Manuscripts in Northumbria in the Eleventh and Twelfth Centuries

ANNE LAWRENCE-MATHERS

In the century after the Norman conquest a new elite came to power in northern England, in the old Anglo-Saxon kingdom of Northumbria. The processes of assimilation are followed here through a detailed study of the libraries which belonged to the religious institutions of the region and their surviving manuscripts. The changes in the perception and writing of the region's history are discussed, together with the production of the manuscripts in which the works survive. Changes in script, illumination and codicology are demonstrated, and investigated as evidence both of new cultural influences and of interaction between the networks of religious houses in the region. The introduction of new religious orders and their interaction with existing cathedrals and monasteries, and the ongoing role of the cults of the region's major saints, are given particular attention, using evidence from the surviving manuscripts.

DR ANNE LAWRENCE-MATHERS is Lecturer in History, University of Reading.

Manuscripts in Northumbria
in the Eleventh and Twelfth Centuries

ANNE LAWRENCE-MATHERS

D. S. BREWER

First published 2003
The Boydell Press, Woodbridge

ISBN 0 85991 765 7

The Boydell Press is an imprint of Boydell & Brewer Ltd
PO Box 9, Woodbridge, Suffolk IP12 3DF, UK
and of Boydell & Brewer Inc.
PO Box 41026, Rochester, NY 14604–4126, USA
website: www.boydell.co.uk

A catalogue record for this title is available
from the British Library

Library of Congress Cataloging-in-Publication Data
Lawrence-Mathers, Anne, 1953–
  Manuscripts in Northumbria in the eleventh and twelfth centuries /
Anne Lawrence-Mathers.
    p. cm.
Includes bibliographical references and index.
  ISBN 0–85991–765–7 (acid-free paper)
1. Northumbria (England: Region) – History – Sources. 2. Northumbria
(England: Region) – Church history – Sources.   3. Northumbria (England:
Region) – Intellectual life – Sources. 4. Manuscripts, Medieval – England
– Northumbria (Region). 5. Manuscripts, English (Old) – England –
Northumbria (Region). 6. Manuscripts, Latin (Medieval and modern) –
England – Northumbria (Region). 7. Books and reading – England –
Northumbria (Region) – History – To 1500 – Sources. 8. Monasticism
and religious orders – England – Northumbria (Region) – History –
Middle Ages, 600–1500 – Sources. 9. Monastic libraries – England –
Northumbria (Region) – History – To 1500 – Sources. 10. Scriptoria –
England – Northumbria (Region) – History – Sources. I. Title.
DA670.N8 L39 2002
942.8'018 – dc21   2002014970

This publication is printed on acid-free paper

Typeset by Joshua Associates Ltd, Oxford
Printed in Great Britain by
St Edmundsbury Press Ltd, Bury St Edmunds, Suffolk

Contents

&❧

Plates

&❧

and *Fellows of University College, Oxford. Photograph by courtesy of the Conway Library, Courtauld Institute of Art.*

16. Oxford, University College, MS 165, p. 9. *By permission of the Master and Fellows of University College, Oxford. Photograph by courtesy of the Conway Library, Courtauld Institute of Art.*

17. Durham, Dean and Chapter Library, MS B IV 5, fol. 1r. *By permission of the Dean and Chapter of Durham.*

18. Oxford, University College, MS 165, p. 26. *By permission of the Master and Fellows of University College, Oxford. Photograph by courtesy of the Conway Library, Courtauld Institute of Art.*

19. Oxford, University College, MS 165, p. 72. *By permission of the Master and Fellows of University College, Oxford. Photograph by courtesy of the Conway Library, Courtauld Institute of Art.*

20. Oxford, University College, MS 165, p. 78. *By permission of the Master and Fellows of University College, Oxford. Photograph by courtesy of the Conway Library, Courtauld Institute of Art.*

21. Oxford, University College, MS 165, p. 143. *By permission of the Master and Fellows of University College, Oxford. Photograph by courtesy of the Conway Library, Courtauld Institute of Art.*

22. York, Minster Library, MS XVI Q 3, fol. 1r. *Copyright Dean and Chapter of York: By kind permission.*

23. Rouen, Bibliothèque Municipale, MS A 321 (444), fol. 1v. *By permission of the Bibliothèque Municipale de Rouen. Photograph by Thierry Ascencio-Parvy 2002.*

24. Durham, Dean and Chapter Library, MS B II 8, fol. 1v. *By permission of the Dean and Chapter of Durham.*

25. Durham, Dean and Chapter Library, MS B II 7, fol. 12r. *By permission of the Dean and Chapter of Durham.*

26. London, British Library, MS Add. 38817, fol. 6r. *By permission of the British Library.*

27. London, British Library, MS Royal 8 D XXII, fol. 2r. *By permission of the British Library.*

28. Durham, Dean and Chapter Library, MS A III 4, fol. 4v. *By permission of the Dean and Chapter of Durham.*

29. London, British Library, MS Royal 6 C VIII, fol. 26r. *By permission of the British Library.*

30. London, British Library, MS Add. 35180, fol. 3r. *By permission of the British Library.*

List of figures

&❧

Acknowledgements

&❧

The study of the manuscripts discussed in this book would not have been possible without the assistance and patience of the staffs of the following libraries: Corpus Christi College, Cambridge; Jesus College, Cambridge; Trinity College, Cambridge; the University Library, Cambridge; the Cathedral Library, Canterbury; the Dean and Chapter Library and the University Library, Durham; the British Library; the Bodleian Library, Oxford; the Bibliothèque Nationale, Paris; the Bibliothèque Municipale, Rouen; the Cathedral Library, Winchester; and York Minster Archives. I thank also all the owners and custodians of manuscripts who gave permission to publish photographs of manuscripts in their care.

The generous assistance of the Marc Fitch Fund, and of the Research Endowment Trust Fund of the University of Reading, is gratefully acknowledged.

The work on which this book is based owes much to the guidance of Professor Michael Kauffmann who, when Director of the Courtauld Institute of Art, was my supervisor. I am indebted also to fellow medievalists and colleagues in the School of History and the Graduate Centre for Medieval Studies at the University of Reading. Particular thanks are due to my husband, Pete Mathers, for his support and enduring interest. All remaining errors are the responsibility of the author.

Editorial Conventions and Abbreviations

&%

I n describing the constituent parts of letters, strokes of ordinary height
are referred to as minims, those which extend above the height of
minims are referred to as ascenders, while those which extend below the
ruled line are called descenders; finally, the rounded parts of letters are called
bowls.

The following abbreviations have been used (full details, where relevant,
are given in the Bibliography):

BL	London, British Library
BM	Bibliothèque Municipale
DCL	Durham, Dean and Chapter Library
EHR	*English Historical Review*
fol.	folio (of manuscript)
Libellus	*Historia Dunelmensis Ecclesiae* (the *Libellus de Exordio atque Procursu Istius, Hoc est Dunelmensis, Ecclesie*) by Symeon of Durham
MS	manuscript
PL	*Patrologia Cursus Completus, Series Latina*, ed. J. P. Migne, 221 vols., Paris 1844–64
r	recto (of manuscript)
UL	University Library
v	verso (of manuscript)

Introduction

&❧

In recent years, a number of scholarly works have used studies of groups of manuscripts as evidence for building up impressive analyses of medieval intellectual and spiritual life at a range of English centres. Prominent amongst these have been Teresa Webber's study of the canons of Salisbury and their books, and Alan Coates's work on the book collections of Reading abbey (T. Webber, *Scribes and Scholars at Salisbury Cathedral c.1075–c.1125* and A. Coates, *English Medieval Books*, both Oxford, Clarendon Press, respectively 1992 and 1999). Of these, this present work perhaps has most in common with Coates's, in knowingly taking on a broad area of study, as against the perhaps better-established study of the manuscripts of a particular cathedral or monastic house within a fairly short period of time.[1] Indeed, the aim of this book is ambitious, in seeking to build up a picture of the establishment of monastic intellectual and spiritual culture within a very large geographical region where, arguably, it did not previously exist, and to carry this picture not only through a relatively long period of time (something over a century, though the exact dates necessarily vary from place to place) but also through two successive reforming movements, those of the Augustinian canons and of the Cistercians. If it is added that by 1166 some forty-four new houses had been founded (and this total does not include minster churches or the cathedral of York itself), the ambition may appear to verge on recklessness.

Nevertheless, the argument of this book is that there is a real value to looking across the particular region of Northumbria, in the century following

---

[1] A few examples would be: R. M. Thomson, *Manuscripts from St Albans Abbey 1066–1235*, Woodbridge, 1982; K. Waller, 'Rochester Cathedral Library: An English Book Collection Based on Norman Models', *Les Mutations socio-culturelles au tournant des xie–xiie siècle. Colloque internationale du CNRS: Le Bec-Hellouin, 11–16 juillet 1982*, Paris, 1984, 237–50; E. McLachlan, *The 'Scriptorium' of Bury St Edmunds in the Twelfth Century*, New York, 1984; also J. M. Sheppard, *The Buildwas Books: Book Production, Acquisition and Use at an English Cistercian Monastery, 1165–c.1400*, OBS, 3rd series 3, Oxford, 1997 (though this has perhaps more in common with Coates).

the Norman Conquest, precisely because this stark contrast offers a unique context within which to study the development of monastic and intellectual culture, through an analysis of the manuscripts, scriptoria and libraries which were at its heart. Each section of the book therefore develops from examinations of the surviving manuscripts, paying particular attention to their illumination, scripts and textual contents. The results of this analysis are then placed within the larger context of the social and political development of the Northumbrian 'region' or 'province' (to use the terms favoured by contemporary writers) in the century c.1066–c.1166. What emerges, complementing existing studies of the secular aristocracy, is a picture of a distinctive monastic culture, which reached a peak in the career and writings of Aelred of Rievaulx (d. 1167). The analysis of the surviving manuscripts established that this culture had two striking central characteristics. First, houses belonging to different orders cooperated closely in the dissemination of texts and the spread of artistic styles across the region. This involved strong links between the Cistercians and the 'traditional' Benedictines, as well as the Augustinians. Secondly, and closely related to this cooperation, the new monasteries were strongly influenced by Northumbria's eminent monastic past, an influence which reached them through both the cult of St Cuthbert, the region's greatest saint, and the writings of the Venerable Bede.

It is not possible for this work to give an in-depth palaeographical and art-historical analysis of all the surviving manuscripts of relevant date from all the Northumbrian monastic and religious houses. Even if Durham were to be taken on its own, this would probably be physically impossible in one volume, but fortunately the eleventh and twelfth-century manuscripts of Durham have been particularly well studied, and it is possible for the present book to build on that work, without repeating what has been well done elsewhere.[2] Rather, as stated above, this study seeks to use both palaeographical and art-historical analysis as tools, with which to build up a historical overview of the creation of a new kind of culture within a distinctive region of eleventh and twelfth-century England.

The most important task for this Introduction, therefore, is to provide a background for the individual chapters which follow by looking at the political identity and development of Northumbria in the period across the Norman Conquest, especially since, of all the regions or earldoms which

---

[2] The fundamental work is that by R. A. B. Mynors, *Durham Cathedral Manuscripts to the End of the Twelfth Century*, Durham, 1939. More recent work includes: A. C. Browne, 'Bishop William of St Carilef's Book Donations to Durham Cathedral Priory', *Scriptorium* 42, vol. ii, 1988, 140–55; and M. Gullick, 'The Scribe of the Carilef Bible: A New Look at Some Late-Eleventh-Century Durham Cathedral Manuscripts', in L. Brownrigg, ed., *Medieval Book Production: Assessing the Evidence*, Los Altos Hills, 1990, 61–83.

made up late Anglo-Saxon England, Northumbria was the one most recently annexed and the one most severely affected by the Conquest. Indeed, the border with Scotland was by no means stable throughout the period, both east and west of the Pennines, making relations with the Scots almost as crucial as relations with the conquerors, at least for Northumbria above the Tees, and making the actual territorial extent of Northumbria somewhat variable. The relatively wealthy region of Lothian had probably been lost to the Scots only some fifty years before the Conquest,[3] and Durham chroniclers, at least, preserved memories of lost territories and possessions well into the twelfth century. During Stephen's reign the eastern border was again especially vulnerable, with David, king of Scots, effectively controlling the area down to the Tees, according to William of Newburgh, and succeeding in establishing first his son, Henry, and then his grandson, William, as 'comes Northumbriae'[4] (here meaning probably only the same area, also called by William of Newburgh 'Aquilondis regio', as opposed to William's own region of 'Eboracensis provincia').[5] To the west, the situation was still more debatable. The kingdom of Strathclyde maintained its independence into the eleventh century, and it was only in the reign of David that the Scottish kingdom established direct control over all the region of Galloway. The territory which came to be known as Cumberland changed between 'English' and Scottish domination several times both before and after the Conquest, being also successfully claimed by David, for a time.

By contrast, Yorkshire, originally the kingdom of Deira, then the Scandinavian kingdom of York, called by William of Newburgh 'Eboracensis provincia' and 'provincia Deirorum', remained both far more stable and more Anglicised.[6] Higham, amongst others, has pointed out that whilst Yorkshire, for all its size and its division into three Ridings, was treated by the late Old English government as a shire, this was not the case for Bernicia, where the kings of the Wessex dynasty, and Cnut, had no royal estates, burhs or mints. Indeed, Higham calls eleventh-century Bernicia 'more like a client-kingship than an integral part of England'.[7] Moreover, political power in Northumbria was still more complex, and fluid, than this two-part division would suggest. The Scandinavian invasion of the late ninth century had turned the old kingdom of Deira into a fairly coherent

---

[3] N. J. Higham, *The Kingdom of Northumbria AD 350–1100*, Stroud, 1993, 230. Stenton, however, took a different view: F. M. Stenton, *Anglo-Saxon England*, 3rd edn, Oxford, 1971, 370.

[4] William of Newburgh, *Historia Rerum Anglicarum*, lib. I, cap. xxiii. See William of Newburgh, *The History of English Affairs, Book One*, ed. and trans. P. G. Walsh and M. J. Kennedy, Warminster, 1988, 100–1.

[5] Ibid. 98 and 76.   [6] Ibid. 118.

[7] Higham, *The Kingdom of Northumbria*, 226.

'Viking' kingdom, arguably the most Scandinavian of all the Anglo-Saxon regions. By contrast Bernicia, united with Deira at the time of the invasion, was effectively split off and fragmented, with power divided between Scandinavian leaders, the Anglo-Saxon dynasty based on Bamburgh and the Community of St Cuthbert. This was still largely the position when Northumbria was annexed by Athelstan and Eadred in the mid-tenth century, and Stenton argues that until Cnut's conquest in 1016, 'the country between the Tees and the Scottish border seems to have been ruled almost continuously by the successive heads of the same native Northumbrian family' who were 'regarded as possessing a hereditary claim to rule in the north'.[8] This is basically the view put forward by the *Historia Regum*, which breaks off its narrative to explain, probably originally under the year 952, about the succession of earls who ruled the 'provincia' of the Northumbrians 'statu regum Northanhymbrorum deficiente'.[9] There were at first two earls, one based north of the Tyne, the other in York. However, the family of Waltheof I, although their main base was in Bernicia, are said to have gained control over the whole province, and kept it at least until Cnut engineered the murder of Earl Uhtred, thus starting a feud between this dynasty of earls and a powerful Anglo-Danish family, based in York, which was to affect the politics of Northumbria until well after the Norman Conquest. Nevertheless, Uhtred's family are stated to have retained the title of 'comes Northymbrensium' until Siward, under the aegis of Harthacnut, killed Earl Eadulf, and became earl 'totius provinciae Northanhymbrorum, id est ab Humbra usque Tuedam'. This leaves a good deal of ambiguity, especially as it ignores Cnut's appointment of Eric as earl in Northumbria, narrated by all the versions of the Anglo-Saxon Chronicle, although suggesting that Siward's total earldom was larger than Eadulf's.[10] Nevertheless, the effect of this murder was apparently to reunite Northumbria under first Siward, then Tostig, then (after a major rebellion caused partly by Tostig's elimination of another member of the Bamburgh dynasty) from 1065 onwards Morcar. Although Morcar is stated to have given

[8] Stenton, *Anglo-Saxon England*, 417.

[9] The *Historia Regum* is generally attributed to Symeon of Durham. For this passage, see *Symeonis Monachi Opera Omnia*, ed. T. Arnold, Rolls Series 75, 1882–5, 2 vols, vol. ii, 196–9 (cited henceforth as Arnold). For discussion, see D. Whitelock, 'The Dealings of the Kings of England with Northumbria in the Tenth and Eleventh Centuries', in P. Clemoes *et al.*, eds., *The Anglo-Saxons: Studies Presented to Bruce Dickins*, Cambridge, 1959, 70–88; and D. Rollason, ed., *Symeon of Durham, Historian of Durham and the North*, Stamford, 1998. The 'Preface' to the *Historia Dunelmensis Ecclesiae*, also attributed to Symeon, uses with familiarity the terms Northumbria, Bernicia and Deira. Like the other works discussed here, the term 'Northumbrians' is used for those living in Yorkshire as well as Durham and Northumberland. See Arnold, i, 98–101 and 108–10.

[10] Arnold, ii, 198.

Osulf, son of the murdered Earl Eadulf, an earldom north of the Tyne, he himself retained the 'dukedom'.[11]

This account gives some idea of the complexity of Northumbrian politics at the time of the Norman Conquest, though it omits the important presence of Siward's youngest son, Waltheof, whose mother was a member of the Bamburgh dynasty. It also gives some idea of the twelfth-century perception of these events from Bernicia, a perception which becomes even stronger as the author/compiler of the *Historia Regum* goes on to tell the story of the earls after the Conquest. We are told: of Morcar's imprisonment by William I; of the brief tenure of Osulf's earldom by Copsi, former lieutenant of Tostig; of Osulf's murder of Copsi and subsequent death; of one Cospatric, a member of the Bamburgh dynasty in the female line, who obtained from William an unspecified 'comitatum Northymbrensium' before fleeing into Scotland; of Waltheof, Siward's son, who, after his rebellion, was imprisoned (and subsequently executed); of Walcher, William I's choice as bishop of Durham, who now held the earldom also until he was murdered in 1080 (by a group led by one Eadulf Rus, grandson of Earl Uhtred's son Cospatric); of Albric who abandoned the earldom and went home; and of Robert de Mowbray, who was involved in the failed rebellion of 1095 against William Rufus. Finally, we are told, 'rex junior Wilhelmus, hodieque rex Henricus, Northymbriam in sua tenet manu'.[12] It should be stressed that this story, complex though it is, is an over-simplification since it omits not only those holding lesser office in York but also Robert Cumin or de Comines, who was, as cap. cliii narrates, sent by the Conqueror 'Northymbris ad aquilonalem plagam Tine' as 'comes' and whose murder at Durham in 1068 led to savage reprisals against the region.[13] What becomes apparent, at least as part of the problem, is the paucity of the terminology available to the twelfth-century chronicler, who uses 'comes' both for those exercising power in Bernicia alone and for those who governed all of Northumbria (except for Morcar, who is called 'dux' to distinguish him from his 'junior earl' in Bernicia). This is clearly complementary to the later views of William of Newburgh, who also sees the whole of Northumbria as a unit whilst distinguishing Yorkshire as a 'province' within it. Neither makes the status of the western areas clear, but both are united in referring generally to the rest of England as 'the southern provinces' or 'the regions south of the Humber'. This confirms again the sense of the separate identity of Northumbria, something which emerges also very strongly in the writings of Richard of Hexham and, especially, of Aelred of Rievaulx.

---

[11] Ibid.   [12] Ibid. 199.   [13] Ibid. 186–7.

The preceding account makes it clear that, whilst it is valid to think of late-eleventh and twelfth-century Northumbria as a 'province' or region with an identity and a very old-established political tradition of its own, to leave the analysis at that point would be an over-simplification. The equally old-established traditions of separatism and genuine cultural variation between Yorkshire and the northern area also continued to be of real importance in conditioning the local society into which the new monasteries and priories were introduced, and thus in helping to determine the patterns of monastic settlement. Finally, what emerges from both the *Historia Regum* and William of Newburgh as well as, in a somewhat different way, the historical and hagiographic writings of Aelred of Rievaulx, is the effective acceptance that the region between the Tweed and the Tyne, as well as Cumberland in the west, constituted border territories especially prone to invasions and raids by the Scots.[14] New monastic foundations in these regions were particularly in need of powerful patronage and this emphasises, if it were needed, the unique political and spiritual status of Durham, a theme which will be taken up in several of the chapters which follow.

Finally, it is also important to stress the theme of royal policy, especially as it was this, when confronted directly by the conservative and separatist traditions sketched above, which contributed most to the fact that by the 1070s large areas of Northumbria had been devastated and left, at best, sparsely populated and with their economy severely damaged. The worst instance of deliberate military attack on the peasant population as well as on their leaders was the Conqueror's 'harrying of the north' in the winter of 1069–70. This came after a sequence of attacks, focusing on the killing of Earl Robert de Comines with his army in Durham early in 1069, and the later killing of Robert fitz Richard, one of the two castellans of York. The attempted punitive attack on Durham failed, but York was sacked by the Conqueror, who subsequently built a second castle there, with a second garrison. Early in September of the same year events in Northumbria became still more dangerous for the Normans, when a large fleet, led by the brother and sons of Swein, king of Denmark, arrived in the Humber and was met by Edgar Atheling, last heir of the Anglo-Saxon royal dynasty, with a number of Northumbrian leaders who had taken refuge with him in Scotland, and by Earl Cospatric, whose brief tenure has already been mentioned, 'cum totis viribus Northymbrorum, unanimiter omnes contra Normannos congregati'.[15] This is not the place to tell the story, but the outcome was disastrous for the Northumbrians. York was burnt, including the cathedral, and Aldred, the last Anglo-Saxon archbishop of York, died (though apparently of natural causes). The church at Jarrow was

---

[14] For further discussion of this, see Chapter 6.   [15] Arnold, ii, 186–7.

burnt. Durham, abandoned by the bishop, the 'chiefs of the people' and their followers in the face of the approaching Norman army, was looted, before being finally deserted by Bishop Ethelwin, who decided to flee into exile. A large part of the remaining aristocracy of Northumbria also went into exile, with Edgar Atheling, in Scotland. But for the peasants escape was more difficult, and the picture of the *Historia Regum* is grim. William led his army to devastate the countryside, slaughtering both the farmers and their stock. He also gave the retreating Danes permission to seize whatever supplies they wanted for the winter. The author goes on to describe at least one year of terrible famine, with some surviving by selling themselves into slavery, some eating whatever they could, including turning to cannibalism, and some dying even while attempting to get away. According to the *Historia Regum* the land between York and Durham was left without anyone to farm it for nine years, and the empty villages became bases for thieves, who made travelling very dangerous.[16] This picture may seem exaggerated, but chroniclers from as far away as Evesham record the arrival of refugees from the north, and the death of others on the journey,[17] and the evidence of Domesday Book for Yorkshire, though still debated, strongly suggests that the region was far from complete recovery even some sixteen years later.[18]

The *Historia Regum* also makes it very clear, however, that the king of England was not the only one to inflict damage on Northumbria. Attacks by the Scots were relatively frequent, and the invasions of the twelfth century have already been mentioned. Malcolm III, in 1070, took advantage of the vulnerability of the whole region to lead an army through Cumberland to sack Teesdale, Cleveland, Holderness and the territory of St Cuthbert. The church at Wearmouth was burnt, as were other churches, and many of the defenders were killed. This raid also turned into something worse when Malcolm heard of Cospatric's counterattack on Cumberland, and the Scottish army were ordered to kill or enslave everybody they could catch. The account concludes that, even at the time of writing, every little village and every cottage in Malcolm's territory still had English slaves.[19]

All this must further have emphasised Northumbria's difference from the more peaceful, wealthy (and densely populated) regions further south. It also helps to explain why the Normans were at first slow to establish new

[16] Ibid. 188.

[17] See R. H. C. Davis, 'Bede after Bede', in C. Harper-Bill, C. J. Holdsworth and J. L. Nelson, eds., *Studies in Medieval History Presented to R. Allen Brown*, Woodbridge, 1989, 103–16.

[18] See especially W. Farrer, 'Introduction to the Yorkshire Domesday', in W. Page, ed., *Victoria County History of the County of York*, London, 1912, vol. ii, 133–90; J. le Patourel, 'The Norman Conquest of Yorkshire', *Northern History* 6, 1971, 1–21; and H. Jewell, *The North–South Divide*, Manchester, 1994, 86–91.

[19] Arnold, ii, 190–2.

monasteries in their territories, despite the rapid establishment of baronies in Yorkshire and the creation of outposts of royal power, such as Newcastle and the castle at Durham, further north. When monasteries were founded, they faced very distinct problems; questions of achieving stability in a region with a depressed economy and a very unsettled political situation made it necessary to make the most of all assets, whether economic or spiritual, and to balance the requirements of differing groups of patrons. It is perhaps over-simplistic to say, as Higham does, that 'the new northern monasteries were as much a manifestation of southern dominance and intrusion as were the several castles of the Norman baronage'.[20] The importance of links with the past emerges, inevitably, most strongly at York and Durham, but those links were not insignificant, and they affected the history in this period of churches such as Wearmouth, Jarrow, Tynemouth, Lindisfarne, Hexham, Whitby, Beverley and Ripon, as well as wholly new monasteries such at St Mary's, York. The struggle between the archbishops of York and of Canterbury over the issue of primacy may appear remote from the concerns of this study. But it made books and documents take on particular significance, as histories and archives were scrutinised for proof of York's independence, and as accounts of the struggle were composed. The dispute thus led 'foreign' incomers to study the history of the cathedral and diocese to which they had come, and to argue for its separate institutions and identity. Arguably, if York had been wholly subordinated to Canterbury then a central element in the regional identity of Northumbria would have been lost. Nevertheless, York was no more immune to the problems of the reign of Stephen than it had been to those of the Conquest. It was Thurstan, the same archbishop whose tenacious defence of the rights of York was celebrated by Hugh the Chanter, who rallied the army which halted the advance of the Scots into Yorkshire in 1138, a success celebrated in further chronicles and poems.[21] When Stephen appointed his nephew, William fitz Herbert, as archbishop of York in 1141, the Cistercian abbots and Augustinian priors of the region acted together, with the support of the bishops of Durham and Carlisle, to have him replaced by Henry Murdac, abbot of Fountains. This move was further resisted by Stephen, while Fountains was attacked and burnt by a mob who were attempting to murder Murdac.[22] Ecclesiastical reform and royal policy could thus also become dangerously entwined in this region.

[20] Higham, *The Kingdom of Northumbria*, 251.

[21] See Hugh the Chanter, *The History of the Church of York, 1066–1127*, ed. and trans. C. Johnson *et al.*, Oxford, 1990.

[22] For this affair see D. Knowles, 'The Case of St William of York', *Cambridge Historical Journal* 5, 2, 1936, 162–77 and 212–14; C. H. Talbot, 'New Documents in the Case of St William of York', *Cambridge Historical Journal* 10, 1, 1950, 1–15; and D. Baker, '"Viri Religiosi" and the York Election Dispute', *Studies in Church History* 7, 1971, 87–100.

Equally crucial as a link between past and present was Durham. After 1083 its new monks faced a complex task, since a large proportion of them were newcomers to the region, who were put into possession, with the bishop, of the cathedral relics and lands which had been controlled by the Community of St Cuthbert. This was perhaps the most successful and longest-established clerical and aristocratic group of the region, since it could demonstrate a continuous existence going back to the flight of the monks from the long-destroyed monastery of Lindisfarne, in the late ninth century. Their control, with the bishops, of both the relics and the lands of St Cuthbert made them a force recognised by all the rulers who competed for the region in the tenth and eleventh centuries.[23] This wealth and power was, however, in the Anglo-Norman period, largely the prerogative of the bishops, and the monks seem to have experienced various insecurities. Moreover, political tension surfaced very clearly at Durham. The assassination of Bishop Walcher has already been mentioned; but the next bishop, William of St Calais, who transformed the Community of St Cuthbert into a priory of Benedictine monks, went into exile five years later following his opposition to the accession of William Rufus. The Scottish incursions of the 1130s affected Durham seriously, and in the 1140s the cathedral was the scene of sieges, stormings and military action when the Scottish chancellor, William Cumin, seized the bishopric for nearly three years.[24] Through all this Durham remained the seat of St Cuthbert's shrine, and its bishops and monks were vitally interested in maintaining both its possessions and its traditional status and power, something which again led to careful reading and use of surviving histories and records, as well as the production of new ones.

The newest element in the ecclesiastical politics of Northumbria was introduced by the Augustinian and Cistercian houses. These were leaders of reform everywhere in the first half of the twelfth century, and as new orders, as well as new houses, their history was short, if celebrated. But what was distinctive about their presence in Northumbria was not only their clear prominence, at least in Yorkshire, but also their links with the more traditional houses. They showed a strong interest in the history of the region, transmitted both by Bede and by the more recent Durham historians, as well as producing new historical works, such as foundation histories and William of Newburgh's *Historia Rerum Anglicarum*. They also played a very

---

[23] See particularly L. Simpson, 'The King Alfred/St Cuthbert Episode in the *Historia de Sancto Cuthberto*', in G. Bonner *et al.*, eds., *St Cuthbert, His Cult and His Community to AD 1200*, Woodbridge, 1989, 397–412; and G. Bonner, 'St Cuthbert at Chester-le-Street', ibid. 387–96.

[24] There is a full account in the *Historia Dunelmensis Ecclesiae Continuatio usque ad Electionem Willelmi de Sancta Barbara*, in Arnold, i, 135–60. For a more impressionistic account, see *Dialogi Laurentii Dunelmensis Monachi ac Prioris*, ed. J. Raine, Surtees Society 70, 1880, 1–61.

important part in the economic revival of the region, particularly in the reorganisation and expansion of agriculture, their increasing wealth making it possible for some of them to take in very large numbers of recruits.[25] But, despite their focus on the management of their estates and the implementation of ideals of reform, they also took seriously the training of recruits, the reading and study of scriptural and theological texts and the building up of libraries. Thus many of the monastic houses of the region, with Durham perhaps foremost, show a strong duality in their interests. On the one hand they appear as proponents of Northumbria's eminent monastic past, while on the other they were committed to the newest developments in theological scholarship, as study of their books shows. It is thus the argument of this book that the study of manuscripts and an enquiry into the intellectual and spiritual culture of Northumbria in the century after the Conquest are intimately interrelated. Moreover, no study of all the surviving manuscripts from the region in this important period has previously been attempted. The late-eleventh-century manuscripts of Durham have been the subject of considerable analysis and argument recently, focusing in particular on the question of whether the place(s) of their production can be identified.[26] But even in the case of Durham, the twelfth-century manuscripts have been surprisingly little studied. C. M. Kauffmann gives full descriptions and analyses of the most art-historically important, and sets them valuably into the context of the development of English Romanesque illumination;[27] and Mynors's *Durham Cathedral Manuscripts* catalogues and analyses the surviving manuscripts, and gives perceptive comments on links in script and illumination, as well as thorough identifications of texts. But neither of these impressive books is concerned to study the post-Conquest manuscripts as a complete group, nor to put them into the wider context of intellectual history. The neglect of the surviving manuscripts of this period from other Northumbrian houses has been almost complete, despite the identification of catalogues from Whitby, Rievaulx and, most recently, St Mary's, York, and despite the listings of identifiable manuscripts given by N. R. Ker.[28] The

---

[25] See D. M. Robinson, *The Geography of Augustinian Settlement in Medieval England and Wales*, British Archaeological Reports, British Series 80, 2 vols., Oxford, 1980, and H. E. Hallam, *Rural England 1066–1348*, Glasgow, 1981, 187–92.

[26] R. M. Thomson, 'The Norman Conquest and English Libraries', in P. Ganz, ed., *The Role of the Book in Medieval Culture*, Bibliologia 4, Brepols-Turnhout, 1986, 27–40; and Gullick, 'The Scribe of the Carilef Bible'.

[27] C. M. Kauffmann, *Romanesque Manuscripts, 1066–1190*, Survey of Manuscripts Illuminated in the British Isles 3, London, 1975.

[28] N. R. Ker, *Medieval Libraries of Great Britain: A List of Surviving Books*, Royal Historical Society Guides and Handbooks 3, 2nd edn, London, 1964. The Whitby catalogue is published in *The Whitby Cartulary*, vol. i, Surtees Society 69, 341. The Rievaulx catalogue is given by M. R. James in *A Descriptive Catalogue of the Manuscripts in the Library of Jesus College, Cambridge*,

reasons for this are not hard to understand: most of these houses have only small numbers of surviving manuscripts, and none of them offer miniatures or historiated initials. Nevertheless, these manuscripts offer a very significant resource for understanding the development of monastic and intellectual culture in this region during an important period of transition.

For this reason, this study adopts a deliberately interdisciplinary approach. At its heart are the detailed analyses of the groups of surviving manuscripts, discussing both illumination and script. These, together with analyses of texts, demonstrate a striking degree of contact and cooperation between houses of differing orders, and throughout the region. An examination of the chronicles and histories composed across Northumbria is also undertaken here, in order to establish whether their authors and compilers had come to share a view of history by the end of the period studied. Finally, individual attention is given to the career of one of the most important authors produced by the region in the twelfth century, Aelred of Rievaulx, who was particularly influential in bringing together concepts of Northumbria rooted in the past (of which his own family had been a part) with the advanced ideals of the reformers. Through these varying analyses, the question of the production and collection of manuscripts is examined in detail, but it is hoped that something more also emerges. The manuscripts are put into their social and political contexts, and thus demonstrate their full importance for a detailed understanding of the developing spiritual and intellectual culture of northern England.

Cambridge, 1895, 44–52. On the recently identified catalogue of St Mary's, York, see R. Sharpe et al., *English Benedictine Libraries*, Corpus of British Medieval Library Catalogues 4, London, 1996.

⚬❅

CHAPTER ONE

The influence of the past

I

t has been frequently stated that in 1066 there were no monasteries north of the Humber.[1] This is literally true, but perhaps undervalues what had been achieved during the tenth and eleventh centuries. Its implication of a complete rupture with the monastic past may also do an injustice to Durham, as the centre where both traditions and more material remains still provided a link with the past.[2] Moreover, the group of monastic newcomers introduced to Durham by Bishop William of St Calais were at pains to emphasise these links, and to represent themselves as continuing the monastic traditions of St Cuthbert and Lindisfarne.[3] For these reasons, it is important for this enquiry to begin with a survey of those remnants of the great libraries of the Northumbrian Renaissance which still survived in the late eleventh century, and to make some attempt to understand how these books were regarded and used.[4]

There is no doubt that the losses had been very great. Lindisfarne had suffered one of the earliest recorded Viking attacks in Britain, in 793, and in

---

[1] See for instance F. Barlow, *The English Church 1066–1154*, London and New York, 1979, 177; and Higham, *The Kingdom of Northumbria*, 219–20.

[2] Durham's position as heir to the lost monastery and see of Lindisfarne has been extensively discussed. See particularly: E. Kitzinger and D. McIntyre, *The Coffin of St Cuthbert*, Oxford, 1950; and the papers collected in C. F. Battiscombe, ed., *The Relics of Saint Cuthbert*, Oxford, 1956. More recent studies are edited by Bonner *et al.*, *St Cuthbert*.

[3] This is stated uncompromisingly by Symeon of Durham, in the Preface to the *Libellus de Exordio atque Procursu Istius, Hoc est Dunelmensis, Ecclesiae*, or *Historia Dunelmensis Ecclesiae*, in Arnold, i. This is customarily abbreviated to *Libellus*. For discussion see B. Meehan, 'Insiders, Outsiders and Property at Durham around 1100', *Studies in Church History* 12, 1975, 45–58; A. J. Piper, 'The First Generations of Durham Monks and the Cult of St Cuthbert', in Bonner *et al.*, *St Cuthbert*, 437–46; M. Foster 'Custodians of St Cuthbert: The Durham Monks' Views of Their Predecessors, 1083–*c.*1200', in D. Rollason *et al.*, eds., *Anglo-Norman Durham 1093–1193*, Woodbridge, 1994, 53–67; and D. Rollason, 'Symeon of Durham and the Community of Durham in the Eleventh Century', in C. Hicks, ed., *England in the Eleventh Century*, Harlaxton Medieval Studies 2, Stamford, 1992, 183–98.

[4] The question of the books owned by the Community of St Cuthbert and their bishops is discussed also by Bonner, 'St Cuthbert at Chester-le-Street'.

830–45 the monks were forced to move to Norham, carrying with them such religious treasures as the relics of St Cuthbert, a carved stone cross and the Gospel book now known as the Lindisfarne Gospels.[5] Over the following century and a half they and their successors continued to guard these treasures, occupying a number of sites, before finally establishing a new cathedral centre at Durham in 995. During this time, they remained under the leadership of a series of bishops, who maintained their monastic status, although the rest of the Community of St Cuthbert, as they came to be known, gradually took on the character of a group of secular clerks. Despite later criticisms, the group, with the bishops, both maintained the books brought from Lindisfarne and added to the collection.[6] However, before looking in detail at what is known of these books, it is necessary to establish the fates of the libraries of the other great monastic houses of the region.

The quality of the scriptorium of Wearmouth–Jarrow in the eighth century is demonstrated by its surviving products, such as the Codex Amiatinus and the St Petersburg Bede.[7] Some indication of its size and productivity is given by the number of skilled scribes who collaborated on the surviving books, and by letters from continental clerics requesting copies of the works of Bede.[8] From these, it would appear that Wearmouth–Jarrow's reputation was almost as great as that of York. The first Viking attack came in 794, according to the Anglo-Saxon Chronicle, and archaeological excavations have confirmed that it was severe. Evidence of burning was found at both sites, and at Jarrow the fire burnt fiercely enough to melt the glass of the windows.[9] Both sites were temporarily abandoned. The sources are sparse for the following period, but it is clear that all hope of reviving the site had been lost by the late ninth century. Early in the tenth century Benedict Biscop's bones were exhumed from Monkwearmouth and taken to Thorney as part of a widespread removal of northern relics to southern monastic centres.[10] In the early eleventh century the sacrist of Durham, Alfred Westoue, was able to identify the burial places of the saints whose relics he was seeking at Jarrow, and to

[5] Symeon, *Libellus*, lib. I, cap. xii and lib. II, cap. vi. See Arnold, i, 39 and 56–8.
[6] The Preface to the *Libellus* contains the most severe criticisms of the Community: see Arnold, i, 8–9.
[7] These are now: Florence, Biblioteca Medicea Laurenziana, Amiatinus 1; and St Petersburg, Public Library, Cod. v. I. 18.
[8] See R. G. Gameson, 'The Royal 1. B. vii Gospels and English Book Production in the Seventh and Eighth Centuries', in R. G. Gameson, ed., *The Early Medieval Bible*, Cambridge, 1994, especially 44 and n. 89.
[9] R. Cramp, 'The Window Glass from the Monastic Site of Jarrow', *Journal of Glass Studies* 17, 1975, 88–95; and 'Excavations at the Saxon Monastic Sites of Monkwearmouth and Jarrow, Co. Durham: An Interim Report', *Medieval Archaeology* 13, 1969, 21–65.
[10] Higham, *The Kingdom of Northumbria*, 222.

remove the relics to Durham, and it seems that some Wearmouth–Jarrow books had already, at some stage, passed to Durham.[11]

The disappearance of the Anglo-Saxon books of Whitby and of Tynemouth has been complete. The latter was attacked and destroyed in 800, and any hope of monastic reoccupation must have ended in the 870s, when Healfdene, leader of the Great Danish Army, made the site his own base.[12] Tynemouth was an important centre of pilgrimage, and correspondingly wealthy, but nothing survives of its library. From Whitby, also destroyed during this period, books had been sent to the missionary, Boniface, and the skill of its scribes is suggested by a number of inscribed stones found at the site.[13] At Whitby, also, however, the library was lost. All the houses so far discussed were coastal foundations, and thus particularly vulnerable to the piratical raids which characterised early Viking attacks. The inland centres of Ripon, Beverley, Hexham and York survived longer, but suffered severely during the conquest of most of Northumbria by the Great Danish Army in the 860s and 870s. The see of Hexham had already lapsed in the 820s and was merged with that of Lindisfarne.[14] None of the abbey's books are known to survive, and if any were transferred to the Community of St Cuthbert there is now no trace of them. Hexham's relics, however, were also moved by Alfred Westoue, partly to Durham, and partly to new locations within the church, which he seems to have partially restored.[15] The destruction of Ripon is also not well recorded, though its abandonment is demonstrated by Oswald's refoundation in the tenth century, whilst he was archbishop of York; this refoundation was not a success.[16] The library of Ripon also disappeared, including Wilfrid's luxurious copy of the Gospels, 'written in letters of gold on purple parchment and illuminated'.[17]

While Wilfrid's restoration of the church at York is described in some

[11] On the books, see Bonner, 'St Cuthbert at Chester-le-Street'; and Mynors, *Durham Cathedral Manuscripts*, 13–23. The question of the Wearmouth–Jarrow books is discussed by M. P. Brown, 'The Lindisfarne Scriptorium', in Bonner *et al.*, *St Cuthbert*, 153 and n. 9.

[12] Symeon, *Libellus*, lib. II, cap. vi; Arnold, i, 56.

[13] Sir Charles Peers and C. A. Ralegh Radford, 'The Saxon Monastery of Whitby', *Archaeologia* 89, 1943, 27–88.

[14] See J. Raine, ed., *The Priory of Hexham*, vol. i, Surtees Society 44, 1863, xlii–xliii (references henceforth are to vol. i unless indicated otherwise). For more detailed discussion of Hexham see Chapter 9 below.

[15] Aelred of Rievaulx, *On the Saints of the Church of Hexham*, in Raine, *Hexham*, 173–203, at 190–9. For comment and a short paraphrase see Raine, *Hexham*, liii–lv.

[16] For Oswald's career, see the *Life of St Oswald* in J. Raine, ed., *The Historians of the Church of York and Its Archbishops*, Rolls Series, 3 vols., London, 1879–94, vol. i, 399–475. For Oswald's attempt to settle monks at Ripon, see ibid. 462–3. No trace of the arrangement survived at the time of the Norman Conquest.

[17] C. B. L. Barr, 'The Minster Library', in G. E. Aylmer and R. Cant, eds., *A History of York Minster*, Oxford, 1977, 487.

detail by Eddius Stephanus, his gifts to its altars are outlined in glowing but general terms, concentrating on altar cloths and vessels; it would appear that no book equivalent to the Ripon Gospels was given to York. Nevertheless, there was an organised school from the 730s, supported by an extensive library made famous by Alcuin.[18] Archbishop Albert, according to Alcuin, travelled in both Frankia and Italy in search of books and exemplars. Alcuin's poetic description of the library names forty authors, implying that the majority of their works were available at York, as well as stating that this is not a complete list. The Church Fathers, including those of the Eastern Church, were well represented, as were Anglo-Saxon writers such as Aldhelm and Bede. The classical collection included fundamental works on history, rhetoric, grammar and poetry, as well as Christian Latin poetry by an impressive list of authors. Altogether, according to Alcuin, the writers of Rome, Greece, the Hebrews and Africa were all represented.

As with the other inland centres, York was not seriously affected by the early raids, but the campaign of 866–7 was different. York was captured by the Great Army, and both the city and the minster were severely damaged by fire.[19] How much of the library was lost is not recorded, but the text of one service book which may be associated with York, Egbert's Pontifical, must have survived, as it was copied in the tenth or eleventh century, the copy surviving as Paris, Bibliothèque Nationale, Lat. 10575. Certainly from the eleventh century is the surviving volume of the York Gospels, but this is not a York product; it was made at Canterbury and brought to York by Wulfstan.[20] This fact may suggest either that book production at York was known to be at a low ebb, or simply that Wulfstan wished to bring an impressive gift with him. An early sixteenth-century inventory lists about ten Gospel books, all in the minster treasury, and all believed to be of Anglo-Saxon and Anglo-Norman origin.[21] Of these, the York Gospels is now the sole survivor, but it is possible that some of the books lost after the Reformation were of early Anglo-Saxon origin, and the survival of Egbert's Pontifical supports this. For the library books, however, there is evidence that some of the collection did survive Danish attacks, only to be destroyed by the Normans. The minster was burnt in 1069, along with much of the

[18] Barr, 'The Minster Library', 488–9.

[19] Anglo-Saxon Chronicle, sub anno 867 (868 C), ed. and trans. D. Whitelock in English Historical Documents, Volume 1, c.500–1042, London, 1979, 191. See also Libellus, Arnold, i, 50–1 and 54–5.

[20] This is now Minster Library, Add. 1. It contains a short stint by Eadui Basan of Christ Church, Canterbury (see D. H. Turner, 'Illuminated Manuscripts', in D. H. Turner et al., eds., The Golden Age of Anglo-Saxon Art, British Museum, 1984, 72); it also contains work by a hand identified as that of Archbishop Wulfstan (d. 1023).

[21] See Barr, 'The Minster Library', 489–90.

city of York, and Florence of Worcester, well informed about York, commented 'In the library of St Peter's . . . now there is nothing . . . for these treasures . . . were destroyed by the savagery of the Danes and the violence of William the Bastard.'[22] This may well be an exaggeration, given the survival of the Gospel books, but other twelfth-century writers also comment on the loss of the York library, and nothing is now known to survive of the works listed by Alcuin.[23] Archbishop Thomas of Bayeux is known to have given books to the minster, probably mostly liturgical, but in the absence of a cathedral priory there would be no need for a communal library.[24] It seems likely that, in the late eleventh century, the minster clergy had private book collections, as they certainly did in the twelfth century.[25]

From this survey, it is clear that the unique survival of the library of Durham needs to be explained. The circumstances of the Community of St Cuthbert in the ninth and tenth centuries, whilst they were resident at Norham and Chester-le-Street, will therefore be examined in order to assess their opportunities to maintain and add to their book collection. They had, in fact, enjoyed a period of relative security at Norham, but were forced to flee again in 875, by Healfdene and the Great Danish Army. This new period of wandering was brought to a successful end, however, when they were established at Chester-le-Street, with extensive landholdings.[26] Indeed, these estates remained so extensive that N. J. Higham has recently suggested that they were established by mutual agreement, as a buffer between the Danish kings of York and the Anglo-Saxon rulers based at Bamburgh.[27] Even in the early tenth century, when further disruption was caused in the region by the interventions of the Irish and Breton Norse, the Community of St Cuthbert survived. They suffered the loss of some of their landed wealth, but were still powerful at the time of King Athelstan's annexation of Northumbria in 927. Indeed, this was recognised by Athelstan himself, who visited the shrine in 934, and gave impressive gifts, including a set of four books. The importance of this event for the clerks is demonstrated by the copying of a poem in praise of Athelstan into one of the early Gospel

---

[22] Ibid.

[23] Ibid.

[24] For a detailed discussion of York, see Chapter 5 below.

[25] The best-known example is that of Hugh, dean of York, who took his book collection with him to Fountains in 1134. See D. Knowles, *The Monastic Order in England, 960–1216*, 2nd edn, Cambridge, 1963, 237. The precentor and *magister scholarum*, positions established by Archbishop Thomas I of Bayeux, would also presumably have needed book collections. See Hugh the Chanter, *The History of the Church of York*, 11.

[26] See the *Historia de Sancto Cuthberto*, paragraphs 13, 21–4, trans Whitelock, in *English Historical Documents*, 286–8. The full text is given in *Symeonis Dunelmensis Opera et Collectanea*, vol. i, ed. Hodgson Hinde, Surtees Society 51, 1868, 138–52.

[27] Higham, *The Kingdom of Northumbria*, 183.

books owned by the Community (now Durham, DCL, A II 17), and by the account of the visit in the *Historia de Sancto Cuthberto*, nearly contemporary with the event.[28]

The wealth of the Community by the end of the tenth century is demonstrated by the construction of a new cathedral church at Durham, after the move from Chester-le-Street in 995, brought about once again by renewed Danish invasions. The construction of expensive stone churches on several estates, such as those at Staindrop and Norton, is also impressive. The old church of Chester-le-Street was also rebuilt in stone in the 1050s.[29] At the same time, the clerks were also able to resist attempts by the new rulers of Northumbria to impose a more communal form of life upon them. Indeed, Symeon of Durham, writing early in the twelfth century, suggested that much of the aristocracy of Northumbria was proud to claim to be related to members of the Community of St Cuthbert.[30] Evidence for this is given by the story of one bishop of Durham, whose daughter married into the semi-royal house of Bamburgh. Her husband was made earl of Bamburgh and Yorkshire in 1006, by Ethelred II, but his wife took the veil at Durham.[31] It was also during this later Saxon period that the relics of Durham, already the greatest collection in Northumbria, were further added to, as described above. Even the unsuccessful importation of monks from Peterborough to Durham, described by Symeon of Durham, may have led to the introduction of new texts, and Symeon certainly states that the sacrist and scholarly relic-collector, Alfred Westoue, also ran a semi-monastic school for boys at Durham.[32]

The final problem is the extent of the disruption suffered at Durham during the Conqueror's 'pacification' of the north. His severity is effectively summed up by Higham thus: 'By 1075 . . . York was burnt and pauperised, its population decimated, and the members of Northumbria's several regional aristocracies were dead or had fled.'[33] The impact on the library of York Minster has already been suggested. In the case of Durham, Symeon, writing within living memory of 1069/70, stated that the clerks had fled from Durham, seeking safety ironically in their original home of Lindisfarne. When they returned to Durham, the cathedral church had been looted, but they had carried their greatest treasures with them. These may have included

---

[28] See Hinde, *Symeonis Opera*, 149–50.

[29] See E. Cambridge, 'Early Romanesque Architecture in North-East England: A Style and Its Patrons', in Rollason *et al.*, *Anglo-Norman Durham*, 141–60, for a full discussion of the problems of dating these buildings.

[30] Symeon, *Libellus*, lib. II, cap. xii; Arnold, i, 65.

[31] *De Obsessione Dunelmi*, full text printed in Hinde, *Symeonis Opera*, 154–8.

[32] Symeon, *Libellus*, lib. III, cap. vii; Arnold, i, 87–8.

[33] Higham, *The Kingdom of Northumbria*, 233.

the DCL A II 17 Gospels, which survives in fragments and the Lindisfarne Gospels themselves. Just what was lost is not clear, but they did, after long lawsuits, receive financial compensation from William himself.[34] Durham, then, suffered relatively minor losses. Its estates seem to have been impoverished for some time, although evidence is sparse, since the region is not included in Domesday Book. However, neither this nor the description of the looting of the cathedral suggest any major losses of books. It is even possible that the first 'Norman' bishop, Walcher (1071–80), a secular priest from Lotharingia, may have introduced some new books.

What is certain is that books were being brought into Northumbria from an unexpected source, some at least of which, together with those who brought them, were later to be brought to Durham. The Evesham chronicler recorded the arrival of starving Northumbrian refugees, and it may perhaps have been their arrival, and thus stories about conditions in the north, which led Aldwin, prior of Winchcombe, with two monks from Evesham, to set off for Northumbria.[35] Symeon gives a detailed account of their departure, taking with them 'one ass only, which carried the books and priestly vestments which they required for the celebration of the divine mystery.'[36] It seems clear that Aldwin was familiar with Bede's *Historia Ecclesiastica*, though whether a copy of this was carried by the donkey, with the liturgical manuscripts, is not stated by Symeon.[37] The 'pilgrims' went first to the earl of Northumbria, but were summoned to Durham by Walcher, who gave them the ruined monastery of Jarrow. In the Preface to the *Historia Dunelmensis Ecclesiae* it is hinted that this was from the start a temporary arrangement, whilst the bishop had monastic buildings constructed (presumably those at Durham).[38] However, in the main narrative, book III, chapters xxi and xxii, the suggestion is rather that Aldwin and his companions came with the intention of visiting and, if possible, reviving the ancient sites described by Bede. These two chapters relate how they settled first at Jarrow, building crude shelters there, and gathered recruits both from Northumberland and 'the South', the larger number being again supported by Walcher, who granted them the vill of Jarrow, and the estates around it. Reinfrid's move to Whitby, and Aldwin's to Melrose, presumably once Jarrow was judged to be securely established, are described as if they were individual initiatives. But when the move to Melrose failed, it seems that Walcher again intervened,

---

[34] Symeon, *Libellus*, lib. III, cap. xv. See Arnold, i, 100–1.

[35] For the most recent discussion of their importance, see J. Burton, 'The Monastic Revival in Yorkshire: Whitby and St Mary's, York', in Rollason *et al.*, *Anglo-Norman Durham*, 41–65, at 41–52. The events leading up to their journey are discussed by Davis, 'Bede after Bede'.

[36] Symeon, *Libellus*, lib. III, cap. xxi; Arnold, i, 108–9.

[37] For detailed discussion of this question see Chapter 5 below.

[38] Symeon, *Libellus*, Preface; Arnold, i, 9–10.

summoning Aldwin and his companion, Turgot, to Wearmouth, where the buildings appear to have been even more ruinous than at Jarrow. Here again recruits were gathered, also from 'far away' and again the bishop granted the monks both Wearmouth itself and the land around it. Symeon takes pains to suggest that, at both Jarrow and Wearmouth, the bishop was a generous patron and the monks accepted his authority.[39]

These details are important. They establish that at least basic liturgical and monastic texts will have been obtained for both Jarrow and Wearmouth. Moreover, that trained monks were recruited, perhaps especially from the Winchcombe area, some of whom may well have been able to act as scribes. Finally, their acceptance of the bishop's patronage helps to explain how it was possible for Bishop William of St Calais to move the new communities from both sites, and to re-establish them, presumably with their books and scribes, at Durham itself. It is clear that, in the case of Reinfrid and his recruits, who had, by their move to Whitby and then to York itself, moved into the sphere of the archbishops of York, there was no assumption of authority on the part of the bishops of Durham.

One final point should be made about the books assembled at Durham on the eve of the Norman Conquest. At least in what survives, there is a striking absence of copies of basic patristic works, and it is tempting to link this to the clerks' rather secular, aristocratic mode of life, as suggested by Symeon.[40] Indeed, the story of the expulsion of the Peterborough monks seems to support this view. The evidence of this absence of patristic works may appear strong support for Symeon's story, since it goes further than the general poverty or outdatedness of the holdings of such works in Anglo-Saxon libraries. However, this rather simplistic image is contradicted by the career of Alfred Westoue, mentioned above. In the accounts of both Symeon and Reginald of Durham, Alfred emerges as an almost saintly individual, and very learned about both the saints and the old monastic sites of Northumbria. He was clearly familiar with Bede's *Historia Ecclesiastica* and *Lives of St Cuthbert*, and Symeon's description of his school suggests a knowledge of Latin grammar and perhaps poetry. Finally, if Symeon's assertion that Alfred

---

[39] For more detailed discussion on this point, see Burton, 'Monastic Revival', 42–5; and A. Dawtry, 'The Benedictine Revival in the North: The Last Bulwark of Anglo-Saxon Monasticism', *Studies in Church History* 18, 1982, 87–98. The general picture is given by Knowles, *Monastic Order*, 159–71.

[40] The surviving books are catalogued by Mynors, *Durham Cathedral Manuscripts*, 14–31. For discussion see also Bonner *et al.*, *St Cuthbert*. The Durham books may be compared with N. R. Ker's remarks on Anglo-Saxon monastic libraries in his *English Manuscripts in the Century after the Norman Conquest*, Oxford, 1960, 4–9. These comments may also be compared with the listings given by H. Gneuss, 'A Preliminary List of Manuscripts Written or Owned in England up to 1100', *Anglo-Saxon England* 9, 1980, 1–60.

observed the night hours is anything more than special pleading, it is possible that he had some knowledge of the Benedictine Rule.[41]

However, any books for private reading acquired by Alfred would have remained his own property, and would have passed to his heirs. This was certainly the case with the ex-monastic church of Hexham, granted to Alfred in gratitude for his activities. At his death, this passed to his son, Eilaf, who retired to it in 1083, when William of St Calais set up his new Benedictine priory at Durham.[42] Provision was also made for other clerks who refused to join the priory and abandon their families in 1083, and they too would have departed, taking personal property with them. Thus, whilst this can only be hypothesis, the absence of later Anglo-Saxon copies of patristic works in the Durham collection cannot necessarily be taken as evidence of the clerks' ignorance. In turning to the surviving books themselves, Mynors's impressive work makes a detailed catalogue here redundant. Instead, attention will be paid to the nature and extent of the collection which belonged to the shrine by 1083, in order to establish what would have been available to the new monastic community.

Perhaps the most impressive group would be the early biblical manuscripts. Oldest of all is the fragment of a sixth-century Italian copy of Maccabees, now part of DCL B IV 6. From the seventh century is the Gospel of John, written in Northumbria, and now at Stonyhurst College. This became known to the monks of Durham only in 1104, when it was found in St Cuthbert's coffin, and they continued to keep it with the relics, protected inside two leather bags. The impressive collection of insular Gospel books included one of the cathedral's treasures, the Lindisfarne Gospels, now BL Cotton Nero D iv. Its origin was recorded in a colophon by Aldred, the late-tenth-century provost of the Community, who also supplied an Old English gloss, although he describes it as being made by men attached to the monastery of Lindisfarne for God and St Cuthbert, rather than specifically for the church, which may suggest that it was intended in fact for the shrine.[43] The Durham Gospels, now DCL A II 17, was also at Chester-le-Street in the tenth century, when names and other annotations were made in the margins. It seems that it was already at that date bound up with nine leaves from another Northumbrian Gospels, now fols. 103–11, written in the distinctive script of Wearmouth–Jarrow. The volume seems to have been passed to the

---

[41] See Symeon, *Libellus*, lib. III, cap. vii; Arnold, i, 87–8; and Reginald of Durham, *Libellus de Admirandis Beati Cuthberti Virtutibus Quae Novellis Patratae sunt Temporibus*, ed. J. Raine, Surtees Society 1, 1835, at cap. xxvi, pp. 57–60.

[42] For detailed discussion see Chapter 11 below. On the provision of estates for the expelled clerks see Rollason, 'Symeon of Durham and the Community of Durham', 191–2.

[43] Aldred's colophon is on fol. 259r.

monks in this compound condition.[44] Other fragments are more difficult to interpret, but seven leaves, now dispersed between DCL A II 10, C II 13 and C III 20, were originally part of another seventh-century Gospels; its condition at the time of the Conquest is unclear. However, DCL A II 16 is an eighth-century copy of the Gospels which was certainly at Durham in the twelfth century, and may be presumed to have been part of the collection in 1083.[45]

In the case of other early manuscripts and fragments, the difficulty is to determine the date of their acquisition. The eighth-century copy of the Pauline epistles, now divided between Cambridge, Trinity College, B 10 5 and BL Cotton Vitellius C viii was certainly at Durham by the fourteenth century when it, together with the eighth-century copy of Cassiodorus' *Commentary on the Psalms*, now DCL B II 30, were attributed to the hand of Bede.[46] This would suggest that the manuscripts were believed to have been in the library at Durham from an early date, but there is no proof. Finally, there are two leaves of an eighth-century copy of Leviticus, believed by Mynors to have been part of a Pentateuch, now in DCL C IV 7, and one leaf of an eighth/ninth-century Northumbrian Lectionary, now in DCL A IV 19. These last contain no evidence on their early history.

As was mentioned above, Aldred, priest and provost of Chester-le-Street in the third quarter of the tenth century, added a gloss and colophon to the Lindisfarne Gospels. His hand is also found in Oxford, Bodleian, Bodley 819, an eighth or ninth-century Northumbrian copy of Bede's *Commentary on Proverbs*. This would suggest that this book also was held in high esteem by the Chester-le-Street community, and would have been passed on as a communal possession to the priory of Durham. Aldred's hand occurs in one other manuscript, DCL A IV 19, the 'Durham Rituale'. The nucleus of this is an early tenth-century Collectar, written out in southern England, but based upon that which was used by the Augustinian canons of St Quentin in Vermandois, France. Why precisely this text was chosen is not known, but Aldred glossed this manuscript, and added four prayers forming part of a mass for St Cuthbert. He also recorded that he did so in 970, whilst accompanying Bishop Ælfsige, at Oakley Down in Dorset.[47]

Other books do not contain Aldred's hand, but can definitely be assigned to the possession of the Community of St Cuthbert for other reasons. BL Cotton Domitian A vii is the *Liber Vitae* of Durham. Its basis is a list of some 3,150 names, copied out in letters of silver and gold at Lindisfarne in the

[44] Mynors, *Durham Cathedral Manuscripts*, 15.
[45] Ibid. 18–20.　　　　　　　　　　　　　　　　　　　　　　[46] Ibid. 20–1.
[47] C. Hohler and A. Hughes, 'The Durham Services in Honour of St Cuthbert', in Battiscombe, *Relics*, 155–91, at 157.

ninth century. It was taken up by the monks of Anglo-Norman Durham, added to, and kept on the high altar in a rich cover. Other liturgical manuscripts raise complex questions which will be discussed below, but Sidney Sussex Δ 5 1 5, part II, is an eleventh-century Pontifical which was at Durham by the late twelfth century, and may have been acquired by a pre-Conquest bishop.

Forming a special category are the books associated with King Athelstan, and his gifts to the shrine of St Cuthbert at Chester-le-Street.[48] The anonymous *Historia de Sancto Cuthberto* was first compiled at Chester-le-Street in the mid-tenth century.[49] This records Athelstan's visit in 934 and lists the books he gave as: a Missal, two copies of the Gospels, and the *Life of St Cuthbert* in verse and prose. Of these, Cambridge, Corpus Christi College, MS 183 has generally been accepted as the *Life of St Cuthbert*, despite some difficulties over the dating; however Rollason has recently proposed that Corpus 183 and the Sidney Sussex Pontifical may have come to Durham only after the Conquest, and from south-west England.[50] It was certainly at Durham by 1080, as a contemporary hand copied a land grant by Bishop Walcher onto its last leaf. The Missal is lost, but Mynors identifies BL Cotton Otho B ix as one of the Gospels. It was of ninth/tenth-century Breton origin and, although it was almost completely destroyed in the Cotton fire, descriptions make clear that it, like Corpus 183, had a miniature showing Athelstan and St Cuthbert. In this case, the miniature had an accompanying inscription, recording its presentation by the king.[51]

Still more problematic is a group of Anglo-Saxon manuscripts which was at Durham by the later twelfth century, but whose exact date of acquisition is not known. The oldest is perhaps Lambeth Palace MS 325, a copy of the *Letters and Poems* of Ennodius, written in tenth-century Caroline minuscule. The appearance of the text in the Durham catalogue, and the existence of a twelfth-century Cistercian copy, perhaps from Fountains, suggests that this was at Durham by the mid-twelfth century. In a similar category are: DCL B IV 9, a complete *Works* of Prudentius; Cambridge UL Gg III 28, Ælfric's *Catholic Homilies*, in Old English and therefore less likely to have been

[48] For detailed discussion of this group see S. Keynes, 'King Athelstan's Books', in M. Lapidge and H. Gneuss, eds., *Learning and Literature in Anglo-Saxon England*, Cambridge, 1985, 170–201.

[49] For discussion of its authenticity see A. Gransden, *Historical Writing in England c.550 to c.1307*, vol. i, London, 1974, 76–8; and Simpson, 'The King Alfred/St Cuthbert Episode'.

[50] D. Rollason, 'St Cuthbert and Wessex: The Evidence of Cambridge, Corpus Christi College MS 183', in Bonner *et al.*, *St Cuthbert*, 413–24.

[51] See R. Deshman 'Anglo-Saxon Art after Alfred', *Art Bulletin* 56, 1974, 176–200; Keynes, 'King Athelstan's Books', 170–9; A. Lawrence, 'Alfred, His Heirs and the Traditions of Manuscript Production in Tenth Century England', *Reading Medieval Studies* 13, 1987, 35–56, at 49.

acquired after 1083; Oxford, St John's College, MS 154, a collection of school texts in Latin and Old English, in an early eleventh-century hand; DCL A IV 28, an eleventh-century copy of Bede's *On the Apocalypse*, which was used as an exemplar at Durham in the twelfth century; and two liturgical fragments of the early eleventh century (one leaf of a Psalter, now in Durham, Misc. Charter 5670, and tables and verses on the Kalendar, now in Bodleian, Digby 81).

All this suggests a library impressive in certain areas and strikingly blank in others. Early biblical manuscripts are well represented, most particularly Gospels, although the absence of Psalters is perhaps surprising.[52] There are hints of the presence of at least some of the works of Bede, though it is hard to believe that the clerks had no copy of the *Historia Ecclesiastica*, and no copy of Bede's prose *Life of St Cuthbert* before that given by King Athelstan. Suggestions of a school, at least in the time of Alfred Westoue, are supported by the school books. Ælfric's *Catholic Homilies* may have been either for private reading or for use as the basis of preaching. There are also suggestions, from both the tenth and eleventh centuries, of interest in maintaining up-to-date liturgical books. Perhaps most striking is the almost complete absence of major patristic works, and the presence of relative rarities such as the Ennodius. Any image of lax clerics uninterested in reading is contradicted by several pieces of evidence. The activities of Alfred Westoue and his son, both called 'larwa' or scholar, have already been discussed. The existence of annotations in the Prudentius, in a number of tenth and eleventh-century hands, also suggests the presence of some scholarly individuals. This might, very tentatively, suggest that, whilst the oldest books, and certain categories of school books, liturgical books, and all gifts to the shrine, were regarded as the property of the saint, others were individual or family property.

One area clearly under-represented in this survey so far is that of historical (and hagiographical) writing. Anglo-Saxon books in this category were presumably replaced by twelfth-century compositions such as those of Symeon and Reginald. However, a brief outline can be supplied. The twelfth-century handlist of books, included in DCL B IV 24, has a list of books in Old English, which includes a laconic reference to 'two chronicles'.[53] These are not identified, but Symeon's 'charter-roll of the church, showing the munificence of kings and persons in religion' is likely to be the

---

[52] The mid-twelfth-century book-list gives a long list of Psalters apparently in the hands of individual monks. Presumably members of the Community of St Cuthbert were still more likely to have their own Psalters. See *Catalogi Veteres Librorum Ecclesie Cathedralis Dunelm*, ed. B. Botfield, Surtees Society 7, 1838, 6–7.

[53] Ibid. 5.

compilation known as the *Historia de Sancto Cuthberto*, which was first put together in the mid-tenth century, then brought up to 995 after the move to Durham. In addition to this, Symeon also refers to a list of bishops, to the 'statutes and privileges of King Guthred', and to material also found in the early twelfth-century *Miracles and Translations of St Cuthbert*.[54] Finally, the compiler of the twelfth-century *Historia Regum*, attributed to Symeon of Durham, seems to have used a chronicle for the period 848–1118 which included information on the see of Durham; the exact nature of this source is, however, not known.[55]

If the manuscripts surveyed here are at all representative of what was taken over by the new monastic community in 1083, then certain general observations can be made. First, while the collection was clearly strong in the area of early Northumbrian Gospels, there is a striking absence of any of the beautifully decorated Gospels and Psalters associated with the tenth-century revival of monasticism in the south. At least one such book reached York, brought by Wulfstan, but Durham remained unaffected. This absence makes the group of books given by King Athelstan the more outstanding, especially as the two usually accepted as members of the group both had full-page miniatures showing the king and St Cuthbert. The Breton origin of Athelstan's Gospel book makes it a rarity in a collection otherwise heavily dominated by Northumbrian books. This raises the question of other books brought to Durham from outside Northumbria. The Wessex Collectar acquired by Bishop Ælfsige has already been mentioned; more problematic are a pair of books, both containing Hymns and Canticles, which appear to have been written and illuminated at Canterbury (now DCL B III 32 and BL Cotton Julius A vi). However, as these are generally argued to have come to Durham after the Conquest, they will be considered together with books almost certainly brought to Durham from Canterbury at that time.[56]

Finally, there is one other important observation which should be made. This is that, at least in the surviving manuscripts, there is no evidence of

[54] Edited by Arnold, i, 229–61 and ii, 333–62. Also edited by J. Hodgson Hinde, for Surtees Society 51, 1868, 158–201. For discussion see B. Colgrave, 'The Post-Bedan Miracles and Translations of St Cuthbert', in C. Fox and B. Dickins, eds., *The Early Cultures of North-West Europe*, Cambridge, 1950, 305–32.

[55] For detailed discussion of the sources drawn upon see Gransden, *Historical Writing in England*, 112, 122, 142–50; D. Whitelock, 'After Bede', Jarrow Lecture, Jarrow, 1960; and M. Lapidge, 'Byrhtferth of Ramsey and the Early Sections of the *Historia Regum* Attributed to Symeon of Durham', *Anglo-Saxon England* 10, 1981, 97–122.

[56] For a more detailed discussion of this group of books see A. Lawrence, 'The Influence of Canterbury on the Collection and Production of Manuscripts at Durham in the Anglo-Norman Period', in A. Borg and A. Martindale, eds., *The Vanishing Past: Studies of Medieval Art, Liturgy and Metrology Presented to Christopher Hohler*, British Archaeological Reports, International Series 3, Oxford, 1981, 95–104.

organised book production at Durham on the eve of the Norman Conquest. If the clerks of St Cuthbert had Psalters or copies of fundamental patristic works, they presumably took them away with them when they were dispersed. What is certain, and will be studied in detail below, is that Bishop St Calais took effective steps to provide just such books.

For this chapter, one last question remains: what was the attitude of the Anglo-Norman monks towards these Anglo-Saxon books? Here the main sources of evidence are again Symeon and Reginald, together with annotations in the surviving books themselves. These make clear that the most prized books were those directly connected with St Cuthbert himself: the Lindisfarne Gospels, celebrated as the medium through which St Cuthbert worked a miracle, and known as 'the Gospels which fell into the sea'; and the Stonyhurst College Gospel, found in St Cuthbert's coffin in 1104 and kept, according to Reginald, as one of the treasures of the shrine, to be shown to particularly favoured pilgrims.[57] More confusing is the book referred to by Symeon as 'the very book out of which [Boisil] instructed [Cuthbert] . . ., and which, after so many centuries, exhibits even at this present time a remarkable freshness and beauty'.[58] From the context, this cannot be the Lindisfarne Gospels. The likelihood must be that it is the Stonyhurst Gospel, but Symeon does not state that it was found in St Cuthbert's coffin: however, the references to its remarkable state of preservation are very reminiscent of those applied to the body of St Cuthbert. Almost as important was the *Liber Vitae*, which was kept on the high altar, and added to periodically with the names of patrons, or of those with whom confraternity agreements had been made.

Symeon also makes it clear that he has several works by Bede available, including both the *Lives of St Cuthbert* and the *Historia Ecclesiastica*, upon whose method he appears to be modelling himself. However, he gives no details of the volumes, so that their age and origin cannot be inferred.[59] His evident respect for Bede, however, does make it likely that, if Durham had possessed any books directly connected with Bede, Symeon would have mentioned it whilst discussing Bede's scholarly activities and the monastic education then available.

Of the other early books, DCL A II 17 has no twelfth-century annotations to match those from the tenth century; but the addition to DCL A II 16 of a twelfth-century forgery, purporting to be a contemporary copy of a bull of Gregory VII to St Calais, authorising the foundation of the priory, at least suggests that the antiquity of this book was respected. Of the other early

---

[57] Reginald, *De Admirandis*, cap. xci, pp. 197–201.
[58] Symeon, *Libellus*, lib. I, cap. iii; Arnold, i, 22.
[59] Ibid. lib. I, cap. viii, xiii, xiv and xv, pp. 29–30 and 39–46.

books, DCL B II 30, the eighth-century copy of Cassiodorus' *On the Psalms*, was repaired and perhaps rebound in the twelfth century.

Evidence of attitudes towards the later Anglo-Saxon books, as might be expected, is sparser. However, Bishop Walcher at least seems to have been interested in King Athelstan's copy of Bede's *Lives of St Cuthbert*, and in the office for the saint which it contained. As has already been noted, a copy of a lease granted by Walcher was added into the book. Moreover, the office it contained was copied at Durham after the Conquest, the copy perpetuating a scribal error found in Cambridge, Corpus Christi College, MS 183.[60] This evidence makes it all the more interesting that the text of the *Prose Life* found in Corpus 183 diverges from that of the post-Conquest copies of the text, such as Oxford, University College, MS 165. In addition, the *Verse Life* was less widely copied, but here again later Durham copies, such as those in Bodleian, Fairfax 6 and Digby 175, do not derive from Corpus 183. All this would suggest that the Durham scribes of the late eleventh and twelfth centuries believed they had more authentic copies of the texts, from other sources.[61] BL Cotton Otho B ix has been too badly damaged for evidence of twelfth-century use, if any, to have survived.

Of what might be called the library books, Lambeth Palace MS 325, the Ennodius, has no twelfth-century annotations, but it was presumably still in use, if it was indeed used as the exemplar for a Fountains copy. DCL B IV 9, the Prudentius, has glosses from both the eleventh and twelfth centuries. And DCL A IV 28, Bede's *On the Apocalypse*, was also the exemplar for a twelfth-century copy, this time one for Durham itself. One point which may perhaps be made is that all these books were in Latin. How long the Old English books remained in use is not clear, but the implication of the laconic list added to the book-list in DCL B IV 24 is that they were no longer read by the second half of the twelfth century.

In conclusion, although the number of surviving books is low, and other evidence, if added in, still only gives a total of some thirty to forty volumes, nevertheless it is clear that the library of Durham was unique in Northumbria in the late eleventh century. It represented the only surviving remnants of the great libraries of the past, and it contained at least the nucleus for an impressive collection. This inheritance from the past gave it an advantage over the libraries which must have been growing at the new houses of Whitby and St Mary's, York; and the monks of Durham, seeing themselves as the successors to the monks of Lindisfarne, were proud of the books which were part of the connection with that past.

---

[60] Hohler and Hughes, 'The Durham Services', 157.
[61] For detailed discussion see Chapters 2 and 3 below.

&❧

CHAPTER TWO

Durham and the Norman world

PART I
The books of William of St Calais

The material presented in the previous chapter has put Durham forward almost as a last surviving bastion of the great days of the North-umbrian Church. Certainly, its library can be argued to have repres-ented, by the 1070s, the last great collection of the books produced during that earlier period; and moreover, as was suggested above, there is evidence that those books were still in use, and were, at least in some cases, highly valued. It would be possible to put forward an argument that Durham remained relatively unaffected by the Norman Conquest, and even by the conqueror's punitive military expedition into the north. In such an argument, the appointment of Walcher (1071–80) as bishop of Durham would be seen as a conscious response to the local traditions and circumstances of Durham. For Walcher was not a Norman abbot, but a Lotharingian secular priest, who apparently planned to reorganise his cathedral clergy as a community of regular canons, a type of organisation already widely introduced into south-ern England before the Conquest, and indeed patronised by both Edward the Confessor and Harold.[1] Even Walcher's murder at Gateshead, together with members of his household, could be presented as evidence of the continuing power exercised by the local Anglo-Norse aristocracy, not yet substantially displaced by the creation of a new land-holding group.[2]

Central to such a view would be the writings attributed to Symeon of

---

[1] Harold's foundation at Waltham was itself granted to Durham by the Conqueror, perhaps as a support to Walcher. For discussion of the patronage of canons in the late Saxon period, see J. Barrow, 'English Cathedral Communities and Reform in the Late Tenth and the Eleventh Centuries', in Rollason *et al.*, *Anglo-Norman Durham*, 25–39.

[2] See Symeon, *Libellus*, lib. III, cap. xviii–xxiv; Arnold, i, 105–17. However, the *Historia Regum*'s account of the close cooperation between Walcher and Earl Waltheof is rather in tension with this picture. See *Historia Regum*, *sub anno* 1072, paragraph 160, in Arnold, ii, 200.

Durham, who, in the early twelfth century, produced a *Historia Dunelmensis Ecclesiae*, and to whom is attributed the Durham chronicle known as the *Historia Regum*.[3] It is Symeon who tells in detail of the coming of the three monks from the south-west; monks who came from the region where Anglo-Saxon churchmen such as Wulfstan II of Worcester had retained positions of power and responsibility; and monks of whom two, Aldwin the prior and Elfwy the deacon, bore Anglo-Saxon names.[4] Symeon's point, naturally enough, was that it was the new monastic community, although largely southern in origin and formed by a Norman bishop-abbot, which was the true heir to the monasticism of St Cuthbert. For the recruits gathered and trained at Wearmouth and Jarrow were to be brought to Durham by William of St Calais in 1083 when, in an act of episcopal power sanctioned by papal and royal authority, he replaced the Community of St Cuthbert with a priory of Benedictine monks. However, Symeon's whole account is shaped in such a way as to show that, whilst monasticism remained the ideal for the Community of St Cuthbert, and was indeed maintained by the bishops and by heroic individuals such as Alfred Westoue, the majority of the Community, through passage of time and difficult circumstances, lapsed from this ideal. Moreover, by 1083 they had lapsed so far that, when offered the opportunity to take up monasticism, all but one of them refused.

Aird has recently suggested that Symeon's account of the events of 1083 is seriously distorted, and that more of the members of the Community joined the new priory than Symeon admits; Rollason's objection that such a distortion, written well within living memory of the events, is unlikely, does seem more convincing, especially when the political and economic situation of Durham by 1083 is considered. A political arrangement whereby all the senior members of the Community were asked effectively to sever their links with the 'civil society' of the region by repudiating their families and their homes and placing themselves within a theoretically enclosed institution from which all women were strenuously barred (apparently even as pilgrims or visitors), and within which they would be expected to submit to the abbatial power of the bishop, would not be strikingly attractive and yet could not be taken as an insult. Men in the probable position of chaplain, vicar or unmarried son of a senior member, like those discussed by Aird, would presumably have more to gain and considerably less to lose. Moreover, no

---

[3] On the identity and work of 'Symeon of Durham' see Gransden, *Historical Writing in England*, 116 and 148–51. More recently, see Rollason, *Symeon of Durham*, especially papers by Rollason, Gullick, Story and Sharpe.

[4] See Chapter 5, and references there. On the question of the Northumbrian revival as an expression of pro-Saxon feeling, see Dawtry, 'The Benedictine Revival in the North'.

violence was necessary, although the savage effectiveness of the king's armies against 'rebels' had been recently very memorably demonstrated. The full members of the Community were apparently given the perfectly polite alternative of retirement, with their family, to a prestigious estate such as Eilaf's Hexham. Finally, the fact that it was no less a figure than the dean who joined the new priory is suggestive; who better to act as symbolic guarantor of the rights of the departed members, and to show that the Community retained a representative close to the bishop and the saint during the period of transition?[5]

All this clearly raises the question of how the arrival of Bishop William of St Calais, and his subsequent actions, should be interpreted. Do they represent a return to a better past, and thus an idealised continuity, as Symeon of Durham suggests? Or should they be seen as a break with the past, and therefore also with its cultural traditions? In seeking to suggest answers to these questions, an examination of the books surviving from the period can play a very important part. In the first place, the origins of the books themselves, whether they came from outside Durham, and if so from where, may suggest centres with which the new monastic community of Durham had important ties. Secondly, if some of the books can be shown to have been produced at Durham, stylistic analysis can provide evidence about the training of those who made them and, more tentatively, about the tastes of those who commissioned them. Finally, the choice of texts can provide evidence on the spiritual and intellectual life of those who used them.

Some sixty manuscripts, attributable to the late eleventh or early twelfth centuries, have been identified as having belonged to Durham in this period. Originally there were certainly more, since a surviving mid-twelfth-century book-list gives a total of some four hundred volumes for the library books alone, without including liturgical manuscripts and those kept by the sacrist or on the altars. Indeed, of the forty-six to forty-nine

---

[5] The exact organisation and constitution of the Community of St Cuthbert remain rather obscure. The use made of the tenth-century Collectar obtained in Wessex by Bishop Aldhun is discussed by Alicia Correa, *The Durham Collectar*, Henry Bradshaw Society 107, 1992, especially 77; but few other insights are available. Genuine attachment to the cult of St Cuthbert is suggested by the collection of miracle stories which were subsequently taken up by the monks; see Chapter 4 below. Symeon is concerned mostly with questions of the decay of monastic practice and of the married status of the 'clerks'. For contrasting views see Rollason, 'Symeon of Durham and the Community of Durham'; and W. M. Aird, 'St Cuthbert, the Scots and the Normans', in M. Chibnall, ed., *Anglo-Norman Studies XVI: Proceedings of the Battle Conference, 1993*, 1994, 1–20, especially 19–20. For recent discussion see Aird, *St Cuthbert and the Normans, The Church of Durham 1071–1153*, Woodbridge, 1998, ch. 3 (especially 115–23); but see also the review by D. Rollason, *English Historical Review* 115, 463, 929–30.

volumes given to the monks by Bishop William of St Calais only half, some twenty-three volumes, have been tentatively identified.[6] However, the existence of the list of St Calais's gifts, and of the later book-list, help to demonstrate that Durham is well provided with evidence for the development of the monastic community and its library.[7] Before moving into a detailed analysis of the texts, scripts, decoration and annotation of the surviving manuscripts, therefore, it will be of value to attempt some analysis of this background.

What is central here is the contradictory situation established at Durham. On the one hand, the imposition of a Norman abbot, and an almost complete replacement of the cathedral clergy, had been carried out with a thoroughness unequalled anywhere in southern England, except perhaps at St Augustine's, Canterbury, after its attempted rebellion against Lanfranc. Moreover, the new Norman bishop, William of St Calais, was no obscure figure in the Anglo-Norman Church, but rather a protégé of Odo of Bayeux, one of the most powerful churchmen in the country. Indeed, William was a trusted member of the Conqueror's court, a leading administrator, and very possibly the director of the great Domesday Survey in the last years of the reign.[8] His appointment to Durham then, and his rapid actions once there, seem to mark a deliberate change of policy and, presumably, a determination to establish a secure base for Norman power in the far north of England. On the other hand, this new monastic community was itself, as has been argued above, concerned to present itself as the true successor to the Lindisfarne of St Cuthbert. The preface to Symeon's *Historia Dunelmensis Ecclesiae* calls Lindisfarne 'the mother church of all the churches and monasteries of the province of the Bernicians', with the clear implication that this proud title has been inherited by Durham.[9] Indeed, this preface stresses the interest taken by both Walcher and William of St Calais in the distinguished past and traditions of their new see. In the south, Lanfranc might doubt the authenticity of many Anglo-Saxon saints, and remove their feasts from his new calendar; some new abbots, such as Paul of St Albans, might go so far as to treat the relics of some Anglo-

---

[6] The classic analysis and identification of these books is that by Mynors, *Durham Cathedral Manuscripts*, 32–45. For a more recent discussion see Browne, 'Bishop William of St Carilef's Book Donations to Durham Cathedral Priory'; this is primarily concerned with the arrangement and significance of the list of the bishop's books given in the surviving volume of his Bible, now DCL A II 4.

[7] For a list of books available in the mid-twelfth century, see DCL B IV 24, fols. 1r–2r. This is printed in *Catalogi Veteres*, 1–10.

[8] For this suggestion see P. Chaplais, 'William of St Calais and the Domesday Survey', in J. C. Holt, ed., *Domesday Studies*, Woodbridge, 1987, 65–77.

[9] Symeon, *Libellus*, Arnold, i, 7.

Saxon saints with scorn.[10] But at Durham, the glory of its past was vouched for by no less an authority than the Venerable Bede.[11]

The books and documents from Durham's past are explicitly put forward by Symeon as the means by which contact with the 'great traditions' of that past was maintained, across the radical change in regime. Bishop Walcher is stated to have read Bede's *Historia Ecclesiastica* and his *Life of St Cuthbert* to 'learn the history' of his see.[12] William of St Calais, more generally, is described as studying 'earlier documents' on the history of the see.[13] But it is interesting to note that, whilst the argument which William is stated to have used with the king in order to justify his decision to move the monks established at Wearmouth–Jarrow to Durham was a purely practical one, having to do with the size and resources of the see, the argument presented to the Pope was very different. Here, the stress is on 'what the bishop had discovered in books with respect to the church.'[14]

Some sense of the importance of the writings of Bede for the new monastic community may be gained from Symeon's own stated method of work, where he seems to model himself on the methods of Bede. Bede's own writings are, of course, the explicit starting point for the writing of this new history, and they are to be supplemented with 'other treatises', 'old books', the 'statutes and privileges' of Durham, the 'charter-book' of the church, and, again like Bede, with reliable oral testimony.[15] In handling the latter, Symeon, like Bede, is always careful both to name his source, and to present his credentials as a reliable witness. Indeed, it is clear that Symeon has been through the 'old books' for he draws not only on the tenth-century compilation known as the *Historia de Sancto Cuthberto* and on miracle stories about St Cuthbert, later than those told by Bede, but also upon the colophon written in the Lindisfarne Gospels, and the *Life of St Cuthbert*.[16]

[10] For a discussion of Norman attitudes to Anglo-Saxon saints, see S. Ridyard, 'Condigna Veneratio: Post-Conquest Attitudes to the Saints of the Anglo-Saxons', in *Anglo-Norman Studies IX. Proceedings of the Bible Conference 1986*, Woodbridge, 1987, 179–206, at 180, 196–206.
[11] At the time of the Conquest, Durham almost certainly possessed the splendid copy of Bede's *Prose Life of St Cuthbert*, given by King Athelstan, and now Cambridge, Corpus Christi College, MS 183. Symeon also had access to a copy of the *Historia Ecclesiastica* which was not that later given by Bishop St Calais (now DCL B II 35), and which appears to have preserved some early readings. For discussion see Chapter 10, and references there.
[12] Symeon, *Libellus*, Preface; Arnold, i, 9.
[13] *Libellus*, 10.   [14] Ibid.
[15] These references are scattered through the Preface, Apology, and lib. I, cap. i, of the *Libellus*, in which the author sets out his task and his approach.
[16] The material from the *Historia de Sancto Cuthberto*, and the miracle stories, are to be found especially in lib. II, cap. x–xviii; Arnold, i, 61–77. Quotations from the *Life of St Cuthbert* are especially prominent in lib. I, cap. x and xi, pp. 32–8. For a much fuller analysis of Symeon's use of his sources, see the contributions by Rollason, Meehan, Piper, Story and Sharpe in Rollason, *Symeon of Durham*.

However, even within this theme of continuity, there is evidence of the different attitude introduced by William of St Calais. The copies of Bede's works read by Bishop Walcher seem to have been those already available at Durham. Indeed, the preferred copy of the *Life of St Cuthbert* seems to have been that believed to be the copy presented to the shrine by King Athelstan. The evidence for this is that a liturgy for St Cuthbert, introduced under Bishop Walcher, was originally composed in Wessex, and was to be found at Durham in the Athelstan manuscript, now Corpus 183.[17] By contrast, copies of both the *Historia Ecclesiastica* and the *Life of St Cuthbert* survive in the hands of scribes closely associated with William of St Calais.[18] The first is almost certainly the 'historia anglorum' included in the list of St Calais's donations, and has been identified as the main portion of DCL B II 35, which still survives at Durham.[19] What is particularly interesting here is that, whilst endorsing the importance of Bede, St Calais was at pains to have a new copy made, by a scribe working closely with him, and that it was this new copy which then became the exemplar for subsequent copies of the work.[20] The copy of the *Life of St Cuthbert* is less clearly associated with St Calais, since it is now in the Bodleian Library (Bodley 596), and seems to have belonged to Canterbury in the medieval period; moreover, the text is not included in St Calais's donations. However, there is no doubt about the Durham origin of the book since its distinctive style of script and initials occur in a number of other Durham books, as I shall argue below; and it is the oldest surviving copy of a recension of the text which seems to stem from Durham in this period.[21] The suggestion that Bodley 596 was St Calais's personal copy of the work comes from Michael Gullick. The strongest evidence for such a link is the inclusion, in a different hand, of material relating to St Julian, since St Calais had previously been abbot of St Julian's, Le Mans. However, before attempting a detailed analysis of the surviving books, it is important to assess St Calais's collection overall, and the evidence it offers.

St Calais's library

Most important of all is the list of St Calais's own donations. This is on fol. 1 of the surviving volume of St Calais's great two-volume Bible, now DCL A II

---

[17] Hohler and Hughes, 'The Durham Services', 157.

[18] These are now DCL B II 35 and Bodleian, MS Bodley 596 respectively.

[19] A reproduction of the list of St Calais's books is given by Gullick in 'The Scribe of the Carilef Bible' (see also Plate 1).

[20] For the dissemination of the text, see *Bede's Ecclesiastical History of the English People*, ed. B. Colgrave and R. A. B. Mynors, Oxford, 1969, xlvi–lxi.

[21] On this, see B. Colgrave, *Two 'Lives' of St Cuthbert*, Cambridge, 1940, 24–5.

4, and was almost certainly added into the Bible at Durham (see Plate 1). Indeed, other work by the scribe exists at Durham, although I do not believe, *pace* Thomson, that this scribe was the scribe of the Bible itself.[22] What the list does demonstrate is the thoroughness with which St Calais set out to provide what he presumably identified as the books necessary to form a working collection for the new monastic life introduced at his cathedral. Broadly, they consist of: eight liturgical books (Breviaries, Antiphoners, Missals and a Gradual) presumably representing St Calais's choice of liturgical material; other texts necessary for the running of a benedictine house (Rule, Customary, Martyrology, and such basic works as Prosper, Smaragdus and the *Lives of Egyptian Monks* as well as two volumes for reading at Matins); a collection of sermons and homilies; and a set of twenty-two works by the Fathers of the Church, ranging in length from Augustine's three-volume *Commentary on the Psalms* to shorter works such as Jerome's treatise *On Hebrew Names*, or Gregory's *Pastoral Care*. In other words, the collection is very much in line with Ker's analysis of the types of texts introduced into English libraries by the Norman abbots and bishops.[23] However, there are some touches of individuality. The presence of Origen's *On the Old Testament* suggests wider theological reading than was common, while the choice of three *Commentaries* by Bede (on Mark, Luke and the Song of Songs) as well as the *Historia Anglorum* suggests further recognition of the importance of Bede for re-establishing a sense of monastic tradition at Durham. Also interesting are the final elements of the list, again suggestive of relatively wide reading, and consisting of Pompeius Trogus, Julius Pomerius, Tertullian and Sidonius. It is tempting to link this with the impressive 'classical collection' in the mid-twelfth-century book-list, and to suggest that St Calais established an interest in the study of the classics at Durham.

If the list in DCL A II 4 offers some insight into those texts which St Calais regarded as fundamental for his new foundation, and, more tentatively, into his own intellectual interests, the next problem is to gain some sense of the sources upon which he drew in building up his collection. The first step, clearly, is the identification of surviving volumes from St Calais's donation, a task made more difficult by the absence of any means of identification, such as 'second folios', in the list itself, and by the absence of any inscriptions in surviving Durham books.[24] However, the hard work of identification was

---

[22] Thomson, 'The Norman Conquest and English Libraries', 37.

[23] Ker, *English Manuscripts*, 4–15.

[24] The only exceptions are: A II 4 itself; B II 13, the second volume of St Calais's copy of Augustine's *Commentary on the Psalms*, which has the well-known historiated initial showing the bishop and his artist; and B II 14, the third volume of the same work, which has a colophon by the scribe, William, dedicating his work to the bishop.

impressively done by Mynors, and the remarks offered here are based upon his work, and upon his suggested identification of twenty-three volumes. In each case, the identification rests upon the isolation of a text named in the St Calais list, in a volume datable by its style, and sometimes by more definite evidence, to the episcopate of St Calais. In fact, whilst Mynors's identifications have generally been accepted by subsequent writers, what has proved more controversial is the question of the place or places where the books were made.[25] Fortunately, a complete answer to this question is not necessary for the present study, nor do I believe that it is possible. What is important is that, as the colophon in DCL B II 14 makes explicit, the books given by St Calais will have been purchased or ordered by him, and at his own expense.[26] There is, therefore, no *a priori* reason to assume that they were made by members of the monastic community at Durham itself. At the opposite extreme, while some of St Calais's books were almost certainly made by scribes from Normandy and Canterbury, this does not mean that none of these books was produced at Durham.

It was Mynors who first drew attention to the importance of the statement by Symeon that St Calais, whilst in exile in Normandy, sent books and other treasures back to Durham, before returning himself.[27] The exile was for political reasons, again showing St Calais's involvement in great affairs of state, and lasted from 1088 to 1091. The statement that the books were sent to Durham from Normandy has generally been taken to imply that they were books acquired in Normandy, and therefore, presumably, the work of Norman scribes and artists. However, this can only be hypothesis. The other interesting question which arises is that of the timing of St Calais's gifts of books. At first glance, the unified list in A II 4 suggests that they were given as a group, presumably at the bishop's death. However, several factors contradict this. Firstly, the small alterations and departures from its own ordering principles in the book-list itself suggest that the scribe was bringing

[25] The most recent discussions are those of Thomson and Gullick; see notes 19 and 22 above. They come to fundamentally different conclusions, since Thomson argues that St Calais's manuscripts were produced in a scriptorium established at Durham, while Gullick argues that the majority of the manuscripts which show work by Norman-trained scribe-artists who also worked for Norman houses will have been made in Normandy, presumably during St Calais's exile. Ker is guarded on the question of the emergence of an organised scriptorium at Durham; see *English Manuscripts*, 23–5. Kauffmann takes a similar position; see *Romanesque Manuscripts*, 19–20. Thomson also has recently moved to a more cautious view (pers. comm. 1996).

[26] The text is as follows: 'Hoc exegit opus Guillelmus episcopus illo/ Tempore quo proprio cessit episcopio./ Materies operisque labor reputantur eidem./ Materies sumptu sed labor imperio/ Nominis eiusdem confors Willelmus et idem/ Perstitit ut fieret arte labore manu/ Pontificisque sui tanto fervebat amore/ Ut labor ipse foret eius amore eius.'

[27] Mynors, *Durham Cathedral Manuscripts*, 32.

the list up to date on more than one occasion, or else listing books which were already scattered in several locations, rather than being kept together.[28] Secondly, there is Symeon's evidence, mentioned above, which states that some books at least were given in 1091. Finally, there is the argument of practicality. If texts such as the Benedictine Rule, the Martyrology and the liturgical books were indeed intended by St Calais to lay down the basis for the monastic life and liturgy at Durham, it would make little sense for him to hand them over only on his deathbed. Instead, a piecemeal set of gifts, starting with a rapid acquisition of the fundamentals or of 'approved' editions of basic works, not already available at Durham, and then supplemented by various gifts, would make more sense. In this model, some of the more unusual texts may indeed have been acquired by the bishop originally for his own reading, and thus passed on to the monks subsequently. Such a pattern might also help to explain the duplication of Augustine's *Commentary on St John's Gospel* which exists at Durham in two copies of the late eleventh century; one might have been acquired by the monks, the other, as the list suggests, by St Calais.[29]

Symeon's account suggests that St Calais moved with speed and decision to establish his new priory. The evidence of the list, and of the surviving books, shows that he also had clear views about the nature of the Benedictine life which he wished to establish. As was outlined above, the new monastic groups at Wearmouth–Jarrow were established by Aldwin and his two companions from Evesham. Their books also presumably came from that area, supplemented, perhaps, by Northumbrian patrons such as Bishop Walcher or Earl Roger de Mowbray (the main patron of the new community at Tynemouth).[30] Symeon's description of their living conditions hardly suggests that copying of books can have been undertaken on any very large scale, but some of their work may survive. The 'Martyrology and Rule' in the A II 4 list has been identified with DCL B IV 24. This contains the Rule in both Latin and Anglo-Saxon, in versions which appear to have originated in the south-west.[31] Each is the work of a different scribe, both using versions of Anglo-Caroline minuscule. However, although they were probably the work

[28] The latter is the opinion of Browne; see his 'Bishop William of St Carilef's Book Donations to Durham Cathedral Priory', 149.

[29] The two books are now DCL B II 16 and B II 17. The former is in the distinctive hand of a scribe who worked chiefly for St Augustine's, Canterbury; see T. A. M. Bishop, 'A Canterbury Scribe's Work', *Durham Philobiblon* 2, 1, 1955.

[30] For discussion, see A. J. Piper, 'The Durham Cantor's Book (Durham, Dean and Chapter Library, MS B. IV. 24)' and M. Gullick, 'The Scribes of the Durham Cantor's Book (Durham, Dean and Chapter Library, MS B.IV.24) and the Durham Martyrology Scribe', both in Rollason *et al.*, *Anglo-Norman Durham*, 79–110.

[31] See note 30.

of English-trained scribes from the south, it seems likely that the Latin version at least may have been written out in Northumbria. At any rate, its opening initial and display script, on fol. 74v, uses a purple pigment and a decorative motif which are found in a number of contemporary Durham manuscripts (see Plate 2). Another important text in this composite volume, however, has a different and significant origin. This is a copy of Archbishop Lanfranc's *Monastic Constitutions*, originally written for Christ Church, Canterbury, and here copied in the distinctive script introduced to the Christ Church scriptorium under the aegis of Lanfranc himself.[32] This choice of customal presumably came from St Calais, and again demonstrates the Anglo-Norman ecclesiastical culture to which he belonged, and his association with its leading figures. That these basic texts were in use by the prior or precentor by the time that St Calais went into exile is demonstrated by the fact that a letter from the bishop to his monks, and intended to be read to them during his exile, was added into fol. 14r, a blank page, on the verso of which is the opening of the Rule, in Old English.

Links with Canterbury

The evidence of the works bound up together in DCL B IV 24 thus suggests that St Calais was prepared to make use of books made for or by the monks whom he assembled at Durham, but that he wished to bring his priory into line with the monasticism imposed by Lanfranc at Canterbury. Other surviving books present further evidence of St Calais's respect for Lanfranc, and for the library being built up at Christ Church. Perhaps most significant is Cambridge, Peterhouse, MS 74, the manuscript which has been identified as St Calais's *Decreta Pontificum*.[33] This is a copy of the canonical material brought to Canterbury by Lanfranc, and known as the 'Collectio Lanfranci'.[34]

[32] For the scribe and his work see Ker, *English Manuscripts*, 25–32. St Calais's acquisition of books from Canterbury is discussed in Lawrence, 'Influence of Canterbury'. K. D. Hartzell, 'An Unknown English Benedictine Gradual of the Eleventh Century', *Anglo-Saxon England* 4, 1975, 131–44, argues that the Gradual, now Durham UL Cosin V v 6, was probably acquired from Christ Church, Canterbury, at the time of St Calais's establishment of the cathedral priory. Thus, although this book is not strikingly similar to other late-eleventh-century Christ Church manuscripts, it may constitute further evidence of St Calais's reliance on Lanfranc's Christ Church.

[33] This is item 21 on the A II 4 list. For the dissemination of the text in England see R. Somerville, 'Lanfranc's Canonical Collection and Exeter', *Bulletin of the Institute of Historical Research* 45, 1972, 303–6. St Calais's use of this collection is suggested in the text known as the *De Iniusta Vexatione Willelmi Episcopi Primi*; see Arnold, i, 171–94. For discussion see Barlow, *The English Church 1066–1154*, 145–6 and 282–6; and M. Philpott, 'The *De Iniusta Vexacione Willelmi Episcopi Primi* and Canon Law in Anglo-Norman Durham', in Rollason *et al.*, *Anglo-Norman Durham*, 125–37.

[34] On the text, see M. Gibson, *Lanfranc of Bec*, Oxford, 1978, 139–40.

This manuscript is in a hand not found in any other Durham manuscript, but also not characteristic of Canterbury. Its immediate origins are therefore unclear, but the influence of Lanfranc is again represented by the text, and marginal notes and additions demonstrate that the book was in use at Durham by c.1100.[35]

Much more difficult to interpret are manuscripts with a certain or probable Canterbury origin, but with no discernible link with St Calais. Three books belong to this category. Neither the Gradual (Durham UL Cosin V v 6) nor the Hymnal with Calendar (BL Cotton Julius A vi) can be firmly identified with the liturgical manuscripts given by St Calais. Moreover, the absence of twelfth-century Durham inscriptions in these books makes it possible that they were only acquired later; however, since they belong to a category of books not fully represented in the twelfth-century book-list they may have been kept by a different official from the main book collection, so that the absence of these inscriptions cannot be conclusive. The Gradual seems almost certainly to be a product of Lanfranc's Christ Church since Hartzell identifies the hand of the neums with that of the neums in another probable Christ Church manuscript, now Dublin, Trinity College, MS 98, and Gameson identifies the distinctive coloured display capitals as of Christ Church type. The Calendar and Hymnal is a compound manuscript, with the metrical Calendar being early eleventh-century in date, while the glossed Hymnal is mid-eleventh century. Both are linked to Christ Church, predominantly by the style and iconography of the Calendar drawings, and they were bound together by the time they appear in the later Durham library catalogues. The willingness of Christ Church to part with such an attractive manuscript may perhaps be linked to Lanfranc's rather radical reform of the calendar, but this can only be speculation. Equally tantalising is DCL B III 32, a compound manuscript consisting of a Latin Hymnal and of Ælfric's Grammar. Contents, script and illuminations, as in the other two manuscripts, demonstrate the Canterbury provenance, but this manuscript may only have come into the Durham library in the eighteenth century. Moreover, Gameson has questioned the traditional attribution to Christ Church, although he does accept this as a Canterbury product.[36] In these circumstances, these manuscripts may suggest that Canterbury books enjoyed a certain prestige at Durham – but they cannot be used as evidence of St Calais's preferences.

Considerably more interesting for the present inquiry are surviving copies

---

[35] Mynors, *Durham Cathedral Manuscripts*, 43–4.
[36] Ibid. 28–9. See R. G. Gameson, 'English Manuscript Art in the Late Eleventh Century: Canterbury and Its Context', in R. Eales and R. Sharpe, eds., *Canterbury and the Norman Conquest: Churches, Saints and Scholars 1066–1109*, London and Rio Grande, 1995, 117 and n. 77. See also: 102, n. 28; 111, n. 55; 131, n. 135.

of patristic works which can be identified with items on St Calais's list, and which have connections with Canterbury. In this category also there are three books: DCL B II 10, B II 16 and B II 22. The first of these is a copy of the letters of Jerome, and is the work of a Christ Church scribe and artist; the script is in the distinctive style already mentioned, and the initial is very similar in construction, style and motifs to those in several surviving Canterbury manuscripts.[37] Equally distinctive, though very different in style, is B II 16, a copy of Augustine's *Commentary on St John's Gospel*. This is in the distinctive late-eleventh-century script of St Augustine's and, although its initials are unusual, its text also links it strongly to Canterbury. Its rubrics and marginal annotations/alternative readings are all, in wording and format, the same as those in Cambridge, Trinity College, B 4 2, the late-eleventh-century copy of the same text from Christ Church. Moreover, Christ Church manuscripts of this period frequently have such boxed marginal annotations, and B 4 2 has alternative readings not copied into B II 16. All this suggests very strongly that B II 16 is a Canterbury product and, whilst the initials are unusual, their strong, chalky colours may be found in contemporary Norman manuscripts, and their figure style may be compared with Cambridge, Trinity College, O 2 51, a copy of Priscian from St Augustine's.[38] The evidence thus suggests that these two books were produced in the Canterbury scriptoria and subsequently, though soon after their making, brought to Durham. B II 22 raises rather different problems. It is a copy of Augustine's *City of God*, and its script and minor initials are the work of a scribe – artist who worked on several Durham manuscripts, as will be argued below. However, this book also is very probably copied from a Canterbury exemplar, and its main initial is almost certainly the work of an artist who provided initials in a set of manuscripts for Christ Church.[39] Just where this manuscript was copied cannot be proved, but the initial suggests that a scribe who produced

[37] For detailed comparisons see Lawrence, 'Influence of Canterbury', 97–8 and Plates 8.12 to 8.15. Gameson attributes the initials to an artist whose hand he also identifies in: Cambridge, Trinity College, B 4 9, B 4 26 and B 5 26; BL Arundel 16; and, more tentatively, Cambridge, Trinity College, B 39. See 'English Manuscript Art in the Late Eleventh Century', 117 and n. 78. Webber identifies the scribe as collaborating also on a collection of Anselm's works, from the 1120s, now Oxford, Bodleian, Bodley 271. See 'Script and Manuscript Production at Christ Church, Canterbury, after the Norman Conquest', in Eales and Sharpe, *Canterbury and the Norman Conquest*, at 151, n. 26.

[38] For a similar conclusion as to their style see R. G. Gameson, 'English Manuscript Art in the Mid-Eleventh Century: The Decorative Tradition', *Antiquaries Journal* 71, 1991 64–122, at 93–4. In his study of the Canterbury manuscripts, Gameson discusses this manuscript's use of historiated initials, and adds the tentative suggestion that the artist of B II 16 also executed the illustrations in a herbal of probable St Augustine's origin, now Oxford, Bodleian, Ashmole 1431. See Gameson, 'English Manuscript Art in the Late Eleventh Century', 126, 137 and 139.

[39] See Lawrence, 'Influence of Canterbury', 98–100, Plates 8.18 to 8.31.

manuscripts for St Calais and Durham was sent to Canterbury to copy this work, and that it was there given an initial by a Christ Church artist (see Plate 3). Of the manuscripts associated with St Calais then, two of the most practical are directly associated with Archbishop Lanfranc, and three demonstrate the bishop of Durham's respect for the libraries being built up at Canterbury under Lanfranc's scholarly influence. Other aspects of St Calais's career have also left their trace on the books and muniments of Durham, and it is this question which will be investigated next.

The introduction of scribes

First, it seems clear that St Calais would have needed the services of several scribes, not only to copy books for him, but also to help with the administrative work in which he was engaged, both as bishop of Durham and as director of the great Domesday Survey. Both professional scribes and secretary-chaplains are recorded in the late eleventh century, and, as other Norman abbots seem to have brought companions and fellow monks to their English houses, to help them in introducing the changes they deemed necessary, it seems almost certain that St Calais would have done the same.[40] Indeed, Bishop Walcher's fate demonstrated that a 'foreign' bishop of Durham was in need of especially strong support. However, scribes and secretaries working under the direction of the bishop in this way by no means constitute a 'Durham scriptorium'. (The term 'scriptorium' is here used to denote a collaborating group of scribe-artists, working at a particular

[40] At Abingdon, Abbot Rainald (1084–97) seems to have brought with him from Jumièges a scribe and artist who produced a copy of the Gospels for presentation to Jumièges, now Rouen, BM, MS 32 (A 21). At St Augustine's, Canterbury, Scolland seems to have brought at least one scribe-artist from Mont-Saint-Michel, whose work appears in Cambridge, Corpus Christi College, MS 276, together with the work of an English scribe. At Christ Church, Lanfranc seems to have been accompanied by two Norman scribes, one of whom may be the Maurice to whom Anselm wrote about books for Le Bec (see Gibson, *Lanfranc*, 76). For further discussion on this point see A. Lawrence, 'Anglo-Norman Book Production', in D. Bates and A. Curry, eds., *England and Normandy in the Middle Ages*, London and Rio Grande, 1994, 79–94, at 89–91. The working relationship between Anselm and his biographer, Eadmer, is well known. Professional scribes were employed at St Albans by Abbot Paul (1077–93) and at Abingdon by Abbot Faricius (1100–17) (see Barlow, *The English Church 1066–1154*, 236–7). At Norwich, the sacristan, Norman, seems to have acted as secretary and scribe to Herbert Losinga, bishop c.1095–1119; while Losinga also employed a wandering monk called Alexander to act as a professional scribe at Norwich (Barlow, 240–1). Alexander discusses the career of the scribe Antonius at Fécamp and Mont-Saint-Michel (*Norman Illumination at Mont St Michel 966–1100*, Oxford, 1970, 235–6); while the Durham *Liber Vitae* records an agreement with Gregory the Scribe, of Bermondsey, in the late eleventh century (see *Liber Vitae Ecclesiae Dunelmensis*, Surtees Society 13, 1841, 33). A variety of arrangements are suggested by Anselm's letters about the copying of Bec manuscripts for Canterbury (Gibson, *Lanfranc*, 171).

religious house.) Evidence of the existence of such a group must be sought in the surviving manuscripts, and so the question arises of whether such a scriptorium was formed during St Calais's episcopate. Crucial here are the other manuscripts associated with St Calais, and the question of whether any of them can be argued to have been made at Durham. If Canterbury books are obviously excluded from this putative group, so must be any others which can be proved to have originated from centres outside Durham. Unfortunately, this is by no means a straightforward question, in a situation in which many individuals were, as has already been argued, moving both from Normandy to England, and within England. In these circumstances, a more fruitful approach will be to seek to identify a group of manuscripts which can be linked together by their script and initials, and which can be associated with both St Calais and Durham. Those manuscripts which do not fall into this group, but which are still associated with St Calais, *may* then give evidence of the other sources upon which he drew in building up his book collection.

Gullick has already published a detailed analysis of the most 'Norman' of St Calais's books, arguing that these represent the volumes acquired by the bishop in Normandy and sent from there to Durham.[41] I do not agree with all Gullick's attributions and arguments, and it is therefore necessary to discuss these books also here, rather than being able to deal with them briefly. The situation is also complicated by Thomson's argument that all these 'Norman' books were, in fact, made by Normans working at Durham, especially since this question does not seem capable of resolution.[42] The books, and the evidence concerning them, will therefore be considered here according to the approach outlined above.

One place to start is with the scribe, William, who has left a record of his name and of his personal association with William of St Calais in a piece of Latin poetry which he inserted as a colophon in a book he copied for the bishop, during the latter's exile. This is now DCL B II 14, and is the third volume of St Calais's copy of Augustine's *Commentary on the Psalms*. The lines of poetry are ambiguous in some ways, but seem to state definitely that this volume, at least, was written during the bishop's exile, and that St Calais paid for the materials. There is also a suggestion of personal devotion to the bishop on the part of the scribe, but there is no definitive statement about

---

[41] Gullick, 'The Scribe of the Carilef Bible', *passim*. Gullick's recent attribution of work in a set of Durham manuscripts, in which other scribes also worked, to Symeon of Durham leads to a related conclusion, namely that there was a productive group of scribe-artists assembled at Durham, beginning in the episcopate of St Calais. See 'The Hand of Symeon of Durham: Further Observations on the Durham Martyrology Scribe', in Rollason, *Symeon of Durham*, 14–31.

[42] See note 22 above.

where the copying was done.[43] Nevertheless, William's script is wholly Norman in style, as are the initials in the manuscript, and there is evidence that William worked for St Calais over a period of some years, including some time at Durham. This evidence was presented by Bishop and Chaplais, who argue that B II 14 represents early work by William, who subsequently copied a diploma of Duncan, king of Scotland (d. 1094) and another of King Edgar, datable to 1095, for Durham. Bishop and Chaplais further demonstrate that William copied Bede's *Historia Ecclesiastica*, in the version which is now the core of DCL B II 35, for St Calais. Like the writs, this also looks like later work by William, and therefore probably done in the 1090s – a point which puts the acquisition of a personal copy of this text interestingly late in the bishop's career.[44] It is tempting to speculate that St Calais encountered both William the scribe, and what he regarded as a good text of Bede, between 1088 and 1091, in Normandy: but there can be no proof.

Gullick has made further attributions to William,[45] including the list of sixty-seven Durham monks in BL Cotton Domitian VII, fol. 45; this is the Durham *Liber Vitae*, and the list is datable to 1099–1109. Thus, the list was drawn up after St Calais's death, and suggests that William stayed on at Durham after the death of his patron. Moreover, it seems probable that such a list would be drawn up by a member of the community, which may suggest that William became a monk at Durham in the 1090s. Gullick also attributed DCL B II 6 to William; this is another St Calais volume, a collection of short works by Ambrose. The attribution is convincing, and the script seems perhaps closer to that of B II 14 than that of B II 35. However, whilst Gullick attributes the whole volume to William, the change of pen and of style on fol. 81r makes me believe, with Mynors, that there is a change of hand there.[46] The new hand is also Norman in style, though a little cruder than William's, and completes the last four folios of the book in an increasingly untidy fashion.

One scribe may then be seen as first working for William of St Calais and then being established as a member of the community at Durham. However, the works attributed to him are, on the whole, associated with the bishop, and thus cannot be taken as evidence for the existence of a scriptorium at the priory. The situation is rather different with another scribe, whose name is not known, who seems to have copied books for the bishop, but also worked

---

[43] Chaplais takes the colophon to suggest that the scribe was at Durham whilst St Calais was in exile. See T. A. M. Bishop and P. Chaplais, *Facsimiles of English Royal Writs to AD 1100*, Oxford, 1957, no. 9 and Plate VIII. Gullick lists B II 14 as a 'Norman' book ('The Scribe of the Carilef Bible', 69). For the text of the colophon, see note 26 above.

[44] Bishop and Chaplais, *Fascimiles of English Royal Writs*, no. 9 and Plate VIII.

[45] Gullick, 'The Scribe of the Carilef Bible', 68–9.

[46] Mynors, *Durham Cathedral Manuscripts*, 41.

at the priory. This analysis is further complicated since much of the work of this putative scribe has been identified as being by Symeon of Durham himself by Gullick who, in the recent article already cited, has argued that authorial corrections in the earliest surviving copy of the Libellus (now Durham UL Cosin V ii 6) as well as annotations in the Martyrology, identify the scribe as Symeon (see note 41). This is convincing but again I do not entirely agree with Gullick's analysis of scribal work in the 'library' books, so shall set out my own views here and in Part II of this chapter. The hand in question is small and distinctive, though neither strongly Norman nor Anglo-Caroline, and equally distinctive initials appear together with his writing, suggesting that he may have been responsible for both.[47] The next section of this chapter will therefore discuss manuscripts which contain work by this scribe, concentrating on the question of whether they provide evidence for the establishment of an active scriptorium at Durham in the late eleventh century. A full analysis of their style and illumination will be given in Part II of this chapter, when they will be discussed together with the other surviving manuscripts from the period. The present analysis will start with a text almost certainly copied at the direction of St Calais, the Martyrology and pericopes incorporated into DCL B IV 24 (fols. 12–45). The hand here is small and rather cramped-looking, with minims appearing heavy in relation to the overall size of the script. The decoration is minimal, consisting of plain red capitals.

The same hand recurs in Bodleian, Bodley 596 and Digby 175, both copies of Bede's *Life of St Cuthbert*. Of the two, Digby 175 is identified as the oldest surviving Durham copy of the text (if Corpus 183 is excluded as being of Wessex origin), while Bodley 596, as stated above, is argued by Gullick to have been St Calais's personal copy of the work.[48] A link with St Calais would help to explain the presence, on fols. 207–13, of a *Life of St Julian of le Mans* and an office for St Julian, the latter added by a le Mans scribe. The duplication of the main text, with differing additions, suggests commissions by different patrons, and Digby 175 may perhaps represent work by this scribe, on behalf of the priory of Durham, as opposed to the bishop. The monks would thus acquire a copy of this very important text, in a version associated with St Calais, and subsequently to be further copied, both for Durham and elsewhere. Bodley 596 also has two major initials, on fols. 175v and 177, in the distinctive style and palette used by this scribe. They will be discussed in Part II of this chapter, together with those of all the other surviving manuscripts of the period.

[47] His work is discussed, and further attributions are made, by Gullick 'The Scribes of the Durham Cantor's Book'.
[48] Ibid. 98.

Still more impressive, and again connected with St Calais, is DCL B II 22, the copy of Augustine's *City of God* whose major initial was drawn by a Canterbury artist (though perhaps painted by the Durham scribe-artist, in his usual colours). This long work is copied by the scribe with impressive uniformity, in both script and minor initials. However, if the Martyrology and B II 22, at least, are evidence that this scribe produced some of St Calais's books, other manuscripts demonstrate that he also collaborated with a large and diverse set of other scribes. The majority of these collaborative manuscripts are also associated with St Calais, and are still in the Durham library. The Martyrology Scribe's strong connections with Durham therefore make it almost certain that Durham was the location for this collaborating group of scribes. Further proof for this hypothesis comes from the wide range of scripts found in these books, a range which would fit the diverse group of monks assembled at Durham by St Calais. Finally, the link with Durham is still further reinforced if Gullick's identification of this scribe as Symeon, precentor and historian of the priory, is correct.[49]

The importance of the Martyrology Scribe

The books now to be discussed are those in which I believe the hand of the Martyrology Scribe appears, collaborating with other scribes. Gullick's suggestion that he was none other than Symeon of Durham is interesting, but again not capable of definite proof. I shall therefore restrict myself to discussing the following books: DCL B III 9, the letters of Gregory the Great, a St Calais book; B II 21, the letters of Augustine, also a St Calais book; B IV 13, Gregory on Ezekiel, another St Calais book; and B IV 7, Augustine's *De Caritate*, not a St Calais book, but another major patristic work. Perhaps most problematic is B III 9. Here, initials in the style of the Martyrology Scribe occur in fols. 1r, 1v, 194v and 199v. But fol. 53v has an unusual initial S in a rather different style, which includes two profile heads, something which does not appear in the Martyrology Scribe's initials. Furthermore, fol. 37v has another S, this one painted rather than drawn in red outline, and with an early version of the stylised foliage motif named the 'clove curl' by Mynors, which is characteristic of Durham manuscripts, but which does not usually occur in the Martyrology Scribe's work.[50] The script is difficult to analyse: throughout, the style is, in a general way, that of the Martyrology Scribe, yet the size and spacing are larger than in the manuscripts previously discussed, and the script is less perfectly regular than in B II

[49] Ibid. 104–8.
[50] The term is Mynors's, see *Durham Cathedral Manuscripts*, 7. For Gullick's most recent views, see 'The Hand of Symeon of Durham', especially 24–31.

22. One way of interpreting this might be that the Martyrology Scribe supplied headings and some initials, while other scribes copied the text and added other initials. Whilst the text is in a style based on the Martyrology Scribe's own, the initials are more varied. If this is indeed the case, then the Martyrology Scribe may have influenced, or perhaps taught, other scribes at Durham. This would make his work, unlike William's, strong evidence of the establishment of a scriptorium at Durham. Moreover, as B III 9 is a St Calais book, it seems that the Martyrology Scribe was training other scribes at Durham before St Calais's death in 1096.

Also complex is DCL B II 21. This collection of Augustine's letters is different at several points from the Christ Church copy, and was not taken from a Canterbury exemplar. Moreover, the majority of the book is in a small, rather rough Norman hand, and the main initial, on fol. 12r, is in the style of Robert Benjamin, the Norman artist who painted the main initials in DCL B II 13, volume ii of St Calais's copy of Augustine's *Commentary on the Psalms*. This being so, it is rather surprising to find the Martyrology Scribe providing a substantial stretch of the text, from fol. 30 to fol. 58. Minor initials throughout the book are in a style found in a number of books of this period, written in varying hands, which have the twelfth-century Durham *ex libris* (see Part II below). The probability then is that this also is a Durham product, and that Durham thus had a scriptorium, with a distinctive decorative repertoire, in the late eleventh century. If so, there is some likelihood that Robert Benjamin, like William the scribe, travelled to Durham, if it was indeed he who executed the major initial in this manuscript.

DCL B IV 13, like the previous two manuscripts, is gathered in quires of ten leaves, another feature of these Durham books. Like B III 9, its main initials and opening rubrication are in the style of the Martyrology Scribe. However, this manuscript contains work by a number of mediocre scribes, several of whom appear to be following the style of the Martyrology Scribe, again suggesting his central role in the establishment of a scriptorium at Durham. Again, characteristic forms of stylised foliage, which will be discussed below, recur on minor initials throughout the volume. In a similar way, B IV 7 contains work by a number of hands and some of them, as in B II 21, are very Norman in appearance. Here, there are none of the characteristic initials in red outline and colour-wash, but the opening *incipit* is in the style of the Martyrology Scribe, and a hand very close to his takes over on fol. 13r, and continues to fol. 19v. Moreover, both in the main initial and in the initial rather awkwardly inserted on fol. 12v, there are the characteristic stylised foliage motifs found on the minor initials of the other manuscripts in this group.[51]

[51] See Part II below.

The evidence presented thus makes it possible to argue, not only that a scriptorium was established at Durham during the episcopate of St Calais, but also that the Martyrology Scribe may have had a position of some responsibility within this scriptorium. Moreover, while the Durham manuscripts overall do exhibit the wide stylistic range described by Ker, it would appear that moves towards establishing a 'house style' were gradually taking shape, and that the Martyrology Scribe played an important part.

The Norman books

However, the books discussed in detail so far constitute only ten of the twenty-three volumes identified by Mynors with items on the list of St Calais's gifts. As was stated above, several others have no conclusive evidence about where they were made, but they can be shown to contain work by scribes or artists who mostly worked for other houses. Of these, the largest group are those in Norman hands, and which do not contain work by scribes who can be placed at Durham, or initials using characteristic motifs. Pre-eminent amongst these is the great Carilef Bible, DCL A II 4, which, as Gullick has most recently argued, was almost entirely written by a scribe who worked mostly for Bayeux Cathedral, and in collaboration with other Bayeux scribes.[52] Its initials are also by one artist, who worked not only for Bayeux and for St Calais, but also for St Ouen, and for Osbern, bishop of Exeter.[53] Gullick has also identified the hand of the Carilef Bible scribe in DCL B II 17, another copy of Augustine's *Commentary on St John's Gospel*, which is wholly Norman in style, and was perhaps acquired by St Calais in Normandy, duplicating the copy from Canterbury.[54]

Gullick also argues that A II 4 and B II 17 in fact form part of an interlocking group of manuscripts, all made for St Calais in Normandy, by a group of scribes and artists presumably brought together at St Calais's request. However this may be, the rest of the manuscripts in question, DCL B II 13 – B II 14, B III 1, B III 16, B III 10 and B II 11 are certainly Norman in both script and decoration. I would also agree that B III 1 and B III 10 (Origen's *Homilies* and Gregory's *Moralia in Job*, respectively) are mostly by the same scribe. Their initials are by different hands, but they both show characteristic Norman 'scalloped' decoration (see Figs. 1 and 2). However, since this scribe also worked for Jumièges, Exeter and St Albans,

[52] See Gullick, 'The Scribe of the Carilef Bible', *passim*.
[53] Ibid. 64–5. See also F. Avril, *Manuscrits normands XI–XIIème siècles*, Rouen, 1975, at no. 33; and T. S. R. Boase, *English Art 1100–1215*, 2nd edn, Oxford, 1968, 26 and 29, and Plates 4 and 5.
[54] Gullick, 'The Scribe of the Carilef Bible', 69.

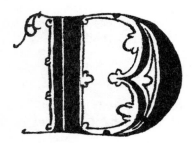

FIG. 1 Initial D from Durham, DCL,
MS B III 1, fol. 106v

FIG. 2 Initial B from Durham, DCL,
MS B III 10, fol. 31v

it seems likely that he was a professional.[55] I would also agree that DCL B II 13, B II 11, and B III 16 (Augustine's *Commentary on the Psalms*, opuscula by Jerome, and Rabanus Maurus) all contain work by another scribe. However, these manuscripts are more complex, since their initials contain foliage motifs popular at Durham. Gullick does not link the scribe with other manuscripts made for Norman centres, and the same hand seems also to occur in DCL B II 6, which is described as a Durham product by Gullick.[56] It has already been suggested that Robert Benjamin, the Norman artist of B II 13 who, like William the scribe, expresses his admiration for St Calais, may (also like William) have travelled to Durham. In these circumstances, all that can be said for certain is that these manuscripts had been assembled at Durham by the time of St Calais's death, and that they, like any of those responsible for their production who did travel to Durham, may well have been influential in the development of the scriptorium at Durham.

Before leaving the question of manuscripts produced by Norman scribes and artists, however, DCL B II 9, another St Calais manuscript, should be considered. This is a copy of Jerome's *Commentary on the Minor Prophets*, which shows several variations from the Canterbury copy of the same work, and is wholly Norman in appearance.[57] It appears to be in one hand throughout, though the writing is not completely regular, and it has major initials drawn in brown ink outline, with touches of red, on a light green ground. François Avril has suggested that these initials are by the artist of the initials of Rouen, BM, MS 1406, a collection of saints' *Lives*, made for St

---

[55] Gullick, 'The Scribe of the Carilef Bible', 63.   [56] Ibid. 68.
[57] The Canterbury copy is now Cambridge, Trinity College, B 3 5.

FIG. 3 Initial D from Durham, DCL,
MS B II 2, p. 34.

FIG. 4 Initial B from Winchester,
Cathedral Library, MS 2, fol. 4v

Ouen at the order of Abbot Nicolas (1042–92).[58] This comparison is convincing, but I cannot accept Gullick's argument that the script and initials of B II 9 are by Hugo Pictor.[59] However, as neither script nor major initials in exactly this style occur in other Durham manuscripts, it does seem possible that this book also was acquired by St Calais in Normandy.

Conclusion

The last three 'St Calais' manuscripts are DCL B III 11, B II 2 and A III 29. They raise similar problems to the 'Norman' group just discussed, since there is no clear evidence about where they were made. However, they all show English hands, and B II 2, a collection of homilies, has initials with a type of stylised foliage found in a number of twelfth-century Winchester books (see Figs. 3 and 4).[60] In the circumstances, they may be imports from Wessex or Mercia, or the work of monks who had come north in response to the call of Aldwin and his companions. However, this discussion of the manuscripts

[58] See Avril, *Manuscrits normands*, at no. 35. See also A. C. de la Mare, 'A Probable Addition to the Bodleian's Holdings of Exeter Cathedral Manuscripts', *Bodleian Library Record* 11, 1983, 79–83.

[59] Gullick, 'The Scribe of the Carilef Bible', 74–5.

[60] See, for comparison, Winchester Cathedral MSS 4 (Cassiodorus) and 5 (Jerome). Related foliage is also found in Winchester Cathedral MS 20 (Hegisippus). For related arguments on the significance of such foliage motifs for the attribution of manuscripts see J. J. G. Alexander, 'Scribes as Artists: The Arabesque Initial in Twelfth-Century English Manuscripts', in M. B. Parkes and A. G. Watson, eds., *Medieval Scribes, Manuscripts and Libraries. Essays Presented to N. R. Ker*, London, 1978, 87–116.

associated with St Calais has made it possible to put forward some conclusions. The first, and most important, is that the evidence suggests that an active scriptorium was formed at Durham by 1096. Secondly, scribes associated with St Calais himself appear to have taken part in the work of this scriptorium. Thirdly, in the case of the Martyrology Scribe, a 'St Calais' scribe appears to have acted almost as director of the scriptorium, and to have taken some steps towards introducing a more unified style of script and initials. More generally, it would appear that, at least in those books which may have been ordered and paid for by St Calais, there is less influence from Winchcombe and Evesham than might have been expected. Indeed, whilst a number of English hands have already been noted, it would appear that, for St Calais, the most important sources of texts and scribes were Lanfranc's Canterbury, and a group of Norman houses which, interestingly, did not include Bec or Caen, but did include Bayeux and St Ouen.

PART II
Manuscript illumination at Durham, c. 1083–c. 1099

Part I of this chapter was concerned to discuss the evidence for the establishment of scribes at Durham, and to attempt to identify those manuscripts which could be argued to have been produced by them. These books were also distinguished from those brought into Durham, by St Calais or others, from other sources. Having attempted to establish this distinction, it is now important to look at the style of the manuscripts argued to have been produced at Durham, and in particular at their illumination, in order to establish whether a 'house-style' of manuscript production and decoration was established at Durham before 1100. Of the various groupings of books already discussed, two thus become particularly important: those which were produced by scribes associated with St Calais, and located at Durham, and those which can be linked with these books (primarily by palaeographical and art-historical features) and thus putatively located at Durham. The characteristics of these manuscripts will therefore be discussed, together with their links with, and differences from, the other, contemporary, manuscripts associated with Durham. Some overlap with the preceding discussion will be necessary, for the problem of the origin of any book remains relevant. However, a point worth emphasising is that, however diverse their origins, all these manuscripts could still constitute a pool of figures and motifs on which future illuminators could draw.

This observation leads on to another very important point, which can seem so obvious that it is easy to overlook. This is that virtually all the Durham manuscripts of this period, even those from Canterbury, show what are fundamentally Norman styles, motifs and colour-usages. Given the emphasis at Durham on restoring the glories of the past, this may seem curious, especially as Durham possessed some strikingly illuminated tenth-century manuscripts, most notably the *Life of St Cuthbert* which Bishop Walcher had consulted. However, it may not be unimportant that this manuscript (now Cambridge, Corpus Christi College, MS 183) was recorded in the Durham sources as having been presented by King Athelstan, the hero of the Wessex dynasty, and even showed the king, with St Cuthbert, in a miniature. Such associations may have been unwelcome after 1083. What does seem certain is that Bishop St Calais had new copies of both the *Life of St Cuthbert* and of Bede's *Historia Ecclesiastica* made, by Norman or North French scribes and artists. This may suggest that the prevalence of Norman illumination represents something more than a coincidence. It would seem that St Calais preferred to patronise scribes and artists who worked in styles with which he was familiar, though it also seems that the emphasis was on the provision of 'good' and impressive copies of fundamental books, rather than on the imposition, or attempted imposition, of any uniform style.

With these general points established, this section will begin by examining the illumination of those manuscripts of whose origins something is known. Others will be discussed in terms of the stylistic features they exhibit, and of whether these features can be located at specific centres in Normandy or England. Special attention will be paid to those which can be argued to have been produced at Durham, and especially to whether they exhibit any common or recurring features. This examination will add further support to the arguments based on script, which found evidence for the existence of a productive scriptorium at Durham before the death of St Calais.

The obvious place to start is with DCL A II 4, the surviving volume of St Calais's Bible, which contains the list of his books. This manuscript is linked both with Bayeux, where St Calais had risen to prominence as one of the circle gathered by Odo, bishop of Bayeux, and with Rouen, the ducal capital in Upper Normandy. It is generally accepted to have been commissioned by St Calais during his exile in Normandy, 1088–91. Its scribe seems to have worked mostly for Bayeux, since François Avril has found his hand in a Sacramentary for the use of Bayeux (Paris, Bibliothèque Mazarine, MS 404/729): and Gullick has found it in a copy of Gregory's *Moralia in Job* from Bayeux (Bayeux Cathedral, MSS 57–8), and in the Bayeux Cathedral entry in the Mortuary Roll of Abbot Vitalis, who died in 1122.[61] Gullick has also found his hand in DCL B II 17, which was probably St Calais's copy of

---

[61] See Gullick, 'The Scribe of the Carilef Bible', and Part I above.

Augustine's *Commentary on St John's Gospel*, and in Bodleian Library, Bodley 810, the Exeter copy of Lanfranc's 'Canonical Collection', which also contains work in a Canterbury style. The illumination of the Bible also forms part of a complex set of attributions, but unfortunately they are different ones. The Bible contains no miniatures, as is common with Norman books, but has a set of brightly coloured and distinctive historiated initials. There is general agreement that the artist of these also executed the historiated initials in the St Ouen copy of Augustine's *Commentary on St John's Gospel* (Rouen A 85/467), and Avril has convincingly argued that another St Ouen manuscript, now Rouen Y 21/233, has a half-page miniature in a very similar style.[62] However, even if the style can be located at St Ouen, the Bible artist, like the scribe, worked for a range of patrons. Avril finds his hand in: an Exeter manuscript (Bodleian, Bodley 301); in the Bayeux *Moralia* mentioned above; and in an unprovenanced manuscript in the Bibliothèque Nationale (Lat. 7963). All these comparisons are convincing.[63]

These networks of attributions are complex, and suggest that it was not uncommon for scribes and artists to be brought together for particular patrons, on an *ad hoc* basis. What is more important for the present enquiry is that there is no evidence that the Bible artist travelled to Durham, nor that his figure style appears in any other Durham manuscript. However, one point which has not previously been made is that the type of 'acanthus' foliage used by the Bible artist does appear in another Durham manuscript. This is DCL B III 16, Rabanus Maurus' *Commentary on St Matthew*, written by at least two 'Norman' hands, neither of which is that of the Bible scribe. Its main initial is an M, composed of coils of foliage. This is rather softer in appearance than the Carilef Bible initials, since it is drawn in red and green outline, rather than the black favoured by the Bible artist. However, the foliage is elongated, as is that of the Bible artist and, more importantly, the leaves are made as are those in the Bible, and are joined to the stems in the same very characteristic way (see Figs. 5 and 6). The minor initials in this manuscript are also painted in red, green and blue, and are decorated with scallop patterns, some articulated with fine lines, and with small, bud-like florets (Fig. 7). These motifs certainly belong to the repertoire of Norman (rather than Anglo-Saxon) illumination, but are almost universal in Norman books. I have found them in manuscripts from Lyre, Le Bec, St Evroult, Jumièges, Fécamp, St Ouen and Mont-Saint-Michel. It is thus clear that this is a 'Norman' book, and unclear where the illumination was executed. However, work by its main scribe also appears in DCL B II 6, B II 11, and B II 13 (vol. ii of Augustine's *On the Psalms*). It would seem, therefore, that the illuminator of B III 16

---

[62] Avril, *Manuscrits normands*, nos. 33 and 34.
[63] Ibid. under no. 33, at 44.

FIG. 5 Leaf motifs from Durham, DCL,
MS A II 4, fol. 2v

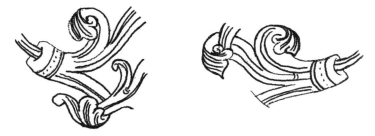

FIG. 6 Leaf motifs from Durham, DCL, MS B III 16, fol 2r

FIG. 7 Initial E from Durham, DCL, MS B III 16, fol. 6r

formed part of a group of scribes and artists working for St Calais, whether at Durham or elsewhere, and that he chose to imitate the foliage in the initials of the Bishop's Bible.

The other manuscript which can be ascribed with certainty to St Calais's exile is DCL B II 14, vol. iii of Augustine's *On the Psalms*, which is the companion volume of B II 13. It has been argued that these books were produced both at Durham and in Normandy, but I do not propose to enter into this argument. What is important here is that William, the scribe of B II 14, can be placed at Durham after St Calais's return there, where he produced more work (as was seen above), and that these two manuscripts share certain types of initials which recur in the Durham books. Unusually, the name of the artist of the major initials of B II 13 is known, since he executed an initial showing himself at the feet of his patron, and surrounded by an inscription in which his name is given as Robert Benjamin. Figures are, in fact, rare in his initials, and are less incisively drawn than those of the Bible artist, but his palette and colour usage are similar. His initials are made up of the elements common in Norman illumination, combining panelled sections, dragons, lion-masks, interlace terminals, coils of acanthus foliage and parti-coloured grounds. However, his style does have distinctive elements, which add up to an impression of heaviness. His panelled sections are rather loosely con-structed, with the bowls of letters large in relation to their stems; his dragons have small, round heads with a corrugated outline, on bulky bodies marked with dots along the spine; and his foliage has rather small leaves, with simple bases, long stems, and rows of heavy dots. Like Gullick, I would argue that Robert Benjamin's work is found in other Durham manuscripts.[64] However, I disagree with some of Gullick's attributions, and also believe that Robert Benjamin had followers, or at least artists who worked in related styles, at Durham. This makes detailed discussion necessary.

Like Gullick, I believe that Robert Benjamin executed the main initial of B II 14, the companion volume to B II 13 (see Plate 4). The letter-construction, the dragons and the foliage are all very similar to those in B II 13.[65] However, I do not believe that Gullick's assertion that Robert Benjamin also executed the arabesque initials in these two books is capable of proof, since they use a repertoire very different from that of the inhabited initials. Furthermore, I cannot accept that the major initial of DCL B III 1 is by Robert Benjamin. Its trellis-like construction is quite different from his panel-and-dragon constructions, the lion-mask is very different from his, especially in the execution of the eyes, and the colouring is different. For these reasons, I shall discuss these initials separately. However, unlike Gullick, I would argue that the main initial of DCL B II 21 (St Calais's copy of Augustine's letters) is either by Robert Benjamin or by a very similar hand (see Plate 5). The loose, panelled construction and the dragons are very

[64] For Gullick's attributions of initials to Robert Benjamin, see 'The Scribe of the Carilef Bible', 69.
[65] A preliminary version of my own attributions is given in Lawrence, 'Influence of Canter-bury', 95–6.

close, although it must be admitted that the foliage is more abundant and lacks the distinctive dots, and that the purple pigment is less good here than in B II 13. Since the minor initials of B II 21 contain a number of motifs which recur in Durham books, two of which are very distinctive, it may be best to consider the artist of B II 21 as an imitator, something which would raise interesting questions about the methods used to train illuminators. Also interesting are initials in DCL B II 35 (St Calais's copy of Bede's *Historia Ecclesiastica*), and B IV 7, not a St Calais book, but a patristic work, a copy of Augustine's *De Caritate*. The script of the former has been convincingly attributed to William, the scribe of B II 14, and it has an initial on page 72 which has been attributed to Robert Benjamin (see Plate 6). However, the dragons of which this is largely composed are smaller, thinner, and more crisply drawn, while the foliage lacks the distinctive dots and bases. Indeed, this seems to me a different hand, the same as that of the initial on fol. 25r of B IV 7 (see Plate 7). Since the other initials of the latter show the same distinctive features as those of B II 35, there seems a good case for regarding both of these initials as the work of an artist located at Durham, and drawing upon the same repertoire as Robert Benjamin. It should be noted that the origin of B II 35, as with all this group, is still under debate. Gullick has more recently come to regard it as a Norman product, imported into Durham.[66]

It may now be appropriate to return to DCL B III 1, the manuscript whose main initial was attributed by Gullick to Robert Benjamin. This is St Calais's copy of Origen's *Homilies*, and I do agree with Gullick that the same scribe also wrote most of DCL B III 10 (St Calais's copy of Gregory's *Moralia in Job*, vol. i). The major initials in the two books also show similarities, although I would argue that neither is by Robert Benjamin. Both share a very bright palette, using red, blue, green and bright yellow, without the acid green, buff and purple of the previous initials. Moreover, they show very similar patterns in their upright stems. Each consists of two thin uprights, around which acanthus foliage coils in patterns, reminiscent of the frames found in late Anglo-Saxon manuscripts. What has not been pointed out before is that, while such trellis-elements are used as frames in Mont-Saint-Michel books (see Alexander, *Norman Illumination at Mont St Michel 966–1100*, Plate 30), they are used to constitute whole initials only at Jumièges, where they are very popular. Indeed, of the Jumièges books at Rouen, these trellis-initials are found in no less than five, out of perhaps twenty surviving books attributable to the late eleventh century (Rouen, BM, A 102, A 298, A 88, A 195 and U 61).[67] Two of these, A 298 and U 61, also

---

[66] See M. Gullick, 'The Origin and Importance of Cambridge, Trinity College R. 5. 27', *Transactions of the Cambridge Bibliographical Society* 11, part 3, 239–62, at 244 and n. 18.

[67] For reproductions see Avril, *Manuscrits normands*, nos. 27, 33, 47.

have lion-masks similar to those in B III 1, while the beak-heads which form part of the upper terminals of the initials in both B III 1 and B III 10 are very similar to one another. On these grounds, it seems probable that the main initials of B III 1 and B III 10 are by the same hand, and that this artist had a Jumièges background. However, he had no imitators at Durham, and the arabesque initials are of common Norman types.

Also to be classed as a wholly Norman work, which had no direct followers at Durham, is DCL B II 9, St Calais's copy of Jerome's *Commentary on the Minor Prophets*. This book also has been included in a complex network of attributions, resulting in Gullick's argument that its scribe-artist was none other than Hugo Pictor.[68] This seems unlikely, at least in the case of the initials of B II 9, which are very different from Hugo Pictor's signed work in Bodleian, Bodley 717 and Paris, Bibliothèque Nationale, Lat. 13765. They are also very unlike the miniatures in Rouen Y 109/1408 and A 366/539, which Avril, following Pächt, has convincingly attributed to Hugo Pictor.[69] For this reason, I would see B II 9, with Avril, as the work of an artist who also illuminated manuscripts for St Ouen, in the time of Abbot Nicholas (1042–92). These other manuscripts in his style are: Rouen, BM, Y 41/ 1406, a collection of saints' *Lives* apparently produced at the order of Nicholas; and Rouen, BM, A 47/464.[70]

The eleven books discussed so far in this chapter contain between them the bulk of the more impressive illumination to be found in Durham books of this period. It will be clear that they contain no miniatures, and that historiated initials are to be found only in the Bible, and in vol. ii of Augustine's *On the Psalms* (B II 13). Thus there would appear to be a striking lack of interest in pictorial narrative in these books. Only one manuscript attributable to St Calais's patronage contains the popular author-portrait type of initial, and that is B II 22, the copy of Augustine's *City of God*. Here the script, and the arabesque initials, are the work of the man I have called the Martyrology Scribe, but the author-portrait initial is almost certainly the work of a Canterbury artist. I have discussed this initial in detail elsewhere, arguing that it is the work of the artist of the secondary initials in Cambridge, Trinity College, R 15 22 and B 3 4, and in Cambridge UL Ii III 12, all Christ Church manuscripts.[71] An additional point, worth making here, is that the colouring of the author-portrait initial in DCL B II 22 is different from that in the Christ Church group, but the same as the minor initials in B II 22. It therefore seems that this initial was drawn by a

---

[68] Gullick, 'The Scribe of the Carilef Bible', 75.
[69] Avril, *Manuscrits normands*, nos. 43 and 44.
[70] Ibid. no. 35.
[71] Lawrence, 'Influence of Canterbury', 98–100.

Canterbury artist but painted at Durham, or by a Durham artist. This is particularly interesting since something similar may have happened in the case of DCL B II 16, another copy of Augustine's *Commentary on St John's Gospel*. This is entirely written by a St Augustine's scribe, and has unusual initials. Besides the common dragons and lion-masks, they also contain, or are partially composed of, active human figures, drawn in a wiry style, which may be compared with the 'gymnastic' initials found at Canterbury. However, the colours used to paint these initials are quite unlike Canterbury work. They include the deep acid green and bright orange very frequent in Norman manuscripts, together with the sort of thick, chalky pastel colours found in late eleventh-century books from Mont-Saint-Michel and Fécamp.[72] Moreover, there are similarities between the ochre-greens, thick use of paint, and complex colour-contrasts used to suggest highlights in B II 16 and the fully painted work in Oxford, University College, MS 165 – although the latter makes much more use of dark blue, a very expensive pigment. These connections are admittedly rather tenuous, but if accepted they may suggest that the curious initials of DCL B II 16 mark the beginning of a type of painting at Durham which was further developed in Univ. 165, which is the luxurious, illuminated copy of the *Life of St Cuthbert* almost certainly produced at Durham *c.*1100.[73] By contrast, DCL B II 10, St Calais's copy of Jerome's letters, is entirely a Christ Church, Canterbury, product, which found no followers at Durham.

All these manuscripts, whether from Normandy, Canterbury, or unknown centres, have represented styles and motifs which originated outside Durham, and were thus being introduced, together with Benedictine monasticism and Anglo-Norman Church politics. Some new suggestions have been made here about the origins of some of their features, but there has also been an interest about whether they took root at Durham. Moreover, in the cases of both the dragon-and-acanthus initials, and of the 'scalloped' type of minor initial, it has been argued that this did indeed happen. It is therefore now time to turn to those books which it can plausibly be argued were produced at Durham, and to look at the range of initials and decorative motifs they contain.

[72] On the letter, see Avril, *Manuscrits normands*, nos. 9 and 14. Jonathan Alexander gives a clear analysis of the colours used in Mont-Saint-Michel manuscripts: see especially *Norman Illumination at Mont St Michel 966–1100*, Oxford, 1970, 205–9. Colour reproductions of the Mont-Saint-Michel initials are given in Michel Delalonde, *Manuscrits de Mont-Saint-Michel*, Rennes, 1981.
[73] Gameson compares the painting style of DCL B II 16 with the enigmatic eleventh-century Troper, now BL Cotton Caligula A xiv; and with Cambridge UL Ii 3 33, a Canterbury copy of Gregory's *Registrum Epistolarum*, datable to 1079–1101. See 'English Manuscript Art in the Mid-Eleventh Century', 90–5.

The connecting link in the majority of these manuscripts is formed by the work of the Martyrology Scribe. What is particularly interesting, in books where writing by him occurs, is the almost universal appearance of a type of initial distinctive in both style and colour. This type of initial is well illustrated by DCL B II 22, the *City of God*, whose main initial was discussed above, and which was entirely written by this scribe. The larger initials in this style serve here to mark the opening of some of the books into which the text is divided. They are firmly drawn in bright red outline, a technique found also in Norman manuscripts, and use an unusual palette of bright red and blue, purple and soft yellow. Major portions of the letters are formed by precise curves or straight lines, and are almost always panelled; minor elements, such as the tail of Q, or the stem of round d, may be formed by sprays of outsize foliage. Dragons and lion-masks do occur, but are rare, and the initials are characterised by sinuous coils of fleshy foliage, terminating in simple groups of petals and berries. These are left in plain vellum, and set against grounds filled with areas of distinctive colour. This gives the initials a statuesque effect in reproduction, since liveliness is created by the bright colours. Almost identical initials are found in: Bodley 596, a copy of the *Life of St Cuthbert* written by this scribe, possibly for St Calais; in DCL B III 9, St Calais's copy of Gregory's *Registrum*, partly written and stongly influenced by this scribe (see Plate 8); and in DCL B IV 13, St Calais's copy of Gregory's *Commentary on Ezekiel*, again partly written by this scribe. Ironically, the one text wholly written by this scribe in which these initials do not appear is the Martyrology after which he is named (DCL B IV 24, fols. 13–44v).

What is also very interesting is that these initials, although they appear in two manuscripts produced by groups of cooperating scribes who were presumably monks of Durham, were not taken up by any other illuminator, nor used in manuscripts of the next period such as Univ. 165.[74] Instead, it was the smaller, arabesque initials executed by this artist which were extremely influential. They are also very precisely painted, and they deploy a small repertoire of very distinctive foliage motifs which continued to be used at Durham into the twelfth century.

The first is a simple, outsize leaf, usually used as an enlarged terminal at the top or bottom of a letter (see Figs. 8–11). Related to this type of leaf is a composite floret which has been discussed and named the 'flame motif' by Gullick (see Figs. 12–14).[75] The last example introduces also the third element of this repertoire, a small, curved cross with round terminals, used to decorate the narrow portions of letters, in place of the more usual circle-

---

[74] Presumably for this reason they are not discussed in detail by Mynors in *Durham Cathedral Manuscripts*.

[75] Gullick, 'The Scribes of the Durham Cantor's Book', 96.

FIG. 8 Initial N from Oxford, Bodleian,
MS Bodley 596, fol. 183v

FIG. 9 Initial F from Durham, DCL,
MS B III 9, fol. 22r

FIG. 10 Initial I from Durham, DCL,
MS B II 22, fol. 42v

FIG. 11 KL monogram from Durham,
DCL, MS B IV 24, fol. 7v

and-bar motif (see Figs. 15 and 16). As in B IV 13, these last two motifs frequently occur on the same initial. It should perhaps be emphasised that, simple though it is, this decorative repertoire stands out in certain ways from the majority of the arabesque decoration to be found in late-eleventh-century Norman and Anglo-Norman manuscripts. This tends to repeat basic, very popular motifs (see Figs. 17–21). The same motifs are used, in varying forms, in manuscripts from Le Bec, St Ouen, and Préaux. I do not know the minor initials of Mont-Saint-Michel manuscripts, but Jonathan Alexander illustrates the same types of motifs: Plate 46 of *Norman Illumination* shows an initial with very standard scallops and floret.[76] What emerges from this comparison is that the motifs used by the Martyrology Scribe are drawn from the general repertoire of Norman illumination, but are handled by him in a

---

[76] See Alexander, *Norman Illumination*, Plate 46.

FIG. 13 Flame motif from Durham, DCL,
MS B IV 24, fol. 7r

FIG. 12 Flame motif from Durham,
DCL, MS B III 9, fol. 27v

FIG. 14 Flame motif from Durham,
DCL, MS B IV 13, fol. 53v

FIG. 15 Initial N from Durham, DCL,
MS B II 22, fol. 78v

FIG. 16 Simple circle-and-bar motif

simpler manner, and on a larger scale relative to the overall size of the initials. If specific comparisons are sought, the best appear to come from Jumièges, where the practice of drawing initials in red outline is also found, but the Jumièges examples are not by the same hand, and are not close enough for it to be certain that they are more than coincidence (see Figs. 22–6).

This repertoire seems to have been influentially used at Durham by the Martyrology Scribe, and there the 'flame motif' and the curved-cross became particularly important. The earliest appearance of the former may be in the Latin copy of the Benedictine Rule which begins on fol. 74v of DCL B IV

FIG. 17 Initial I from Rouen, Bibliothèque
Municipale, MS U 3, fol. 39r

FIG. 18 Initial A from Rouen, Bibliothèque
Municipale, MS I 69, fol. 154r

FIG. 19 Initial H from Rouen, Bibliothèque
Municipale, MS U 61, fol. 170r

FIG. 20 Initial C from Rouen, Bibliothèque
Municipale, MS A 296, fol. 172v

24, a text not in the Martyrology Scribe's hand and which may originate in
the West Midlands.[77] The implications of this are further discussed in
Chapter 3; here it is important to note that, whatever the origins of the
individual motifs, they were almost certainly derived from Norman sources,

---

[77] This is discussed in detail by Piper, 'The Durham Cantor's Book'.

FIG. 21 Initial A from Rouen, Bibliothèque Municipale, MS A 259, fol. 53v

FIG. 22 Initial P from Rouen, Bibliothèque Municipale, MS 102, vol. i, fol. 5v

FIG. 23 Initial H from Rouen, Bibliothèque Municipale, MS A 28, fol. 64v

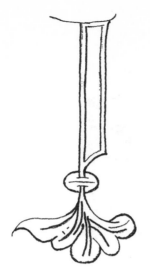

FIG. 24 Initial I from Rouen, Bibliothèque
Municipale, MS A 366, fol. 21v

FIG. 25 Initial I from Rouen, Bibliothèque
Municipale, MS A 278, fol. 44r

FIG. 26 Floret motif from Rouen, Bibliothèque
Municipale, MS A 102, vol. iii, fol. 118r

and they played a major part in the repertoire of the developing scriptorium
at Durham. Two other manuscripts will demonstrate how these motifs took
root at Durham, and show some of the ways in which they were used. They
have both already been mentioned, and the first is DCL B II 21, St Calais's
copy of Augustine's letters. This has a main initial in the style of Robert
Benjamin, and its minor initials are mostly plain. However, the flame motif
appears as a terminal on a round-d on fol. 15v, and the curved cross appears
on fol. 158r. These disparate elements are most likely to have been brought
together at Durham, and to have been used together by scribes and artists in a
new scriptorium, drawing upon the various models available to them. The
same argument can also be made in the case of DCL B IV 7. This is not a St
Calais book, and is often dated to 1100. However, its script, in several hands,

FIG. 27 Initial M from Durham, DCL, MS B IV 7, fol. 31v

FIG. 28 Initial S from Durham, DCL, MS B III 9, fol. 87v

is still Norman in character, and it has a rather scratchy dragon-initial of Norman type on fol. 25r (see Plate 7). Its opening initial, on fol. 3r, is a large arabesque, which combines several versions of the curved-cross with other, more generally used, foliage motifs. Furthermore, an initial P on fol. 13r has a large flame motif tail, while an M on fol. 31v has both an elaborate flame motif and a curved-cross (Fig. 27).

Further evidence that the manuscripts containing these motifs represent work in an emerging house-style at Durham is provided by DCL B III 9, St Calais's copy of Gregory's *Registrum*. This contains a number of initials by the Martyrology Scribe which have already been discussed. However, in addition to the established repertoire, something new appears on fol. 87v (Fig. 28). This is an initial S, which has as a lower terminal an elaborated flame motif, which includes two early versions of the clove-curl motif which became so popular in Durham books in the twelfth century. Mynors does not mention this initial, but he perhaps had it in mind when he stated that initials in this manuscript 'can be connected in style . . . with Durham books of the early XIIth century'.[78]

It has been necessary for this chapter to examine a large number of details. Nevertheless, the procedure has succeeded in identifying a group of manuscripts which were almost certainly written and illuminated at Durham during the episcopate of St Calais. Another interesting feature which has emerged is that, despite the almost certain presence at Durham of monks from the West Midlands, traditionally seen as a bastion of Anglo-Saxon tradition, both the manuscripts brought to Durham and those produced there are strongly Norman in their illumination. Finally, it has been argued that certain distinctive motifs are already popular in Durham manuscripts of the late eleventh century. All these points are important in themselves, but they will also form the basis for the discussion of the early-twelfth-century manuscripts which will form the next chapter.

[78] Mynors, *Durham Cathedral Manuscripts*, nos. 41, 39.

☙❧

Manuscript production at Durham in the early twelfth century

In the previous chapter, it was argued that organised production of manuscripts began at Durham before the end of the eleventh century. Two other important points were made, namely that this production focuses on the work of two scribes who appear to have been introduced into Durham by Bishop St Calais himself, and that it was dominated by Norman styles of script and illumination. In the light of this, it is scarcely surprising that production of high-quality manuscripts continued at Durham in the early twelfth century, and that some elements of a house-style began to emerge, though more markedly in illumination than in script. What is very surprising is that this illumination, rather than developing the Norman styles already introduced, shows strong Anglo-Saxon elements in both style and technique. Thus, the main task of the present chapter will be to identify those manuscripts which are datable to the early twelfth century, and to discuss their relationships with one another, in order to clarify the patterns of development of manuscript production at Durham. But a second theme will be the nature and origin of the style of illumination which dominated at this time.

PART I

Script and initials

The script of Durham manuscripts of this period has been analysed or commented upon by several writers. Mynors made observations and suggestions on some manuscripts, but found few books which could definitely be linked together. In all, he identifies forty-two manuscripts as datable to the first half of the twelfth century, and he points out that the great majority of these each show work by several different scribes.[1] In only a few cases does he

---

[1] See Mynors, *Durham Cathedral Manuscripts*, nos. 52–93.

suggest that the same hand can be identified in more than one book. Ker confirms this impression (shared also by the present writer) of a large number of different hands, varying rather widely in style and quality. Indeed, Ker points out that it is impossible to give any overall characterisation of script at Durham in the early twelfth century, as there is almost no stylistic coherence.[2] Nevertheless, this conclusion is in itself very interesting and suggestive. Ker and Piper identify thirty-two manuscripts as 'Durham' books datable to the early twelfth century, including four books not discussed by Mynors. These add more hands to the overall picture. It is extremely difficult to be precise, since many hands are poor and variable, and some seem to appear for only very short passages. Nevertheless, it can be argued that some fifty different hands, the majority rather unimpressive, appear in Durham manuscripts from this time. This is not the pattern which would be produced by a small number of expert scribes working together to copy and illuminate books, paid for and presumably directed by the bishop or prior. Instead, what is strongly suggested is that the majority of the monks, together, perhaps, with at least some of the clerks attached to the bishop's household, made a contribution to the production of books. More recently, Gullick has convincingly argued that Symeon of Durham played a directorial role in the Durham scriptorium in this period, copying almost no complete texts but rubricating, annotating and correcting in eighteen surviving manuscripts, mostly patristics but including the 'presentation copy' of his own *Libellus*, now Durham UL Cosin V ii 6, as well as copying documents and charters datable as late as *c.*1128. Gullick also observes that these manuscripts are further interlinked by the work of other scribes whose hands are recognisable, as well as by their decoration, points closely related to the analyses which follow here.[3]

The evidence also suggests that the library of Durham grew rapidly in the first half of the twelfth century. It has already been seen that the surviving evidence produces a total of no more than about thirty books taken over by the priory from the Community of St Cuthbert. To these, St Calais's gift added some forty volumes of types which would appear on the mid-twelfth-century book-list. The forty-eight Psalters grouped together in the book-list were perhaps given individually by monks, while gifts from priors came to a further nineteen books.[4] Nevertheless, the book-list contains some four hundred volumes, meaning that a further two hundred and fifty books had

[2] Ker, *English Manuscripts*, 23–5.

[3] See Piper, entry for 'Durham', in N. R. Ker and A. G. Watson, *Medieval Libraries of Great Britain: Supplement to the Second Edition*, Royal Historical Society Guides and Handbooks 15, London, 1987, and Gullick, 'The Hand of Symeon of Durham', especially 20–2 and 25–31.

[4] See *Catalogi Veteres*, 5–9.

been collected or produced by the monks, and it should be remembered that liturgical books are not included in the book-list. Of course, it cannot be simply assumed that all two hundred and fifty books were produced by the priory. The book-list distinguishes gifts of books, but makes no mention of any purchases. Thus, it cannot be known whether no purchases took place, or whether the compiler of the list simply regarded it as unimportant. One thing, however, can be said, and that is that the resources of the priory were put under strain by Ranulf Flambard. St Calais had failed to allocate estates specifically for the priory's expenses, an omission which seems not to have caused problems during his lifetime. But Flambard had very considerable expenses in his career as bishop; his building projects included not only those already discussed – there was also his foundation of St Giles's Church and Hospital -- and still he was able to offer Henry I a bribe of 1,100 marks, according to Hugh the Chantor.[5] It is thus hardly surprising that Flambard seems to have made use of his opportunity to deprive the monks of resources which they felt were rightfully theirs, a deprivation apparently only ended by a deathbed repentance and restitution.[6] There is no suggestion that Flambard imposed hardship upon the monks, but nevertheless, their capacity to purchase a large number of books must be in some doubt.

In approaching the surviving books then, it is possible to assume that a large proportion of them will be the products of the Durham scriptorium, and that that scriptorium will have utilised the work of monks, presumably directed by those who were in charge of scriptorium and book collection. This means that codicological evidence will be important, in order to discover whether unified processes of book production underlie the stylistic variations of script and illumination. However, perhaps the best place to start is with a manuscript whose affiliations with other Durham books have already been the subject of some discussion, and that is the collection of *Lives*, now DCL B IV 14.

DCL B IV 14 and its group

B IV 14 itself is a complex manuscript, and it will first be worthwhile to give a brief account of it. It consists of twenty-five gatherings, of which thirteen are gatherings of ten, a type common at Durham in the late eleventh century.[7] There are also three gatherings of twelve, with the rest being

[5] See Hugh the Chanter, *The History of the Church of York*, 46.

[6] See *Durham Episcopal Charters, 1071–1152*, ed. W. H. Offler, Surtees Society 179, 1968, 107–11.

[7] For an analysis of the manuscript and its texts see Mynors, *Durham Cathedral Manuscripts*, no. 55.

eights. The texts consist of five main saints' *Lives*, those of Gregory the Great, Martin of Tours, Nicholas of Myra, Dunstan, and Augustine (of Hippo), together with associated shorter texts and additions. These texts did not originally exist as separate volumes. Only once does a new text begin with a new quire, and that is the *Life of St Dunstan*, which begins on fol. 201r, at the opening of quire xxi. Here there is also another change of hand, and a change from thirty-two lines per page to the more cramped format of forty-four lines per page. However, the written space remains approximately the same and, when this text ends, on fol. 218v, in the middle of quire xxiii, it is immediately followed by the *Life of St Augustine*, in a round, upright hand. This at first follows the forty-four lines per page format but, at the end of quire xxiii, there is a reversion to the thirty-two line format, and the text, like the volume, ends in this format. Thus, if the *Life of St Dunstan* was ever intended to form a separate volume, it was soon incorporated into the group of texts which form B IV 14.

In both script and illumination, B IV 14 presents a very varied appearance. It contains work by perhaps eight different scribes (Mynors does not give a figure), some still using versions of Norman styles, others a script which is becoming recognisable as that of Durham in the early twelfth century. Patterns of pricking and ruling vary slightly throughout the book, though they are all simple, and all ruling is in hard point. Some of the work in the manuscript is of high quality: but some is rather poor. A final curious feature is that the first two quires, distinguished as a and b by Mynors, appear to be a contemporary replacement of the original quire i. Thus, the overall impression is of a book produced at some speed, with long stretches, including the whole of the *Life of St Martin*, supplied by good scribes, but with shorter stretches and pieces in hands which are very uncertain. There is no real attempt at a uniform appearance. Instead, the impression is of one scribe following another to copy out a set of major saints' *Lives* in one long volume. Care is shown in the correcting of the scribes' work, and in the incorporation of supplementary texts into the volume. For instance, the *Life of St Martin*, and Gregory's account of his miracles, is followed by the story of a miracle which took place at the saint's translation in 1008. Similarly, the *Life of St Nicholas* is followed by an account of his translation to Bari in 1087, and the *Life of St Augustine* is again followed by an account of his translation to Pavia. Again, on fol. 237 is added the spurious 'Letter of Pope Leo on the translation of St James the Greater to Spain'. This interest in the translations of saints is very appropriate for a Durham manuscript which would have been produced at around the time of the ceremonial translation of St Cuthbert into the new cathedral, in 1104.

Finally, the affiliations of the texts in B IV 14 are interesting, where they can be traced. Mynors points out that the version of Gregory's *Liber de Miraculis S. Martini* found in B IV 14 has an omission in book I which is also found in Le Mans, BM, MS 10, as well as in other French manuscripts.[8] It is thus possible that St Calais may have obtained the exemplar for this text, using his links with Le Mans, as already seen in the additions to Bodleian, Bodley 596. The source of the *Life of St Dunstan* is unknown, but it is interesting that it ends imperfectly in chapter 16, as does BL Harley 56, the slightly later copy of the same text from St Mary's, York. However, B IV 14 does not have the marginal diagram of the tomb of Oda of Canterbury, found in Harley 56. It is thus most likely that they both descend from the same exemplar, rather than that B IV 14 served as exemplar for Harley 56. In view of this fault, it seems unlikely that the exemplar came directly from Canterbury, yet the diagram in Harley 56 suggests knowledge of Canterbury tombs. Perhaps all that can be said is that this work would have been widely distributed in England at the end of the eleventh century, and that a faulty copy reached Durham.

Besides its texts, the other factor which makes B IV 14 so interesting is that several of its scribes and artists can be identified in other Durham manuscripts. Mynors pointed out that the hand of the *Life of St Dunstan* is very similar to some of the six or seven hands found in DCL B IV 5, a collection of short works by Ambrose. However, it is possible to take this a little further, and to argue that the scribe of the *Life of St Dunstan* also wrote B IV 5, fols. 83r–92v. Moreover, the initial on fol. 201v of B IV 14, which is rather unusual in that manuscript (Fig. 29), has close parallels in B IV 5, most particularly an initial Q on fol. 57v (Fig. 30).

Elzbieta Temple was the first to point out another correlation, namely, that the scribe of the *Life of St Martin* in B IV 14 (fols. 112–69) is none other than the scribe of the illustrated *Life of St Cuthbert*, now Oxford, University College, MS 165.[9] This attribution is convincing, and indeed, this scribe also contributed another section to B IV 14, namely the end of the preceding *Life of St Gregory the Great*, fols. 100–11v. The same scribe can also be found in DCL B IV 7, a copy of Augustine's *De Caritate*, again containing work by several hands. His hand appears first on fol. 12v, where he supplies the rubric for tractate II. Then, on fol. 13v, he takes over the main text. In both B IV 7 and B IV 14 he repeats an unusual trick with the incipits; the letters are widely spaced laterally, so that they overflow the allocated lines, and the text of the incipit is completed by running it vertically down the right-hand margin. This trick is not found in Univ. 165, but it seems likely that B IV 7

[8] Mynors, *Durham Cathedral Manuscripts*, no. 55.
[9] E. Temple, 'A Note on the University College *Life of St Cuthbert*', *Bodleian Library Record* 9, 6, 1978, 320–2.

FIG. 29 Initial D from Durham, DCL,
MS B IV 14, fol. 201v

FIG. 30 Initial Q from Durham, DCL,
MS B IV 5, fol. 57v

represents early work by the scribe. The hand is rather variable there, and the initial on fol. 25r (where the unusual incipit also occurs) is a twelve-line S, consisting of a twisted dragon on a parti-coloured ground, still very Norman in appearance. This is all the work which can be attributed to this scribe with any degree of certainty, but his work appears to have been very influential at Durham, and to have contributed considerably to the upright, rounded, almost curvilinear appearance of Durham script in this period, where it begins to develop towards a recognisable style. Both B IV 7 and B IV 14 show the scribe's work in a somewhat pointed style (see Plate 9); but in Univ. 165 it is very round, with ascenders shorter in relation to the height of minims. In this style it is copied in DCL B II 18, a copy of Augustine's *De Verbis Domini*. Here, the main initial is a sixteen-line round E, still based on Norman styles of construction and stylised foliage, but definitely twelfth-century in its symmetrical coils of plant stem, and large, confident, foliate terminals. The script also is written with a broader nib, and is beginning to take on a more standardised appearance. A similar point may be made about Durham UL Cosin V ii 6, the early copy of Symeon's *Libellus* datable to the beginning of the twelfth century.

DCL *Hunter 100 and its group*

Hunter 100, like Univ. 165 and B IV 14, is one of the very few Durham manuscripts of this period which has figurative illustrations and historiated initials. Like B IV 14 and Univ. 165 also, its script has been analysed by other writers, most particularly Ker. Mynors sees the work of several scribes, whom he calls 'expert', but does not go into detail. More recently, Gullick has identified Symeon of Durham as the scribe of what are now fols. 1–42v.[10] Ker called the main scribe of Hunter 100 'very expert', and identified him as the scribe of the *Life of St Cuthbert* in Bodleian, Digby 20, fols. 194–227.[11] In both manuscripts the writing is very small and compressed, but regular and clearly legible. This has the effect of reducing flourishes, abbreviation signs and other potentially distinctive features, but nevertheless the overall appearance and balance of the hand is recognisable.

There are no other Durham manuscripts which contain work which can be identified with certainty as by this scribe, but several have very similar hands, which were perhaps influenced by the Hunter 100 scribe. One such appears in B IV 5, the collection of short works by Ambrose mentioned above in relation to B IV 14. The main hand has already been discussed, but another appears on fol. 71r and another on fol. 93r, both of which have a general similarity with that of Hunter 100. Another very similar hand appears in B IV 7, supplying short passages on fols. 10r–12v, although the rubrics, as already argued, appear to be in the style of Univ. 165. However, DCL B IV 4 presents work by another, even more expert scribe, who works on an even smaller scale. This hand appears in a separate quire, containing extracts from other Fathers, added as an appendix after the main text, which is Ambrose's *Hexaemeron*. The hand here is minute but beautiful, and may perhaps itself have influenced other Durham hands, although it appears in no other surviving manuscript.

The significance of decorative motifs

The brief analysis of scripts given above has demonstrated that two influential styles of script may be distinguished at Durham in the early twelfth century. Moreover, these styles, although different, often appear together in the same manuscripts. Thus, an interlocking group has been proposed, consisting of Univ. 165, Digby 20, Hunter 100, Cosin V ii 6, and B IV 14, B IV 5, B IV 7 and B II 18, with B IV 4 as an addition. These manuscripts are further linked together by their use of a small set of distinctive foliage motifs. The simplest

---

[10] Mynors, *Durham Cathedral Manuscripts*, no. 57, and Gullick, 'The Hand of Symeon of Durham', 27.   [11] Ker, *English Manuscripts*, 24.

of these, merely an idiosyncratic use of the popular motif called by Mynors the 'frilled curl', has been sketched above as it appears in B IV 14 and B IV 5 (Figs. 29 and 30). A very similar initial, which adds green to the gaudy palette of red, purple and yellow, occurs on fol. 8r of B IV 7, and may be by the same hand. However, more widespread, and more representative still of Durham styles of book production in this period, is the motif discussed by Gullick, and called by him the 'flame motif'.[12] (Surprisingly, Mynors does not mention this motif in his analysis of Durham ornament.) What is particularly important about this motif is that it first appears in manuscripts associated with St Calais, and continues in use in books datable to the episcopate of Flambard. After that, however, it disappears, its place being taken by the clove curl and split petal, which first appear in the early-twelfth-century books, but reach their peak around the middle of the century.[13]

The flame motif appears in four of the manuscripts associated with St Calais, namely DCL B IV 24, B III 9, B IV 13 and B II 21; Gullick has also argued that it appears in a simple form in a fifth such manuscript, DCL B II 6. It is most commonly used as a finial, appearing only very rarely within the bowl of a letter, and its varying early forms are shown in Figs. 31–5. In all these early appearances, it occurs in books containing work by scribes who, it has been argued, were based at Durham, at least temporarily, and working in Norman styles. It is thus reasonable to see it as being developed by the group of scribe-artists active at Durham in the period following the Conquest; however, its appearance in two separate sections of St Calais's compound 'Martyrology and Rule' (B IV 24) raises more complex questions. Gullick argues that the Calendar of B IV 24 was written by an English scribe, but one whose hand also appears in the Durham *Liber Vitae*, and who must therefore also have been based at Durham, perhaps being one of the new monks brought there in 1083. The flame motif appears on several of the KL monograms of the Calendar, but it also appears again in conjunction with work by another English scribe, decorating the opening initial of the Latin text of the Benedictine Rule on fol. 74v (Figs. 34 and 35). This copy of the Rule forms a separate item, on different parchment, within B IV 24, and cannot be proved to be a Durham product. It is therefore possible that the motif was taken up and developed by scribe-artists at Durham from its simple start in B IV 24's Latin copy of the Rule (although it may of course be that the initial was only completed once this text had been brought to Durham).

Wherever its exact origin may have been, the motif was clearly established at Durham in the late eleventh century, and subsequently appears frequently in the group of early-twelfth-century manuscripts discussed here, providing

[12] Gullick, 'The Scribes of the Durham Cantor's Book', 95.
[13] These terms were coined by Mynors. See *Durham Cathedral Manuscripts*, 6–8.

FIG. 31 A characteristic flame motif

FIG. 32 Flame motif from Durham, DCL, MS B II 21, fol. 12r

FIG. 33 Flame motif from Durham, DCL, MS B IV 13, fol. 53v

FIG. 34 Flame motif from Durham, DCL, MS B IV 24, fol. 74v

FIG. 35 Variant of flame motif from Durham, DCL, MS B IV 24, fol. 7r

further evidence for their production in a large scriptorium active at Durham in this period. It is fairly frequent in B IV 14, executed by several different hands, including once in the section written by the Univ. 165 scribe (Figs 36 and 37). Perhaps most significantly, it is used in the historiated initial on fol. 170v, which is by the artist of Univ. 165, the well-known illuminated copy of the *Life of St Cuthbert* (Fig. 38). This would seem to confirm, not only that Univ. 165 is a Durham product, but also that its main artist received some training at Durham. Further evidence pointing to the same conclusion will be discussed in the next chapter. For the moment, it is sufficient to note that the flame motif occurs at least six times in Univ. 165 itself, and is one of only a very limited repertoire of motifs used there, thus tying the manuscript still closer to the Durham scriptorium, although the decorated initials on which it appears do not seem to be by the artist of the miniatures (see Fig. 42 for another recurring motif, and Figs. 43–44 for variants of the flame motif).

This motif occurs very frequently also on the secondary initials of Bodleian Digby 20, another copy of the *Life of St Cuthbert*, this time written out by the scribe of Hunter 100, as noted above. Still more significantly, both Digby 20 and Hunter 100 use the same variant, and simplified, form of the motif (see Figs. 39–41). In this variant form, it appears again in DCL B IV 7 and B IV 4, already discussed as linked into this interrelated group by their scripts. It is thus possible to argue that the flame motif was a dominant element in the decoration of both major and secondary initials in manuscripts produced at Durham in the transitional period from the last years of St Calais's episcopate into the twelfth century. Moreover, it is potentially helpful as dating evidence within the sequence of Durham manuscripts, since, in manuscripts which show more fully Romanesque styles of initial decoration, together with more uniform and distinctive script, this motif is increasingly reduced to smaller size and to a minor role. Examples of this are found in DCL B II 18 (a copy of Augustine's *De Verbis Domini*), B II 26 (Augustine's *De Trinitate*) and A I 10 (a collection of shorter works by several authors). Of these, B II 18 is probably earliest, its script being modelled on that of the scribe of Univ. 165 as argued above, and with small versions of the flame motif appearing on several secondary initials. B II 26 is similar in both characteristics (see Fig. 45), but also shows the new and very distinctive Durham motif of the clove curl. Finally, A I 10 is a beautiful volume, with fully painted historiated initials in a developed Romanesque style, dating most probably from *c.*1130, and here the flame motif appears only in vestigial form, as a terminal on minor initials.

As suggested above in the discussion of B II 18, the dominant place of the flame motif in the repertoire of the Durham scribe-artists was gradually taken over by new motifs, particularly the clove curl (already mentioned) and the

FIG. 36 Flame motif from Durham,   FIG. 37 Flame motif from Durham,
DCL, MS B IV 14, fol. 19v   DCL, MS B IV 14, fol. 143v

FIG. 38 Variant of flame motif from Durham, DCL, MS B IV 14, fol. 170v

split petal, both of which, as Mynors noted, reach their fullest development around the middle of the twelfth century. However, they both first appear in manuscripts which belong to the early/transitional group under discussion, thus further confirming that the Durham scriptorium was developing its own style and repertoire in this period. Of the two, the clove curl is more popular. Its earliest appearance is perhaps in DCL B IV 5, the collection of short

FIG. 39 Prototype flame motif from
Oxford, Bodleian, MS Digby 20,
fol. 196r

FIG. 40 Prototype flame motif from
Durham, DCL, MS Hunter 100,
fol. 6v

FIG. 41 Leaf motif from Durham, DCL, MS Hunter 100, fol. 62v

works by Ambrose linked by its scripts to B IV 14, as discussed above.[14] Here
it appears amongst the stylised foliage on the decorated initial which opens
the final text, the *De Paschali Mysterio*, on fol. 121r (Fig. 46). In B II 26 it is
already in its fully developed form, as on fol. 117v (Fig. 47). Intermediate
between the two is perhaps B III 3, Augustine's *De Quaestionibus*, perhaps of
the 1120s (e.g. fol. 4v). The split petal, though less frequent in appearance, is
equally recognisable, but Mynors found its earliest appearances only in
Durham books of *c*.1150, where it already appears in elaborate forms.[15]
However, simple versions of the motif do in fact appear in two early-twelfth-
century manuscripts: B IV 15, a copy of the *Etymologies* of Isidore of Seville;
and BL Harley 4688, containing commentaries by Bede. Both are confirmed
as Durham products by their codicological format and their scripts.[16] Thus
the development of this motif also can be traced within the Durham
scriptorium itself, showing that the scribe-artists active there continued to
develop their own distinctive repertoire of decorative motifs into the twelfth

[14] Mynors, *Durham Cathedral Manuscripts*, no. 41.

[15] Ibid. 6–8.

[16] Ibid. nos. 59 and 63. Gullick has rejected DCL B IV 15 as early twelfth century, partly on
the grounds that its text, Isidore's *Etymologies*, is not listed in the mid-twelfth-century book-list in
B IV 24. However, this is unconvincing, since that list includes two versions of the work, both in
the main list and grouped with three other works by Isidore. See Gullick, 'The Origin and
Importance of Cambridge, Trinity College R. 5. 27'; and *Catalogi Veteres*, 2.

FIG. 42 Characteristic curved-cross motif

FIG. 43 Leaf motif from Durham, DCL, MS B II 18, fol. 7v

FIG. 44 Flame motif from Durham, DCL, MS B II 18, fol. 9v

FIG. 45 Flame motif from Durham, DCL, MS B II 26, fol. 10v

century (Fig. 48). This argument is important, since the motif occurs by the second half of the twelfth century in manuscripts from a wide range of Northumbrian monastic houses, thus confirming a network of links between their libraries and scriptoria, as will be discussed in later chapters.

The Durham Josephus and links with St Mary's, York

The importance of the distinctive motifs used on decorated or arabesque initials is shown also in discussing DCL B II 1, the Durham Josephus. This is a handsome manuscript, which cannot be identified with any of the items on the list of St Calais's gifts, and whose script and decoration place it outside the groups of Durham manuscripts already examined. It also contains no clear dating evidence and has usually been placed, on stylistic grounds, in the early twelfth century. Gullick has argued for a late-eleventh-century date, on the grounds that two of the hands which appear in B II 1 have features in common with the scribe of Great Domesday.[17] This date would, however, make the figure-initial on fol. 237v surprisingly early in view of its firm, Romanesque line. Gullick suggests a comparison with the figure-initials in Hunter 100, but this in itself would make an early-twelfth-century date more convincing. If the manuscript's date is debatable, still more so is its script,

---

[17] M. Gullick, entry for DCL B II 1, in *Anglo-Norman Durham 1093–1193: Catalogue for an Exhibition of Manuscripts in the Treasury, Durham Cathedral*, Durham, 1993, 6–7.

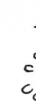

FIG. 46 Clove-curl motif
from Durham, DCL, MS B
IV 5, fol. 121r

FIG. 47 Clove-curl motif
from Durham, DCL, MS B
II 26, fol. 117v

FIG. 48 Split-petal motif
from Durham, DCL, MS B
IV 15, fol. 23r

which is in at least six different hands, none of which can be clearly located at Durham.

All of the scribes used English styles of script, and Gullick argues that another two of them show features found also in manuscripts from Winchcombe and Evesham. This leads him to suggest that these scribes may have been amongst the recruits gathered at Wearmouth and Jarrow by Aldwin and his companions who were, of course, moved to Durham by St Calais. This is an attractive suggestion, but still more attractive is the possibility that these scribes were recruited by Reinfrid and Stephen, and were ultimately part of the new foundation of St Mary's, York, which had rapidly attracted large-scale patronage. This story is told and analysed in more detail in the next chapter; here it is sufficient to note that the closest stylistic connections of B II 1 are with the best of the small group of books surviving from St Mary's. Most strikingly, one of the scribes of B II 1 also contributes a major section to what is almost certainly the St Mary's copy of Bede's *Historia Ecclesiastica*, now Cambridge, Trinity College, R 5 27. A hand very similar to this is also found, as Gullick observes, in a York charter preserved at Durham.[18] Moreover, the text of Josephus found in B II 1 is faulty, having a section originally missing in book IX of the *Jewish Antiquities*, which was supplied later. This is a significant lacuna whose appearances in other northern twelfth-century copies of the text Gullick has discussed in a recent article where, incidentally, he redates B II 1 to the middle of the twelfth century.[19] Particularly interesting here is the fact that another twelfth-century copy of the same text, still at York and of northern origin (now York Minster XVI A 7) has the same lacuna.[20] None of these points provides solid evidence, but it does seem at least possible that B II 1 was a product of the

[18] *Catalogue for an Exhibition of Manuscripts in the Treasury, Durham Cathedral Durham*, 1993, 6–7.

[19] Gullick, 'The Origin and Importance of Cambridge, Trinity College R. 5. 27', especially 253–6. See also Mynors, *Durham Cathedral Manuscripts*, no. 85.

[20] Ibid.; M. Gullick, pers. comm.

scriptorium of St Mary's, York, and was brought to Durham in the twelfth century, and at some point fairly soon after its production if it is accepted that it is the 'Josephus Antiquitatum' which is the fifth item on the twelfth-century book-list found in B IV 24.

Further evidence, of a rather difficult sort, is provided by the arabesque initials of B II 1. These do not use any of the distinctive Durham motifs discussed above, but nor are they close to the initials of Cambridge, Trinity College, R 5 27 (or indeed of BL Harley 56, another York manuscript which is closely related to R 5 27). Instead, they use large, bold versions of the distinctive foliage used at St Augustine's, Canterbury, both before and after the Norman Conquest. In the form in which it appears in B II 1, the foliage is closest to that in early-twelfth-century St Augustine's manuscripts, such as Cambridge UL Kk 1 17 (Figs. 49 and 50). The similarity is not strong enough to argue that the artist of the B II 1 initials must be a St Augustine's artist, but foliage of this type is rare in twelfth-century manuscripts, and some connection with St Augustine's seems possible. It cannot be suggested that a Canterbury exemplar was borrowed for the text, and that these initials were copied from the exemplar, since the contemporary Canterbury copy of this work does not have the omission found in B II 1. In short, this book is puzzling, but it stands outside the group of Durham manuscripts whose development has been explored, and can perhaps best be seen as a York product which came to Durham soon after it was made. It is important to note, however, that the borrowing of exemplars from Canterbury appears to have continued in the early twelfth century. This is attested by DCL B IV 6, which contains Augustine's *De Haeresibus* in a very distinctive version found in an eleventh-century Christ Church book (now Cambridge, Trinity College, B 3 25) and also in a twelfth-century copy from Rochester.[21]

PART II

Figurative illumination in Durham manuscripts in the early twelfth century

The analysis of scripts and foliage decoration in the previous section produced some very interesting results, which help to define the context within which figurative illumination developed at Durham. These may be briefly summarised here. First, it should be emphasised that, despite the strains imposed by Ranulph Flambard on the priory's financial resources, it is

---

[21] The Canterbury copy is now Cambridge, St John's College, 8 i. For DCL B IV 6 and its affiliations see T. Webber, *Scribes and Scholars at Salisbury Cathedral c.1075–c.1125*, Oxford, 1992, 72–3.

FIG. 49 Detail of initial H from Durham, DCL, MS B II 1, fol. 31r

FIG. 50 Detail of initial P from Cambridge, University Library, MS Kk 1 17, fol. 84r

clear that there was a rapid production of a large number of manuscripts at Durham in this period. Under these circumstances it is scarcely surprising that the surviving manuscripts show virtually no use of highly expensive materials such as gold or silver. Indeed, the pressure to build up a well-stocked, up-to-date library appears to have been such that many who wrote only unpractised, or even irregular, hands were pressed into service. Some of their stints were very short, suggesting that all who could contribute were asked to do so, in whatever time was available for them. However, the situation was not merely chaotic. A core group of scribe-artists can be isolated, whose distinctive work appears in the set of interrelated manuscripts previously discussed. It was in their work that a small set of distinctive foliage motifs first appeared, on arabesque initials, drawing upon motifs used in St Calais's books. Moreover, these scribe-artists were influential at Durham, and their styles, in both script and arabesque initials, were copied by others. Thus, the medley of hands and styles to be found in any one book gradually declined and, perhaps by the second decade of the twelfth century, a recognisable 'house style' had emerged.[22]

Figurative illumination was rather rare in St Calais's books, but it was predominantly Norman in style when it did appear, confirming again St Calais's preference for Norman texts, styles and editions, even of the works of Bede.[23] Nevertheless, St Calais's two-volume Bible must have been a striking and impressive book. Such complete Bibles were apparently only very rarely produced, especially as luxury-books, in late Anglo-Saxon England. St Calais's Bible was thus something very new in post-Conquest England, and was presumably a prestigious possession for the new priory.[24] The initials of the surviving volume ii contain the largest array of figures amongst the Anglo-Norman books at Durham, and this immediately raises a question: were these figurative initials used as models at Durham after 1100, as foliage motifs were? This is a question to which it will be necessary to return, but one point can be made. The analysis of the flame motif and its usage showed that it occurred, not only as the main decoration on a large number of secondary initials but also as an integral part of the historiated initial which opens the *Life of St Nicholas* in DCL B IV 14 (fol. 170v), and which is by the artist of the miniatures in Univ. 165 (see Plate 14). This suggests that this artist may well have been trained at Durham, as well as playing an influential part in the Durham scriptorium. Whether he was also the scribe-artist of the text and minor initials of Univ. 165 cannot be proven, but it is at least a very interesting possibility.

The raising of this question means that it is necessary to give some account of the range of figurative illumination to be found in books which were

---

[22] On the emergence of a 'house style' of script see Ker, *English Manuscripts*, 23–5.

[23] For discussion of this group of illuminations, see Boase, *English Art*, 24–8; and Kauffmann, *Romanesque Manuscripts*, 19–20. The exception to this Norman style is the major initial of DCL B II 22, which is in the distinctive style found in manuscripts and wall-paintings at Christ Church, Canterbury, attributed to the early twelfth century. See Lawrence, 'Influence of Canterbury'.

[24] On this, see W. Cahn, *Romanesque Bible Illumination*, Ithaca, 1982.

available at Durham from the time of St Calais. The Bible, with its repertoire of historiated and inhabited initials, has already been mentioned.[25] The other relevant books are: DCL B III 10, B II 16, B II 13 and, possibly, B II 22 and B II 1. B II 13 is St Calais's copy of the second volume of Augustine's *On the Psalms*. Here, human figures appear in nine initials, all apparently the work of the same hand. The artist is Robert Benjamin, who gives his name in an inscription in fol. 102, incorporated into the well-known initial showing the artist as a monk, kneeling at St Calais's feet. Another historiated initial occurs on fol. 181v, perhaps a form of author portrait, though oddly treated; here, a nimbed figure is seated inside an eight-line high initial O, and is receiving a book from the Manus Dei (see Plate 10). A more marginal case occurs on fol. 222v, where a figure is seated inside an initial P, making a gesture signifying teaching or instructing. In the other six cases the figures have no apparent narrative or illustrative content, and simply climb or pursue one another through coils of foliage, or through the panelled structure of the letters themselves. In one more unusual case, on fol. 203v, human heads are used as terminals, a practice which became more common in English manuscripts in the first half of the twelfth century. Similar initials, though drawn without Robert Benjamin's energy, occur in DCL B III 10, St Calais's copy of Gregory's *Moralia in Job*; here also the figures simply clamber up letter and foliage. In B II 16 the initials, like the script, are in a late Anglo-Saxon style. The script identifies this manuscript as a product of St Augustine's, Canterbury, but the initials are puzzling. One, on fol. 79, uses heads in medallions set into the letter, in a manner reminiscent of Canterbury work (though more associated with Christ Church).[26] However, the figure style is rather different from most known St Augustine's examples, being more closely related to the miniatures of the Troper, BL Cotton Caligula A xiv. This is of unknown origin, but has some links with Christ Church, Canterbury.[27]

DCL B II 1 and B II 22 are more dubious, since in each case the figure initials may be later than St Calais's time. In the case of B II 1, it seems likely that the book was made in the early twelfth century, and possibly at St

---

[25] For a complete list of the illuminated initials see Mynors, *Durham Cathedral Manuscripts*, no. 30.

[26] For discussion and reproductions of these Canterbury initials see C. R. Dodwell, *The Canterbury School of Illumination, 1066–1200*, Cambridge, 1954: and A. Lawrence, 'Manuscripts of Early Anglo-Norman Canterbury', in *British Archaeological Association Conference Proceedings, 5, 1979*, 1982, 101–11. The most recent discussion is Gameson, 'English Manuscript Art in the Late Eleventh Century'.

[27] A similar opinion is expressed by Gameson, 'English Manuscript Art in the Mid-Eleventh Century'. More recently, Gameson has also tentatively suggested a similarity with the herbal, now Oxford, Bodleian, Ashmole 1431. See 'English Manuscript Art in the Late Eleventh Century', at 126, 137 and 139.

Mary's, York. The ink outline drawing of a human figure which forms an initial on fol. 237v certainly appears early twelfth century, rather than Anglo-Norman.[28] B II 22 may be St Calais's copy of Augustine's *De Civitate Dei* (although B II 17 is perhaps the more likely candidate). Its text is written by the Martyrology Scribe who appears to have been introduced to Durham by St Calais, but its main initial, though touched with the distinctive combination of yellow, mauve, red and light blue used by the Martyrology Scribe in his own initials, is clearly in the same style as a set of early-twelfth-century manuscripts made for Christ Church.[29] This initial, on fol. 27v, shows Augustine, nimbed and in bishop's robes, writing, flanked by two heads in medallions which, like Augustine himself and the heads which act as terminals to the letter, are drawn in a very distinctive way.

After this outline of figurative illumination in the late-eleventh-century books, it is time to turn to those of the early twelfth century. Here, perhaps unsurprisingly, most of the books with figurative illumination are the work of the distinctive scribe-artists already discussed. Bodleian, Digby 20, fols. 194–227, is a copy of Bede's *Life of St Cuthbert*. Its main initial contains an author-portrait of Bede, softly drawn in red and black outline, and filled with washes of soft green (see Plate 11). Ker identified the scribe of Digby 20 as being also the scribe of DCL Hunter 100,[30] and Alexander attributes this initial to the artist of Hunter 100.[31] In this, Alexander is going further than Kauffmann or Boase, and a direct comparison will be helpful. The obvious comparison is with the author-portrait initial on fol. 43r of Hunter 100, showing Helperic of Grandval (see Plate 12). Here, there are significant similarities, most particularly in the ways the bodies are conceived and handled. In both, the hair is treated as a set of rounded clumps, and both faces show the same long, sharp-pointed noses. The handling of shoulders, knees and thighs is also very similar. Finally, the draperies, despite the differences in their handling, have one distinctive feature in common, and that is a way of handling folds or pleats in the hems. This is most used in Hunter 100, occurring eight times in this one figure, but it occurs once on the hem of Bede's habit in Digby 20, and once on the fabric draping his lectern. It is thus very difficult to say conclusively whether the initials are by the same artist, but they are certainly closely related.

[28] The exact date of acquisition of this manuscript is unknown; but it must have been at Durham by the late twelfth century, when missing portions of text were supplied in a Durham hand. See Mynors, *Durham Cathedral Manuscripts*, no. 85.

[29] See Lawrence, 'Influence of Canterbury', 98–100, and Plates 8.18 to 8.31.

[30] Ker, *English Manuscripts*, 23–5, and 'Note', in *Bodleian Library Record*, 1954–6, 6.

[31] J. J. G. Alexander, entry for Univ. 165, in J. J. G. Alexander and E. Temple, *Illuminated Manuscripts in Oxford College Libraries. The University Archives and the Taylor Institution*, Oxford, 1985.

In fact, Hunter 100 contains a relatively large repertoire of figures, in both miniatures and initials, across its various sections. Most striking are the miniatures illustrating cautery scenes, on fols. 119 and 120. These are in two registers, some framed. All are drawn in ink, but some are touched with colour, like the author-portrait, giving them a softer appearance.[32] The treatment of hair and faces is very similar to that in the author-portraits already discussed, while these figures, like Bede, have small pot-bellies, often teardrop-shaped. The distinctive hem-pattern occurs again, as do jewelled bands on belts and hems. However, some elements in these cautery scenes suggest that their model was very different from that of Digby 20. The figures take up bolder and more energetic poses; the handling of faces, and particularly of profiles, is more varied, and there is more sense of three-dimensional solidity. In all these ways, the cautery scenes of Hunter 100 move away from the Anglo-Saxon elements in Digby 20. The representation of the figures is also slightly more solid, with thighs more strongly outlined by clinging drapery, and torsos showing two oval, pectoral areas. However, these more Romanesque features are taken further in the cautery illustrations than elsewhere. On fols. 2–7 are drawings of the Signs of the Zodiac, illustrating a calendar, and on fols. 61v to 64v are small outline drawings of constellations. The small size of both, and of the latter especially, means that they are fairly plainly handled, but both groups show several of the features already discussed. In general the outline here is dry, with lines used in pairs, one dark and one light, on draperies and muscles: while faces are smoother, with neat features and smaller ears. However, the hair, torsos and thighs are still treated as in the cautery figures, and the distinctive fold pattern appears in the drapery. In the astrological figures especially, elements of two contrasting styles appear. One may be typified by the figure of Aquarius, which is very firmly, almost harshly, drawn, with emphasis on the protruding stomach, and on checker-patterned bands. The contrasting style has much softer and more varied outline, reminiscent of early eleventh-century Anglo-Saxon style, and boot-button eyes, a combination reminiscent of Digby 20. It would be tempting to explain these differences as the work of two different artists, but the features of both styles are found together in the initial on fol. 52, constructed of a master beating a pupil. In other words, the style of Hunter 100 presents a curious blend of diversity and coherence. It is impossible to identify with any certainty the work of a number of different hands, each with a coherent, repeatable style, and yet the use of stylistic elements is more varied than would normally be expected within one stretch of work by one artist. Perhaps the most satisfactory explanation is that Durham housed, at

---

[32] For discussion, see Kauffmann, *Romanesque Manuscripts*, at no. 27.

this time, a small group of artists who were practiced at the techniques of outline drawing and colour-washing, but whose style was still fluid and relatively eclectic. Thus, the images of the exemplars could be influential, and so also could other available stylistic models. This may very tentatively give further support to the idea of artists receiving some sort of training at Durham itself.

By contrast, however, the contemporary, illuminated copy of Bede's *Life of St Cuthbert*, now Oxford, University College, MS 165, exhibits a high degree of stylistic coherence. The narrative illustrations of this manuscript, and their relation to the text, are discussed in detail in a separate chapter. Here, what is at issue is their place within the development of illumination at Durham. In terms of technique, they fall into two groups. The first group is of fully painted work, and includes: the opening miniature of Bede writing, and presenting his work to the abbot and monks of Lindisfarne; the author-portrait initial of Bede which opens his introductory Letter; and the inhabited initial on fol. 5, which opens the main text. The second group consists of fifty-five coloured outline drawings, one for each chapter of Bede's text, and one for each of the added miracle stories.[33] The style of the drawings is most clearly related to that of Hunter 100 but the figures are distinctive in several ways. First, they are more elongated than those of Hunter 100. Faces also tend to be longer, and with rounded jaws, while eyebrows are more smoothly curved, and mouths are slightly fuller. The artist shows a marked preference for three-quarter faces, dominated by characteristically large eyes and long jaws. These features look forward to figure styles such as that of the St Albans Psalter, but are here less clearly formed.[34] Also very interesting is the way in which robes articulate bodies. The prominent, teardrop-shaped stomachs are here, although more softly treated than in Hunter 100, while the outlining of long oval areas on thighs and torsos is taken much further. Hems still swirl softly, though any Anglo-Saxon fluttering is curtailed, and the distinctive pattern appears occasionally in draperies, though as part of a varied system, rather than being a mannerism.

This description thus reasserts what other writers have argued, that these drawings show a mixture of Anglo-Saxon and Romanesque characteristics. The relationship between them and the illustrations of Hunter 100 is, however, rather difficult to clarify, and it is hoped that the preceding

[33] For discussion, and reproductions of the majority of these, see M. Baker, 'Medieval Illustrations of Bede's *Life of St Cuthbert*', *Journal of the Warburg and Courtauld Institutes* 41, 1978, 16–49.

[34] The style of the figurative illustrations in the St Albans Psalter (Hildesheim, Basilika St Godehard, s.n.) is extensively discussed in O. Pächt, C. R. Dodwell and F. Wormald, *The St Albans Psalter/Albani Psalter*, London, 1960. See also Kauffmann, *Romanesque Manuscripts*, at no. 29; and Thomson, *Manuscripts from St Albans Abbey*, no. 72.

annotation provides some basis for making an attempt. Univ. 165's stylistic coherence suggests that its outline drawings are predominantly the work of one artist, with a developed style. This in turn suggests that the figures in Hunter 100 which show similar characteristics were influenced by those of the Univ. 165 artist. Indeed, it is possible that one artist who worked on Hunter 100 also assisted the main artist of Univ. 165. Some of the healing miracles, most particularly the story of the healing of the sick nun, are illustrated by miniatures containing shorter figures, with beady eyes, and less well articulated draperies. Clearly, this could be the result of increasing pressure on the artist as he reached the later parts of the work, but these figures, and especially those on page 88, are very similar to some of those in Hunter 100 (see Plate 13). If they do represent the work of a second artist, then he was presumably subordinate to the Univ. 165 artist, and it is tempting to suggest that the relationship was one of master to pupil. Such a relationship would help to explain the rather unconfident appearance in Hunter 100 of motifs from Univ. 165.

There are two further sources of evidence which suggest that the work of the Univ. 165 artist was highly regarded at Durham. They come firstly from DCL B IV 14, the volume of saints' *Lives* which it was argued above was linked to the translation of St Cuthbert, since it shows a marked interest in the translations of other saints.[35] This contains only one historiated initial, for the *Life of St Nicholas*, whose translation to Bari had taken place as recently as 1087,[36] and this initial has figures in the distinctive style of the Univ. 165 artist (see Plate 14). The presence of this initial in such a position, together with the choice of this artist for the *Life of St Cuthbert*, does suggest that he held a prominent position amongst the scribes and artists at Durham. The initial in B IV 14 is unusually plain in appearance. The figures are simply placed on the plain vellum surface, inside the loops of the B. The letter itself is not panelled, nor in the form of a trellis, and it has no interlace terminals. Instead, the foliage is reduced to a series of neat palmettes, reserved in plain vellum against a coloured ground, while the letter is punctuated at its mid-points by small medallions, containing rosettes. The restraint of this arrangement is hard to parallel exactly, and is extremely unusual at Durham. As the text contains the *Life* of a saint with Italian connections, it is possible that this unusual letter is influenced by Italian initials, where small white foliage patterns are used against coloured grounds.[37] However, another possibility is that there is a slight connection with Canterbury. In Canterbury initials of

---

[35] See pages 66–69.
[36] Temple, 'Note', at 322, also links this initial with the Univ. 165 artist.
[37] See, for example, O. Pächt and J. J. G. Alexander, *Illuminated Manuscripts in the Bodleian Library Oxford*, vol. ii, *Italian School*, Oxford, 1970, Plates I–V.

*c.*1100 such small medallions are frequent, as are figures and beasts 'high-lighted' with rows of small circles, a trick found in both Univ. 165 and B IV 14.[38] Indeed, one feature of the B IV 14 initial appears to be related directly to the Canterbury initial in B II 22, and that is the use of terminals in the form of grotesque, semi-human heads, with coloured lines projecting from their mouths.[39] Such a link would again suggest a group of artists at Durham engaged in developing a figural style, and making detailed use of the models available to them on the spot.

The fully painted miniature and initials of Univ. 165 have been less discussed, but they also present evidence of the artist's status. The miniature on fol. 1v/p. 2 is considerably smaller than the page on which it is placed, and has a strong frame (see Plate 15). This has suffered from flaking, but uses a fully painted acanthus frieze, which is itself related to that used in the initial of B IV 14. The figure drawing here is clearly related to that in the line drawings, and the handling of both seated and standing figures may be compared to those in the illustration of St Cuthbert giving hospitality to the angel, on page 26, strongly suggesting that the same artist designed both. Perhaps the most striking feature of both miniature and initials, however, is the use of colour. Bright red and pink in frame and decorative elements are set against a bright blue ground. The monks' habits are in shades of blue, grey and green, enlivened with touches of red-brown, yellow, white and gold. Gold is also used on the hems of garments and draperies, adding to the very static effect of the standing figures. This use of colour is reminiscent of Anglo-Saxon luxury books.[40] It was, however, taken up in some Norman scriptoria, most particularly Mont-Saint-Michel and Fécamp, although Norman artists were never quite so bold in their colour contrasts.[41] What can be said here is that both painting and outline drawings in Univ. 165 show considerable late Anglo-Saxon influence, making it very interesting that Margaret of Scotland had bequeathed a Gospel book, almost certainly of Anglo-Saxon workmanship, to Durham, and others may have existed.[42] Such

[38] See Lawrence, 'Manuscripts of Early Anglo-Norman Canterbury', Plates XXXIII, A and C, XXXIV, A, C and D.

[39] For Rochester manuscripts with comparable foliage see Boase, *English Art*, Plate 19 and 61–4.

[40] On colour effects in Anglo-Saxon painting, see J. J. G. Alexander, 'Some Aesthetic Principles in the Use of Colour in Anglo-Saxon Art', *Anglo-Saxon England* 4, 1975, 137–54.

[41] For colour usage in Mont-Saint-Michel manuscripts, see Alexander, *Norman Illumination*, 205–9.

[42] On St Margaret's illuminated Gospels, see the *Life of St Margaret*, printed as Appendix III in *Symeonis Dunelmensis Opera et Collectanea*, ed. J. Hodgson Hinde, vol. i, Surtees Society, 1868, at cap. xi, p. 250. St Margaret's career raises another interesting possibility, through her correspondence with Archbishop Lanfranc. This demonstrates that a group of Canterbury monks was sent to Scotland at Margaret's request, before 1089. Baker believes that their

a mixture was not unusual in England *c.*1100, and has been analysed at Canterbury, in some detail, by Francis Wormald.[43]

A final problem is represented by the fully painted inhabited initial, on page 9 of Univ. 165 (see Plate 16). This is loosely drawn, in a manner reminiscent of Robert Benjamin's initials, and its stem has a rather wobbly outline. The bowl of the P is filled with coils of rubbery acanthus, on a parti-coloured ground, and moving through these is an elongated lion. Its palette is the same as that of the miniature. In all this it is different from the initial in B IV 14 discussed above. Amongst contemporary Durham initials, this looseness of outline is perhaps most closely paralleled in DCL B IV 5, a copy of Ambrose's *De Officiis*. The opening initial here is an energetic N, partly composed of a large, dragon-like bird, and filled with a range of human figures and grotesques (see Plate 17). Rows of small circles, like those found in Univ. 165 and B IV 14, are used on the beasts in the B IV 5 initial. Moreover, the clothed figure in the lower part of the N is similar in both profile and drapery to figures in B IV 14 and Univ. 165. It is thus possible that the inhabited initials in both B IV 5 and Univ. 165 are also by the St Cuthbert artist. This grouping is further added to by analysis of the initials in the two early-twelfth-century copies of Symeon's *Libellus*, now Durham UL Cosin V ii 6 and BL Cotton Faustina A v, fols. 25–98.[44] The animal forms, acanthus panels, highlighting and use of colour in the major initials of these two manuscripts are indeed similar to those of the group under discussion, suggesting that they are all the work of one artist who thus seems to have worked on several of the most prestigious manuscripts to have survived from the Durham scriptorium of the very early twelfth century (for the flame motif, used frequently in Cosin V ii 6, see Fig. 56).

The final examples of figurative illumination which may be classified as '*c.*1100' are two more initials. These are the figure-initial on fol. 237v of B II 1, already discussed above, and an author-portrait initial on fol. lv of Cambridge, Jesus College, Q B 11, a Priscian. Of these, the Priscian initial

settlement, whether at Dunfermline or elsewhere, would have been disrupted when both Malcolm and Margaret died in 1093; but their son, Edgar, received another group of Canterbury monks from Anselm. The presence of these monks in association with the Scottish court might well have given Durham access to books, or even artists, of Canterbury origin, especially given the links between Durham and the Scottish royal house. See D. Baker, '"A nursery of saints": St Margaret of Scotland Reconsidered', in D. Baker, ed., *Medieval Women*, Studies in Church History, Subsidia 1, Oxford, 1978, 119–42.

[43] F. Wormald, 'The Survival of Anglo-Saxon Illumination after the Norman Conquest', *Proceedings of the British Academy* 30, 1944, 127–45.

[44] See M. Gullick, 'The Two Earliest Manuscripts of the *Libellus de Exordio*', in Rollason, *Symeon of Durham*, 106–19, at 111. The colours in the Cosin manuscript are perhaps more subdued in their overall effect, but the use of red, pink, blue and white against grey, black and yellow parallels that in Univ. 165.

shows general similarities to the figures already discussed, being small and executed in tinted outline drawing. It is not the work of the St Cuthbert artist, but clearly fits into the Durham milieu, suggesting again the presence of a small group of artists working and developing together. The figure initial in B II 1, the Durham Josephus, is rather different in style, although it is again an outline drawing, this time in plain black ink. Analysis of the initials and script of this manuscript shows it to have connections with St Augustine's, Canterbury, and, more closely, with St Mary's, York.[45] This figure appears more definitely Romanesque, and may have been a later addition, but its place of execution cannot be ascertained.

This completes the listing and analysis of the material covered by this chapter. In conclusion it is necessary to place this material into the context of the development of illumination at Durham. Elzbieta Temple proposed that the illumination of Univ. 165, B IV 14, Hunter 100 and Digby 20 should all be seen as the work of one artist.[46] This would have the advantage of simplifying considerably the model for the introduction of this new figural style at Durham. All that would be necessary would be the arrival of a trained artist, who could execute the greatest part of the surviving illumination. However, detailed analysis of the illumination makes acceptance of this model difficult. The artist of Univ. 165 *et al.* does appear as dominant, and as entrusted with the most prestigious surviving works. But, while his style does introduce a more Romanesque approach to the figure, he also uses motifs which were integral to Durham illumination, and which suggest that he accepted some Durham influence, or training, rather than simply arriving from outside. Also striking is his use of Anglo-Saxon features and technique, now clearly acceptable at Durham. Moreover, he appears to have worked with a collaborating group of other artists, whose precise number cannot be known, but in which there appear to have been a minimum of three individuals. To at least one of these the St Cuthbert artist may have been a teacher; the relationship with the others is necessarily vague, especially as nothing approaching precise dates can be established, other than for the two copies of Symeon's *Libellus*. It was, then, this small group who dominated the painting-style of the Durham scriptorium in the early twelfth century. The task for a future chapter will be to see how far this phase influenced the illumination of the succeeding period.

[45] See Chapter 5.   [46] Temple, 'Note'.

&❧

CHAPTER FOUR

Pictorial narrative and the cult of St Cuthbert

Oxford, University College, MS 165

I t has long been recognised that the contents of this manuscript, which focus exclusively on the life and miracles of St Cuthbert, make Durham its most likely place of origin. Indeed, the network of palaeographical and art-historical affiliations, previously discussed, make it virtually certain, as has been seen, that this manuscript was produced by an active group of scribes and artists, working in the cathedral priory at Durham, and drawing upon types of script and decorated initial which evolved in the 1080s and 1090s. Having established that this manuscript can be considered a product of the Durham scriptorium, it is now time to look at the circumstances of its production, and at its significance for any analysis of the development of the cult of St Cuthbert at Durham.

At first sight, Oxford, University College, MS 165 appears to be a representative of the category of book designated the 'libellus' by Wormald, and its production to be clearly linked with the establishment of a community of Benedictine monks to serve the shrine of St Cuthbert.[1] However, the position is by no means as straightforward as these arguments imply. First, and perhaps most important, Univ. 165 is not a shrine-book of the classic type described by Wormald thus: 'libelli . . . are entirely devoted to the saint, and besides the life and miracles contain also prayers, masses and even the musical portions of the Office.'[2] Now, Univ. 165 contains only: Bede's *Vita Prosaica*; two standard miracles derived from the *Historia Ecclesiastica*; a selection of seven later miracles covering the period from the reign of Alfred to 1080 (this is the period during which the shrine was served by the community of St Cuthbert); and a *Verse Life* (not Bede's) with invocations.[3] This absence of any liturgical material is puzzling. The libellus presented to the shrine in the 930s by Athelstan contained such material, which is known to have been used by Bishop Walcher, but rejected by St

---

[1] F. Wormald, 'Some Illustrated Manuscripts of the Lives of the Saints', *Bulletin of the John Rylands Library* 35, 1952, 248–66.

[2] Ibid. 249–50.

[3] See Colgrave, *Two 'Lives'*, 26–7.

Calais.[4] Thus, in the time of St Calais, new liturgical material was created (which has been discussed in a previous chapter) and which must have been available to the scribe of Univ. 165. Its absence here suggests either that Univ. 165 is a rather strange sort of libellus (especially as Durham already had a classic example of the genre), or that it was intended as something rather different. Probably the most satisfactory explanation is, as David Farmer argues, that Univ. 165 was created for private devotional use by a high-ranking devotee of St Cuthbert.[5] This would also help to explain how the book came to be in the possession of the Augustinian priory of South-wick, Hampshire, in the later Middle Ages. As this house was only founded c. 1130, Univ. 165 cannot have been originally made for it, and it seems unlikely that the bishop or prior of Durham would accept that a major treasure of their chief shrine should be given to an obscure house with no special connection to St Cuthbert. An individual patron does seem the most likely intermediary.

The suggestion that Univ. 165 was created for an individual patron also helps to explain why it should be produced at a relatively unlikely point in the development of the new Benedictine community. That is, had a shrine-book been seen as a priority for the new community, St Calais might be expected to have ordered one, after his perusal of the 'old books' of his church, and his rejection of Corpus 183, but there is no evidence that this happened. On the other hand, if the creation of such a book was projected c. 1100 then it seems curiously premature. At that time, the east end of the new church would be substantially complete, while work continued on the nave. It would thus be possible to hold services in the choir, and the setting for the new shrine may well have been ready – but the relics were still in their old location, and not to be translated for several years. It would appear more logical that a new shrine-book would be created for the new shrine when it was complete. However, Univ. 165 cannot be such a book, as it has no mention of the translation of 1104, or of the triumphant demonstration of St Cuthbert's incorrupt body. It therefore seems most likely that Univ. 165 was created in response to a request from an influential patron, and not at a time chosen by the community of Durham.

This suggestion helps to explain some of the book's puzzling features. However, there remains one serious problem, and that is the origin of its very full set of pictures. These consist of a historiated initial with an author-portrait of Bede, a full-page, two-tier, dedication miniature, and no less than fifty-five miniatures, one for every chapter of the prose *Life* and subsequent

[4] See Chapter 5; and Hohler and Hughes, 'The Durham Services'.
[5] See D. H. Farmer, 'A Note on the Origin, Purpose and Date of University College, Oxford, MS 165', Appendix D to Baker, 'Medieval Illustrations', at 46–9.

miracles, whose style has already been discussed.[6] Univ. 165 thus contains the earliest surviving pictorial narrative cycle for the *Life of St Cuthbert*, and, since it is the only one to illustrate the seven post-Bedan miracles, it may also be called the fullest.[7] Moreover, the illustrations for the post-Bedan material use the same compositional techniques and narrative strategies as do the miniatures for chapters 1–48, as will be demonstrated below. However, Malcolm Baker's analysis of the surviving cycles demonstrates that the two surviving late-twelfth-century cycles do not descend directly from Univ. 165, though they are closely related to it.[8] Baker makes two further detailed arguments relevant to this chapter. The first is that, between Univ. 165 and the later cycles there is an intermediate cycle, of the mid-twelfth century. The second is that this intermediate cycle did not derive directly from Univ. 165, but from a slightly earlier, and even fuller, cycle which Baker argues must lie behind Univ. 165, but which apparently did not have illustrations for the post-Bedan miracles.[9]

A new examination of the text and illustrations of Univ. 165 suggests that the compositional principles used in it are coherent and consistent, and that the evidence for a fuller cycle underlying some of Univ. 165's compositions is not fully convincing. However, it does seem inherently unlikely that no narrative cycle for St Cuthbert would have been created at Durham until a request for an illustrated *Life* was received from a patron; and, if it is true that Univ. 165 left Durham relatively soon after its completion, then it follows that another, related, cycle must have remained behind to serve as model for the late-twelfth-century cycles. Wormald's discussion of Univ. 165 is extremely lucid, and makes no attempt to come to a final conclusion on the question of whether it is based on an earlier model, though he cites hints which suggest that it may be.[10] He does, however, make two general observations about illustrated copies of saints' *Lives*, as a category of book, which point in two different directions in the case of Durham. In the first

---

[6] See Kauffmann, *Romanesque Manuscripts*, at no. 26.

[7] See, for comparison: BL Add. 39943; Cambridge, Trinity College, O 1 64. For details, see Kauffmann, *Romanesque Manuscripts*, 67.

[8] See Baker, in note 5 above.

[9] There is no final answer to this problem, as there is no way of knowing how many sets of these illustrations have been lost. There is also no way of knowing exactly when Univ. 165 came to Southwick, although it must have done so between *c.*1130 and the thirteenth century, when the Southwick inscription was entered. Southwick appears to have been given an unusual set of books by a patron, as M. R. James notes, of which Univ. 165 may perhaps have been a part. These included a copy of the Old English version of Bede's *Historia Ecclesiastica*, and other material in Old English, as well as an eleventh-century Paterius (Ker, *Medieval Libraries*, 181). Given the nature of these texts, it may be that they were no longer required by their original owner(s). Whether this applied also to Univ. 165 can only be speculation.

[10] Wormald, 'Illustrated Manuscripts', 259–61.

place, he argues that the creation of such books is almost always associated with major Benedictine abbeys, and with movements for their reform or refoundation.[11] This would tend to link the creation of a St Cuthbert cycle with the establishment of Benedictines at Durham. However, in the second place, Wormald argues that, although the narrative cycles only appear in books from the late tenth century, in almost every case this stage was preceded by the growth of a cycle in other media, on precious objects associated with the shrine, and most probably in wall paintings.[12] This argument goes against Baker's hypothesis that the Community of St Cuthbert was unlikely to have had a narrative cycle since 'it was not until 1083 that a community existed that might have supported an active *scriptorium*'.[13]

Sadly, almost nothing is known of the appearance or decoration of St Cuthbert's shrine in the original church at Durham. However, both the *Historia de Sancto Cuthberto* and Symeon's *Historia Dunelmensis Ecclesiae* preserve accounts of some of its treasures. Both state that King Athelstan, on his visit to the shrine, 'beautified it with gifts . . . of various kinds as an ornament to [St Cuthbert's] church.'[14] There is no description, but both sources make it clear that the 'ornaments' were distinct from the gifts of land, silver and confirmation of privileges. The *Historia de Sancto Cuthberto* also enumerated the books given by Athelstan, of which the shrine-book, Corpus 183, was one.[15] Both sources are primarily interested in gifts of land, but it is interesting that they agree in associating gifts of 'treasures' and 'ornaments' with southern kings, or their representatives. Another donor of such gifts was Cnut, whose treasures are not described;[16] but the dark hints dropped by Symeon about Bishop Egelric's thefts suggest that the 'ornaments' accumulated at the shrine by the mid-eleventh century were considerable.[17] More details are given, however, by both Symeon and one of the post-Bedan miracles in Univ. 165 itself, of Earl Tostig Godwinsson and his wife, Judith of Flanders, and of their gifts to the shrine. The only objects described in detail are a large rood, comprising a crucifix with accompanying figures of the Virgin and St John, which sounds very like those carved in the late Saxon churches of southern England;[18] and an illuminated Gospel book, with a precious cover, stated by the miracle story to be still in the church of Durham, and which again sounds as if it would be of southern origin.[19] The

[11] Wormald, 'Illustrated Manuscripts' 256.
[12] Ibid. 253–4.
[13] Baker, 'Medieval Illustrations', 29.
[14] Simeon, *Libellus*, lib. II, cap. xviii; Arnold, i, 75.
[15] *Historia de Sancto Cuthberto*, Arnold, i, 211.
[16] Ibid. 213. Symeon's account is based upon this; ibid. 90.
[17] Ibid. 92–3.   [18] Ibid. 95.   [19] Ibid. 245.

suggestion that 'art-treasures' of southern origin or type were intoduced into Durham in the tenth and eleventh centuries is especially interesting since surviving descriptions of the chief shrines, such as those of St Swithun at Winchester and St Etheldreda at Ely, suggest that the reliquaries at least were richly decorated, and that Ely contained large 'images' (possibly statues) of Etheldreda and other saints.[20] Thus, it does seem likely that the Community of St Cuthbert would have possessed a range of images of their great saint. Clearly, it is a large step from this to a coherent, narrative cycle based upon Bede's *Prose Life*, but such pre-Conquest images may have helped to fix the iconography of St Cuthbert, which certainly appears quite developed already in Univ. 165, and to include emphases not present in Bede's text.[21]

This suggestion that images made for, or belonging to, the Community of St Cuthbert may have contributed to a narrative pictorial cycle created for the Benedictines of Durham is strengthened by the fact that it would parallel the situation found in the texts copied into Univ. 165. These have been discussed in detail, most particularly by Colgrave but also, more recently, by Aird.[22] What is especially interesting is that it is possible to argue that, in the case of the post-Bedan miracle stories found in Univ. 165, material origin-ally created by or for the Community of St Cuthbert was seen in the process of being adapted to the needs of the new priory. As this process is clearly very important, it is worth attempting to trace the stages involved. The first, obviously enough, was the acquisition of Bede's texts themselves, and here Colgrave's analysis of the surviving manuscripts produces some very import-ant results. None of the surviving copies is older than the tenth century, but Colgrave demonstrates that the tenth century copies, none of which originated at Durham, contain several misunderstood words and sentences, and omit several short passages, some of them containing important points.[23] By contrast, a group of three manuscripts, of which Univ. 165 is

[20] King Edgar is said by Wulfstan to have given 300lbs. of gold, as well as silver and gems, to make a reliquary for St Swithun; see R. N. Quirk, 'Winchester Cathedral in the Tenth Century', *Archaeological Journal* 114, 1957, 28–71, at 38. The reliquary was decorated with scenes of the Life of Christ, and 'many other matters'. On the images and sculptures at Ely, see S. Ridyard, *Royal Saints of Anglo-Saxon England*, Cambridge, 1988, ch. 6.

[21] A marked element in the illustrations of St Cuthbert in Univ. 165 is the representation of the saint in three different modes: an active young man in secular dress; a tonsured monk, still youthful and active; and a white-haired bishop, carrying a book and a staff. These formulae, at least, may be related to established iconographies of the saint. The last is in accord with the surviving wall-painting in the Galilee Chapel, Durham Cathedral; and with the form in which the saint is regularly described in twelfth-century visions. For the latter, see particularly Reginald, *De Admirandis*, cap. xxiii, xxxviii, lviii, lix.

[22] Colgrave, 'The Post-Bedan Miracles'; and Aird, 'St Cuthbert, the Scots and the Normans'.

[23] Colgrave, *Two 'Lives'*, 45–7.

one, all seem to have been produced at Durham *c.*1100, and all contain the same version of the *Prose Life*, which does not have any of the deficiencies of the tenth-century books.[24] Indeed, this version of the text is so good that, as Colgrave argues, it must derive from an examplar very close to the archetype (Bede's original). This makes it almost certain that, amongst the books brought from Lindisfarne, there was an early copy of the *Life of St Cuthbert*, and that possession of this treasure also passed to the Benedictines in 1083. The absence of the book from the mid-twelfth-century book-list is no impediment to this argument, since such a book would be kept apart from the library books, and would not appear listed with them. It is striking that this early book-list mentions only two copies of the *Life*, one in the books of William de Nunnewick, the other amongst the books of Prior Thomas.[25]

The next stage was the collection of further miracles, and there is evidence that the Community of St Cuthbert was active in this field, as it was in building up its collections of relics and treasures. Central to this argument is the curious, composite text known as the *Historia de Sancto Cuthberto*.[26] This combines accounts of St Cuthbert's life and miracles with stories of the saint's translations, and notices of grants of land and other benefactions made to the saint and his shrine. The major part of it seems to have been compiled in the mid tenth century, and a final section, adding further information on the ninth century and bringing the whole thing up to date, was added in the reign of Cnut (1020–35).[27] The whole is almost certainly the 'charter-book, with records of gifts' extensively used by Symeon and apparently studied by Bishop St Calais.[28] It adds four important miracles to Bede's collection, namely St Cuthbert's protection of King Alfred; the tempest, with waves of blood, which stopped the attempt to take St Cuthbert's body to Ireland; the depredation of the Danes, and the punishment of Onlafbald; and the story of the invading Scots swallowed up by the earth.[29] These stories are briefly told, but their selection and context is important. All focus on major demonstrations of St Cuthbert's power, by which he also preserved his community and its inheritance. The *Historia de Sancto Cuthberto* thus suggests that the Community was active in collecting stories about the saint, and in compiling an account of his continuing involvement with them. Further material was also put together after the Conquest, but before the arrival of the Bene-

[24] Colgrave, *Two 'Lives'*, 47–50.
[25] See *Catalogi Veteres*, 1–10.
[26] The text is printed in Arnold, i, 196–214. A fair copy of it passed into the possession of the priory, and was used by Symeon.
[27] See Simpson, 'The King Alfred/St Cuthbert Episode'.
[28] 'Preface' to *Libellus*, in Arnold, i, 10. See also lib. II, cap. xvi, p. 72.
[29] These are respectively sections 14–19; 20; 22–3; and 33 in Arnold's edition.

dictines, as was demonstrated by Craster, and this would also seem to have been available to Symeon and his fellows.[30]

The next, and most difficult, stage was the transformation of the material in the *Historia de Sancto Cuthberto* into elaborated miracle-stories, for formal addition to Bede's text. Colgrave demonstrates that the four *Historia de Sancto Cuthberto* stories were rewritten, and added to three later stories, to produce a clear group of seven, all the work of one author.[31] The later three are of the same general type as the first four, and they bring the story down to the 1070s. The problem is thus whether this group was composed in its present form by the Community of St Cuthbert, or by the Benedictines. Colgrave argued for the latter, and has been followed by all subsequent writers: disagreement is therefore difficult.[32] However, the case made is not entirely watertight. It has already been pointed out that these miracle stories must have been composed in this form after 1070. They must also have been complete before Symeon worked, as he quotes from them (a point also made by Colgrave), and assumes that they are readily available to his readers, in the first instance the bishop and priory of Durham.[33] Colgrave's main basis for arguing that they were the work of one of the Benedictines comes from Miracle 6, the story of how, in the aftermath of the massacre of Robert de Comines and his army, the bishop and Community fled to Lindisfarne, taking St Cuthbert's body with them.[34] The point here is that the author of the Miracle Story states that those who carried the coffin have since become, like himself, 'fratres' at Durham.[35] However, while the argument for Benedictine authorship is thus strong, Symeon's version of the story suggests something rather different. Symeon states that these 'porters' were the source of the story, but rather pointedly omits to call them monks, referring to them simply as 'those who, on this occasion, carried the shrine'.[36] Now Symeon is generally extremely precise about his witnesses, stating their connection to Durham, if any existed. Thus, if he had viewed them as monks, it seems most likely that he would have said so. The omission was presumably deliberate, since he had the Miracle Story before him. There is another, admittedly slender, piece of evidence which points in a similar direction. The author of

[30] H. H. E. Craster, 'The Red Book of Durham', *English Historical Review* 40, 1925, 504–32.
[31] Colgrave, 'Post-Bedan Miracles' 326–7.
[32] Ibid. 327.
[33] For instance, Symeon begins his account of St Cuthbert's appearance to King Alfred thus: 'Sed qualiter ibi manifesta visione sanctus ei Cuthbertus apparuerit, et ejus suffragante auxilio subactis hostibus regnum receperit, quoniam alibi plene per ordinem scriptum habetur, hic non esse repetendum videtur' (Arnold, i, 62).
[34] Colgrave, 'Post-Bedan Miracles', 327.
[35] The version of the text found in BL Harley 1924 is printed in Arnold, i, 245–7.
[36] 'Illi qui tunc feretrum portabant'; see *Libellus*, lib. III, cap. xv; Arnold, i, 101.

the Miracle Story refers, quite unproblematically, to the presence of women and children amongst the Community as they crossed to Lindisfarne. But Symeon goes out of his way to add the explanation that 'all the people of the Saint' had joined the flight.[37] These two differences would seem to suggest that the Miracle Story author was a member of the Community of St Cuthbert, for whom it was natural to accept the presence of women and children, and who refers to members of the Community as 'fratres', while Symeon equally consistently uses 'clerici'.[38]

If the Miracle Story group was written by a member of the Community of St Cuthbert, it may help to explain the variations in the post-Bedan contents of the Durham group of early twelfth-century manuscripts previously referred to. These are as follows: Bodleian, Bodley 175 has the *Prose Life*, with the usual two additions, the *Metrical Life*, the *Lives* of St Aidan and St Oswald, also from Bede, and only one post-Bedan story, that of St Cuthbert and King Alfred; Bodleian, Digby 20 (fols. 194–222v) has the *Prose Life*, the two additions, and the first five of the group of seven, several of the latter in shortened versions; and Univ. 165 itself is different again, as it has a long hymn in place of the *Metrical Life*, and all seven of the Miracle Stories, in their full versions. All this suggests two things – first, that there was a considerable demand for copies of the *Life of St Cuthbert* at or from Durham in the late eleventh and early twelfth centuries, and second that the contents of such books were not fixed, but open to considerable variation. One element in this variation was presumably the wishes of the patron for whom the book was destined (none of these have the character of shrine-books). But another may well have been that the Benedictines had taken over from the clerks a collection of several texts and sources, of which no 'official edition' as yet existed. This would be supported by the evidence of Bodleian, Bodley 596. This manuscript has already been discussed as part of the books datable to the time of St Calais, and as the work of the Martyrology Scribe.[39] Indeed, it is linked to St Calais himself, since, in addition to the *Prose* and *Metrical Lives of St Cuthbert*, it also contains the *Life* and office of St Julian, of whose house at Le Mans St Calais had been abbot. What makes the manuscript so interesting is that it combines an unusual variant of the *Prose Life* with a copy of the *Historia de Sancto Cuthberto*.[40] This means that, in the late eleventh century,

---

[37] See Colgrave, 'Post-Bedan Miracles', 325; and Arnold, i, 100: 'quarto die ad ipsius insulae aditum, comitante omni ejus populo, pervenit'.

[38] For instance, in lib. III, cap. vi, Symeon discusses the election of the 'clericus', Eadmund, as bishop, and how he was subseqently made a monk; his attitude towards the 'clerici' is suggested by the statement that: 'Et dum illorum unicuique durum esset mundi gaudia deserere, blandimenta saeculi relinquere, voluptates abjicere, grave erat ad suscipiendum sanctitatis officium consentire' (Arnold, i, 85).

[39] See Chapter 2 above. [40] See Colgrave, *Two 'Lives'*, 24–5.

Durham possessed at least three versions of the *Prose Life*. One was the putative early copy whose presence was deduced by Colgrave, one was the tenth-century Wessex text presented by Athelstan, and the third was the recently copied version in Bodley 596, of unknown origin.[41] It would therefore seem that there was a deliberate decision to acquire a copy of this variant version, and to add to it the *Historia de Sancto Cuthberto*, before the decision in favour of using the early version as an exemplar for further copies was taken. In other words, this again supports the idea of careful collection and scrutiny of material relating to St Cuthbert by the scholars of Durham, perhaps under the aegis of Symeon, who was an 'acknowledged expert' on the cult.[42]

The argument thus far may now be summarised. Seven main points have emerged, which are as follows:

1. It seems likely that the treasures of the shrine of St Cuthbert, when it was transferred from the clerks to the monks, would have included images of the saint.
2. In the mid-tenth century and in the first half of the eleventh century the clerks maintained a written record of the gifts made to their saint, and of the striking ways in which he protected them.
3. This was supplemented, after the Conquest, by the writing of a brief chronicle.
4. The group of seven Miracle Stories, written between the Conquest and 1100, were composed by a member of the Community of St Cuthbert.
5. There is evidence of considerable activity in the collection and editing of material relating to St Cuthbert, by the first generation of Durham monks.
6. This activity forms the background to the production of a group of at least three manuscripts at Durham *c.*1100, all using the same edition of the *Prose Life* but making different selections from the other available material.
7. None of these three manuscripts was intended as a shrine-book, and that they all seem to have left Durham before the fourteenth century (they do not appear in the very full fourteenth-century catalogue).

It is now possible to turn to the illuminations of Univ. 165, and to see to what extent they fit into this sequence of events. The first stage will be to examine the relationship between the narrative miniatures and the texts. Physically, this is straightforward. Each miniature is inserted between the

[41] On the early copy see Colgrave, *Two 'Lives'*, 45–7.
[42] See Gransden, *Historical Writing in England*, 115–16.

heading for each of Bede's chapters, or each Miracle Story, and the opening of the text. With very few exceptions they are broader than they are high, and thus tend to occupy a rectangular strip running across the page. Finally, they are not separated from the text by a frame (with the exception of the miniature for chapter 1), but fill all the available vertical space, frequently obtruding into the space allocated for the decorated initial for each chapter, and sometimes overlapping the nearest lines of text. This is a form of text–image spatial relationship well established by 1100, and Jonathan Alexander is surely correct in stressing the close relationship of narrative heading, picture and text as especially suitable for private reading and meditation.[43]

In looking at the narrative or illustrative relationship between images and text one factor becomes extremely clear, and that is that the designer of the miniatures knew the text very well. Both Malcolm Baker and Jonathan Alexander demonstrate that the images are not based on the narrative heading only, but contain a great deal of specific detail, based on the section of text being illustrated.[44] However, the extent of the knowledge displayed goes further, for there are several places where the illustration for one chapter draws on details, particularly of St Cuthbert's actions and modes of behaviour, derived from other chapters. Examples of this occur in the miniatures for chapters 9, 18 and 22. In the miniature for chapter 9, St Cuthbert stands at the left, preaching to a group of roughly dressed peasants, on the right. All this is as described in the text, and follows Bede's emphasis on St Cuthbert's devotion to teaching the laity.[45] But what is not derived from this chapter is that Cuthbert is shown leaning on a sturdy staff, with a top like a crutch. This is presumably a reference to chapter 8, where the reader is told of St Cuthbert's illness and cure (neither of them illustrated in the miniature), and of how St Cuthbert was left with a permanent weakness in his leg. The miniature for chapter 18 is also striking, as it appears to depart from the text.[46] Bede tells in some detail of how St Cuthbert and his helpers found water by digging a pit, which became a permanent water-supply. Surprisingly, the miniature shows St Cuthbert striking a rock-face with a pick-axe, as water gushes out. This prompts speculation about whether the designer of the miniature was drawing on images of the story of Moses, but the explanation comes from the next chapter, where Bede comments on the miracle of chapter 18, and equates it with St Benedict bringing water from

[43] J. J. G. Alexander, *Medieval Illuminators and Their Methods of Work*, New Haven and London, 1992, 85.

[44] See Baker, 'Medieval Illustrations', 33–4; and Alexander, *Medieval Illuminators*, 85.

[45] Univ. 165, p. 33; Colgrave, *Two 'Lives'*, 184–7.

[46] Univ. 165, p. 58; Colgrave, *Two 'Lives'*, 216–21.

the rock.[47] If correct, this would suggest that the designer knew the whole text, before he began work on individual miniatures. Finally, the miniature to chapter 22 seems to refer back some distance, to chapter 18. The text of chapter 22 describes St Cuthbert's preaching on Farne, and refers to Boisil's prophecy that Cuthbert would be made a bishop. The miniature, however, is more circumstantial, and shows St Cuthbert preaching from inside his cell, leaning out through a small window, as described in chapter 18.[48] Thus again the designer's thorough knowledge of the text is demonstrated, but so, as in the previous two examples, is something else. What is apparent is that there is no attempt to create an exact visual equivalent for the text. Rather, certain aspects of St Cuthbert are selected for repeated emphasis, in a way which means that some miniatures illustrate only a surprisingly small part of the text they accompany, while others add scenes or details not found in the text. Since this cannot be the result of ignorance of the text, it must be a deliberate choice, and is therefore important.[49]

The repeated emphases are comparable to those found in other contemporary saints' *Lives* and may be summarised as follows:

1–2. St Cuthbert had special gifts of contact with angels, and of prophecy.
3–5. St Cuthbert was a powerful healer, a protector of his community, and could communicate with animals.
6–8. St Cuthbert was an energetic teacher, a true monk and a scholar.

Of these groups, the core, 3–5, follow closely the emphases of the texts. But 1 and 2 are illustrated in sometimes surprising ways, which tend to focus attention on St Cuthbert as an individual of very exceptional status, and 6–8 start from a textual basis, but move away from it, with 8 having virtually no textual support. Thus, while all of these areas develop aspects of St Cuthbert's sanctity, and may be seen as offering guidance for the meditations of the reader, at least four do this in ways which differ from Bede's emphasis. However, before the significance of this can be discussed, it is first necessary to prove the point.

In the case of the representations of St Cuthbert's contacts with angels, four miniatures are relevant, those for chapters 2, 4, 7 and 17. The first shows St Cuthbert's first encounter with an angel, who arrives on horseback, then tells St Cuthbert how to cure a severe inflammation of his knee. All these elements are represented in the miniature, which also emphasises the friendly and equal contact between St Cuthbert and the angel.[50] In the case of chapter

---

[47] Colgrave, *Two 'Lives'*, 222 and 223.   [48] Univ. 165, p. 67; Colgrave, *Two 'Lives'*, 228–31.
[49] For comparison with the representation of other saints see B. Abou-el-Haj, *The Medieval Cult of Saints: Formations and Transformations*, Cambridge, 1994, especially 33–60.
[50] Univ. 165, p. 12; Colgrave, *Two 'Lives'*, 158–61.

4, the miniature follows the text in suggesting that only St Cuthbert can see the angels with the soul of St Aidan, and it incorporates the figures of three sleeping shepherds, and shows St Cuthbert as communicating his vision to them.[51] The dual emphasis of the chapter is thus neatly encapsulated. However, it is the last two images which are perhaps the most striking. The text of chapter 17 emphasises St Cuthbert's expulsion of demons from the island of Farne, and only in passing does it mention that he had angelic help in moving large stones. In the miniature, however, there is no reference to demons; rather, St Cuthbert and an angel are shown together in the act of building his cell.[52] The miniature for chapter 7 goes even further (see Plate 18). The text's story here is of how St Cuthbert, while a monk at Ripon, gave hospitality to an angel unawares, and was rewarded with bread from heaven. In Bede's narrative, St Cuthbert follows all the requirements of hospitality in the Rule: 'Nam lavandis manibus aquam dedit, pedes ipse abluit, linteo extersit, fovendos humiliter manibus suo in sinu composuit.'[53] This gives the reader a mental image of St Cuthbert kneeling to wash the angel's feet, as Christ had the apostles'. But the miniature shows St Cuthbert seated companionably beside the angel, holding only the latter's hand in his bosom. This had the effect of emphasising St Cuthbert's equality with the angel, even at the expense of his humility.

The representations of St Cuthbert's prophecies are equally interesting. Here, the relevant miniatures are those for chapters 4, 11, 12, 13, 15, 24, 27, 28 and 34. To these, as a related category, may be added prophecies about Cuthbert, which include chapters 1, 6 and 8 (the prophecy referred to in the text of chapter 22 is not illustrated). It would be tedious to describe these one by one, so the main points will be made by discussing 13, 15, 24 and 34. In all of these, as also in those not examined in detail, the designer of the miniatures shows considerable skill in condensing the moment of vision or prophecy, and its effect upon others, into an effective image. The miniature for chapter 13 shows St Cuthbert standing at the left, leaning on his staff, and beckoning to a group of people who are distracted by a phantom fire, just as the saint predicted. They are beginning to pay attention to St Cuthbert, and, in the centre of the image are two pointing figures, who demonstrate the effectiveness of the saint's teaching.[54] In a similar way, in the miniature for chapter 15, the saint is shown as calmly predicting the recovery of a dangerously sick woman, who duly appears in the second part of the image, already well. Thus, the moment of healing is given second place to

---

[51] Univ. 165, p. 18; Colgrave, *Two 'Lives'*, 164–7.
[52] Univ. 165, p. 55; Colgrave, *Two 'Lives'*, 214–17.
[53] Univ. 165, p. 26; Colgrave, *Two 'Lives'*, 174–9.
[54] Univ. 165, p. 43.

St Cuthbert's foreknowledge.[55] Again, in the miniature for chapter 34, a complex story, which includes both a vision and a prophecy, is condensed into a striking image. The first part shows the moment of vision, as St Cuthbert, seated at table, drops his knife, and is discussed by his companions. At the right, the subject of the vision is simply shown. This has the effect again of stressing how St Cuthbert affected others.[56] The same emphasis is found in miniatures such as that for chapter 27, or chapter 28. Most striking, however, is the image for chapter 24 (see Plate 19). There are two elements, separated from each other by a narrow space. At the left is a small tower, with a lookout peering eagerly from an opening at its top. At the right, St Cuthbert sits in conversation with Abbess Ælfflæd. The text of this chapter falls into two parts. In the first, St Cuthbert prophesies to Ælfflæd about the death of her brother, King Ecgfrith, and about his own future. The second part tells of the fulfilment of both prophecies.[57] Here again, what the artist appears to have done is to focus on the moment of prophecy, showing St Cuthbert in the act of making his prophecies, in response to Ælfflæd's entreaties (she holds out both hands open towards him, he responds with a gesture of his right hand). The artist has also provided visual reminders of the contents of the prophecies. Although St Cuthbert is not yet a bishop, he is holding in his left hand a large and prominent crozier, presumably a reference to his prophecy about himself; and the lookout is presumably a reference to the prophecy that Ecgfrith's heir is to be looked for from the islands of the sea (the relevant words would be: 'Cernis hoc mare magnum et spaciosum quot abundet insulis?').[58] Thus in this case, as in the rest of this category of miniatures, the artist's approach is consistent, and seems aimed at emphasising St Cuthbert's visionary and prophetic powers, rather than illustrating the whole narrative.

The two categories so far examined have suggested that the artist was working from a thorough knowledge of Bede's text, whilst bringing out consistently the impressive extent of St Cuthbert's powers. In the cases of the saint's dealings with animals, the healing miracles and the stories of preaching trips, as in the stories of how St Cuthbert was consistently fed and protected by God, the miniatures in general follow the text. However, the miniatures' emphasis on St Cuthbert as both teacher and scholar exceeds the text. The first, small, example comes in chapter 8, which deals with St Cuthbert's seven days of reading John's Gospel with the dying Boisil. Bede's text makes it clear that the book belonged to Boisil, and makes no mention of what happened to

[55] Univ. 165, p. 47.
[56] Univ. 165, p. 94; Colgrave, *Two 'Lives'*, 260–5.
[57] Univ. 165, p. 72; Colgrave, *Two 'Lives'*, 234–9.
[58] Colgrave, *Two 'Lives'*, 236.

it subsequently. But the miniature shows St Cuthbert holding the book open on his lap, and showing it to Boisil.[59] This has the effect of making St Cuthbert the apparent possessor of the book, and seems to accord with Symeon's stress on the links between the cult of St Cuthbert and books. This may appear an over-interpretation, but from this point on a book becomes the saint's most frequent attribute when he is shown seated, just as the heavy staff appears when he is represented standing. The first example comes in chapter 15, the story of the distant healing of the reeve's wife, whilst Cuthbert was prior of Melrose. Here, the text focuses on the arrival of the reeve, and on St Cuthbert's departure with him on horseback. But the left-hand part of the two-part miniature shows the reeve kneeling to St Cuthbert, who has a book open on his lap, a detail not mentioned in the text.[60] Again, something similar happens in the case of chapter 26, which deals with St Cuthbert's life as a bishop (see Plate 20). Bede describes St Cuthbert's prayers, admonitions and teaching by example, but makes no mention of scholarship. The miniature, however, shows St Cuthbert reading a large book, which is supported on a lectern identical to the claw-footed lectern shown in the dedication miniature and historiated initial at the opening of the manuscript. (The second part of the miniature shows St Cuthbert standing, with his staff.)[61] There is no need to labour the point, but a book appears as St Cuthbert's attribute again in the miniatures for chapters 28, 29 and 30. In other words, it is particularly associated with St Cuthbert as bishop of Lindisfarne. There is another detail, again going beyond the text, which appears in the same sequence of miniatures. This is that the saint's hair is now shown as white, and more wavy than previously. Clearly, the interpretation of these details can only be a matter of hypothesis. But what is striking is that these miniatures appear to draw on a visual tradition for the representation of the saint which is not simply based on Bede's text, but which emphasises him as a bishop, with waving white hair, and with a book, a crozier and a staff as his attributes. This is also the form in which St Cuthbert appeared in the twelfth-century visions of him, listed and described by Reginald of Durham in the third quarter of the century.[62] Thus it seems likely that here the artist was drawing on an established Durham tradition, in all probability deriving from the traditions and treasures preserved by the Community of St Cuthbert.

At this point, the examination of Univ. 165 increasingly touches on areas explored in the cases of other illustrated saints' *Lives* by Barbara Abou-El-Haj, Magdalena Carrasco and others.[63] This is the question of the extent to which Univ. 165 and its miniatures may be seen as representing the aspirations and problems of the community which produced it. However, what is puzzling is that the kinds of miracles especially emphasised by Abou-El-Haj, that is, occasions on which the saint, after death, continued to wreak powerful and terrifying vengeance on those who trespassed against his or her relics, property and community, are illustrated *only* in Univ. 165, amongst the Durham St Cuthbert *Lives*. Why this should be so can only be a matter for speculation. The simplest explanation is that Univ. 165 was produced, as argued above, at a time of considerable work on the texts relating to the cult, and was put together at the request of a patron. The decision to include a miniature for each section of the prose contents would then be at the request of the patron, and might help to focus meditations on the text. At some later point, however, as the post-Bedan material continued to grow and be repeatedly re-edited, as Colgrave demonstrates, the decision was apparently taken to restrict illustration to the oldest texts, those of Bede.[64] However this may be, it does seem that Univ. 165 gives its seven post-Bedan miracles an equal status with Bede's text, by illustrating them in the same way and on the same scale. These miniatures thus take on considerable interest as evidence of the view of St Cuthbert propagated by the Benedictines of Durham *c.* 1100. Their relationship to the text is also important, as discrepancies may suggest differences of view between the composer of the texts and the designer of the miniatures.

As the texts of the seven miracles, as they are given in Univ. 165, have not been published, and the miniatures were not discussed by Baker, it will be necessary to examine them in some detail. In the case of Miracle 1, the story falls into three sections: the first deals with King Alfred's encounter with a mysterious pilgrim; the second tells of St Cuthbert's appearance to the king in a vision; and the third deals with the fulfilment of the saint's promises and Alfred's devotion to him. Of these, the miniature illustrates primarily the first, showing St Cuthbert appearing, Christ-like, as a pilgrim (with his staff) to King Alfred, who is shown as an enthroned king rather than as a fugitive, in accord with St Cuthbert's subsequent promise. In other words, this miniature seems to use the same illustrative approach as those of the earlier prophecies already discussed.[65]

[63] See: Abou-el-Haj, *The Medieval Cult of Saints*, and 'Bury St Edmunds Abbey between 1070 and 1124: A History of Property, Privilege and Monastic Art Production', *Art History* 6, 1983, 1–29; and M. Carrasco, 'Spirituality in Context: The Romanesque Illustrated Life of St Radegund of Poitiers (Poitiers, Bibl. Mun., MS 250)', *Art Bulletin* 72, 1990, 414–35; also R. Blumenfeld-Kosinski and T. Szell, eds., *Images of Sainthood in Medieval Europe*, Ithaca, 1991.

[64] See Colgrave, 'Post-Bedan Miracles'.   [65] Univ. 165, 135–43.

Miracle 2 is the story of the final abandonment of Lindisfarne in 875, and of the attempted transporting of the saint to Ireland, which is prevented by a tempest and by waves which turn to blood (see Plate 21). Here again the miniature follows the principle of focusing on the moment of revelation of the saint's power, showing a storm-tossed ship, with the waves rising high, and the people of St Cuthbert watching as the miracle is accomplished. In the miniature, as in the text, there is no reference to Symeon's story about the Lindisfarne Gospels.[66] However, whilst the text speaks of the bishop as accompanied by monks or brethren, the miniature shows them in what appears to be secular dress. In this detail the designer of the miniatures seems to follow Symeon in implying that the community, once they had left Lindisfarne, ceased to be true monks, while the text does not acknowledge the distinction.[67]

The same distinction occurs between the text and miniature in Miracle 3. Here the story is of Scula and Onlafbald, two followers of the pagan king Ragnald, and of how Onlafbald, who takes away St Cuthbert's property, and attempts to enter the church at Chester-le-Street whilst denigrating the saint, is struck down and dies in agony. In the miniature, Onlafbald is shown defying the saint, and rushing towards the shrine with drawn sword, before turning away and beginning to fall. Again, the moment of power is clearly represented, but the guardians of the shrine, although one is tonsured, appear to be in secular dress.[68] The miniature for Miracle 4 is different however, since no clerics are represented. Instead, this is the story of how a marauding army of Scots was swallowed up by the earth: and what is expressed by the miniature is a certain contempt for the Scots. They are shown as barefoot, and wearing shaggy skins and pagan bonnets, in a manner reminiscent of twelfth-century Northumbrian accounts of the 'Picts', for instance the story of the Battle of the Standard.[69] Furthermore, they are shown as being driven by the victorious Anglo-Saxons into the mouth of a pit, which looks like a simplified form of representations of hell-mouth.[70]

Both text and miniature for Miracle 5 follow the pattern set by Miracle 3. Here the miscreant is Barcwith, a soldier of Earl Tostig, and his crime is to infringe the rights of sanctuary of Durham. The text goes on to describe how, after the death in agony of Barcwith, the earl and his followers make offerings at the shrine. But the miniature focuses only on the punishment of Barcwith,

---

[66] See Symeon, *Libellus*, lib. II, cap. xi and xii; Arnold, i, 64–7.
[67] Univ. 165, p. 143.
[68] Univ. 165, p. 149.
[69] See Chapter 6 below for discussion of Durham attitudes to the Scots. For the miracle, see Univ. 165, 153–6.
[70] Univ. 165, p. 153.

and again shows the keepers of the shrine in non-monastic dress.[71] In both 6 and 7 the distinction does not arise, since Miracle 6 makes it clear that those who carried the shrine to Lindisfarne in 1069/70 were soldiers at the time, while the action of 7 takes place at night, whilst the soldier-thief is alone in the church.[72] One final point may be made about the texts and the miniatures in this group; this is that in 3, 5 and 7, that is all the stories in which sacrilegious individuals are struck down, it is soldiers and followers who infringe and are punished. As a result their superiors are generally chastened, and, in the case of Tostig, make offerings to the saint. This is in contrast with the very bold line taken by Symeon, in his story of William the Conqueror's visit to Durham. According to Symeon, the Conqueror doubted that St Cuthbert's body was truly at Durham, and was planning to execute the leaders of the people of the saint for suspected fraud. However, St Cuthbert struck him down, and forced him to flee both church and town, retreating in disarray beyond the Tees.[73] It is Symeon's second story of the Conqueror which reverts to type, telling of the punishment of the tax-collector, Ralph, and of the king's repentance and gifts to the church.[74]

The explanation for the difference can only be hypothetical, but it may be of relevance that Symeon was writing after the death of the Conqueror, when the kingdom was firmly in the hands of Henry I, and when the main problem for the priory was to establish its rights with the new bishop, Ranulf Flambard. By contrast, if the author of the Miracle Stories was indeed a clerk, writing in the last years of the Community of St Cuthbert, the greater reticence of his stories, as of the *Historia de Sancto Cuthberto*, may be explained. By the time of Bishop Walcher, the community had managed to come through a series of sudden and dangerous changes of regime, charted in the Miracle Stories. First there is the tenth-century Anglo-Danish regime of the Scandinavian kings of York, represented by Ragnald and his followers Scula and Onlafbald. Then comes the conquest by the Wessex dynasty, which reaches its own crisis with Tostig's occupation of the earldom, 1055–65. Next comes the Conquest, and the oppressions of the Norman army. Each of these is dealt with, and St Cuthbert's repeated protection of his Community and lands is emphasised, but the writer does not feel secure enough to deal with the conqueror as robustly as does Symeon. Instead, in the story of the greedy and sacrilegious Norman soldier, resident in the castle built by the conqueror for Walcher, this individual is actually given permission to spend the night in the church. This story cannot be identified with any of Symeon's,

[71] Univ. 165, p. 157.
[72] Univ. 165, p. 164.
[73] Symeon, *Libellus*, lib. III, cap. xix; Arnold, i, 106.
[74] Ibid. cap. xx; Arnold, i, 107–8.

and Colgrave suggests that it may come from the time when the whole community of Durham was punished by the Norman army after the assassination of Walcher.[75] But it would fit as well into the stories of Walcher's difficult and intrigue-ridden episcopate, when he was living in the castle, protected by the garrison, and becoming increasingly involved in the power-struggles of the region, as he attempted to fulfil also the role of the earl.[76] If this is the case, then the very decision to collect and retell these miracle stories may reflect the insecurity of the Community, particularly after the execution of the Anglo-Saxon Earl Waltheof as a traitor.

From all this it is now possible to put forward some conclusions. The first is that Univ. 165 appears as a product of a period when the benedictine community was actively involved in promoting the cult of their leading saint, and in studying and editing all the material available on him. The post-Bedan miracles incorporated into Univ. 165 testify to this activity, but come from an early stage in the production of copies of the chosen edition of the *Life*, and may well have been written by a member of the Community of St Cuthbert, in the last years of its existence. However, the miniature cycle is more hybrid. On the one hand, it is based upon a thorough knowledge of the texts, and appears to draw upon a traditional iconography for St Cuthbert, which was very probably already established at Durham before 1083. On the other hand, it consistently emphasises some aspects of St Cuthbert as described by Bede, at the expense of others, and even adds themes, particularly St Cuthbert's scholarship and association with books, not mentioned by Bede. Finally, its attitude to the Community of St Cuthbert is different from that of the author of the Miracle Stories, since it consistently represents them in secular clothing, rather than as 'fratres'. It would appear then that the miniature cycle represents the viewpoint of the Benedictines, and must have been designed, at least in this form, after 1083. The only remaining problem is the issue raised by Malcolm Baker, that is, whether the cycle of Univ. 165 represents a sometimes clumsy contraction of an ex-tremely full cycle.[77] The difficulty here of course is that the argument depends on how one reads the text, but the existence of an even fuller cycle does not seem to be a necessary conclusion from the evidence of Univ. 165.

This argument may be briefly set out as follows. First, Baker argues that, as the later versions of the cycle frequently use two separate scenes where Univ. 165 has only one compound image, Univ. 165 represents a conflation of a fuller cycle which was more faithfully copied in the later works.[78] Of course,

[75] Colgrave, 'Post-Bedan Miracles', 327.
[76] See Symeon, *Libellus*, lib. III, cap. xxiii and xxiv; Arnold, i, 113–18.
[77] Baker, 'Medieval Illustrations', 26–7.
[78] Ibid.

it is equally possible that the later artists, using more lavish formats and working in more public, formal contexts, chose to expand Univ. 165's condensed and sometimes selective imagery (or that the compiler/designer of an intermediary cycle did so). Secondly, the inconsistencies which Baker finds in some miniatures, and which he sees as caused by unsuccessful selection from a fuller pictorial narrative, can equally (and more economically) be accounted for by a slightly different reading of the text and image. The miniature for chapter 24, which Baker sees as one such case, has already been discussed, as has that for chapter 2. In the case of chapter 3, where St Cuthbert saves the monks on the drifting rafts, I would disagree with Baker's reading. His argument is that Bede is making the point that Cuthbert's prayers were *more* effective than those of the monks, and that therefore some image of the monks also praying would be important.[79] However, Bede states that God merely delayed answering the monks' prayers, in order that the jeering peasants might be taught a more thorough lesson.[80] Thus, the miniature, by showing St Cuthbert in the midst of the peasants, who wonder as the boat begins to change direction (shown by the flapping sail), focuses in once again on St Cuthbert as preacher and teacher, and resists any apparent criticism of the monks. Finally, in the miniature for chapter 40, where the transport of the saint's newly dead body back to Lindisfarne is combined with a representation of the signaller and watcher, the compression is both effective and very much in line with the focus and economy of the miniatures in general.

Thus, as Jonathan Alexander also suggests, there is no need to hypothesise an earlier, fuller cycle.[81] Rather, an intelligent and literate designer seems to have worked from the texts, creating a set of miniatures which fulfil very well the requirements of the format and apparent function of Univ. 165, and drawing upon a traditional picture of the saint, perhaps from wall-paintings or other media. Either Univ. 165 itself, or something very close to its designs, then remained at Durham at least until the middle of the twelfth century, when a revised version was created. It is of course possible that the production of the cycle found in Univ. 165 was associated with the preparation of the new shrine, ready for the translation of 1104. Indeed, the emphasis on the large and small reliquaries, their arrangement and appearance, in the miniatures for the Miracle Stories may suggest this, but this can only be speculation. What can be suggested, as Pächt, Baker and Alexander have argued, is that the designer was familiar with images of the types found in other late-eleventh-century illustrated saints' *Lives*, and that he

[79] Ibid.
[80] Colgrave, *Two 'Lives'*, 162–4.
[81] Alexander, *Medieval Illuminators*, 85.

may have taken an illustrated *Life of St Benedict* as a particular compositional model.[82] With this, and with the textual and visual material available at Durham at the turn of the century, a book was created which embodies much of the activity and ethos of the Benedictines, as they took possession of their saint, and prepared to install him in their grand new church.

---

[82] O. Pächt, *The Rise of Pictorial Narrative in Twelfth-Century England*, Oxford, 1962, 14–18.

CHAPTER FIVE

&❧

The Benedictine revival
in Northumbria

In attempting to trace the development of a regional intellectual culture
in post-Conquest Northumbria, the question of the Benedictine revival
poses one of the most difficult problems.[1] The surviving foundation
narratives, cartularies and chronicles have long been acknowledged as
complex, sometimes contradictory, and difficult to clarify; and this is
especially the case with the great black-monk houses of Yorkshire.[2] The
two fullest and most reliable narratives are those of Symeon of Durham and
Hugh the Chanter; but Symeon was little interested in events beyond the
lands and diocese of Durham, while Hugh was primarily concerned to tell the
story of Archbishop Thurstan's great struggle against Canterbury's claims to
primacy (1115–40).[3] For the present study, what makes the problem much
greater is the almost complete loss of the late-eleventh and early-twelfth-
century manuscripts of these houses. Thus, all that can be attempted in this
chapter is a brief outline of the process of the establishment of Benedictines
in Northumbria outside Durham; and of the evidence which can be gleaned
from their surviving manuscripts. Despite the difficulties, the subject is
important, as York represents a major centre of religous and cultural
development, whose relations with Durham have not been entirely clarified.

The story begins with two separate initiatives. The first is that of the
Conqueror and his successors who, with the support of their barons, moved
to establish in Northumbria a scattering of monasteries of the kinds with
which they were familiar. The second is that of Reinfrid, Aldwin and Ælfwig,
the three monks from Evesham and Winchcombe, who between them were
instrumental in founding or refounding, with varying degrees of success,
Wearmouth–Jarrow, Streoneshalch/Whitby, and St Mary's, York. Their

---

[1] The classic account is that of Knowles, in *Monastic Order*, 165–71. See also D. Baker, 'The
Desert in the North', *Northern History* 5, 1970, 1–11.

[2] The problems of the early sources for Whitby and St Mary's, York, have recently been greatly
clarified by Burton, 'Monastic Revival'.

[3] For Hugh's account, see Hugh the Chanter, *The History of the Church of York*.

attempts at Melrose, Lastingham and Hackness ultimately failed, while the monks established at Wearmouth–Jarrow were removed into Durham by St Calais. But Whitby and St Mary's grew and prospered, with St Mary's receiving a level of patronage from both the royal house and leading Norman nobles which gave it wealth and power equalled amongst Northumbrian monasteries only by Durham.[4] What is perhaps surprising, is that the archbishops of York, unlike the bishops of Durham, at first played little part in this movement. They were preoccupied for some time with the repair and reconstruction of their cathedral, and the reorganisation of its chapter and liturgical life.[5] However, as this was achieved, and as reforms were also undertaken at the ancient minsters of Beverley and Ripon, as well as at Hexham, the activities of the archbishops began to form a major element in the complex network of new houses which was taking shape.[6] This chapter is an attempt to examine the type and degree of intellectual life established at the monasteries which formed this network, and the extent of their interconnection with one another.

One theme prominent in this story, which helps to give the monasticism of Northumbria a distinctive character, is that of the search for the eremitical life. This seems to provide the original initiative even for the Conqueror's foundation of Selby, although there are less flattering interpretations also. The main source on Selby's foundation is the twelfth-century History, and this tells of Benedict, a monk of Auxerre.[7] According to the story, Benedict received a vision from St Germanus, after which he absconded from Auxerre with a few followers, and the abbey's chief relic, a finger of St Germanus. He and his followers landed first in the south-east, but eventually arrived at Selby in 1069, at the time when the Conqueror was in the north with his army, intent upon eliminating further resistance throughout the region. Benedict settled under a great oak, on some marshy land belonging to the king, and so came to the notice of the sheriff of Yorkshire. The sheriff was sufficiently impressed by the small group of hermits, and their relic, that he brought Benedict before the king, at York. The Conqueror granted Benedict leave to

[4] For the emergence of Whitby and St Mary's, see Burton, 'Monastic Revival'. For gifts made to St Mary's by Rufus, see Christopher Norton, 'The Buildings of St Mary's Abbey, York, and Their Destruction', *The Antiquaries Journal* 74, 1994, 256–88, at 280–3.
[5] For the state of affairs in York at the time of the Conquest, see J. M. Cooper, *The Last Four Anglo-Saxon Archbishops of York*, Borthwick Papers 38, York, 1970. For the extent of the damage to the city and cathedral in 1069/70, see Hugh the Chanter, *The History of the Church of York*, 11.
[6] The key figure in this development was Thurstan, archbishop of York 1114–40. See D. Nicholl, *Thurstan, Archbishop of York 1114–1140*, York, 1964.
[7] See *Historia Selebeiensis Monasterii*, in J. T. Fowler, ed., *Selby Coucher Book*, Yorkshire Archaeological Society, Record Series 10, 1891. See also R. B. Dobson, 'The First Norman Abbey in Northern England', *Ampleforth Journal* 74, 1969, 161–76.

build a monastery, and a large amount of land to support it, and Benedict was ordained abbot of Selby in 1070 by the archbishop of York. No precise reason for the foundation is stated in the surviving text of the charter, but it is interesting that contemporaries appear to have seen it as an act of penance. However, Orderic Vitalis depicted William I as recognising, on his deathbed, that the harrying of the north was the worst of all his oppressions of the Anglo-Saxons, and was followed in this by William of Malmesbury. It is therefore possible that Selby, like Battle, was intended as an expiation.[8]

Northern England, like the south, thus had a royal abbey founded in association with a war of Conquest; but Selby, unlike Battle, was at first very isolated. It was another thirteen years before Durham became a Benedictine priory, and longer still before the first group of monks was installed at York. Where the first recruits came from is unknown, and nothing survives of Benedict's small buildings at Selby. A link with the archbishops of York is demonstrated by Domesday, which shows the abbot of Selby as a subtenant, holding seven carucates in the archbishop's rich manor of Sherburn-in-Elmet. This was taken further when Rufus placed Selby under the authority of the archbishop. Prominent growth and large-scale buildings came at the end of the century, when Benedict retired to Rochester, and Hugh de Lacy became abbot (1097). By this time, major building was under way at York, but Hugh seems to have looked to Durham as his example, for one of the nave piers at Selby is a copy of the famous piers of Durham, and the design of Selby is clearly influenced by Durham.[9] Some indication of Selby's local prominence is the fact that in the twelfth century it supplied an abbot to Holy Trinity, York, and received abbots from St Augustine's, St Mary's and Pontefract.

Of Selby's library, little can now be known. No book-list or catalogue survives, and Selby produced neither a known scholar, nor a chronicler of the calibre of Symeon or Hugh the Chanter, from whom information could be gleaned. Only two twelfth-century manuscripts from Selby can now be identified (by Ker). One, BL Add. 36652, is a set of Paschal Tables with brief annals, which dates from the second quarter of the twelfth century. The script is good, but not distinctive; and the one decorated initial is a six-line-high T, executed in a rather friable pale blue, and very simple in design. The

[8] See *The Ecclesiastical History of Orderic Vitalis*, ed. and trans. M. Chibnall, vol. iv, Oxford, 1973, 94–5. Janet Burton, however, suggests that Selby may have been intended to function in the north as Worcester and Evesham did on the Welsh border. See *Monastic and Religious Orders in Britain, 1000–1300*, Cambridge, 1994, 276, n. 24.

[9] See Eric Fernie, 'The Romanesque Church of Selby Abbey', in L. R. Hoey, ed., *Yorkshire Monasticism*, British Archaeological Association Conference Transactions 16, 1995, 40–9; and Fernie, 'The Architectural Influence of Durham Cathedral', in Rollason *et al.*, *Anglo-Norman Durham*, 269–82.

other Selby manuscript is a little more distinctive, however, and shows strong signs of being a Northumbrian product. This is Bodleian, Fairfax 12, and is a copy of Bede's *Historia Ecclesiastica*, here called 'Historia de Gestis Anglorum'.[10] The script appears to date from around the middle of the twelfth century, and again shows no distinctive features. However, the textual apparatus, and the opening of the text itself, are handled with a simplicity strikingly reminiscent of contemporary Yorkshire Cistercian manuscripts. There is no contents list, although a number of extra items are added at the end of the text, no title page, and no opening rubric. Capitula are given, although written continuously rather than being set out on their own lines; and there are no display capitals following the initials to the Preface or book I. However, this book does not appear to be a Cistercian product, as three of its decorated initials contain beasts such as dragons, lions and eagles, and one has a small, naked human figure.

These inhabited initials are striking in two ways. First, with their multi-coloured grounds in bright colours, and their heavy acanthus foliage, reminiscent of that found in Norman books, they are curiously old-fashioned. Second, both in this and in their general design and execution, they are very similar to the inhabited initials in a set of copies of the works of Bede from the Augustinian house of Kirkham.[11] Finally, and most distinctively Northumbrian, the initial on fol. 111v has a version of the split-petal motif, though here in the form of a split lozenge (see Fig. 51). This form is rare in Cistercian books, and is perhaps most associated with Durham.[12] In the absence of other Selby manuscripts, there is no evidence on whether Selby had a scriptorium in the twelfth century. The details and stylistic affiliations of this book, however, do seem to suggest links with the Augustinians and with Durham. Its exemplar is unknown, but its text is of the 'Yorkshire' family, the oldest surviving member of which is Cambridge, Trinity College, R 5 27.[13] Finally, although this book cannot give evidence for the existence of a scriptorium at Selby, and may be the product of a scribe and artists who

FIG. 51 Lozenge-shaped split-petal motif from Oxford,
Bodleian, MS Fairfax 12, fol. 111v

[10] For surviving Selby books, see Ker, *Medieval Libraries*.
[11] For these manuscripts, see Chapter 8 below.
[12] A similar conclusion is reached by Elzbieta Temple, in her unpublished thesis: 'The Twelfth-Century Psalter in the Bodleian Library, MS Douce 293', University of London, 1971.
[13] For a full discussion of textual families, see *Bede's Ecclesiastical History*, xlvi–lxi. For analysis of the annotations in the Selby manuscript see Chapter 10 below.

worked for Kirkham, it does demonstrate that someone at Selby was capable of annotating books, and could write a good, clear proto-Gothic hand. On fols. 77 and 78 are two marginal notes, each enclosed in a red box. The first reads: 'Nota quod Lindisfarnensis insula perpetuo habuerit episcopum'; and the second, 'Nota quod Hripensis ecclesia perpetuo habuerit episcopum'. These would seem to suggest that Selby, or a prominent member of the community, maintained an interest in the ecclesiastical politics of the archdiocese of York.

In looking for evidence of links between Selby and other Northumbrian abbeys, the name of its second abbot, Hugh de Lacy, has caused some speculation. It was customary for royal foundations to be supported also by the king's aristocratic followers, and the de Lacy family were prominent in Yorkshire. Indeed, Ilbert de Lacy was perhaps the largest landholder in the West Riding in 1086, holding over 160 manors in that region.[14] Too little is known of Hugh de Lacy for a family connection to be proved, but the de Lacys certainly used some of their extensive holdings to support new monastic foundations. Ilbert's own foundation was at his caput, the strategic- ally important castle of Pontefract, adjacent to a thriving town, one of the few in Yorkshire to have burgesses listed in Domesday.[15] The prestige of this foundation, sited just beside the castle, was enhanced by the fact that it was one of a group of four daughter houses of the prominent Cluniac house of La Charité sur Loire, all founded in England by Norman nobles. Like Selby, Pontefract was at first isolated, as it was founded in 1090 as the only Cluniac house in the north. Its own daughter, Monk Bretton, was founded only in 1154. Whether its fortunes were affected by the fall of the de Lacys in 1106, disgraced after the battle of Tinchebrai, is unclear, but the priory received patronage from a variety of barons. In the 1130s it was chosen by Archbishop Thurstan of York, the patron of Augustinians and Cistercians, for his own retirement.[16] It seems likely that Thurstan would have given Pontefract some of his own books, but there is no surviving evidence on Pontefract's library. That the *lectio divina* was engaged in is suggested by a surviving twelfth-century volume of Augustine, of undistinguished appear- ance; but the evidence goes no further.[17]

Moreover, by 1090 the group of monk-hermits from Evesham and Winchcombe were active in Yorkshire, inspiring both an interest in the

[14] Ilbert de Lacy is numbered X in the list of landholders in Yorkshire in Domesday Book. For a brief biography, and notes on his estate, see M. Faull and M. Stinson, eds., *Domesday Book, 30, Yorkshire*, part 2, Chichester, 1986, Appendix 3, 9W1.

[15] Ibid. 299c. See also Burton, *Monastic and Religious Orders*, 37.

[16] See Nicholl, *Thurstan*, xxiii. It is possible that Hugh also became a monk of Pontefract, ibid. 55, n. 3.
[17] See Ker, *Medieval Libraries*, 153.

eremitical life and the foundation of two great abbeys. This story has been often told, and has been recently analysed and clarified by Janet Burton, so that there is no need to do more here than to summarise the main points. Symeon's *Historia Dunelmensis Ecclesiae* gives two versions of the arrival of Aldwin, Reinfrid and Ælfwig. The longer, and earlier, account is given in lib. III, cap. xxi.[18] Here, Aldwin is depicted as the leader of the group, and as inspired by his reading of Bede with a desire to see the Northumbrian monasteries, although he knows they are in ruins. They have been given permission to come by the abbot of Winchcombe, who allowed them to bring one donkey, with books, vestments and things required for the celebration of mass. In this account, the initiative is taken by Bishop Walcher, who sends for the group, and gives them the site of Jarrow, where they live as hermits, supported by alms. Recruits then arrive, mostly from the south, attracted by unknown means; and Walcher responds by giving the vill of Jarrow, and its surrounding estates, for the foundation of a full monastery. The departure of Reinfrid for Whitby, and the later foundation of St Mary's, York, are briefly told but are of less interest to Symeon than the story of Aldwin and his new recruits, who eventually come to Durham. Much the same story is told in the *Historia Regum*, though in a shorter form, and with emphasis simply on Durham, York and Whitby, as the three great monasteries to emerge from the movement.[19]

The question raised by this account is whether St Mary's, York, and Whitby remained closely linked to Durham, by virtue of their common origins. It is attractive to speculate that they would have done so, and Whitby, St Mary's and Selby all appear on St Calais's confraternity list.[20] However, other evidence suggests that they developed along necessarily different lines, and that their patrons played a very influential part in this. In Janet Burton's analysis, Reinfrid, the ex-soldier who had participated in the harrying of the north, emerges as most dedicated to life as a hermit. Following his move to Whitby he appears to have maintained this emphasis, and to have accepted the patronage of the Percy family, holders of the land on which he and his followers settled. However, growing tensions led a group under the leadership of a monk named Stephen to leave, and to settle finally at the abandoned church of St Olave or Olaf, just outside the walls of York. Stephen and his group appear to have wished to establish a formal Benedictine monastery, of a type possibly resisted by Reinfrid; it is also possible to see the move to York as inspired by a wish for independence from

---

[18] See Arnold, i, 108–10.
[19] See *Historia Regum*, in Arnold, ii, *sub anno* 1074.
[20] See J. Burton, 'A Confraternity List from St Mary's Abbey, York', *Revue bénédictine* 89, 1979, 325–33.

the growing influence of the Percy family. Certainly the little group at St Olave's Church, who soon became the nucleus of St Mary's Abbey, received rapid recognition and gifts from both the Conqueror and Rufus, as well as the majority of the northern barons.[21] Stephen seems to have regarded Whitby as a cell of St Mary's until about 1100; and no formally recognised abbot of Whitby was consecrated until c.1107, when William de Percy became first abbot of Whitby, presumably after the death of Reinfrid. It was perhaps for this reason that no representative of Whitby was present at Durham in 1104 for the translation of the relics of St Cuthbert, although both St Mary's and Selby were represented. Finally, St Mary's rapidly outstripped Whitby in wealth and power, and by the middle of the twelfth century had outstripped Selby also. That Whitby, despite its own growing wealth, remained potentially vulnerable is suggested by the fact that Archbishop Thurstan obtained a papal privilege for its protection in 1125. No such measure was needed for St Mary's.[22]

This wealth and independence seems to have made it difficult for the archbishops of York to influence the policies of St Mary's. Indeed, the archbishops showed relatively little interest in St Mary's itself. The monks' occupation of the site of St Olave's Church was at first contested by Thomas I. However, by 1086 the abbot held five manors in Ryedale from the archbishop. Thurstan, the most active patron of both monks and regular canons, concentrated his patronage on the ancient minsters of Beverley and Ripon, and on developing the Augustinian priories of Nostell and Hexham into something akin to new minsters; he gave each a stall in the cathedral chapter, created a prebend for each, and encouraged patrons to give them extensive groups of parish churches.[23] Meanwhile, St Mary's was embarking on its own expansion in Cumbria, an area in which the archbishops had little influence, except through the Augustinians of Carlisle. St Mary's priory of Wetheral was founded in the 1090s, and was followed c.1120 by St Bee's, on the coast of Cumberland. Both priories were founded and patronised by Ranulf le Meschin, earl of Chester from 1120, and his group of clients.[24] They thus show St Mary's as willing to expand into a new area, and to pursue

---

[21] See note 4 above.

[22] For the papal privilege see Nicholl, *Thurstan*, 98. Selby's loss of status as St Mary's grew is suggested by Rufus' placing of Selby under the authority of the archbishops of York, as well as by the election of Durandus of St Mary's as abbot of Selby in 1125.

[23] See Nicholl, *Thurstan*, 127–39; J. Wilson, 'The Foundation of the Austin Priories of Nostell and Scone', *Scottish Historical Review* 7, 1910, 141–59; W. E. Wightman, 'Henry I and the Founding of Nostell Priory', *Yorkshire Archaeological Journal* 41, 1966.

[24] Ranulph le Mesquin, or Meschin, later earl of Chester, was given the lordship of Carlisle by William Rufus in 1092. See F. Barlow, *William Rufus*, London, 1983, 297–8. Both these foundations were overshadowed in 1123–7 by Stephen's foundation of the wealthy Savigniac house (later Cistercian) of Furness.

its own policies. However, there is no evidence that tension existed between St Mary's and Thurstan until 1132, when Thurstan found himself the unexpected protector of the ejected group of would-be reformers from St Mary's, and founder of the Cistercian house of Fountains.[25]

In the case of Whitby and St Mary's the surviving evidence for their libraries and scriptoria is disappointing.[26] The Whitby Cartulary preserves a late twelfth-century library catalogue on fol. 138.[27] This shows books on related subjects grouped together, which suggests the presence of a librarian, as would be expected by this date. However, both the range and the organisation of the list require some comment, as they are not entirely straightforward. Firstly, the list, though carefully arranged, mostly by author, in three columns, does not always make the number of volumes clear. Some 105 titles are given, but four of these are said to exist in two copies, while 32 are listed as forming just 14 compound volumes. This gives a probable total of some 91 volumes, respectable for a group of perhaps forty monks, but still very small by comparison with Durham, which seems to have had over 500 by the same period. Moreover, it would clearly be very misleading to think of these simply as constituting the 'library' of Whitby in the sense of books available for the *lectio divina*, let alone as constituting all of the books which the abbey needed to function. In the first place, no complete Bibles, or Psalters, or other books of the Bible are included, with the enigmatic exception of three small books, two of individual Gospels (Matthew and John), and one of Exodus, much further down the list, all with a gloss. Similarly, there are almost no liturgical books here, with the exception of two Passionales, one for November and one for January, listed immediately after the two glossed Gospels. Both categories of book were essential, but were presumably kept separately from the volumes listed here; the four exceptions are puzzling, but were perhaps regarded as 'reading' books, rather than being put into the two separate categories. Glosses on books of the Bible are, however, included here, in a small group of five anonymous volumes, two on the Pauline Epistles, two on the Psalter and one on the Song of Songs. Considerably more difficult to explain is the fact that, while the list opens with patristic works, in the way that was usual for the twelfth century, there is nothing by Augustine (usually the largest single contributor to any such list), nothing by Jerome or Gregory the Great (usually almost as popular as

[25] This story is well-known. See, for example: D. Baker, 'The Foundation of Fountains Abbey', *Northern History* 4, 1969, 29–43; D. Bethell, 'The Foundation of Fountains Abbey and the State of St Mary's, York, in 1132', *Journal of Ecclesiastical History* 17, 1966, 11–27.

[26] See Ker, *Medieval Libraries*, 197–8 and 217. For a brief discussion of the St Mary's manuscripts see Temple, 'The Twelfth-Century Psalter in the Bodleian Library', 197–200, 238–41.

[27] See *Whitby Cartulary*, i, Surtees Society 64, London, 1878, 341.

Augustine), and only two works by Ambrose. This would suggest that a portion of the list, perhaps containing also the absent biblical books, is missing; but the fact that the book is a composite, and that the folios of which the list is a part are not in their original position, make this difficult to assess. The absence of a whole set of standard patristic works is made all the more surprising, since the list does contain volumes by two of the Greek Fathers (Gregory Nazianzen and Origen) which are considerably rarer, as well as a small but respectable set of twelfth-century theological works, including two (probably) by St Bernard of Clairvaux, two by Hugh of St Victor and one by Peter Lombard.

Other areas of standard monastic reading, however, *are* well represented, with works of ecclesiastical history, works by Carolingian writers, the works of Cassian, and moralising texts such as Smaragdus' *Diadema Monachorum* and a 'de activa et contemplativa vita', making up some twelve volumes. Also well represented are saints' *Lives*, which are grouped together in a set of eight volumes, beginning, interestingly, with the *Life of St Cuthbert*, although a 'liber Tome de sancta Hilda', presumably of strong local interest, appears in a compound volume in another part of the list. Two other groups of books are perhaps discernible in the main list, namely a small set of books on canon law, and a set of volumes needed for running aspects of the abbey's life. The first consists mostly of a pair of volumes, a copy of the decretals (most likely Lanfranc's canonical collection, acquired at Durham in the late eleventh century) and a copy of the *Panormia* of Ivo of Chartres, also possessed (in duplicate) by Durham; as an addition, there is also an 'exceptiones decre-torum Graciani' lower on the list, in the section which contains most of the 'newer' theological works. The second group is also not systematically organised, but shows works on medicine, astrology, the computus, music and the mass, clustered together with a 'liber consuetudinum'. Again, however, this does not seem like a complete list, in the absence especially of the Rule. Overall, then, this list is puzzling. It would appear that it cannot be complete, but no rationale for its inclusions and exclusions can be suggested, beyond the possibility that its first section may be missing. Second, while it shows some attempt to organise its contents into groups, this is by no means systematically carried through. All this would suggest that, while the usual formal distribution of books at Lent, detailed for instance by Lanfranc, was carried out under the supervision of one of the senior monks, who may have been responsible for the books on this list, the monks of Whitby did not build a library of anything like the dimensions of that at Durham, and perhaps organised their books rather informally.

This does not mean, however, that they were uninterested in acquiring and passing on a good education. The largest group of books on the list, by a good margin, is that of 'libri grammatici', which comprises the last thirty volumes, and which suggests that Whitby's school enjoyed the use of a good and wide-ranging set of textbooks. Actual 'grammar' is represented, as usual, by Priscian and Donatus, with a commentary on Donatus by Remigius of Auxerre. There is also a good set of works combining sacred history with approved poetic style, such as Prudentius, Sedulius, Prosper, Theodulus and Arator, as well as most of the usual 'poetic textbooks', such as Statius, Virgil, Horace, Avianus, Maximianus, Cato and 'Homerus'. As was usual, these make no distinction between classical and post-classical authors, but the Whitby list does suggest an unusually strong interest in the classics, since it includes Plato (probably the *Timaeus*, but still rare) and Virgil's *Eclogae* (here, as at Durham, referred to as *Bucolica*). Also here are the standard works of Cicero, Juvenal and Boethius, though thorough teaching is also suggested by less common volumes such as: the work by Remigius of Auxerre already mentioned; a book of 'Derivationes'; what seem to be 'introductions' to Boethius; and Bernard of Utrecht's commentary on Theodulus.

Finally, several entries on this list strongly suggest that Whitby acquired books or exemplars from Durham. This is not necessarily the case for the eight listed works by Bede, since these were widely available, and the *Super Apocalipsim* does not appear in the twelfth-century Durham book-list; but Durham would be the obvious source for a good text of the *Life of St Cuthbert*. Some of the rarer theological works point in the same direction: Durham also had the Gregory Nazianzen as well as the *Prognosticon* of Julian of Toledo, while a volume of Origen with the same title, 'super Vetus Testamentum' was given by St Calais. Equally, the more unusual school-books, the Plato and the 'Bucolica' appear also at Durham. Most of the other works on the Whitby list are too popular to point to any particular source, but three historical works are more significant. The first to appear is the 'De Situ Dunelmensis Ecclesie'. At first sight, this looks like the Latin title given to an Old English poem praising Durham and its relics, which survives in a part of a late-twelfth-century manuscript of probable Durham origin (now Cambridge UL Ff 1 27) which also contains Symeon of Durham's *Libellus de Exordio atque Procursu Istius, Hoc est Dunelmensis, Ecclesie*; it is most likely that this longer work, perhaps with the poem, is meant. Also interesting is the appearance on the Durham twelfth-century list of a 'Liber de Statu Dunelmensis Ecclesiae' which, in the absence of any clear entry there for Symeon, may be related to the Whitby entry. Equally interesting is a compound volume a little lower on the list, just after the collection of saints' *Lives*, containing an *Imago Mundi* (almost certainly that of Honorius Augustodunensis) and 'Gildas'. This again points to Durham, since the collection of historical works now found in Cambridge UL Ff 1 27 also includes book I of Gildas, *De Excidio Britanniae* (together with the *Historia Brittonum*, believed to be by Gildas in the twelfth century). Moreover, a further collection of historical, geographical and spiritual texts, originally forming part of the same compound manuscript with the 'local' historical works, and also probably copied out at Durham, also contained the *Imago Mundi* (this portion of the collection now forms part of Cambridge, Corpus Christi College, MS 66). This very complex Durham collection was, by *c.*1200, in the possession of the Cistercian house of Sawley, in Yorkshire and therefore considerably nearer to Whitby, and indeed seems to have been widely influential in twelfth-century Northumbria, so the connection with Durham may not be direct. What can be observed here is that Whitby clearly showed an interest in the historical works circulating in the 'province' in the late twelfth century, and seems also to have shared the equally widespread Northumbrian distaste for the very popular work of Geoffrey of Monmouth, who does *not* appear on the Whitby list.

The evidence from St Mary's, York, is rather different. Until recently it was believed that no library catalogue survived. However, Richard Sharpe has recently identified an anonymous fourteenth-century catalogue as that of St Mary's.[28] There is, of course, no means of dating individual entries, but Sharpe points out that the list contains a respectable number of basic patristic works, of the type which a monastic library would normally seek to collect in the first half of the twelfth century, and of glossed books of the Bible, of the type prominent around the mid-century. There is, then, some evidence that St Mary's was active in building up its book collection, in the generations immediately following its foundation. This provides a helpful counterbalance to the otherwise disappointing picture presented by St Mary's. The picture of laxity and unwillingness to reform given by the Fountains narrative may be biased, but it is also true that St Mary's produced no scholar or historian to rival those of Durham, the Augustinians or the Cistercians.[29] Moreover, it was at the minster that a *magister scholarum* was established, while there is no evidence for the existence of a school at St Mary's.[30] Indeed, the most distinguished scholar to study at York in the early twelfth century was Maurice, later prior of Augustinian Kirkham, and he showed no apparent interest in St Mary's. Instead, his three years in York were spent mostly in studying Hebrew with the Jewish community of the city. He spent some

---

[28] See Sharpe *et al.*, *English Benedictine Libraries*.

[29] On the Fountains narratives, see D. Baker, 'The Genesis of English Cistercian Chronicles: The Foundation History of Fountains Abbey', I and II, *Analecta Sacri Ordinis Cisterciensis* 25, 1969, 14–41, and 31, 1975, 179–212. See also Joan Wardrop, *Fountains Abbey and Its Benefactors 1132–1300*, Cistercian Studies 91, Kalamazoo, 1987.

[30] For the *magister scholarum*, see Hugh the Chanter, *The History of the Church of York*, 11.

time with the canons of the minster, but mentions them mostly to criticise their liturgy and chant.[31] It also appears that St Mary's made no endowment to support a scriptorium during the twelfth century. This is in contrast to arrangements made by major southern black-monk houses in this period.[32] The documentary evidence, then, presents a rather contradictory picture. On the one hand it would appear that St Mary's was building up a book collection of the type which might be expected. But on the other there is no record of the existence of a scriptorium, even in the second half of the twelfth century, when some such provision might be expected. The picture is made still more contradictory by the evidence of Leland's *Collectanea*, which certainly suggests that St Mary's had an interesting collection by the time of the Dissolution. Leland noted only two desirable rarities at York Minster, and only seven at Durham, but a surprising twenty-one at St Mary's.[33] On balance, therefore, it would appear that suggestions that St Mary's showed no interest in building up a library in the twelfth century have been over-harsh.[34]

There is one final question to be considered, before turning to the evidence of the books themselves. This is the problem of the after-effects of the split of 1132, which has not previously been considered in this context. Serlo's narrative of the founding of Fountains makes it clear that those who departed from St Mary's included several of the leading members of the community. Those mentioned include the prior, the subprior, the sacrist, the precentor and the almoner, as well as one 'Geoffrey the Painter' and six others.[35] Such a loss must have caused considerable disruption in the life of St Mary's, which could well have affected its development for some time. It is not possible to demonstrate that Geoffrey the Painter was also an illuminator, but the possibility is at least interesting. That paintings of some kind were produced at Fountains itself is suggested also by Serlo. His description of the precipitate expulsion of the reformers, and of their complete dependence on Archbishop Thurstan, suggests that they can have taken nothing with them from St Mary's. Yet he also describes how Henry Murdac, arriving at

[31] See Barlow, *The English Church 1066–1154*, 247 and n. 175.
[32] The employment of professional scribes at St Albans and Abingdon was noted by Knowles, *Monastic Order*, 520. Indeed, Abbot Richard of St Albans (1097–1112) is said to have granted two-thirds of the tithes of the abbey's churches to its scriptorium. See *Gesta Abbatum Monasterii Sancti Albani a Thoma Walsingham*, ed. H. T. Riley, 3 vols., Rolls Series 25, London, 1867–9, i, 69–70, 76. At Winchester, the tithes of a Rectory were granted in 1171 'ad libros transcribendos', while Nigel of Ely gave two churches to the priory 'ad libros faciendos'; see *Catalogi Veteres*, 1, xxiii–xxiv.
[33] J. Leland, *Collectanea*, iii, 1774, 36–7.
[34] See for instance B. Meehan, 'Durham Twelfth-Century Manuscripts in Cistercian Houses', in Rollason *et al.*, *Anglo-Norman Durham*, 439–49.
[35] Walbran, ed., *Manorials of Fountains Abbey*, i, Surtees Society 42, 1863, xxx.

Fountains, was angered to discover images there.[36] It therefore appears that, in the early 1130s, St Mary's housed one monk who was active as a painter, and who was lost in 1132. The split seems also to have created a lasting hostility between St Mary's and the Cistercians. Evidence for this is given by the surviving St Mary's confraternity list, dating from the last quarter of the twelfth century, which survives as fols. 37r–39r of BL Add. 38816. This list is unusually extensive, including as it does over fifty houses, an observation confirmed by Janet Burton.[37] These include a wide range of English monasteries, as well as sixteen Norman and French houses. Moreover, the agreements were concluded with a very wide range of houses. There are four Cluniac priories, no less than nine houses of Augustinian canons, and one which Janet Burton identifies as Gilbertine. Nearly all the local houses are included, with Holy Trinity (York), Whitby, Selby, Durham and Pontefract all appearing, as well as the Augustinians of Bridlington, Nostell, Guisborough, Kirkham and Newburgh. The one group thus conspicuous for their absence are the Cistercian houses. Even the two apparent exceptions in fact confirm this. The first exception is the inclusion of the Cistercian house of Furness; however, Furness was originally founded as a Savigniac house, in the 1120s, and became Cistercian only c.1147. Thus, as the Add. 38816 list clearly preserves a number of early agreements, it is most likely that this agreement was made before 1132. Second, there is the fact that a single monk of Fountains, one Richard Clerembaud, is included by name. However, the entry for this one individual only serves to emphasise the absence of all other Cistercians. It would thus seem that the departure of the reforming group was a blow significant enough to leave resentments which lasted throughout the twelfth century. Two suggestions follow. The first, already mentioned, is that the loss of the prior, the sacrist, the precentor, and an active painter, may well have affected the development of book collection and production at St Mary's. The second is that it would be surprising if St Mary's were actively engaged in exchanging books and exemplars with the Cistercian houses.

In discussing the surviving St Mary's books, the greatest problem is their very small number. Nevertheless, new evidence is emerging, thanks partly to the researches of Gullick, which makes it possible to expand the very disappointing picture previously available. This relates particularly to BL Harley 56, a copy of Osbern's *Life of St Dunstan*.[38] The script and initials of

---

[36] Ibid. 84–6.
           [37] Burton, 'Confraternity List'.
[38] On this manuscript see also A. Lawrence, 'A Northern English School? Patterns of Production and Collection of Manuscripts in the Augustinian Houses of Yorkshire in the Twelfth and Thirteenth Centuries', in L. R. Hoey, ed., *Yorkshire Monasticism*, British Archaeological Association Conference Transactions 16, Leeds, 1995, 145–53, and, more recently, Gullick, 'The Origin and Importance of Cambridge, Trinity College, R. 5. 27'.

this book suggest a date of *c.* 1120. It is thus a fairly early copy of this text, and it has one feature which suggests that it may have been derived from a Canterbury exemplar. This is in the form of a diagram in the margin of fol. 14v, demonstrating the 'pyramid' construction of the tomb of 'beati Odonis'. The annotations on the diagram are in the hand of the text scribe, suggesting that the diagram was copied from the exemplar, which would thus have shown knowledge of the tomb of Oda of Canterbury. It is not possible to demonstrate that the exemplar was borrowed directly from Canterbury, but this must be a possibility. Other features suggesting an early date are that the manuscript is ruled throughout in hard point, and in a very simple pattern. However, the most striking feature of the manuscript is the curious style of its decorated initials. These consist of a nine-line M on fol. 2r, and a fourteen-line R on fol. 2v. The most curious feature is their palette, which is dominated by purple and green, with touches of yellow and red. Blue, usually so common, is absent. The M is competently executed, and again suggests an early date in its use of a motif found frequently in Anglo-Norman manuscripts, decorating the narrow parts of letters. It also has a terminal in the form of a group of berries, or 'bunch of grapes', with hair-like projections. This latter feature is taken much further in the R on fol. 2v, which is striking in several ways. It is clumsy in construction, with the serifs exaggerated in size, and the curves of the R rather loosely drawn. It has several groups of berries, and terminals in the form of round-headed pins. It also has several wedge-shaped 'leaves' or wedge motifs; as well as an unusual form of the split petal.

These latter motifs do not occur in Canterbury manuscripts, and are thus likely to be a part of the repertoire of the illuminator of this manuscript. Was he then a scribe-artist of St Mary's? The manuscript itself is only firmly linked to St Mary's by a late medieval *ex libris*. However, it may well have been at St Mary's for some time before it was thus inscribed, and it is almost certainly a Northumbrian product. Furthermore, Gullick has convincingly linked it with a manuscript now in Cambridge. This is Cambridge, Trinity College, R 5 27.[39] Its provenance is unknown, though it is interesting that it is a copy of Bede's *Historia Ecclesiastica*. It shows the work of two scribes, one of whom writes a hand similar to that of Harley 56. Its major initials are almost certainly the work of the same hand as those of Harley 56. The berries, wedge-shapes and round-headed pins all occur frequently, whilst one initial, on fol. 141v, shows a pure form of the split petal (see Fig. 52). All this suggests very strongly that the two manuscripts are products of the same workshop, which appears to have been active in Northumbria *c.* 1120–30. A

---

[39] Gullick, 'Origin and Importance', 248–50.

FIG. 52 Split-petal motif from Cambridge, Trinity College, MS R 5 27, fol. 141v

location in York is made more likely by Gullick's discovery that a charter now at Durham appears to have been written at York *c*.1110, and is in a hand closely related to R 5 27 and Harley 56.[40] There is no clear evidence on whether or not this workshop or scriptorium was associated with St Mary's, but Harley 56 was presumably made for a well-connected patron, and this, together with the manuscript's connection with St Mary's, makes that house the most likely location. Finally, there is another shred of evidence in Liège, Bibliothèque de l'Université, 369 C. This manuscript has been discussed by Bernard Meehan, who argues strongly that it was copied in the 1120s.[41] It contains a set of works on Roman, Norman and British history, and appears to be copied from Durham exemplars, with its text of William of Jumièges being closely related to that found in Cambridge, Corpus Christi College, MS 139, which has links with Durham and Sawley. The half-page drawing of Woden and his descendants on fol. 88r is also related to the Durham examplar, though Meehan's dating would make it early.[42] By *c*.1200 this book was at Kirkstall, but if Meehan's dating is correct it cannot have been made for that house, which was founded only in 1147/1152. Gullick points out that the initials of 369 C use the wedge-shaped element found also in R 5 27 and Harley 56. Meehan rejects York as the place of origin for 369 C, but cannot demonstrate it to be a Durham product. Since it is certainly Northumbrian, and its initials are related to those already discussed, it seems preferable to regard it as a product of this same workshop. Gullick has also discussed a Homiliary, now York Minster XVI P 12; this has initials clearly related to the group under discussion and which use both the wedge motif and the split petal. It has no clear provenance, and was probably not made for monastic use, raising the interesting possibility that it was made in this highly

[40] Ibid.
[41] B. Meehan, 'Geoffrey of Monmouth, *Prophecies of Merlin*: New Manuscript Evidence', *Bulletin of the Board of Celtic Studies* 28, 1978, 37–46.
[42] Ibid. See also Kauffmann, *Romanesque Manuscripts*, 123.

competent scriptorium for one of the minster clergy, at least one of whom is known to have had a book collection in this period; of this, however, there can be no proof.[43] It is therefore possible to argue that St Mary's did have a scriptorium in the first third of the twelfth century, producing manuscripts in a style which is distinctive, but which shows strong signs of influence from Norman books and from Durham.

The contents of these books are also striking, with their interest in Anglo-Saxon, as well as Norman and Roman history. Indeed, if these manuscripts were made for St Mary's then they suggest a considerable interest in history in that house, even if it did not itself produce a historian. This would suggest that St Mary's shared such interests with Durham; and it is possible that Durham's and Whitby's interest in the classics was also shared at St Mary's. The evidence for this comes from BL Burney 220, a copy of Ovid's *Epistolae ex Ponto*, and Cambridge UL Ee 6 40, a copy of Plato's *Timaeus*. Both these appear in the mid-twelfth-century book-list at Durham, so that Durham may have provided exemplars. Ee 6 40 has a twelfth-century inscription identifying it as the property of an individual monk, before it passed into the collection of St Mary's. This confirms that at least one monk had scholarly interests, but makes its origin uncertain. Of the two, the most clearly Northumbrian is Burney 220. This is dated to the late twelfth century by Ker, but this dating is rather puzzling. Its script is small, upright and rather square, not markedly proto-Gothic; and its initials fit into the first half of the twelfth century, rather than the second half. It is not a high-quality product, its initials appearing rather amateur, and it is not the work of the scribe-artists previously discussed. Nor does it appear to be a Durham book. Nevertheless, it is clearly Northumbrian, and its initials show signs of Durham influence. The first is an M on fol. 4r which contains foliate decoration which looks like a weak version of the Durham clove-curl motif. More conclusive is the H on fol. 7r, which has a terminal in the shape of a simple split petal (Fig. 53). The book appears to have been made for someone of scholarly interests, since the outer margins are left very wide, and comments have been entered onto them. An inscription on its last folio records that it was in the possession of a monk of St Mary's at the end of the medieval period. Its twelfth-century home thus cannot be proved, but St Mary's would appear the most probable location. Given its scholarly nature and rather amateur decoration, it is possible that it was the work of a monk of St Mary's who was interested in the text. What is more certain is that it was the product of the Benedictine revival in Northumbria.

[43] Gullick, pers. comm., and 'The Origin and Importance of Cambridge, Trinity College, R. 5. 27', 258 and n. 44.

FIG. 53 Initial H from London, BL, MS Burney 220, fol. 7r

Only one work can be argued with any degree of certainty to be the product of St Mary's scribes and artists, and that is fols. 21r–39r of BL Add. 38816. This contains the confraternity list already discussed, as well as copies of royal charters relating to St Mary's, and the foundation narrative of Abbot Stephen. The hands of the charters and foundation narrative appear to be of the middle or third quarter of the twelfth century, while those of the confraternity list are of the last quarter of the century. Most of this is competent, plain work, suggesting that, as would be expected, St Mary's commanded the services of several good scribes. Only the charters are given decorated initials, in the standard colours of red, blue and green. The decoration consists largely of groups of simple, curving leaves, symmetrically repeated to produce a tight pattern. There are no split petals or clove curls, but one initial makes repeated use of the round-headed-pin motif (see Fig. 54). Texts such as these were most likely to be copied within St Mary's itself, and this would suggest that at least one artist was available, to decorate these initials which appear to be the work of one hand. However, whilst this shows that the officials of St Mary's had very good copies of 'administrative' texts, there is no evidence here for the existence of a productive scriptorium. Thus, whilst it is now possible to argue that St Mary's may have had a scriptorium in the first third of the century, producing manuscripts of a type and style which link it to Durham, and perhaps Canterbury and Whitby, the evidence for the rest of the century remains extremely unsatisfactory. Only the late library list may suggest that book acquisition continued actively into the second half of the century.

FIG. 54 Initial H from London, BL, MS Add. 38816, fol. 24v

In the case of York Minster, the question of a scriptorium does not arise. Despite the efforts of St Oswald, monks were not established at the cathedral, and the resources of the archbishops remained small compared to those of Canterbury. Ealdred, bishop of Worcester, was appointed to York, as was traditional, in 1060. Although he was required by the Pope to give up Worcester, he did retain twelve of its manors, to add to the resources of the northern archdiocese. He also succeeded in organising the canons of his cathedral into some sort of regular life, under the influence of the Lotharingian reform movement which was popular in England just before the Conquest.[44] He is recorded as having provided fraters for the canons at both York and Southwell, as well as a frater, dorter, and an enlargement of the church at Beverley. This latter gives some idea of his artistic patronage, since it is described as having a painted ceiling, a pulpitum of brass, gold and silver, and a rood of 'German smith-work'.[45] He is not recorded as having given any books to any of his minsters. However, his tenure ended in disaster in 1069, when he died during the Northumbrian rebellion led by Edgar and Waltheof. In the terrible campaign of 1069–70 the cathedral church, like much of York, was burnt by the Norman army, and almost all of its once-great library was destroyed. The possible survival of Egbert's Pontifical and of a group of

[44] See Barrow, 'English Cathedral Communities'.
[45] See Raine, *Historians of the Church of York and Its Archbishops*, vol. ii, 342–54.

Gospel books, discussed in Chapter 1, suggests that some of the treasures kept in the church may have been saved; but Florence of Worcester and other twelfth-century writers believed that it was this fire which finally destroyed what was left of Alcuin's library.[46]

In 1070 the affairs of the minster were thus at a low ebb. When Thomas of Bayeux arrived he found only three canons left, the others having fled or been killed. Moreover, his resources were put under further strain when he was forced to give up Ealdred's Worcester manors, to surrender his claim to authority over the large diocese of Lichfield–Leicester–Lincoln, and to face demands from Lanfranc that he acknowledge the primacy of Canterbury.[47] The condition of his northern manors is demonstrated by Domesday Book. This assesses the Yorkshire manors of the archbishop at about 243 carucates, of which about half are described as waste.[48] Given that the archbishop's resources always needed to be supplemented, even before this disaster, this presents a bleak picture. However, there were some compensations. In return for giving up the claim to Lincoln, Thomas was permitted to retain possession of Southwell and its lands, and was given the priory church of St Oswald, Gloucester. William Rufus also increased his resources by granting the royal abbey of Selby to the archbishop.[49] Furthermore, the 'lands of St Peter', presumably those allocated to the canons, are separately listed in Domesday, and add up to about 270 carucates; while those of St John of Beverley amount to about 190 carucates.[50]

Nevertheless, Thomas I's achievements remain impressive. By 1075 he had restored the church, and the communal refectory and dormitory had been rebuilt. When, in 1075, the church was again destroyed by war, he had a new church built from the foundations upwards; and c.1090 he succeeded in gaining the land at the west end of the new church, where legal meetings were held by the canons, from William Rufus.[51] It also seems likely that he succeeded in transferring the main burials from the old church to the new one, since he was buried in the new cathedral in 1100, next to his predecessor, Ealdred, who was already installed there. He also reorganised the affairs of the cathedral in numerous ways, using his own property to build up the number of canons, and installing both officials to manage the affairs of the cathedral clergy, and archdeacons to aid in overseeing the

[46] Barr, 'The Minster Library', 490 and n. 18.
[47] The story of these adversities is recounted by Hugh the Chanter: for discussion see Hugh the Chanter, *The History of the Church of York*, xxx–xlv.
[48] Faull and Stinson, *Domesday Book 30, Yorkshire*, part 1, 302a,b–304b,c.
[49] Hugh the Chanter, *The History of the Church of York*, 25.
[50] *Domesday Book, Yorkshire*, 302a,b–304b,c.
[51] Hugh the Chanter, *The History of the Church of York*, 10–19.

diocese.[52] His decision to reorganise the canons as a set of individuals, each with his own prebend, is linked by Hugh the Chanter to the economic condition of the diocese. The plan, according to Hugh, was to divide 'some of the lands of St Peter's which were still waste' (this was in the 1090s) into separate prebends. Thus, an increased number of canons could be introduced, enlarging the traditional number of seven, and economic redevelopment would be encouraged, since each new canon would be 'eager to build on and cultivate his own share for his own sake.'[53] His skill in music and song is commented on by several writers, and it was presumably he, together with the dean, treasurer, precentor and *magister scholarum* whom he appointed, who was responsible for formulating, introducing and teaching the new liturgy of the cathedral. In general, he is described by Hugh as having 'adorned and furnished [the cathedral] to the best of his power with clerks, books and ornaments.'[54]

Hugh does not describe these books, and goes on to lament that they, in their turn, were largely lost in another fire, in 1137. Nevertheless, Barr's argument that, despite Hugh's beliefs, they would have been largely liturgical, is convincing.[55] A chapter of the type introduced in the 1090s would have had no need for a communal library; and the thirteenth-century statutes make no reference to such a library. But the cathedral will still have needed books, other than those for divine service. The speed with which Thomas appointed a *magister scholarum* which was done before the reorganisation of the chapter, according to Hugh, suggests an urgent need to begin the training of choristers, clerks and future canons. Assuming that this involved, as at Lincoln at the same time, the education of boys in a 'song school', then Latin primers and other school books will have been needed.[56] That the clerks were expected to be educated beyond this level, is suggested by Hugh's statement that Thomas personally required the *magister scholarum* to give lectures in the cathedral. It also seems that the canons could be married and

---

[52] For an interesting discussion of the post-Conquest chapter, see C. Brooke and R. M. T. Hill, 'From 627 until the Thirteenth Century', in Aylmer and Cant, *A History of York Minster*, 1–43, at 19–28.

[53] Hugh the Chanter, *The History of the Church of York*, 18/19. This suggests that the Chapter were as much involved in economic reorganisation as were the Yorkshire Augustinians. Evidence of considerable revival comes also from the royal demesne lands in Yorkshire. The manors of Aldborough and Knaresborough were worth £2 15s. in 1086, but were at farm to a royal official for £22 in 1129–30; in all of Yorkshire, the Terra Regis and customary payments totalled £262 in 1086, but the sheriff accounted for £471 in 1129–30, despite considerable alienation. See J. Green, 'William Rufus, Henry I and the Royal Demesne', *History* 64, 1979, 337–52, at 348.

[54] Hugh the Chanter, *The History of the Church of York*, 20/21.

[55] Barr, 'The Minster Library', 491.

[56] An account of the Lincoln school is given by Henry of Huntingdon, who was a pupil there. T. Arnold ed., *Henrici Huntendunensis historia Anglorum*, Rolls Series, 1879, 299, 301, 304.

thus, like the much better-recorded canons of St Paul's, responsible for the education of their sons and nephews, both in their households and by attendance at lectures.[57] Thurstan, archbishop of York 1119–40, and a man of education as well as of reforming principles and political skill, was himself a product of this system at St Paul's. Its operation at Lincoln in the late eleventh and early twelfth centuries is briefly described by one such pupil, the chronicler Henry of Huntingdon, whose father was an archdeacon, and who was taught by members of the chapter. Just how large the personal libraries of scholarly canons *could* be is demonstrated by a twelfth-century canon of Lincoln, who gave his collection of 140 books to Le Bec.[58] This example further demonstrates that such men felt under no obligation to give their books to their cathedral church even when a library did exist, as at Lincoln.[59]

The question of the books copied for, or collected by, the archbishops and the canons of the cathedral thus remains complex. It seems clear that there would have been a considerable need for scribes to produce liturgical books and school books. The *magister scholarum* will have needed at least basic patristic and theological works; while the archbishops would presumably have required books of canon law, not least for use in the primacy dispute into which they were plunged. Once the prebendal system was established, the canons, like the archbishops, would have been able to maintain clerks in their households, who were able to act as scribes. By the middle of the twelfth century the chapter was apparently wealthy, its lands, and the wealth of York itself, having recovered from their devastation. But York Minster in this period produced or housed no great scholars. It seems that Archbishop Gerard (1100–8) shared the contemporary concern, shown by many leading churchmen, to establish accurate texts for books of the Old Testament, and that he, like Stephen Harding at Cîteaux, was prepared to draw upon Jewish scholarship to this end. This is suggested by the fact that he had Hebrew texts of selected psalms copied.[60] It is also possible that this work enjoyed some reputation locally since it was at this time that Maurice, later prior of Kirkham, came to York to study Hebrew, and learnt Hebrew letters and calligraphy. Nevertheless, his opinion of the canons of York, and most

---

[57] For St Paul's, see Barlow, *The English Church 1066–1154*, 235, nn. 93, 94, 95.

[58] See R. M. Thomson, *Catalogue of the Manuscripts of Lincoln Cathedral Chapter Library*, Cambridge, 1989, xv.

[59] Another Lincoln example is Philip Apostolorum, a canon who, in 1187, gave six luxurious volumes, including a glossed Psalter, a glossed Gospels, a Bestiary and a Mappa Mundi to Worksop Priory. See X. Muratova, 'Bestiaries: An Aspect of Medieval Patronage', in S. Macready and R. H. Thompson, eds., *Art and Patronage in the English Romanesque*, Society of Antiquaries, Occasional Papers, n.s. 8, London, 1986, 118–44.

[60] Barlow, *The English Church 1066–1154*, 247.

particularly of their chant and liturgy, was uncomplimentary. He even claimed that the minster's text of the Canon of the Mass was corrupt, a claim which may have had some truth in it.[61] Henry Murdac (1147–53) did have scholarly interests, as well as being a leader of the local Cistercian movement, but his tenure was so disrupted by disputes and exile that he can have had little positive effect on the life of the minster. Perhaps more characteristic of the York chapter in the mid-century were William fitz Herbert, nephew of Stephen, treasurer of York, and Henry Murdac's rival; or Robert of Ghent, who combined the office of dean with being Stephen's chancellor. Perhaps the best known for their scholarly interests are dean Hugh, who entered Fountains in 1134 taking his collection of books with him, and Hugh the Chanter, the historian of Thurstan's struggle against Canterbury. Dean Hugh is described as a book-collector and historian, while Hugh the Chanter was skilled in law, was well-read, and could write polished latin verse, as well as his perceptive account of ecclesiastical politics.[62] These are impressive as individual accomplishments, but they do not suffice to present the minster as a centre for major scholarly activity.

The difficulty in coming to any clear assessment of York's contribution to the development of intellectual culture in Northumbria is made far greater by the almost complete absence of surviving late-eleventh and twelfth-century manuscripts from the minster. The most impressive survival is a pair of volumes which constitute two parts of what was probably originally a five-part Bible. This is now York, Minster Library, XVI Q 3 (see Plate 22). It is dated by Ker to the mid twelfth century, but could be as early as the late eleventh. Its script is in two major hands, one rather better than the other. Both show Anglo-Norman features, including an unusual form of the 'bus' abbreviation, but neither can be identified with hands in Durham books. However, a hand which appears for a brief stint, on fol. 21 of part ii, shows characteristics which link it to the Carilef Bible, and thus to Bayeux. This makes it very attractive to identify the Bible as part of the gift of books made by Archbishop Thomas I, himself once a canon of Bayeux, but the Bible (or at least, the surviving parts) have no inscription, and the *ex libris* in part iii comes from the end of the twelfth century. Another puzzling feature is that the decoration is incomplete, with several major initials, such as the 'Beatus B' for the opening of Psalm 1, having never been supplied. Elsewhere, small plain initials have been supplied in spaces rather too large for them, suggesting that a tentative scribe-artist attempted to make good some of the absences. Where more confident minor initials have been completed,

---

[61] Barlow, *The English Church 1066–1154*, 247

[62] For Dean Hugh's correspondence with Symeon of Durham, see Gransden, *Historical Writing in England*, 116; for his books, see Knowles, *Monastic Order*, 237.

their decorative features are those common *c.*1066–*c.*1100; that is, simple scallop patterns, florets and ball-and-bar motifs.

The most common colours are orange-red and dark green, and the green has eaten through the vellum in several places, something which is fairly common in Norman manuscripts but rarer in the twelfth century. Of the completed major initials, perhaps the most distinctive is the twelve-line-high U on fol. 1r of part ii. This is drawn in black ink, has a panelled construction, and is filled with simple stylised foliage of Anglo-Norman type. At the top of the upright is a knot of interlace, terminating in two profile beak-heads. These are of a type unusual in late Anglo-Saxon and Norman work, and are reminiscent of terminals on Franco-Saxon initials; it thus seems possible that this Bible may have had an early exemplar. By contrast, the stylised foliage used on the major initials fits clearly into the Anglo-Norman context. It is drawn in plain ink outline, and has a plumpness and simplicity of outline similar to that in the work of St Calais's Martyrology Scribe, or to that used on initials in some manuscripts from St Ouen, Rouen. However, the foliage, like the script of this Bible, cannot be exactly matched elsewhere. It therefore seems likely that the Bible was produced *c.*1100, by a group of scribes and artists brought together by an unknown patron. The suggestion of an early exemplar makes it tempting to speculate that it may have been copied from an early Bible surviving in York at that date; but of this there can be no proof, and a continental origin is equally likely. Nevertheless, the unpretentious appearance of this manuscript, and the incomplete state of its illumination, would fit well with the difficulties and financial strains experienced in York in the late eleventh century.

The other York Minster manuscript of *c.*1100, Bodleian, Laud Misc. 140, has several points of similarity with the Bible. It is a scholarly manuscript, a copy of Augustine's *De Trinitate*, prefaced by an extract from the *Retractations* and by the letter to Aurelius, all these being carefully identified. Its vellum is of high quality, being white and thin but not brittle, and it is copied in one hand throughout, the script being regular and uniform, and still showing some English characteristics. However, its decoration is very simple, being restricted in the main to titles and rubrics written in plain red minuscule, and to initials also in plain red, with minimal elaboration, and no stylised foliage. There are just three exceptions to this plainness, and what is interesting about these is their rather old-fashioned appearance. They are drawn in ink outline, with details in red, and use a rather sketchy line reminiscent of Anglo-Saxon, rather than Norman, drawing styles. The first, an eight-line d on fol. 2v, has a curving tail in the form of a piece of acanthus foliage also of Anglo-Saxon type, while another D on fol. 85r and a T on fol. 94r are constructed of short, plump dragons of the type found in Anglo-Saxon initials, rather than the more elongated and sinuous Norman types (see Fig. 55). Again there is a strong suggestion that these initials were copied from an old exemplar, though here perhaps an Anglo-Saxon manuscript of the tenth century. The book also has one other very interesting feature, and this is the handling of a serious mistake made by its scribe. Books XI and XII have been copied in the wrong order, although they are given the correct titles. The scribe notes the error clearly in the margin, so that there is no danger of confusion for the reader; and clear quire signatures run in order throughout. Another, smaller, error was the omission of the heading for chapter xvii of book II, which was entered in the margin, in the usual hand. All this makes the book clearly different from the more polished products of Durham, or of the scriptorium tentatively assigned to St Mary's, in whose work such basic mistakes do not occur. It is all the more surprising to find such mistakes in a manuscript written on high-quality vellum, and offering what appears to be a good, scholarly copy of the text, apparently taken from an exemplar of Anglo-Saxon origin. It seems that the most likely conclusion is that the original owner of the book was a man of some scholarly interests, and of some wealth, but without access to an established, high-quality scriptorium. Again, this seems to fit the situation of the clergy of York Minster at the beginning of the twelfth century.

From this examination of St Mary's and York Minster evidence has emerged which is interesting and suggestive, but cannot be conclusive. First, it now seems that St Mary's may have been active in building up a library in the first half of the twelfth century, and may also have had a

FIG. 55 Initial D from Oxford, Bodleian, MS Laud Misc. 140, fol. 85r

scriptorium able to produce books of good quality in a distinctive style. It also seems that members of the community, at least before the disruption of 1132, were active as painters, as well as pursuing interests in history and classical philosophy. The survival of the *Life of St Dunstan*, and of Ovid's *Epistolae ex Ponto* further suggests that the range of books available at St Mary's was in accordance with what was standard in Benedictine houses of the time, especially if the patristics listed in the later catalogue are taken into account. From the minster, the story is dominated by disasters and losses, but nevertheless the picture which emerges is of energetic rebuilding and reorganisation. That not all York's archive had been lost is suggested by the fact that its documents were accepted as genuine by the papal curia, while those of Canterbury were rejected as patent forgeries (as Hugh the Chanter recounts with relish).[63] This accords with the apparent survival of a group of pre-Conquest Gospel books, and suggests that the destruction at York may not have been quite so complete as chroniclers believed. Into this picture, the two surviving manuscripts of *c.*1100 associated with the minster fit rather well, in that they suggest a wish to supply basic books for services and for study, drawn from old exemplars, and executed by rather tentative scribes and artists using inexpensive pigments. In the absence of any surviving eleventh or twelfth-century manuscripts from the alien priory of Holy Trinity the examination of York must stop here: but it is hoped that enough evidence is now available to suggest that previous dismissals of York as a centre for intellectual activity or book production in this period may have been too sweeping.

[63] Hugh the Chanter, *The History of the Church of York*, 192-5.

CHAPTER SIX

&❧

Power and cultural identity

I: Durham and the anarchy

The reign of Stephen, and most particularly the years 1138–44, was a period of crisis in both the secular and the ecclesiastical politics of Northumbria, and of Durham in particular. During the first half of this unstable reign, Northumberland, much of the lands of St Cuthbert (the territory between Tyne and Tees) and Cumbria were effectively annexed by the king of the Scots, David I. Crucial to the success of this expansion was that the Scots gained temporary control of the great fortresses held by the bishop of Durham, namely Norham (which controlled the crossing of the River Tweed) and, briefly, Durham castle itself, regarded as an impregnable fortress after the further defensive works of Ranulf Flambard, who had also ordered the construction of Norham Castle.[1] The loyalty of the bishop and monastic community of Durham (whose prior claimed to deputise for the bishop during vacancies or absences) thus became even more politically important during this period.[2] Moreover, the Scots succeeded in taking Norham Castle by force, and very nearly succeeded in gaining control of the bishopric of Durham by guile. It was the determination of the prior and monks of Durham, fixedly hostile to being controlled by a man whom they saw as a tool of the king of Scots, which played the central role in defeating the Scottish expansion. Thus, it may be argued that it was the political and cultural identity of the community of Durham which determined the history of the region in this period. This chapter will therefore examine this issue, in preparation for a discussion of the books of the period, which will follow in Chapter 7.

---

[1] On Flambard's career and building activities see Simeon, *Libellus*, in Arnold, i, 135–41; and Reginald, *De Admirandis*, 101 and 205; also obituary in *Liber Vitae Ecclesiae Dunelmensis*, ed. J. Stevenson, Surtees Society 13, 1841. See also R. W. Southern, 'Ranulf Flambard', in his *Medieval Humanism and Other Studies*, Oxford, 1970, 183–205; and J. O. Prestwich, 'The Career of Ranulf Flambard', in Rollason *et al.*, *Anglo-Norman Durham*, 299–310.

[2] For the importance of the priors, see W. M. Aird, 'The Origins and Development of the Church of St Cuthbert, 635–1153, with Special Reference to Durham in the Period 1071–1153', unpublished Ph.D. thesis, University of Edinburgh, 1991, 193–259.

Across the twelfth century, the kingdom of England was in process of emerging as a territorial state, held together by the power, and the law, of its king. This placed a particular emphasis on border regions and, during the reign of Stephen, the politics of the Scottish marches and of Bernicia were further complicated by dynastic struggle between Stephen and the empress Matilda, daughter of Henry I. Matilda's mother, Edith-Matilda, was the daughter of Malcolm III of Scotland and of St Margaret, a princess of the royal house of Wessex. David I, Edith-Matilda's youngest brother, was thus Matilda's uncle, and declared his support for her claim to England.[3] As early as 1136 this gave him a reason to invade Cumbria and Northumberland, claiming Cumbria as a rightful possession of the kings of Scots, and Northumberland through his wife, Maud, who was the granddaughter of the last Anglo-Danish earl of Northumbria, and only daughter of Earl Waltheof.[4] Through this marriage, granted to him by Henry I, he had already gained the earldom of Huntingdon, which he retained when he became king of Scots. His early training at Henry I's court also meant that he was familiar with the Anglo-Norman aristocracy of England, and with the Anglo-Norman style of government. Indeed, he introduced Anglo-Normans as chancellor, steward and constable, and began to create an Anglo-Norman landholding aristocracy in the border regions of Lothian and Teviotdale.[5] For all these reasons, a contradictory situation developed in northern England. At the very time when the definitions of territorial boundaries, and of feudal loyalty, were becoming increasingly significant, many of the leading baronial families of the border region, such as Brus, Balliol and Moreville, found themselves holding land from both Stephen and David.[6] Many of them resolved the issue by giving their support to David, and thus Stephen increasingly lost control of the far north. The First Treaty of Durham, in 1136, effectively recognised David's occupation of Cumberland and Northumberland, as well as granting the honour of Huntingdon, with the important base of Doncaster, in Yorkshire, to Henry, David's heir.[7]

---

[3] This was despite the fact that Stephen's wife, Matilda, was also David's niece, as she was the daughter of Eustace III, Count of Boulogne, and of Mary, David's youngest sister. For Genealogical Table, see F. Barlow, *The Feudal Kingdom of England, 1042–1216*, 4th edn, London and New York, 1988, 452–3.

[4] For discussion, see G. W. S. Barrow, *David I of Scotland (1124–1153): The Balance of New and Old*, Stenton Lecture, 1984, Univ. of Reading, 1985; and P. Dalton, *Conquest, Anarchy and Lordship: Yorkshire 1066–1154*, Cambridge, 1994, 203–11.

[5] See Barrow, *David I*; G. W. S. Barrow, 'The Anglo-Scottish Border', in *The Kingdom of the Scots*, London, 1973, 139–61; and J. Green, 'Aristocratic Loyalties on the Northern Frontier of England, c.1100–1174', in D. Williams, ed., *England in the Twelfth Century. Proceedings of the 1988 Harlaxton Symposium*, Woodbridge, 1990, 83–100.

[6] See Green, 'Aristocratic Loyalties', and Dalton, *Conquest*, 203–11.

[7] See R. Lomas, *North-East England in the Middle Ages*, Edinburgh, 1992, 34.

This placed Durham once again effectively on the border between England and Scotland, and made its territory and fortress of great significance. Its strategic importance was marked by the First Treaty of Durham in 1136, and further emphasised in 1139. In this year, the Second Treaty of Durham recognised Prince Henry of Scotland as earl of Northumberland, while stressing that the lands of St Cuthbert were excluded from this.[8] The bishop of Durham was thus placed in a delicate position. Since 1133 the bishop had been Geoffrey Rufus, once Henry I's chancellor, and appointed to Durham by Henry I. His political and administrative skills were therefore high, and it is a testimony to them that, during his episcopate, Durham and the lands of St Cuthbert suffered relatively little disruption. This is confirmed also by Aird's recent analysis, though his contention that the people of St Cuthbert could have allied with the kings of Scots, and did not identify themselves as hostile to the Scots, is a little surprising in the light of the negative image of the Scots given in virtually all the Durham sources and of the expressed views of Laurence of Durham.[9] It may also have helped that the Anglo-Norman chancellor of Scotland, William Cumin, had been Geoffrey Rufus' pupil and protégé as a chancery clerk, and seems to have had the custom of paying friendly visits to Durham. Geoffrey Rufus maintained his loyalty to Stephen until his death, but put up only a weak defence of Norham Castle, and did not intervene in the Scottish invasions and annexations of 1136 and 1138/9. Thus the Scottish army, advancing across Richmondshire in 1138, was only stopped by an army gathered by Thurstan, the archbishop of York. The only comfort which the Durham chronicler could find was to point out that the Battle of the Standard, which forced the Scots to retreat from Yorkshire, was fought near Northallerton, on land belonging to St Cuthbert.[10] This left Durham still effectively the key to the Anglo-Scottish border, and it was at this stage that, late in 1140, Geoffrey Rufus became mortally ill.

It was the subsequent death of Geoffrey Rufus, early in 1141, which was to begin perhaps the most dramatic sequence of events at Durham in the twelfth century. But in order to understand the issues, it is important to consider briefly the religious and cultural aspects of Durham's relations with Scotland. If attention is moved away from dynastic politics, and on to the cult of St Cuthbert, then a different picture emerges, in which Durham appears, not as a stronghold of English royal influence, but as the centre of a network

---

[8] Lomas, *North-East England*, 34–5; Dalton, *Conquest*, 205–8.

[9] See A. Young, *William Cumin: Border Politics and the Bishopric of Durham 1141–1144*, Borthwick Papers 54, York, 1979, 5–10. See also Aird, *St Cuthbert and the Normans*, ch. 6 and especially 231 and 259–65.

[10] Arnold, ii, 293.

of traditions, influences, prayer associations and spiritual allegiances. St Cuthbert himself was an embodiment of the border region, having been born near Lammermuir (then in Northumbria), and trained and educated by Irish monks at Melrose. As prior of Melrose he preached throughout the region, sometimes travelling for a month at a time. Again, as bishop of Lindisfarne, he not only travelled throughout his own diocese, but visited Hexham and Carlisle, as well as maintaining contact with Melrose and the bishop of Abercorn (near Edinburgh). G. W. S. Barrow points out that some thirty-three dedications of churches to St Cuthbert can be traced in S. Scotland by the late twelfth century, and argues that Cuthbert 'may be claimed as one of the greatest and most influential of Scottish saints'.[11] The cult seems to have remained genuinely popular into the eleventh century, although the Community of St Cuthbert lost control of its territories north of the Tweed.[12] In the late eleventh century, the cult received further support from St Margaret, probably influenced by her confessor, Turgot, who was prior of Durham and then bishop of St Andrews.[13] Her husband, Malcolm III, also showed devotion to St Cuthbert, and was the only layman to take part in the ceremonial laying of the foundation stone of the new cathedral of Durham in 1093.[14] The Scottish royal house also entered into confraternity with Durham at this time, on terms which placed them at least equal with King Athelstan, including the stipulation that the anniversary of the deaths of the king and queen should be celebrated as an annual festival.[15] In return, although only precariously, Edgar confirmed and restored to Durham Coldinghamshire and Berwickshire. Even when Ranulf Flambard's hostility to the Scots led to the revocation of this grant, Edgar showed a wish to maintain friendly relations with St Cuthbert and his monks by granting three large estates to them.[16] Moreover, in 1104 it was Alexander, Edgar's brother, who was again the only layman to participate in a major ceremony at Durham, this time the opening of St Cuthbert's coffin.[17] Finally, in the 1130s and 1140s, Coldingham was officially established as a priory of Durham.[18] That popular reverence for St Cuthbert continued is shown by Reginald of Durham's collection of miracle stories. These involve Kirkcudbright in Galloway, a church dedicated to St Cuthbert in Lothian, a chapel at Slitrig, and a church at Cavers in Roxburghshire.[19] Reginald also testifies

[11] G. W. S. Barrow, 'The Kings of Scotland and Durham', in Rollason et al., Anglo-Norman Durham, 311–24, at 312. [12] Ibid.
[13] See Baker, '"A nursery of saints"'; also Barrow, 'Kings of Scotland and Durham', 313.
[14] V. Wall, 'Malcolm III and the Foundation of Durham Cathedral', in Rollason et al., Anglo-Norman Durham, 325–38.
[15] Barrow, 'Kings of Scotland and Durham', 313–15.
[16] Ibid. [17] Ibid. [18] Burton, Monastic and Religious Orders, 35.
[19] Reginald, De Admirandis, cap. lxxxiv–lxxxviii, cxxxvi.

that, at least in Lothian, the 'peace of St Cuthbert' was recognised in and around his churches. Pilgrims also came to Farne and to Durham from Lothian, while the Durham monks took relics of the saint on a preaching tour as far as Perth and Dunfermline.[20]

Besides this network of contacts created by the cult of St Cuthbert, the cultural links between Durham and Scotland can be investigated by examining surviving twelfth-century churches and manuscripts. The evidence of the manuscripts is bafflingly sparse. Only eight Scottish houses show any surviving manuscripts from the twelfth century, and these produce a grand total of some ten volumes. None of them shows evidence of direct influence from Durham, but none of them are from houses which had any recorded direct link with Durham.[21] St Andrews, which might have been influenced through Turgot and the Scottish royal house, has no surviving manuscripts earlier than the thirteenth century; the same is true of Dunfermline. The evidence from Melrose is especially disappointing. Durham's claims to Old Melrose were recognised by David I, although Melrose was eventually refounded by David himself in 1136, as a Cistercian house, the daughter of Rievaulx, of which he was a patron (and where his steward, Aelred, had become a monk in 1134).[22] Only one manuscript survives from Melrose, a short chronicle of c. 1200, now in the Cotton collection.[23] This shows no sign of artistic influence from Durham. Melrose's own daughter, Holm Cultram in Cumbria, shows four twelfth-century manuscripts, of which one uses the Durham split-petal motif. However, since this motif was ubiquitous in Rievaulx books, it is difficult to know precisely by what route it reached Holm Cultram. If it was from Melrose, this still leaves the question of whether Melrose adopted it from Rievaulx or from Durham.[24]

However, if the manuscript evidence is disappointing, Eric Fernie's examination of architectural evidence produces much more positive results. Perhaps most striking is the case of Dunfermline Abbey, in Fife. This was begun in 1128, and was under construction throughout the reign of David I. Its elevation, rib vaults, decorated piers, chevrons and moulding profiles all show Durham influence. Moreover, the four piers with incised decoration seem to have marked the site of the tomb of St Margaret, at the nave altar. Fernie is surely correct in linking this to the use of similar piers at Durham to mark the main sanctuary and transept chapels. It thus seems, as Fernie argues,

[20] Reginald, *De Admirandis*, cap. xxxv, xcvii, xcviii, cii.
[21] See Ker, *Medieval Libraries*, Coupar Angus (54); Holyrood (102); Loch Leven (120); Isle of May (130); Melrose (130); Sweetheart (184).
[22] Burton, *Monastic and Religious Orders*, 72.
[23] Now BL Cotton Faustina B ix, fols. 2–75.
[24] For the Rievaulx manuscripts using this motif, see Chapter 9.

that 'the Scottish crown chose Durham Cathedral as a model for what was evidently intended to be its dynastic burial church'.[25] As far away as Orkney, Earl Ronald chose Durham as the model for the new cathedral at Kirkwall, begun in 1137, only four years after Durham itself was completed.[26]

It thus seems that, from the Scottish point of view, St Cuthbert and his shrine were the focus of general reverence, both popular and royal. It has even been suggested that, in their incursions into northern England, the Scots deliberately avoided attacking Lindisfarne and Durham, out of reverence for St Cuthbert.[27] The strength of the early-twelfth-century links between the Scottish royal house and the cult of St Cuthbert has already been demonstrated. Members of the Scottish baronage were also prepared to enter into feudal agreements with the monks of Durham. Most notably, Prior Roger entered into an agreement in 1131 with Dolfin, son of Uhtred. The prior and convent ceded Straindrop and Staindropshire to Dolfin and his heirs, and in return Dolfin became the liegeman of St Cuthbert, the prior, and the monks.[28] None of this, however, seems to have made any impact on the monastic community's attitude towards the Scots, which was strikingly negative. The Scots are uniformly portrayed as savage raiders, bloodthirsty and destructive. The Durham chronicle, the *Historia Regum*, paints a horrifying picture of the 'ferocity', 'craftiness' and 'savagery' of the Scottish raid into Cumberland and Northumberland, led by Malcolm III in 1070. The chronicler declares that 'the Scots, more savage than wild beasts, delighted in cruelty, as an amusing spectacle' and, after horrific slaughter of children and the elderly, drove off the young into slavery.[29] Similar epithets are used of the raid in 1081, and when Malcolm and his eldest son, Edward, were killed by a Northumbrian force during another raid in 1093, the Durham chronicler wrote: 'In this death the justice of an avenging God was plainly manifested; for this man perished in that province which he had been often wont to ravage, instigated by avarice, for five times he had wasted it with a savage devastation, and carried captive the wretched natives to reduce them to slavery.'[30]

In the use of such language, the author of the *Historia Regum* is not exceptional. His continuator, John, prior of Hexham, who updated the chronicle in the 1160s, goes further. In his account of the Battle of the

[25] Fernie, 'Architectural Influence', 272.
[26] Ibid.
[27] See *Capitula (Liber) de Miraculis et Translationibus Sancti Cuthberti*, in Arnold, i, 229–61, at ch. 10, 338–44.
[28] See Lomas, *North-East England*, 29.
[29] *Historia Regum*, ed. Arnold, ii, 3–283, *sub anno* 1070.
[30] Ibid. *sub anno* 1093. The translations are taken from J. Stevenson, *The Church Historians of England*, vol. iii, part 2, London, 1855, 139 and 159.

Standard, the Scots are again depicted as destructive, fierce and predatory, while the 'Picts', who also supposedly made up part of the Scottish army, are described, quite literally, as naked savages.[31] The anonymous Durham monk, who wrote a continuation of the *Libellus*, does not go as far as this. Nevertheless, his account of the incursions of the 1130s is full of the same hostility towards the Scots.[32] It could thus be argued that the view of the Scots put forward by Durham authors in the twelfth century amounts almost to a negative stereotype.[33] Something similar is also found in the depiction of the Scottish army in one of the miniatures of Univ. 165. This is of considerable importance for understanding the events which took place at Durham from 1141 to 1144.

Briefly, what happened was that William Cumin, King David's chancellor, visited Geoffrey Rufus at Durham at the end of 1140, and realised that he was near to death. Making sure that he had the support of King David, he persuaded the castellans of Durham to hand the castle over to him. He also obtained the support of those baronial families who had given their allegiance to David, and of the senior archdeacon of Durham, Robert, who had recently been humiliated by the prior.[34] It was now early 1141, and King Stephen appeared to have lost the throne of England, having been taken prisoner by Matilda's supporters after the Battle of Lincoln. York was also in turmoil, because of the controversy over who should succeed Archbishop Thurstan, who had died in 1140. The impact of this controversy is discussed in another chapter, but the lack of an effective archbishop of York at this time was also significant for Durham. With Cumin in effective control in Durham, King David arrived, and claimed 'all things' in the name of his niece, the empress Matilda. He also installed Cumin as keeper of Durham. However, Prior Roger, the monks of Durham and Ranulf, nephew of Ranulf Flambard, the other archdeacon, were opposed to Cumin, and refused to elect him as bishop.[35] Cumin and David, with supporters from Durham, therefore set off to Matilda's court, now in London, in order that she might appoint Cumin as

---

[31] John of Hexham, *Continuatio*, in Arnold, ii, 289–95.

[32] *Continuatio Prima*, in Arnold, i, 152–5.

[33] To some extent, this negative stereotype was already present in such older sources as the story of the army of Scots swallowed up by the earth, which was incorporated into the collection of miracles added to Bede's *Life of St Cuthbert* in Durham copies. In Oxford, University College MS 165, the story is illustrated, and the Scots are shown as roughly dressed and barbarous. It is also probable that this negative view was revived, when Durham's hopes of extending its influence into Scotland were increasingly disappointed (I am grateful to Prof. Donald Matthew for this suggestion).

[34] The story is told in a continuation to Symeon's *Libellus*, in Durham UL Cosin V ii 6, fols. 103–13; see Arnold, i, 143–60. The fullest discussion is Young, *William Cumin*.

[35] For a translation of the account, here referred to as *Continuation*, see Stevenson, *Church Historians*, iii, 2, 712–30.

bishop. This plan was forestalled by the people of London, who forced the empress and her court to flee on the very day when the investiture was due to take place. David, Cumin and their supporters managed to reach Durham, bringing the empress's instruction that Cumin should be elected bishop. Nevertheless, Prior Roger and Archdeacon Ranulf still refused to hold a canonical election and, faced with this impasse, David returned to Scotland in 1141, leaving Cumin in Durham as his castellan.[36] Cumin then required oaths of fealty from the citizens of Durham, and from the barons of the bishopric, as *de facto* bishop; he also dispossessed Archdeacon Ranulf and forced him to flee. But the prior and monks, rejecting friendly overtures from Cumin, maintained their refusal to elect him despite their isolation.[37]

The crisis continued through 1142, although military fortunes changed. Stephen was released and David, though he still held Northumberland, lost Huntingdon and the honour of Lancaster. He also seems to have decided that the attempt to control Durham had failed, and withdrew his support from Cumin. Nevertheless, he did not abandon the project altogether.[38] Cumin was, by now, effectively blockading the priory, but Prior Roger escaped, and reached York. Despite armed intervention by Cumin and his supporters, an election was held at York in 1143, with the support of the Pope, and the dean of York, William de Ste Barbe, was elected. In response to this news, Cumin increased his hostility towards the monks. Cumin next decided to take control of the monastery, for fear that the monks would help Ste Barbe to enter Durham. The monks locked themselves into the cathedral, and gathered around the shrine of St Cuthbert. However, Cumin's soldiers stormed the cathedral, attempting to batter down the doors before breaking in through the windows. The monks were powerless, and were taken prisoner, being effectively confined to their domestic buildings, while the soldiers occupied the priory, using the cathedral as a barracks.[39] The most hostile monks, including Laurence, the future prior, were driven out with only the clothes they were wearing. Nevertheless, Cumin seems to have foreseen ultimate failure, as his men now began to strip the diocese of wealth, doing much damage to both Durham and the surrounding region. The end of the affair, which came in August 1144, was ironic. Cumin had allied with William of Aumale, earl of York, described by chroniclers as effectively king

---

[36] Stevenson, *Church Historians*, iii, 2, 720; Arnold, i, 146.

[37] Ibid.

[38] This is demonstrated by the sending of Herebert, abbot of Roxburgh or Kelso, to ask the prior and monastic officials for a final reply about the acceptability of Cumin; and by Cumin's subsequent attempt to trick David into renewing his support. See Stevenson, *Church Historians*, iii, 2, 720–1; Arnold, i, 146–8. For a slightly different interpretation see Young, *William Cumin*, 17.

[39] Ibid.

in Yorkshire; but Ste Barbe obtained the support of David, and of his son, Prince Henry, still earl of Northumberland.[40] It was when Ste Barbe arrived at Durham with Prince Henry and a Scottish army that Cumin was finally forced to surrender, after much of Durham had been destroyed (by the Scots, according to the Durham chroniclers).[41]

These events explain the assertion made at the beginning of this chapter, that it was the Durham monks who played the key role in preventing Durham from becoming a Scottish-controlled diocese. The failure at Durham did not mean an immediate collapse in Scottish control of Northumberland and Cumbria; that was still recognised in 1149, when Henry of Anjou recognised his great-uncle's control of Cumbria, Carlisle and all the land between the Tweed and the Tyne.[42] It was only brought to an end after 1153, when border politics were changed by the deaths of both Stephen and David, and ecclesiastical politics were transformed by the deaths of the Cistercian pope, Eugenius III, of St Bernard of Clairvaux, of Henry Murdac, the Cistercian archbishop of York, and of William de Ste Barbe, bishop of Durham. It was then that William fitz Herbert, nephew of Stephen, was finally able to take up his long-deferred appointment to York, and that the clergy and priory of Durham, with the encouragement of Henry of Blois, elected Hugh du Puiset, treasurer of York and another royal nephew, as their bishop.[43] By doing so, they were effectively rejecting the policies of Henry Murdac, who from 1149 had been seeking David's support, and rejecting also Scottish influence, by choosing a member of the short-lived royal house of Blois. This election thus seems a clear statement of intent by the community of Durham. The more difficult question is why the monks of Durham were so very determined to resist William Cumin.

Historians have tended to the view that the monks of Durham saw Cumin as an 'independent adventurer', and that their rejection of him was based on the determination to uphold their rights and privileges which they displayed with some fervour throughout the twelfth century.[44] In this account, Cumin's role as a stalking-horse for King David is given only a secondary place. However, this view does not entirely match the ideas expressed by the monastic writers of Durham. Both the anonymous monk who continued the *Historia Regum*, and Laurence of Durham in his *Dialogues*, stress that it was the king of Scots who sent Cumin. Laurence stresses this twice:

---

[40] Stevenson, *Church Historians*, iii, 2, 729; Arnold, i, 159.
[41] See Young, *William Cumin*, 26–7.
[42] See Lomas, *North-East England*, 37.
[43] Stevenson, *Church Historians*, iii, 2, 730; Arnold, i, 160.
[44] See Young, *William Cumin*, 10, and Aird, *St Cuthbert and the Normans*, 262.

Cives, Petre, meos Albania fecit egentes,
Quos fecisse rudes juribus, arte nequit.
Ignes non leges, caedes non scita, dolores
Nobis non mores hactena ipsa dedit.
Et dedit horrendum, quod abhorret et ipsa, Cuminum;
Hinc urbs nostra perit; plebs ruit; exul agor.

dum fraude sua ferus ille Cuminus
Hunc adit, Albano rege juvante, locum.[45]

It is thus the fact that Cumin was sent by Scotland, and that he did damage to
Durham and its lands and people, just as Scottish armies did, which is
stressed; the injury to the legal rights of the monks is not mentioned. Clearly,
it might be naive to expect that such a motive would be given prominence in
epic verse, but this does not mean that abhorrence of the Scots should be
discounted as a motive. It is thus of some importance to discover what was
central in the Durham monks' sense of their own identity, in order to
understand their loyalties. The evidence of their books can be central here,
as can their relationship to the cult of their saint.

The surviving Durham manuscripts datable to c. 1 1 2 5–5 5 will be discussed
in detail below. One general point may be made here, namely that they
follow much the same lines of stylistic development as manuscripts from the
great monasteries of southern England, although they are noticeably less
luxurious in their use of miniatures and gold leaf. It is also worth observing
that they are fewer in number than might be expected, suggesting that the
disruption and economic setbacks of the period may have affected the
priory's capacity to produce books. Nevertheless, the texts of many of the
surviving manuscripts, like the evidence of the mid-twelfth-century book-list,
demonstrate that Durham was very much in the mainstream of European
theological and intellectual development, as will be seen.[46] Of more local
interest are no less than six volumes of works by Bede; as well as a *Life of St
Godric*. But surprisingly, there are no illustrated copies of the *Life of St
Cuthbert* surviving from this period, and no new collection of miracles was
made until the 1160s, and then only at the direct instigation of Aelred of
Rievaulx. This slackening in the promotion of the cult has been observed also
by Victoria Tudor, who suggests that the Durham monks may have become
complacent about their saint, and seen no need to make his shrine more
attractive.[47] It may perhaps be complemented by the absence of any major
building project between 1133, when the new cathedral, and the new priory

[45] Laurence of Durham, *Dialogi*, 4 and 12.
[46] See Chapter 7.
[47] V. Tudor, 'Reginald of Durham and St Godric of Finchale: A Study of a Twelfth-Century
Hagiographer and His Major Subject', unpublished thesis, University of Reading, 1979.

on Lindisfarne, were apparently completed, and the 1160s, when Bishop Hugh du Puiset began the work on the Galilee Chapel.[48]

The picture produced by this evidence is complex and interesting. That the Durham monks maintained, and even developed, an interest in Bede is clear; indeed, Bede seems of more interest during this time than St Cuthbert.[49] It is difficult to imagine that the Durham community were becoming less attached to their great saint; but there does appear to have been less fervour than there was at the beginning of the twelfth century. St Cuthbert's association with the border region, and the strength of his cult in Scotland, may have made him an ambiguous figure, at a time when a sense of English identity was becoming sharper amongst the monastic community. It is striking that neither Reginald nor Laurence of Durham attribute Cumin's defeat directly to St Cuthbert.[50] Indeed, the whole episode must have been difficult to assimilate, as St Cuthbert allowed his shrine and his community to be violated by an intruder, and, most difficult of all, they were finally rescued by the Scots. Laurence of Durham omits this aspect of the affair altogether, stressing that Cumin had a sudden change of heart, brought about by God.[51]

Laurence of Durham himself may be taken as an exemplary figure here, as he was highly regarded in Durham, and played an important role in the events of 1141–4. Most of what is known of his life and career comes from his own writings, most particularly the *Dialogues*, his poetic account of Cumin's invasion of Durham, and the *Hypognosticon*, his verse paraphrase of parts of the Bible.[52] He was born at Waltham, and was educated at the priory originally founded there by King Harold. This he describes in glowing terms, as well as going into some detail on his training in composition in Latin verse and prose, the liturgy and singing.[53] Waltham was granted to Walcher, and then to William of St Calais, and it was the latter who expelled the canons and introduced Benedictine monks.[54] While still young, Laurence left Waltham and became a novice at Durham, perhaps because of the changes made by Henry I. He apparently continued his education there; he stresses that he has studied both the trivium and the quadrivium, and mentions Plato, Plotinus

[48] For the dating of the building of the Galilee, see S. Harrison, 'Observations of the Architecture of the Galilee Chapel', in Rollason *et al.*, *Anglo-Norman Durham*, 212–21, at 213.

[49] See Chapter 10.

[50] Reginald is silent on the whole event, while Laurence speaks only of how Cumin was changed 'Gratia solo Dei' (*Dialogi*, 38), even after stressing the desecration of the cathedral (29).

[51] *Dialogi*, 38 and 39.

[52] On his career, see particularly Raine, Preface, ch. ii, *Dialogi* xxvii–xxxviii. Laurence's main account of himself is *Dialogi*, Liber III, 365 to end and Liber IV, 1–179 (41–51). See also A. Hoste, 'A Survey of the Unedited Work of Laurence of Durham with an Edition of His Letter to Aelred of Rievaulx', *Sacris Erudiri* 2, 1960, 249–65.

[53] Ibid.

[54] See Symeon, *Libellus*, lib. III, cap. xxiii; Arnold, i, 113–15.

and Virgil as favoured authors.[55] At some time before 1143, he seems to have travelled in France; he owned copies of the sermons of St Bernard, as well as Psalters with the glosses of Master Anselm and Master Ivo.[56] In 1143, St Bernard and William, abbot of Rievaulx, wrote to Prior Roger of Durham, suggesting that Laurence be elected as bishop of Durham.[57] He was precentor of Durham, and chaplain and 'receiver-general' to Geoffrey Rufus. He also began to make his metrical version of the Bible, completing it in its final form by 1133.[58] Having been expelled from Durham by Cumin, he seems to have gone back to Waltham, but returned in 1143, and wrote his *Dialogues* between then and 1149, when be became prior. In 1153, he took a leading part in the controversial election of Hugh du Puiset and resisted all pressure, including from St Bernard.[59]

He was clearly an influential figure, and may have played some part in the education of Aelred of Rievaulx. Certainly he wrote to Aelred, addressing him as a friend; even though this was a standard part of twelfth-century epistolary composition, it was expected to contain some element of truth.[60] It may have been partly due to his influence that Master Robert of Adington, who had studied at St Victor, gave his books to Durham.[61] The training at Durham of both Laurence and Maurice, another author, who later became a Cistercian at Rievaulx, where he was noted for his scholarship, says much about the intellectual and theological standards of Durham in the first third of the twelfth century.[62] There is also evidence that, whilst Laurence was prior, Durham supported scholars who were not monks. In 1153, Laurence was a leading member of the Durham party which accompanied Hugh du Puiset on his visit to Rome, to put his case to the Pope. Another member of the party, described as a clerk of Durham, was the confusingly named Master Laurence, who was already resident at the priory, and who knew Godric of Finchale. His exact area of expertise is unknown, but he is described as 'Magister', suggesting that he had studied in the schools, and he was considered important enough to be made a member of the embassy to Rome. This status may have been partly based upon his having studied as a

[55] See (52) above.

[56] See G. E. Croydon, 'Abbot Laurence of Westminster and Hugh of St Victor', *Medieval and Renaissance Studies* 2, 1950, 169–71, at 171; and Raine, Preface to Laurence, *Dialogi*, xxxv.

[57] The text of the letter is copied in DCL B IV 24, fol. 74r.

[58] Raine, in Laurence, *Dialogi*, xxx–xxxi.

[59] Ibid. xxxii–xxxiii.

[60] On the letter, see *The Life of Ailred of Rievaulx by Walter Daniel*, ed. and trans. F. M. Powicke, London, 1950, xl.

[61] Master Laurence, who left Durham for St Albans and Westminster, had been a pupil of St Hugh, and may also have been influential. See Croydon, 'Abbot Laurence'.

[62] On Maurice, see F. M. Powicke, 'Maurice of Rievaulx', *English Historical Review* 36, 1921, 17–25.

pupil of Hugh of St Victor, and acted as the master's secretary.[63] In the event he travelled no further than St Albans, where he became a monk, finally achieving the elevated position of abbot of Westminster in 1160. Prior Laurence himself died in France on the return journey to England but, whilst in Rome, he made a positive impression on Pope Anastasius IV, telling him of the miracles of St Cuthbert.[64]

It is unfortunate that Laurence gives no description of education at Durham, as he does for Waltham. Nevertheless, the information presented here is sufficient to demonstrate that the intellectual achievements of the community of Durham could be high. Leading members of the priory were in contact with the schools of both St Victor and of St Bernard of Clairvaux, while alumni of Durham made positive impressions at Rievaulx, Fountains, St Albans and Westminster. Clearly, this is the milieu in which the monks of Durham located themselves, and it represents a positive part of their identity. Its negative element was their scornful rejection of the Scots, and their participation in the construction of what amounts almost to a racial stereotype of the Scots en masse as savage, greedy, uncivilised and destructive. That this was in some tension with the popularity of the cult of St Cuthbert in the Scottish Lowlands seems very likely, and it seems that this was a tension which the monks of Durham found difficult to resolve. A further tension may well have been that the kings of Scots pursued a policy of rebuffing Durham's attempts to recover lost lands and subordinate houses, and kept Durham's representatives out of the Scottish episcopate.[65] Had their attitudes to the Scots been more flexible, as presumably were those of the secular aristocrats who pledged themselves to King David, then the history of the region might have been very different.

---

[63] See Raine, in Laurence, *Dialogi*, xxxi.

[64] Ibid.

[65] I am indebted to Prof. Donald Matthew for this suggestion. The effectiveness of the Durham opposition is corroborated by G. W. S. Barrow, who writes ('The Kings of Scotland and Durham', 322–3): 'If we seek the single most effective obstacle to the achievement of [King David's vision of a Scoto-Northumbrian realm] we must surely find it in the church, community and bishopric of Durham.'

&

CHAPTER SEVEN

Power and cultural identity
II: Durham and its books *c.* I I 20–*c.* I I 60

The previous chapter looked at William Cumin's attempt to annex Durham, with the support of the king of Scots, and at the attitudes towards the Scots manifested by Durham writers of the period. It was argued that the Durham monks both resented Scottish infringement of their rights and territories, and saw themselves as culturally superior to the Scots. The careers of Durham's leading scholars, Laurence of Durham, Magister Laurence and Maurice of Rievaulx were argued to show interest in the schools of France and the monasteries of England – but no interest in Scotland. It even appears that enthusiasm for the cult of St Cuthbert slackened in this period, perhaps as a result of the traumatic events of the early 1140s; while the reputation of the scholarly Bede, a loyal Northumbrian, was undiminished. Two further sources of evidence for Durham's cultural development in the mid-century remain to be examined, namely the library list and the surviving manuscripts.[1]

PART I
The evidence of the library list

This list survives in DCL B IV 24, called the 'Durham Cantor's Book' by Piper and Gullick, and is entered into that compound manuscript in a mid-century hand.[2] Its presence in this book, which contains a selection of texts central to the running of the priory, suggests that it was intended primarily as a working list for the official responsible for the care and distribution of the book collection. Its arrangement certainly suggests that books are listed in the groups in which they were kept and used. For instance, complete Bibles

---

[1] The mid-twelfth-century library list is entered on fols. 1r–2r of DCL B IV 24, and printed in *Catalogi Veteres*, 1–10.

[2] See Piper, 'The Durham Cantor's Book'; and Gullick, 'The Scribes of the Durham Cantor's Book'.

and collections of canon law, which would be amongst the largest books in the collection, are listed first. Towards the end comes a group of Psalters, many with the names of the monks who presented them, and who are currently using them, noted. Towards the middle of the list is what appears to be a large set of school books, on grammar and dialectics, while an attempt has also been made to group the works of the Church Fathers together. There is also a group of books suitable for reading in the refectory which are listed together, and may well have been separately stored. Finally, liturgical manuscripts are not included, and it also appears that books belonging to the shrine of St Cuthbert are missing from this list. Thus, the books listed here appear to be chiefly those available for the school, for novices, for reading aloud in the refectory, for the *lectio divina* and for consultation by the officials and scholars of the priory.

There is no indication of how the books were obtained, and it is interesting that those given by St Calais appear to have been silently integrated with the other books of their kinds, since their authors or titles appear here, but without any mention of St Calais himself. By contrast, there is a brief entry for 'Libri iii Pr. Algari', though their contents are not noted. An impressive collection of medical works, given by 'Magister Herebertus Medicus' is added at the end, after lists of donations made by priors, apparently after the compilation of the main list was completed. The main list appears to have been drawn up after the death in 1137 of Prior Algar, whose books are included, and before the death in 1153 of Prior Laurence, whose donation is listed separately at the end. It therefore seems likely to have been drawn up under Prior Roger (1137–49), and thus at the very time when the life of the priory was suffering disruption. Indeed, it is tempting to link the compilation of the list with the reorganisation and tidying-up which must have been necessary if the cathedral was indeed used as a barracks by Cumin's soldiers in 1143, with the monks confined to their domestic buildings. However, this can only be speculation. What is more certain is the insight into the intellectual culture of twelfth-century Durham given by the authors and titles listed.

The first striking feature of the list is its length. The main list alone gives a total of some four hundred books by *c.*1150, not counting the liturgical books; and to these Prior Laurence added seven, Prior Thomas nine, and a monk called William de Nunnewic another nine.[3] Still more impressive are

[3] The total is perhaps 416, taking literally the compiler's references to multiple copies, and multiple volumes. The actual number of texts is impossible to discern, since numerous books simply have the presence of additional, shorter, texts briefly noted, as in 'Augustinus de Moribus Ecclesiae, cum ceteris'; while 'Libri tres Prioris Algari' is unhelpful. These entries are on pages 2 and 5 of the printed text, respectively.

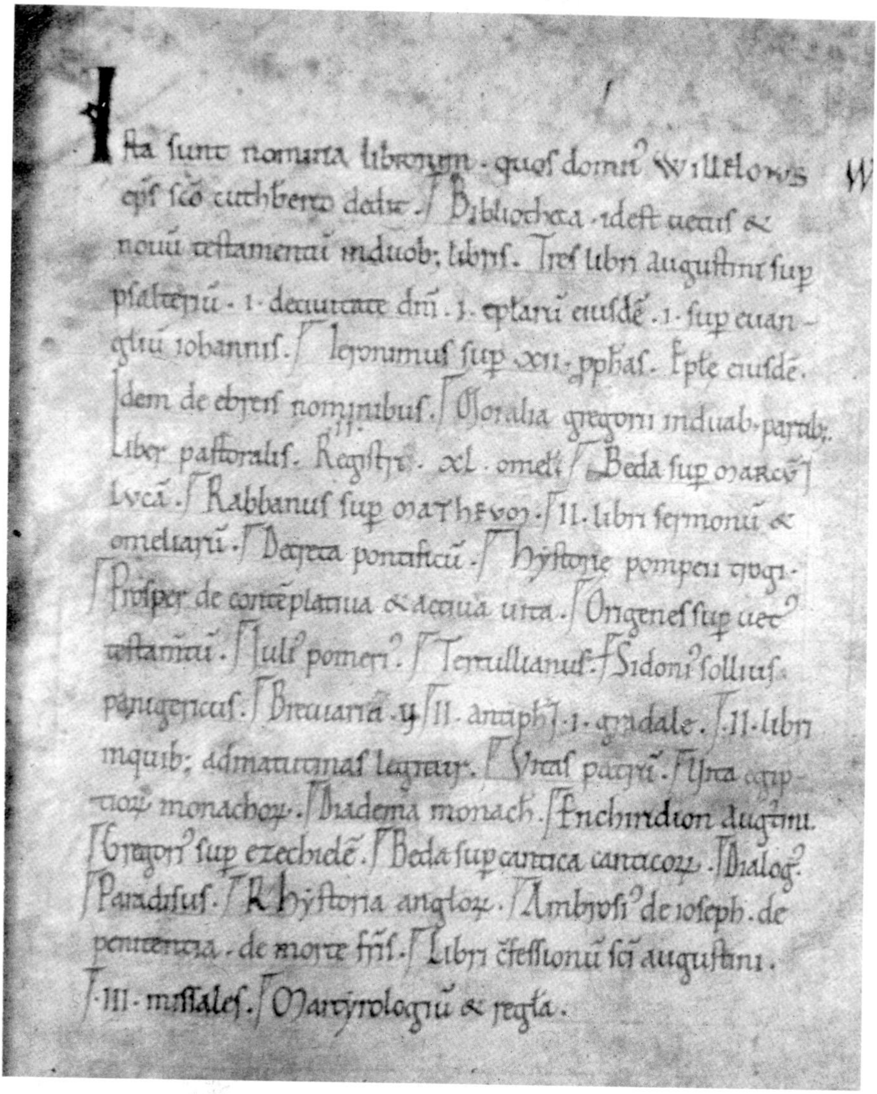

Ista sunt nomina librorum · quos domnus Willelmus
eps sco cuthberto dedit · ¶ Bibliotheca · idest uetis &
noui testamenti induob; libris. Tres libri augustini sup
psalterium · i · deciuitate dm · i · epistularum eiusde · i · sup euan-
gelium iohannis. ¶ Ieronimus sup xii · pphas. Epte eiusde.
Idem de ebreis nominibus. ¶ Moralia gregorii induab; partib;.
Liber pastoralis. Registr · xl · omel ¶ Beda sup marcu ¶
Luca. ¶ Rabbanus sup matheu. ¶ II · libri sermonu &
omeliaru. ¶ Decreta pontificu. ¶ Hystorie pompeii trogi.
¶ Prosper de contemplatiua & actiua uita. ¶ Origenes sup uet
testamtu. ¶ Iuli pomeri. ¶ Tertullianus. ¶ Sidoni sollius
panegericus. ¶ Breuiaria · iiii ¶ II · antiph · i · gradale. ¶ II · libri
inquib; ad matutinas legitur. ¶ Vitas patru. ¶ Vita egip-
tioru monachoru. ¶ Diadema monach. ¶ Enchiridion augtini.
¶ Gregorii sup ezechiele. ¶ Beda sup cantica canticoru. ¶ Dialog.
¶ Paradisus. ¶ R hystoria angloru. ¶ Ambrosi de ioseph · de
penitencia · de morte fris. ¶ Libri cfessionu sci augustini.
¶ III · missales. ¶ Martyrologiu & regla.

Plate 1. Durham, Dean and Chapter Library, MS A II 4, fol. 1r

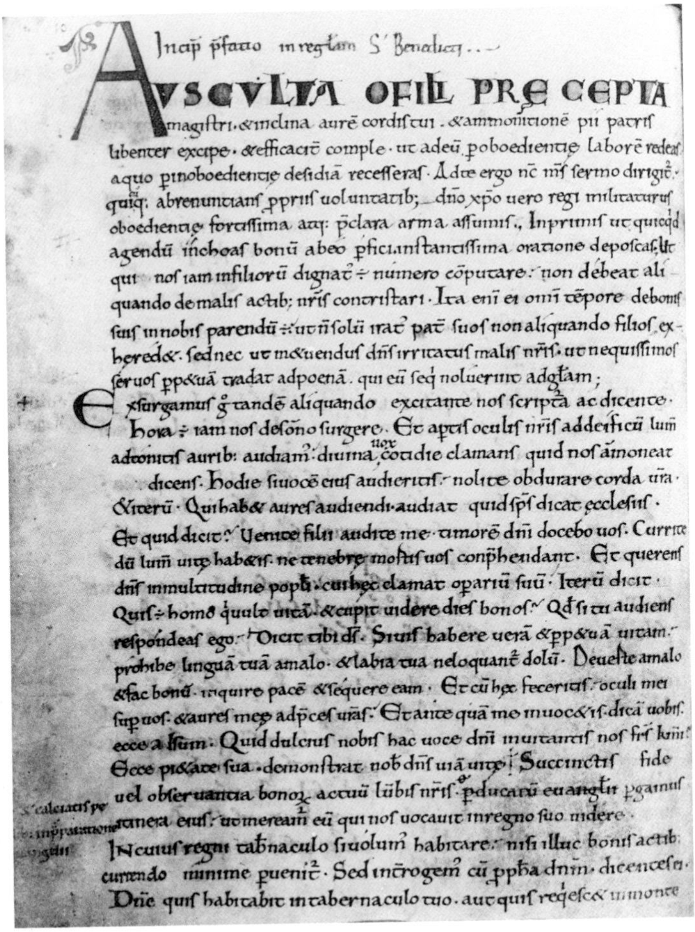

Incipit prefatio in regulam S. Benedicti.

AVSCVLTA O FILI PRECEPTA

magistri. & inclina aurē cordis tui. & ammonitionē pii patris
libenter excipe. & efficacitr comple· ut adeū p̄oboedientiȩ laborē redeas
a quo p̄ inoboedientiȩ desidia recesseras· Ad te ergo nc n̄rs sermo dirigit
quisq; abrenuntians p̄priis uoluntatib; dn̄o xp̄o uero regi militaturus
oboedientiȩ fortissima atq; p̄clara arma assumis· Inprimis ut quicqd
agendū inchoas bonū ab eo p̄ficiaris instantissima oratione deposcas. Ut
qui nos iam in filiorū dignat̄ ē numero cōputare· non debeat aliquando de malis actib; n̄ris contristari· Ita enī et omī tempore de bonis
suis in nobis parendū ē ut nō solū iratus pater suos non aliquando filios ex-
heredet· sed nec ut metuendus dn̄s irritatus malis n̄ris· ut nequissimos
seruos p̄p̄tuā tradat ad poenā· qui eū sequi noluerimus ad glam;

Exurgamus ḡ tandē aliquando excitante nos scriptura ac dicente·
hora ē iam nos de sōno surgere· Et apertis oculis n̄ris ad deificū lum
admonitis auribg; audiam̄ diuina cottidie clamans quid nos ammoneat
uox dicens· hodie si uocē eius audieritis· nolite obdurare corda u̇ra·
Et iterū· Qui habet aures audiendi audiat quid sp̄s dicat ecclesiis·
Et quid dicit? Uenite filii audite me timorē dn̄i docebo uos· Currite
dū lumen uitȩ habetis· ne tenebrȩ mortis uos conp̄hendant· Et querens
dn̄s in multitudine populi· cui hȩc clamat operariū suū· Iterū dicit·
Quis ē homo quī uult uitā· & cupit uidere dies bonos? Qd si tu audiens
respondeas ego· Dicit tibi dn̄s· Si uis habere ueram & p̄p̄tuā uitam·
p̄hibe linguā tuā a malo· & labia tua ne loquant̄ dolū· Deuerte a malo
& fac bonū· inquire pacē & sequere eam· Et cū hȩc feceritis· oculi mei
sup uos· & aures meȩ ad p̄ces u̇ras. Et ante quā me inuocetis· dicā uobis·
ecce adsum· Quid dulcius nobis hac uoce dn̄i inuitantis nos fr̄s kar̄i·
Ecce pietate sua · demonstrat nobis dn̄s uiā uitȩ· Succinctis fide
uel obseruantia bonorū· actuū lūbis n̄ris· p̄ducatū euangelii pargamur
itinera eius· ut mereamur eū qui nos uocauit in regno suo uidere·

In cuius regni tabnaculo si uolumus habitare· nisi illuc bonis actib;
currendo minime peruenit̄· Sed interrogem̄ cū p̄pheta dn̄m· dicentes·
Dn̄e quis habitabit in tabernaculo tuo· aut quis requiescet in monte

Plate 2. Durham,
Dean and Chapter
Library, MS B IV
24, fol. 74v

AVRELII AVGVSTINI DOCTORIS· h
DE CIVITATE DEI
INCIPIT CONT
LORIOSISSIMA

SIVE IN HOC TEMPORE
grinat̄ ex fide uiuens
quā nc expectat p̄p̄at
in iudiciū. deinceps a
ultima & pace p̄fecta
p̄missione debitw. def
deos suos p̄serti fili̇
nū op̄ & arduū. sed di
trib; op̄ sit. ut p̄suade
q̄ sit ut omnia terrena ce
tantia. non humano usurpata fastu sed diuina gr̄a donata o
& editor ciuitatis hui de qua loq̄ instituim̄. inscriptura po
uit. qua dicit̄ ē· Ds̄ sup̄b

Plate 3. Durham,
Dean and Chapter
Library, MS B II 22,
fol. 27v

Plate 4. Durham, Dean and Chapter Library, MS B II 14, fol. 7r

Plate 5. Durham, Dean and Chapter Library, MS B II 21, fol. 12r

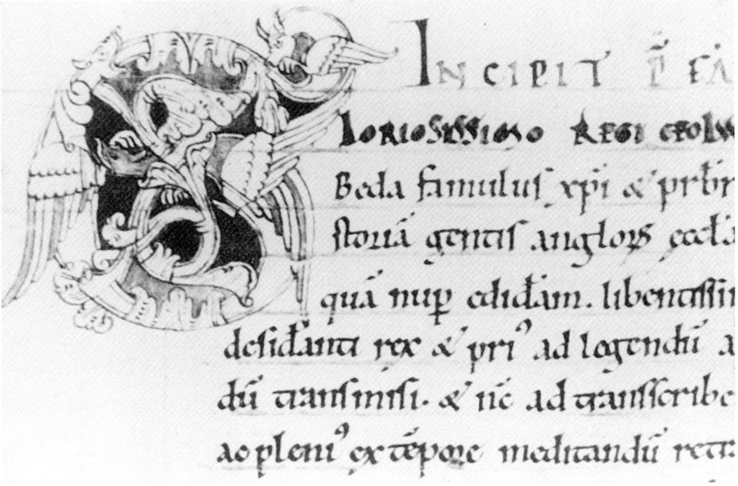

Plate 6. Durham, Dean and Chapter Library, MS B II 35, p. 72

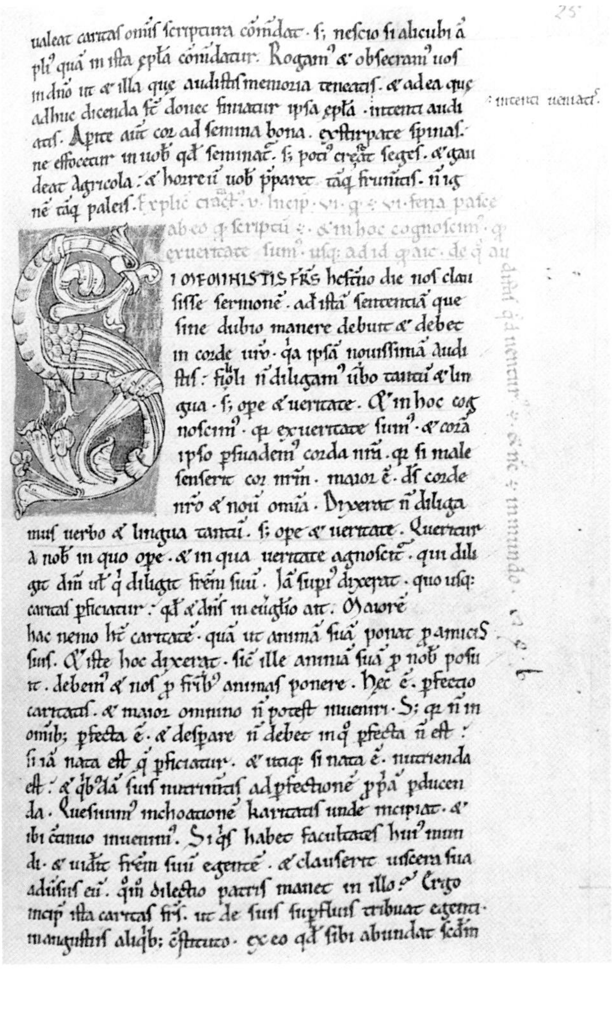

Plate 7. Durham, Dean and Chapter Library, MS B IV 7, fol. 25r

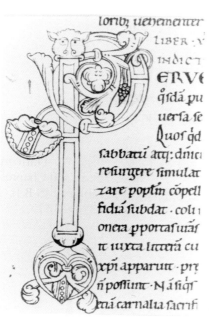

loribʒ uehementer
LIBER · V
INDICT
ERVE
q̃ſdā pu
uerſa ſe
Quor q̃d
ſabbatū atqʒ: dñica
reſurgere ſimulat
zare poptm̃ copell
fidiā ſubdat · col
onera pportas uiā
rt iuxta litterā cu
xp̄i apparuit · pr̃
n̄ poſſunt · Nā ſiq̄
nū carnalia ſacrifi

Plate 8. Durham, Dean
and Chapter Library,
MS B III 9, fol. 1v

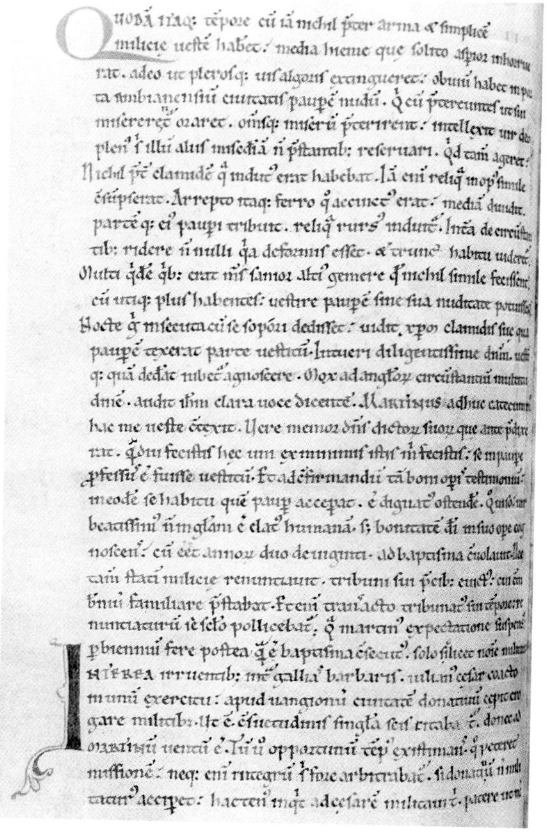

Plate 9. Durham, Dean
and Chapter Library,
MS B IV 14, fol. 113v

Plate 10. Durham, Dean and Chapter Library, MS B II 13, fol. 181v

Plate 11. Oxford, Bodleian, MS Digby 20, fol. 194r

Incipit prefatio helperici coportisse
de arte calculatoria.
QÐ FRATRIBVS ADOLE
SCENTIORIBVS NRIS QVEBRO
CALCVLATORIE ARTIS RVDIMENTA
comuni sermone explicare coepisse· q eit huiusce
qd ñ contempnende ut multi arbitrentur scientie
aliqd ipetere· qi in arte gramatica y ut diuina auxiliam est
munificentia aliquod intradyxeram· nescio q accensi desidic
mstare uehementi coepunt· qñ ea que una uoce deprimp
seru· multor utilitati pturi quecuq; scripto edem· ut siqi
hec ut solet mens humana diuisi edem cursu multa obliuisei
memoria excederit· literaru suffragiis ea qqmodo repara
re ualerent· Q sub cu obniri renitenti id q erat obcen
dem· sup ee scilicet libros de hac eade re· cu dilucide· tñ ut

Plate 12. Durham, Dean and Chapter Library, MS Hunter 100, fol. 43r

tota tanti uiri familia epo potu refectiois
obtulit· qs p ipsi benedictione poculum
mortis euasit· secuta exeplu socr apti petri
que curata a febrib; pdnm· cntnuo surgt
ministrabat illi ac discipulis eius· xxx.

Quoniam puella oleo puncta a dolore capiti laticiq; cum
fuerit.

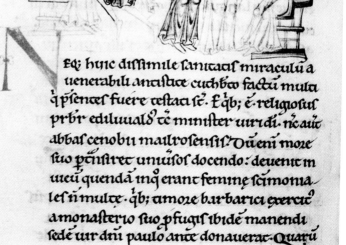

Neq; huic dissimile sanitatis miraculu a
uenerabili antistite cuchbto factu multa
q psentes fuere testati st· E qb; e religiosus
prbr ediluualdo tc minister uiridi· nc aut
abbas cenobii mailrosensis· Qui eni more
suo pnsiret uniusos docendo· deuenit in
uicu quenda inq erant femine scimonia
les ñ multe· qb; amore barbarica exercit
a monasterio suo pfugis ibide manendi
sede uir dni paulo ante donauerat· Quaru

Plate 13. Oxford, University College, MS 165, p. 88

Plate 14. Durham, Dean and Chapter Library, MS B IV 14, fol. 170v

Plate 15. Oxford, University College, MS 165, p. 2

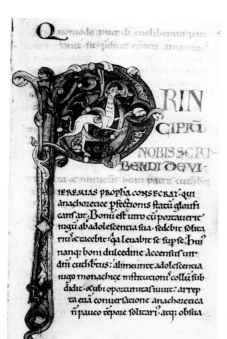

Plate 16. Oxford, University College, MS 165, p. 9

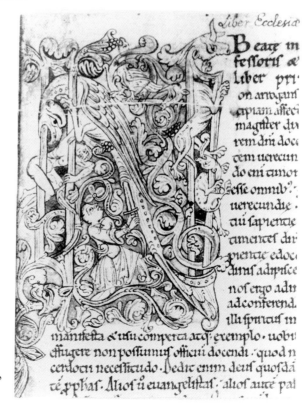

Plate 17. Durham, Dean and Chapter Library, MS B IV 5, fol. 1r

Q[uor]um angl[orum] in hospicio suscipiens dum panem quer[it]
ministrare cernit celestib[us] eor[um] manerium erit...

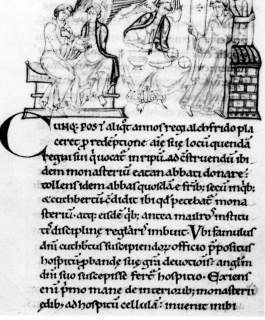

Cuq[ue] post aliq[uo]t annos regi alchfrido pla
ceret p[ro] rede[m]pcione a[n]i[m]e sue locu[m] quenda[m]
regni sui q[uo]cat[ur] in ripu[m] ad [con]struendu[m] ibi
dem monasteriu[m] eata[n] abbati donare:
vollens idem abbas quosda[m] e frib[us] secu[m] inq[ui]b[us]
& cuthbertu[m] [con]didit ibi q[uo]d petebat[ur] mona
steriu[m] atq[ue] eisde[m] q[ui]b[us] antea maiit[er] institu
t[ur] discipline regtar[is] imbuit. Vbi famulus
d[omi]ni cuthb[er]tus suscipiendo[rum] officio p[re]positus
hospicii p[ro]bande sue gr[ati]a deuocio[n]is angl[orum]
d[omi]ni suo suscepisse fert[ur] hospicio. Exiens
eni[m] p[ri]mo mane de interiorib[us] monasterii
edib[us] ad hospicii cellula[m] inuenit in ibi

Plate 18. Oxford, University
College, MS 165, p. 26

scitate illi occasio tolleret increduli[s]. Si
eni[m] eade[m] zona se[m]p adesset: se[m]p ad hanc con
[con]urere uoluissent egroti. & du[m] forte aliquis
ex his n[on] mereret[ur] a sua infirmitate curari:
derogaret i[m]potentie n[on] saluantis. cu[m] ipse
poci[us] e[ss]et salutis indign[us]. Vnde pruida u[er]o
dictu[m] e[st] dispensacione sup[er]ne pietati s[anct]o q[uo]n[iam]
fide[s] credenciu[m] [con]firmata e[st]: mox inuidie
p[er]fidor[um] materia detrahendi e[st] p[ror]su[s] ablata.

Quid de tunica eide[m] elsslede de tuca ecfridi regis &
episcopatu suo p[ra]dixerit.

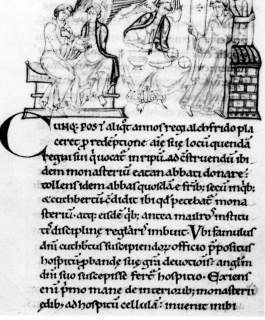

ALIO ITE[M] t[em]pre misit eade[m] reuerentissi
ma uirgo & mat[er] uirginu[m] x[rist]i elsfled.
rogauitq[ue]: uiru[m] d[e]i adiurans in no[m]i[n]e d[omi]ni
ut eu[m] uide[at]. & de necessariis mereret[ur] allo
q[ui]. Qui ascensa cu[m] frib[us] naui: uenit ad in
sula[m] que coquedi fluminis hostio p[ia]cent

Plate 19. Oxford, University
College, MS 165, p. 72

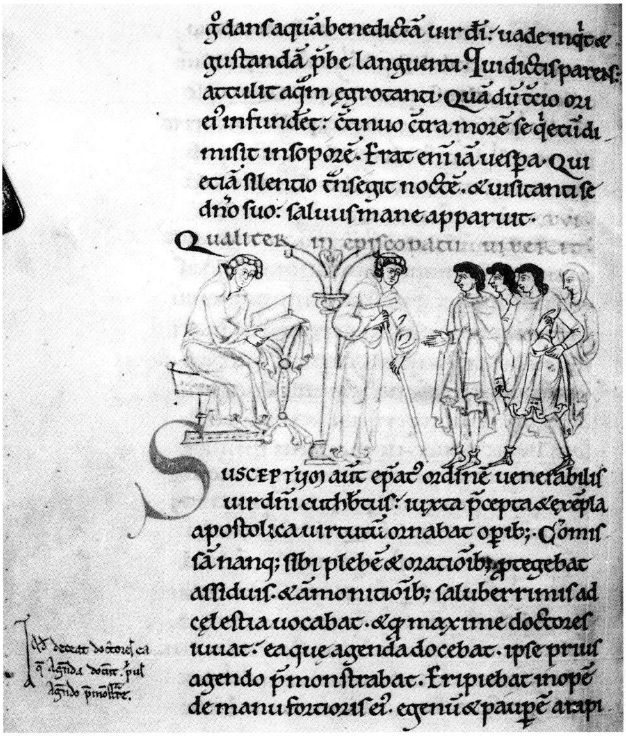

q̄ dans aquā benedictā uir d̄i. uade ɪn q̄ue
gustandā p̄be langueṅti. Q̄uid d̄cōs parei̇t
attulit aq̄m egrotanti. Quā dū d̄ cio orɪ
ei ɪnfundet: et inuio c̄tra more se q̄etū di
misit ɪn sopore. Erat enī ɪā uespa. Qui
ec̄iā silentio tr̄nsegit nocte. & uisitanti se
dn̄o suo: saluus mane apparuit.

Qualiter ɪn episcopatu uɪuerɪt

Suscepto igit̄ aut̄ epat̄ ordine uenerabilis
uir d̄n̄i cuthbꝰ: ɪuxta p̄cepta & ex̄ēpla
apostolica uirtutū ornabat opibꝰ. Commis
sā nanq; sibi plebē & orationibꝰ p̄tegebat
assiduis. & amonic̄oibꝰ: saluberrimis ad
celestia uocabat. & q̄ maxime doctores
ɪuuat: ea que agenda docebat. ipse prɪus
agendo p̄monstrabat. Eripiebat ɪnopē
de manu fortiouis eī. egenū & paupē a rapi

Plate 20. Oxford,
University College,
MS 165, p. 78

bat m̄s̄ficiendo. Illɪnc pagani q̄m detesta
bile sit ɪn humana p̄sumere suꝑbia expuḡ
cadendo: hoc ɪtaq; p̄lio absq; detrɪm̄to
sui exercit̄ c̄fecto: et fredus toci britan
nie ɪp̄iu obtinuit. & q̄m sc̄i c̄fessoris
p̄cepta que susceperat ɪn penuria. memo
rit̄ seruabat ɪn curia: omibꝰ semꝑ &
ubique aduersantiū p̄ualuit moliminibꝰ.

Plate 21. Oxford, University
College, MS 165, p. 143

Plate 22. York, Minster Library, MS XVI Q 3, fol. 1r

etiam olim sepultors cont̄ nos
opuf aggrediendum eſt.

fuerāt ante capt urbacem dece
buum iude & beniamin alii

Plate 23. Rouen, Bibliothèque
Municipale, MS A 321 (444),
fol. 1v

Plate 24. Durham, Dean and
Chapter Library, MS B II 8,
fol. 1v

BEATVS. VIR. QVI. NON ABIIT. IN. CONSILIO. IMPIORVM; ET. CE TERA

Quidā dicunt hunc psalmū quasi psal ione.ēē. spē sci. & ideo ūtulū non habe. alu ineo qd'pm' sit: ordinis sui habe pncipi ū. & pleonasmoy. ēē. ūtulū eū pmū dice. Ance anē nullus sit. Alit. A qud hebreos. & ūnū e

Plate 25. Durham, Dean and
Chapter Library, MS B II 7,
fol. 12r

Plate 26. London, British
Library, Add. 38817, fol. 6r

Durham and its defences.[12] Where St Calais had been an educated monk, trained at Bayeux under Osbern, and interested in scholarship and canon law, Flambard was a royal clerk, criticised by contemporaries as 'almost illiterate'. This was clearly not literally true, since he was, at one stage, head of the king's writing chamber, but he had not studied at any of the rising schools on the continent, nor in any monastic school. He showed no trace of St Calais's interest in books, and the only book he is recorded as giving to the priory was his Breviary, which is entered on the book-list.[13]

In these circumstances the rapid growth of the library, demonstrated by the book-list, and of scholarly activity at Durham, cannot be attributed to episcopal influence, especially as Flambard's successor, Geoffrey Rufus, was another administrator, having been head of Henry I's chancery, and had no recorded scholarly interests.[14] Thus, the considerable activity taking place within the priory must have been primarily the result of the work of priors Turgot (1087–1109), Algar (1109–37), Roger (1137–49) and Laurence (1149–53). The scholarly interests of the latter have already been dealt with in the previous chapter, but less is known of Algar and Roger. Clearly, Algar took over a community of considerable size in 1109. Symeon of Durham states that twenty-three monks from Wearmouth and Jarrow were brought to Durham, and that one of the clerks of St Cuthbert chose to become a monk.[15] The Cosin manuscript of Symeon's work gives seventy-three names of those who joined up to c.1104.[16] This cannot produce an absolute total, since we do not know how many of the founding group of 1083 were still alive in 1104 and Piper has identified problems with both this list and the parallel one in the *Liber Vitae*. Nevertheless, the Durham community was clearly large, and perhaps even rivalled that of Christ Church, Canterbury, estimated at a hundred under Lanfranc.

Not all of these recruits, by any means, can have been fully trained monks, and thus education and training would be a constant necessity. The case of Maurice also demonstrates that oblates were accepted, as was customary, so that a school for boys would be necessary. That children, probably from

---

[12] The assessment of Flambard, by an anonymous author, who was presumably a monk of Durham, stresses the bishop's administrative abilities, and his building projects. His gifts to the Church, in the form of vestments, are listed; but there is no mention of books, or of scholarship. See 'Continuatio Prima', in Arnold, i, at 139–40.

[13] See *Catalogi Veteres*, 6. It was probably an impressive book, as it was in two volumes.

[14] On Geoffrey, see 'Continuatio Prima', in Arnold, i, 141–2. He also gave gifts to the Church, but of these no details are given.

[15] See *Libellus*, lib. IV, cap. iii; Arnold, i, 122–3.

[16] The Cosin MS is Durham UL Cosin V ii 6. The earliest names are nos. 1–73 in the list as printed by Arnold, i, 4–6. For detailed analysis of the list, and other evidence on the numbers of early Durham monks, see A. J. Piper, 'The Early Lists and Obits of the Durham Monks', in Rollason, *Symeon of Durham*, 161–201.

upper-class backgrounds, were taught at Durham seems clear, both from the career of Maurice, and from Victoria Tudor's analysis of those who became hermits associated with Durham.[17] Maurice entered the priory as a child, and learnt so successfully that he became celebrated as a 'second Bede' at Durham for his scholarship. By 1138 he was subprior, and his scholarship was respected also at Rievaulx, to which he subsequently moved.[18] By contrast, several of the twelfth-century Durham hermits had been taken into the priory as children, but apparently failed to reach an academic level which qualified them to become full monks. Reginald of Durham's story of the ex-knight, Robert de St Martin, who became a monk at Durham towards the middle of the twelfth century, may clarify the basic educational attainments required. The new recruit was expected to memorise psalms and prayers, set out (in Latin) in a book which he was required to learn to read. When he failed in this, he experienced considerable criticism.[19] The question of whether the school was open to students from outside cannot be answered. Prior Laurence is believed to have played some part in the education of Aelred of Rievaulx, but this does not necessarily imply that Aelred was a member of the school. Certainly, when the ex-merchant, later St Godric of Finchale, wished to gain some education, he was taught at a school run in a local church in Durham, not at the priory.[20] Indeed, Reginald suggests that such schools were fairly common in the area by the mid-twelfth century, and tells a story about one at Norham.[21] However, the education available in such schools was considerably more basic than that given to the Durham monks; Reginald regards St Godric as poorly educated.

This raises the question of what was regarded as a necessary level of education at Durham, and here the evidence of the book-list is important. As might be expected, there was impressive provision for the teaching of Latin grammar, in the form of eighteen volumes of the works of Priscian. There are also four volumes on rhetoric, and no less than twenty-five on dialectics, the most highly regarded subject of the time. Moreover, there is evidence of study of at least some parts of the quadrivium, in the form of two volumes on arithmetic, one on geometry and two on the astrolabe. There do not appear to be any recognisable works on music, although musical manuscripts will have been needed; these were presumably kept elsewhere. That the books so far discussed were regarded as a school set is suggested by the fact that most

[17] V. Tudor, 'Durham Priory and its Hermits in the Twelfth Century', in Rollason et al., *Anglo-Norman Durham*, 67–78.

[18] See Walter Daniel, *The Life of Ailred of Rievaulx*, 33.

[19] See Reginald, *De Admirandis*, cap. lxxvi, pp. 197–201.

[20] See Reginald of Durham, *Libellus de Vita et Miraculis S. Godrici, Heremitae de Finchale*, ed. J. Stevenson, Surtees Society 20, 1847, ch. 11.

[21] See Reginald, *De Admirandis*, cap. lxxiii, pp. 148–51.

of them occur close together in the list; the pupils of Durham were clearly well-grounded in the trivium, with instruction on the quadrivium available for those judged suitable. It is interesting that the works of Boethius, with multiple copies of commentaries on his works, and three copies or volumes of fables, occur next. These were presumably regarded as basic works, both for practice in reading Latin, and for gaining the rudiments of a Christian education.

However, other parts of the book-list make it clear that far more than basic study was available at Durham by the mid-century. A useful comparison is with the list of twenty-one 'curriculum authors' compiled by Conrad of Hirsau, who was school master in the Cluniac house of Hirsau until his death, *c.* 1150.[22] Conrad himself had been the pupil of Abbot William who, in 1079, had accepted the Cluniac reform, and Conrad's *Dialogus super Auctores* is regarded by E. R. Curtius as giving a valuable insight into teaching and study in reformed monasteries in the first half of the twelfth century. Here, the 'auctores minores', 'rudimentis parvulorum apti', are listed as Donatus, Cato, Aesop, Avianus, broadly matching the Durham listing. The more advanced works, or 'auctores maiores', are divided into: the 'Christian poets', Sedulius, Juvencus, Prosper and Theodulus; the 'Romanos auctores', Arator, Prudentius, Cicero, Sallust, Boethius, Lucan, Virgil and Horace; and Ovid, Juvenal, Persius, Statius and 'Homerus'. Of these all but Juvencus were available at Durham. Moreover, study of grammar and rhetoric may well have included exercises in the composition, as well as the memorising, of Latin verse, as described by John of Salisbury and advocated by Herbert Losinga at Norwich.[23] Occurring near to the list of school books are three copies of Sallust, and further on another group includes Macrobius, Terence, Pompeius Trogus and multiple copies of Cicero and Sidonius. This is a rather mixed set, but Cicero seems to have been read as both a moralist and a stylist, while Sidonius, the fifth-century bishop and patron of monks, was taken as a model for the new poetics of the twelfth century. Ovid is popular, as always, with no less than ten titles, and two copies of the *De Arte Amatoria*; and there are also Maximianus, who was used as a model for rhetorical devices, and a 'Book of Troy' to add to Statius and 'Homerus'. Near to this latter group are also a gloss on Lucan, a gloss on poetry, Quintilian and an unspecified 'Rule of Grammar'.

[22] On Conrad of Hirsau, see E. R. Curtius, *European Literature and the Latin Middle Ages*, trans. W. R. Trask, London and Henley, 1979, 260–1 and 465–7. This may be contrasted, however, with the rather different approach demonstrated by the categorised list of classical authors given in the late eleventh century by Haimeric, in his *Ars Lectoria*. See Webber, *Scribes and Scholars*, 86, n. 21.

[23] Herbert Losinga's instruction of his monks at Norwich, as represented by his letters, is discussed by Barlow, *The English Church 1066–1154*, 240–5.

The Durham book-list is certainly not organised, however, in accordance with Conrad of Hirsau's groupings, and any system, further than the rough groupings outlined above, is hard to discern. The Christian poets are scattered throughout the list, with Prudentius, for instance, occurring between two groups of patristic works, whilst Sedulius and Arator occur next to the *auctores* already discussed. The handling of canon law is also interesting. On the one hand, five volumes occur almost at the head of the list, just after the complete Bibles, suggesting that these also were very large books. However, the earlier canonist, Burchard, appears some way further down, suggesting that this work was kept separately. Nevertheless, there is no suggestion that at Durham volumes of canon law were kept locked up, as they were in Cistercian houses.[24]

Despite the interest in 'auctores' however, the list is dominated, as would be expected, by patristic works and books of the Bible. Some effort, though not a systematic one, has been made to group the former at the head of the list, again suggesting a grouping by size, as these also would be relatively large books. Easily the most popular author is Augustine, twenty of whose works are listed. This is an impressive set, ranging from a collection of short works to the three-volume set of *Commentaries on the Psalms*. Particularly important, it seems, were the *De Civitate Dei, Confessiones, Super Johannem* and *Super Genesim*, as two copies of each were held; but there was no copy of the *De Doctrina Christiana*. Next in popularity is Jerome, the works listed here being the *Epistolae, Contra Jovinianum, De Hebreis nominibus* and *Liber Locorum*, as well as the *Commentaries* on Isaiah, the Twelve Minor Prophets, and the Three Prophets, and the 'Psalterium Jeronimi', a text of which Godric of Finchale also had a copy. Of the works of Gregory, Durham had a two-volume set of the *Moralia* (as well as a separate volume containing Part Three only), two copies of the *Dialogues*, the *Commentary on Ezekiel*, and the *Speculum, Registrum* and *Pastorale*, as well as Paternus on Gregory. The interest in collections of letters occurs again with Ambrose, where the works listed are: *De Officiis, De Patriarchis, Super Lucam, Exaemeron*, and *Epistolae* (in a volume containing also the Epistle of Cyprian). Bede is strikingly popular, with the majority of the major theological works listed, as well as the *Historia Anglorum* and *Lives of the Abbots of Wearmouth*. Bede's *Commentaries* on Genesis, Samuel, the Song of Songs, Mark and Luke, Acts, Epistles and the 'Parabolas Salomonis' are listed, as well as the *De Tabernaculo*; but of his other works, only the *De Temporibus* (in two volumes) appears. Further interest in Bede is demonstrated by an enigmatic *Scutum Bedae*. This patristic

---

[24]   This is justified 'propter varios qui inde possunt provenire errores'. See 'Table', in C. Norton and D. Park, eds., *Cistercian Art and Architecture in the British Isles*, Cambridge, 1986, 333.

collection was somewhat less adventurous, and built up more slowly, than the impressive collection at Salisbury analysed by Webber. Nevertheless, as in the collection of books by 'curriculum authors' already discussed, there is strong evidence that the priory of Durham took its library for the *lectio divina*, as well as for its school, extremely seriously. Indeed, the organisation of the book-list suggests that these two categories may have overlapped.[25]

The Carolingians are represented by Haimo on the Pauline Epistles and on Isaiah, Rabanus Maurus on Matthew, and the *Epistolae* of Alcuin, who was probably also regarded as an author of local historical importance. The *Commentary* on Donatus by Remigius, Haimo's successor at Auxerre, also appears.[26] Perhaps more striking is the number of more 'modern' authors, who include Gilbert de la Porrée (*On the Psalter*), Peter Lombard (the *Sentences*), Hildebert (of Lavardin?) (*Epistolae*), and, perhaps, Hugh of St Victor (in the rather enigmatic form of a *Sententiae Magistri Hugonis*). Much more certain are the *Cur Deus Homo* and *De Meditationibus* of Anselm, and the *Liber de Epistolis* and *Super Canticam Canticorum* of St Bernard of Clairvaux. Further evidence of up-to-date methods of study is provided by the number of glossed books of the Bible, as well as of anonymous glosses. Most popular of all, as was usual, were the Pauline Epistles, and the Psalter.

One final area of interest stands out, and that is history. Numerous 'historical' works occur in the groups already discussed, but, in another section of the list, together with the 'Historia Anglorum' (presumably Bede), are the 'De Gestis Normannorum', a rare chronicle headed 'De Gestis Francorum', and a 'Gesta Pontificum Anglorum', which is presumably William of Malmesbury's.[27] In the separate list of books in Old English there are also two Histories.

The evidence of the book-list, then, demonstrates clearly that the monks of Durham were well supplied with books for the study of the trivium, as well as with fundamental works for the *lectio divina*. Indeed, some were apparently expected to reach a level of some competence both in Latin composition and in their reading of the *auctores*. There are strong signs of special interest in the study of dialectics, the subject achieving fame in the schools of Paris, and of significant efforts to obtain early copies of works by contemporary masters. Overall, there is evidence of a very considerable effort to build up the sort of library considered most valuable in the first half of the twelfth century –

[25] On the importance of Bede, and the popularity of his works, see Chapter 10. For the comparison with Salisbury see Webber, *Scribes and Scholars*, 37–43.

[26] For brief details on these authors, see B. Smalley, *The Study of the Bible in the Middle Ages*, Oxford, 1952, 37–45.

[27] For the strength of historical study and writing at twelfth-century Durham, see the Conclusion, and H. S. Offler, *Medieval Historians of Durham*, Durham, 1958.

presumably aided by the gifts of scholars such as Laurence and Maurice.[28] Nevertheless, the majority of the works included in the main list would have been produced or obtained by the priory, which succeeded in building up a library of some four hundred books by the middle of the twelfth century. This total is not as high as that for Canterbury, for instance, but it apparently started from a very small basis in 1083, and it should be remembered that service books, and others kept separately, are excluded from the list.[29]

Additional evidence

The second part of this chapter will discuss the surviving Durham manuscripts, but first, some additional sources of information should be briefly considered. Perhaps representative of the highest levels of Durham scholarship are the two Laurences, discussed in the previous chapter, and Maurice, the subprior in 1138, whose career has been discussed by Powicke.[30] Prior Laurence's verse works certainly match the interest in Latin composition, Christian poetry, and history, demonstrated by the book-list.[31] However, perhaps Durham's most famous scholar was Maurice, later briefly abbot of Rievaulx. Powicke argued that he wrote the account of the translation of the relics of St Cuthbert in 1104, as well as being the author of a collection of sermons, a collection of letters, and of a set of shorter works listed in the thirteenth-century Rievaulx catalogue as: 'Specula monastice religionis'; 'Apologia'; 'Itinerarium Pacis'; and 'Rithmus'. Other evidence, although more scrappy, points to a fairly high level of activity in this field. The collection known as the *Miracles and Translations of St Cuthbert* was composed by an anonymous Durham author, probably in association with the translation of 1104.[32] This event was also probably the occasion for the composition of special prayers for the mass for St Cuthbert's feast of 4 September, and perhaps for the writing of the sequences 'Verbum Pater' and 'Splendor Christi', which also had specially composed music. Extra antiphons were also written, for insertion into the office for St Cuthbert, found in Corpus 183, the tenth-century copy of Bede's *Life of St Cuthbert*, as well as two new hymns, to old melodies.[33] Another anonymous Durham author wrote the sermon on 'Audivi vocem de caelo' which was added, in a twelfth-century hand, into DCL B IV 12; interestingly, this makes much use of the

---

[28] For the lists of these gifts, see *Catalogi Veteres*, 7–9.
[29] More detailed comparisons with other libraries are given in Chapter 3.
[30] See Powicke, 'Maurice of Rievaulx'.
[31] Laurence's main surviving work is a history of the recent events at Durham, written in the form of a poetic dialogue. This is edited by Raine, in Laurence, *Dialogi*.
[32] For this see T. Arnold, i, 229–64. For Arnold's analysis, see 'Introduction', xxvii–xxxii.
[33] On all this see Hohler and Hughes, 'The Durham Services'.

image of the monk studying, and writing at a desk.[34] Several of Reginald of Durham's miracle stories mention the use of books, and one, datable to 1113 or 1114, describes how St Cuthbert appeared to Bernard, the sacristan of Durham, when he was writing in the monastery.

Finally, there is considerable evidence for continuing interest in the regional past, something which is perhaps surprising in its contrast with the interest in up-to-date study and continental scholarship. This dualism is strongly characteristic, not only of Durham, but of the Yorkshire houses also, and will be discussed further in the Conclusion. Here it may be noted that, assuming that the compiler of the *Historia Regum* was located at Durham, he clearly had access there to a range of chronicles and sources. Chief among these were John of Worcester for the period from 848 to 1119/20, followed by increasing use of Eadmer of Canterbury and possibly William of Malmesbury. As has already been mentioned, William of Jumièges was known and used, as was a copy of the E version of the Anglo-Saxon Chronicle which continued to *c.*1118. The link with Worcester will be discussed further in the next section, but it is worth noting here that material from the *Chronicon* of Marianus Scotus almost certainly also came via Worcester. The *Historia Regum* ended at 1129, but it is possible that it was at Durham that it was re-edited with material from Henry of Huntingdon to produce the *Historia post Bedam*.[35] Further to all this, considerable work in assembling information on the period from the seventh century onwards, and combining it with biblical material as well as lists of Roman and Byzantine emperors, probably copied and compiled by Symeon himself, is shown in the brief chronicle set out on what are now the flyleaves of DCL B IV 22. The copying of the 'Annales Lindisfarnenses et Dunelmenses' onto the margins of the Easter table in Glasgow UL Hunterian T 4 2 (85) was probably also done by Symeon, and again shows related interests and material.[36]

[34] See Mynors, *Durham Cathedral Manuscripts*, no. 59, p. 51.

[35] For a brief analysis of this, see A. J. Piper, 'The Historical Interests of the Monks of Durham', in Rollason, *Symeon of Durham*, 301–32, especially 302–3 and 320–2. See also: P. Hunter-Blair, 'Some Observations on the *Historia Regum* Attributed to Symeon of Durham', in K. Jackson *et al.*, eds, *Celt and Saxon: Studies in the Early British Border*, Cambridge, 1963, 63–118; and H. S. Offler, 'Hexham and the *Historia Regum*', *Transactions of the Architectural and Archaeological Society of Durham and Northumberland* 2, 1971, 51–62.

[36] On this, see J. Taylor, *Medieval Historical Writing in Yorkshire*, St Anthony's Hall Publications 19, York, 1961, and J. E. Story, 'Symeon as Annalist', in Rollason, *Symeon of Durham*, 202–13.

PART II
The surviving books

Two rather different types of manuscript survive from the Durham library of this period. One type is characterised by small size, script which ranges from small to eye-strainingly tiny and makes much use of contractions, and texts which are more related to the needs of serious scholarship than to those of the *lectio divina* as specified by St Benedict.[37] The other type tend to be rather larger (though they rarely reach the size of the St Calais books), to have larger, more formal, less contracted scripts, and to have decorated initials and display scripts which show a continuing development of motifs and characteristics found in the illuminated and decorated manuscripts of the turn of the century.[38] Their texts are dominated by patristic commentaries of the type established as suitable for the *lectio divina*, although they also include volumes of canon law, copies of works by 'local authors' and a few works of recent theological scholarship.[39] There is thus no absolute separation between the groups; and indeed, as might be expected, there is a third, small, group of books which falls somewhere between the two main groups. Nevertheless, the grouping is interesting, and raises a number of questions.

The first, and most difficult, question is whether all the surviving books from this date can be considered as products of a formal, organised, Durham scriptorium. In the case of the more formal manuscripts, with largely patristic texts, the answer to this question, as will be argued below, appears to be yes. But the 'scholarly' manuscripts, by their very nature, are much more difficult to classify. They have scripts which are designed to be legible even at tiny size, and are therefore rather plain and informal; and they have virtually no decoration. Their hands often show general similarities to one another, but often these are of a type which does no more than to suggest that they are of the same period and general region. I have not succeeded in identifying any of these hands with those of the more formal books; though the use of relatively unusual abbreviation signs does form a link between the two groups. It may be, then, that these books were produced by scribes who had some training in the emerging 'house style' of Durham in this period,

---

[37] The main examples are DCL: B IV 12, Sermons, 241 × 173mm; A IV 15, composite vol., 244 × 165mm; B IV 1, Gregory Nazianzen, 203 × 125mm; A IV 34, Gloss on Song of songs, 185 × 109mm; C IV 7, Anon. Glosses, 234 × 147mm; C IV 10, Various contents, 193 × 114mm; and C IV 29, Notes on Priscian and Cicero, 231 × 132mm.

[38] See Chapter 3.

[39] Main examples are DCL: B II 18, Augustine, Sermons, 333 × 234mm; B II 26, Augustine, De Trinitate, 343 × 170mm; A I 10, Commentary on Matthew, 404 × 300mm; B II 7, Jerome, Breviarium in Psalms, 330 × 234mm; and B II 8, Jerome on Isaiah, 411 × 300mm.

discussed by Ker.[40] They are certainly very different from the polished works of the Paris professionals who copied the surviving books given to Durham in the later part of the century by Master Robert of Adyngton, who had studied at the school of St Victor.[41] Moreover, the experience of handling them makes certain things very clear. First, these books are at least as small as modern paperbacks, and several of them were originally only pamphlets, containing relatively short works. Indeed, one survives in a type of 'paper-back' binding,[42] while another, which is still at Durham, is simply a set of small quires, each originally held together by slips or ties of vellum, kept clean and in order by a wrapper.[43] This is presumably, as Mynors says, what is meant by the book-list when it describes volumes as being 'in quaternioni-bus'.[44] They can thus easily be held in the hand, potentially while making notes with the other hand (the use of 'tablets' for note-making in both schools and monasteries is fairly well attested).[45] Secondly, they are not very easy to read even in full daylight, and would be virtually impossible in the gloom of a predawn cloister, one of the major times allocated by St Benedict for reading.[46] The implication, then, is that study was pursued at other times, perhaps those allocated for 'work', and that these books were designed for serious scholars, rather than for those who were first and foremost monks engaged in *lectio divina*. This is interesting, since St Calais had been at pains to give the priory a copy of Lanfranc's Customary, which deals with books and reading only within the context of the *lectio divina*.[47] Clearly changes had taken place since then, very much in line with the other evidence which presents Durham as, in one of its aspects, a bastion of advanced European scholarship.

The texts of these scholarly books are also very interesting, and demonstrate conclusively that the monks and clerks of Durham were in touch with the schools of France and of Paris. One such is a small book, now the second part of the composite manuscript, DCL A IV 15; it has four gatherings, now fols. 17–56 of A IV 15, and it contains an anonymous gloss on the Gospel of

[40] Ker, *English Manuscripts*, 23–5.

[41] See Mynors, *Durham Cathedral Manuscripts*, 78–82.

[42] See note 1 above.

[43] This is now DCL A IV 34.

[44] See *Catalogi Veteres*, 2, 'in iv quaternionibus'; 4, 'in sex quaternionibus'; 9 'in v quaternionibus'.

[45] Magister Laurence of Durham, later abbot of Westminster, clearly made use of them as a student at St Victor. See Croydon, 'Abbot Laurence', 171.

[46] Times allowed for reading in Summer are: 'from the fourth hour until the time of Sext'; 'after Sext and their meal (and before None)'. In Winter they are: 'until the end of the second hour'; and 'after their meal'. The times are set out in detail in ch. 48 of the *Rule of St Benedict*.

[47] See Lanfranc, *Monastic Constitutions*, ed. and trans. M. D. Knowles, Nelson's Medieval Classics, London, 1951.

John. What is unusual about this gloss is its early date. Both Mynors and Ker place the book clearly in the first half of the twelfth century, so this gloss was copied at a time when commentaries on the Gospels were still few. The custom of expounding the Gospels systematically seems, indeed, only to have begun in the school of Laon, under Master Anselm (d. 1117) and his brother Ralph (d. 1131/2).[48] Indeed, it was Anselm who compiled what became the 'Glosa Ordinaria' on John's Gospel, and it was presumably for this reason that later copies of the anonymous gloss, in DCL B III 17 and Cambridge, Trinity College, B I 10, attribute it to 'Anselm'. However, this anonymous gloss is not in fact that of Anselm of Laon, or any other Anselm.[49] The origin of the gloss is unknown, but its existence makes one thing very clear; namely, that Durham before 1150 was in touch with contemporary scholarship as it was developing at the school of Laon and in a few other advanced centres.

Perhaps even more striking is the third book which now makes up A IV 15 (fols. 57–69, two gatherings). This has been examined by Buytaert, who found that it contains the only known copy of what was almost certainly the first version of the capitula and book I of Abelard's *Theologia Christiana*, composed perhaps in 1122–5.[50] It is unclear why the Durham copy stops at the end of book I, having given the capitula for the whole work. But what is important here is that this little book appears to have been copied during Abelard's lifetime, and there is a strong implication that one of the scholars of Durham was in touch with Abelard and his school.

Also very interesting, if less spectacular, are DCL C IV 7 and B IV 16. The former contains a major, anonymous gloss on Plato's *Timaeus*. This was a work which only began to be glossed in the early twelfth century, again starting in France.[51] The author of the C IV 7 gloss knew the comments of Calcidius, who had translated the *Timaeus* into Latin in the early fourth century, as well as a very early twelfth-century French gloss; he did not, however, know the work of William of Conches.[52] Like the practice of glossing the Gospels, that of glossing Plato can be associated with a particular school, in this case that of Chartres. Moreover, although the actual source of the Durham gloss is unknown, it must be an early copy, again putting the

[48] See B. Smalley, *The Gospels in the Schools c.1100–c.1280*, London and Ronceverte, 1985, 3–7.

[49] It is possible that it is that of Rupert of Deutz, which was written *c.*1115, but never circulated widely, though this has not been checked. See Smalley, *Gospels*, 1 and n. 4. See also Mynors, *Durham Cathedral Manuscripts*, at no. 61, 51–2.

[50] P. E. M. Buytaert, 'An Earlier Redaction of the *Theologia Christiana* of Abelard', *Antonianum* 37, 1962, fasc. 4, 481–95.

[51] Mynors, *Durham Cathedral Manuscripts*, nos. 79 and 70.

[52] See P. E. Dutton, '"Illustre Civitatis et Populi Exemplum": Plato's *Timaeus* and the Transmission from Calcidius to the End of the Twelfth Century of a Tripartite Scheme of Society', *Medieval Studies* 45, 1983, 79–119; P. E. Dutton, *The Glosae super Platonem*, Toronto, 1991.

scholars of Durham in contact with the most advanced French trends. In the case of B IV 16, fols. 45–70 constitute an early copy of Jerome's translation of Didymus' *De Spiritu Sancto*. This also was a work newly studied in the early twelfth century, as interest in the Holy Spirit grew, not least in the circles of Abelard. The copy found in B IV 16 is closely related to a slightly later copy from Jumièges, now Rouen, BM, A 343, fols. 83–100, and to another from Rochester, now BL Royal 5 B VII.[53] Although the Durham copy is the oldest of the group, it is not clear that it served as an exemplar for the other two, although it almost certainly did for a lost manuscript, once at Pembroke, Cambridge. However, the up-to-date nature of Durham scholarship is again demonstrated.

The books so far discussed link Durham to the schools of Laon and Chartres, and to Abelard's school in and around Paris. Evidence of a slightly different sort links Durham also to the early stages of the school of St Victor. Master Hugh had a student called Laurence, who published an early version of Hugh's *De Sacramentis*, with the approval of the master. The treatise was prefaced by a letter to Laurence's friend, Maurice, explaining how he was asked to prepare it by his fellow pupils, how he wrote it down from the master's teaching, and how Hugh corrected the tablets each week.[54] Croydon has suggested that this Laurence was the future abbot of Westminster. This would mean that he was none other than the clerk, Laurence, who had been at Durham for some time by 1153, when he supported the scholarly Prior Laurence over the election of Hugh de Puiset as bishop.[55] Maurice would then be the subprior of Durham, whose scholarship, we are told, was famous at Durham, and who was equally respected when he became a Cistercian at Rievaulx (and was briefly abbot of Fountains).[56] That the link with the school of St Victor existed also in the second half of the century, is demonstrated by master Robert de Adyngton, or Edyngton, whose books, in forty-eight wrappers, were given to Durham after having been deposited at St Victor. Perhaps less surprisingly, the works of Anselm were also obtained at Durham in this period, confirming again Durham's contact with Canterbury and its region. Cambridge, Jesus College, Q G 16, is written in several small hands, with plain initials in red or green. Besides several short treatises by Boethius, largely dealing with the Trinity, it contains Anselm's *Monologion*, *Proslogion*, *De Incarnatione Verbi*, *De Veritate*, *De Libertate Arbitrii*, *Cur Deus Homo*, and

---

[53] See L. Doutreleau, 'Étude d'une tradition manuscrite: le *De Spiritu Sancto* de Didyme', in P. Granfield and J. A. Jungmann, eds., *Kyriakon: Festschrift Johannes Quasten*, Münster, 1970, 352–89.

[54] See Croydon, 'Abbot Laurence'.

[55] See Chapter 6.

[56] See Powicke, 'Maurice of Rievaulx'.

other short works. The popularity of Anselm's work at Durham is demonstrated by the existence of another collection, probably contemporary, in Jesus College, Q C 29. This contains the *Dicta*, the *Meditationes*, the *Monologion*, and the *Proslogion*. Here, they are found in the elevated company of Jerome and Augustine, as well as Seneca and a very wide range of short pieces, on prosody, death and the Virgin.[57]

Finally, another group of books is less advanced in its texts, but demonstrates by their nature that Durham did not simply import scholars, but gave very solid training to its own would-be scholars. Maurice seems to have been educated entirely at Durham and both he and Laurence of Waltham, the future prior, may have undertaken some teaching. It is likely that the clerk, Laurence, may also have taught suitable students, even though his exact position is unknown. Relationships between the monks and the bishop's household could be close, as was shown when Laurence of Waltham spent some years as a sort of chancellor to Geoffrey Rufus, apparently living in the castle.[58] DCL C IV 29 testifies to the importance of systematic teaching. It is written in two hands of the early twelfth century, and contains sets of glosses on Priscian, and on the *Rhetoric* of Cicero, taken down from the teaching of a certain 'Magister G.'. The text consists simply of a series of glosses without rubrication, each starting simply with a paraph mark. Much of it makes little sense without an accompanying copy of the works glossed, which are known to have been in the Durham library at this time.[59] Presumably it was composed by a method like that pioneered by Master Laurence from the teaching of Hugh of St Victor, though here at the level of the trivium. The other contents of C IV 7 are similar, being anonymous glosses on fundamental texts by Cicero and Boethius.[60] Finally, the contents of C IV 10 move from advanced work on the material of the trivium, to the study of theology. It opens with a commentary on the Athanasian Creed, then gives two explanations of Prudentius' *Psychomachia*, and glosses on the 'versus Sibille de adventu Domini' and on Sedulius. Its main content is a commentary on Boethius' *De Consolatione*; but it also gives notes on terms used in Roman history, as well as a poem on precious stones.[61] This seems to bear witness to a wide-ranging education.

The manuscripts of this period also demonstrate the strength of the continuing interest in the collection and composition of chronicles at Durham in the 1120s. A copy of William of Jumièges' *Historia Norman-*

---

[57] Mynors, *Durham Cathedral Manuscripts*, nos. 89 and 109.
[58] See *Dialogi Laurentis Dunelmensis Monachi ac Prioris*, Intro., xxi.
[59] See *Catalogi Veteres*, 3 and 4.
[60] Mynors, *Durham Cathedral Manuscripts*, no. 79.
[61] Ibid. no. 80.

norum, in small, prickly hands which show some similarity to that of Digby 20 (now BL Harley 491) is difficult to date; DCL C IV 15 contains the chronicle of Metz (without any title, though a fourteenth-century hand has written 'Chronica Pippini' at the top of fol. 1) and the chronicle of Regino of Prüm.[62] William of Jumièges' work was not rare in early twelfth-century England, and is probably the 'Historia Normannorum' which accompanies Bede's 'Historia Anglorum' on the twelfth-century book-list.[63] The source of the Durham copy is unknown; its script (in two hands) is of Norman derivation, and its initials have only minimal decoration, with no specifically 'Durham' motifs. C IV 15 is equally difficult to place. Each chronicle is copied in one hand throughout, each scribe using the same two-column page layout, and the same red and green for simple, two-line-high initials. The hands are of the same general type, with upright, wiry, rather rounded letter forms, and short, angled serifs. They could be described as 'Anglo-Norman', and they are similar, though not identical, to script found in DCL B IV 15 and B IV 6, so that this volume may well have been copied out at Durham.[64] Its contents are very unusual, and there is no evidence on how they came to be known at Durham. However, they do suggest that the building up of a wide-ranging collection of chronicles was important at Durham.

Cosin V ii 6, the 'presentation copy' of Symeon's *Libellus*, has already been discussed as the product of the organised scriptorium at Durham, probably in the first decade of the twelfth century.[65] Here it is relevant to observe that it continued to be used as an official record of the affairs of the priory. The original hand entered on fol. 6v a list of the bishops of the see from St Cuthbert to Ranulf Flambard, and this was continued in later hands.[66] Fols. 7 to 10 were apparently intended for a running list of the professed monks of Durham. On fol. 7, the original hand entered a list of 'present monks' giving an impressive total of seventy one. The list opens with the familiar names of Aldwin and Turgot, and has Symeon, with a flourished initial S, in thirty-eighth position.[67] Like the list of bishops, it is continued in other hands, ending on fol. 8v, at the top of the third column of names. Fols. 9 and 10 are blank, suggesting that the list fell out of use in the later twelfth century.

---

[62] Ibid. nos. 81 and 86.

[63] *Catalogi Veteres*, 3.

[64] For DCL B IV 15 and B IV 6 see Mynors, *Durham Cathedral Manuscripts*, nos. 77 and 75.

[65] For the script of Cosin V ii 6 see Ker, *English Manuscripts*, 23–5; for analysis of its production at Durham, see contributions by Gullick, Meehan and Rollason in Rollason, *Symeon of Durham*.

[66] For the contents and makeup of the section containing the list of bishops see A. I. Doyle, 'The Original and Later Structure of Durham UL MS Cosin V ii 6', in Rollason, *Symeon of Durham*, 120–7. For the lists of monks and their interpretation see Piper, 'Early Lists and Obits'.

[67] The list is printed in Arnold, i, 4–6.

FIG. 56 Initial A from Durham, University Library, MS Cosin V ii 6, fol. 17v

Interestingly, the list has no Maurice, suggesting perhaps that it was first written out in the 1130s, after he had left for Rievaulx. Another curious point is that, in the later sections of the list, five initials are given for names which were never filled in. Four of these gaps occur between the names Laurentius and Absalon, which form part of the fourth set of names. Laurence and Absalon were apparently entered when it was already known that they were priors, as they are given in capitals, and this makes the missing names all the more puzzling.[68] Whatever may be the explanation for this, the names themselves are interesting, since they include Anglo-Saxon, Scandinavian and Norman-French examples. Of the original seventy-one, twenty-four names are Anglo-Saxon, eight Scandinavian, twenty-four Norman (with William, Robert, and Roger prominent) and the others uncertain. 'Columbanus' is interesting, and might perhaps show Celtic affinities, as might 'Aidan' lower down. Like the list of names, the historical record of the priory is kept up down to the mid-century in later hands. From fol. 98v to fol. 113r the continuators tell the story of Durham, ending with the rout of the usurper, Cumin.

Cosin V ii 6 then forms a link between the manuscripts apparently intended for study, and the grander, larger products of an organised group of scribe-artists whose work continues from Univ. 165, Hunter 100 and the others already discussed. It is appropriate now to turn to these, starting with the simpler examples. Perhaps the most interesting is Cambridge, Jesus, Q G 4, a copy of the sermons of Ivo of Chartres, and of a set of short works by Augustine.[69] It was written by several scribes, in small, wiry hands, similar to those in the 'scholarly' manuscripts already discussed. Its initials are mostly decorated only with small scallops, brackets and knobs, but it has one

---

[68] Laurence was prior 1149–53, and Absalon 1154–1158.
[69] Mynors, *Durham Cathedral Manuscripts*, no. 88.

unusually bulging I, on fol. 43v, which Gullick suggests is the prototype of the curious Durham form of I with a projection from its centre, first discussed by Mynors (Fig. 57).[70] Similarly, Cambridge, Jesus College, Q B 8 is rather plain, but has one decorated initial. Q B 8 is in fact a composite volume, its first part being a set of astronomical pieces, whose initials, like those in some other Durham manuscripts of this period, were never put in. However, its second and longer part contains a collection of sermons by, or attributed to, Augustine. These have no titles or rubrication, but the work opens with a four-line-high red and green D on fol. 19r (Fig. 58). The rather ugly repeated motif of round-headed pins in the centre has already been seen in earlier Durham manuscripts, and recurs in more elaborate, but still rather clumsy, forms in the more luxurious products of the Durham scriptorium.[71]

Next comes a set of manuscripts with slightly more elaborate decoration, making clear use of the Durham motifs already discussed in the previous chapter. London, Society of Antiquaries, MS 7, is a copy of the *Meditations* of Augustine, written in a medium-sized, prickly hand, related to those found in BL Cotton Vitellius D xx, a damaged copy of the *Life of St Cuthbert*, and in DCL B IV 6, a copy of Augustine's *Retractations* and *Confessions*, together with Alcuin's *Dialectics*.[72] Society of Antiquaries MS 7 has initials which show early versions of the clove-curl motif, handled in a way which mixes it with the flame motif, most particularly on fol. 24v (Figs. 59a and b). B IV 6 has only small and insignificant initials; but those of Vitellius D xx, although damaged, show what appear to be examples of the split petal motif. This is clearest on fol. 9v, where the right-hand half of an initial Q survives relatively undamaged, and shows a typical combination of split petal and fleshy curves (Fig. 60). The curving at the tip of the split petal is not distortion, but something found in other early examples of the motif, for instance that in DCL B IV 15. It is found again in two further manuscripts in this group: Bodleian, Laud misc. 392, and DCL A IV 16.[73] A IV 16 is another compound manuscript, its first part being a glossed copy of John's Gospel. The opening initial of the main text is an eleven-line-high blue and green I, with a red split petal forming the central motif in its decorative tail (Fig. 61). The other parts, including Bede's *Commentary on Tobias*, are carefully written but undecorated. The care given to the Bede text is shown by the notes of sources given in red in the margins. A final interesting feature of the

---

[70] M. Gullick, pers. comm.

[71] The four 'round-headed pins' are arranged in a cross, or quincunx, and so may be intended to carry a symbolic meaning.

[72] Mynors, *Durham Cathedral Manuscripts*, nos. 65 and 75.

[73] Ibid. nos. 111 and 100. Gullick has identified work by Symeon in corrections throughout DCL A III 16; see 'The Hand of Symeon of Durham', 26.

FIG. 57 Initial I from Cambridge,
Jesus College, MS Q G 4, fol. 43v

FIG. 58 Initial D from Cambridge,
Jesus College, MS Q B 8, fol. 19r

FIG. 59A Clove-curl motif from London,
Society of Antiquaries, MS 7, fol. 1r

FIG. 59B Clove-curl motif from London,
Society of Antiquaries, MS 7, fol. 24v

manuscript is that the third section, starting on fol. 66 and containing Augustine's commentary on Genesis, contains a long stint from fol. 71v on, in a script modelled on that of the Martyrology Scribe. Bodleian, Laud misc. 392 shows further Durham interest in Hugh of St Victor, containing several of his works. Its style suggests a date in the 1140s. Its main initial is a three-line-high red D, containing another curved split petal, set between curling brackets as in BL Cotton Vitellius D xx, as its central motif.

The manuscripts discussed so far have tended to have only one letter with decoration beyond the rudimentary, if any. They show work by what appears to be a large number of hands, writing rather informally and on a small scale. However, there is also clear evidence that a group of scribe-artists, and

FIG. 60 Split-petal motif from London,
BL, Cotton MS Vit. D. xx, fol. 9v

FIG. 61 Split-petal motif from Durham,
DCL, MS A IV 16, fol. 3r

probably artists, continued to work at Durham, producing books with more
ambitious, and more successful, illumination. One of the simplest of these is
B IV 16, another composite volume. Its first section consists of the twelfth-
century copy of Bede on the Apocalypse. It has been variously dated, but
seems unlikely to be later than mid-twelfth century; Mynors puts it clearly
into the first half.[74] Its script is a good, Durham variant on the recognisable
'English' type of the twelfth century, discussed by Ker; and its initials, the
first of which is reproduced by Mynors, have large and confident clove curls
in red and green.[75] Overall, this is a good-quality book, fitting with the
degree of respect accorded to Bede by the house which owned his relics. By
contrast, the second section of the volume is in a more old-fashioned style,
with taller, rounder script, and initials in red only, with simple and slightly
clumsy decoration of knobs, curving brackets, and the motif called the 'frilled
curl' by Mynors (Fig. 62). The texts are a set of short treatises by various
authors, including Alcuin, mostly on the persons of the Trinity, again
showing the interest in this subject. Finally, the third section is again in a

[74] Mynors, *Durham Cathedral Manuscripts*, no. 70.
[75] Ker, *English Manuscripts*, 23–5; and Mynors, *Durham Cathedral Manuscripts*, Plate 38b.
Further dating indication for at least one part of the manuscript is given by Gullick's identification of corrections and other small contributions by Symeon of Durham on fols. 110r–190v. See
'The Hand of Symeon of Durham', 29.

FIG. 62 Clove-curl motives from Durham, DCL, MS B IV 16, fol. 15r

new hand, somewhere between the first two in style, and here the initials again use clove curls, now in a rather thin and elongated form. Thus, the implication of the components of this manuscript is that each part was the work of one scribe, each of whom did the initials for his own work, decorating them with motifs drawn from the stock current at Durham. This was presumably the standard, and most convenient, practice.

However, there is also a set of manuscripts, those with the fullest and most sophisticated illumination, where work by the same hands recurs, in collaboration. One of the most striking of these is B II 8.[76] It is a copy of Jerome's *Commentary on Isaiah*, which once had a medieval note stating that it was kept in the cupboard by the infirmary door, for reading in the refectory. As might be expected, it is considerably larger than the books so far discussed, its size equalling that of the Carilef books. It is datable only by style, generally to c.1130, though Piper places it amongst the thirty-two manuscripts classified as '12th c in'.[77] What is most striking about it for this analysis is the number of other Durham books with which it connects. It is gathered in quires of ten, a practice common at Durham since the late eleventh century, and has traces of other early characteristics.[78] Like B II 26, its initials are frequently wholly or partly composed of human figures and animals, drawn in outline and set against strongly coloured grounds. Some of these are still multi-coloured, though grounds wholly of a strong blue are again beginning to dominate. The practice of composing initials in this way can be traced back to very early examples, such as the Corbie Psalter, but enjoyed a revival in the early twelfth century, most famously demonstrated by

---

[76] Mynors, *Durham Cathedral Manuscripts*, no. 68, Plate 42a and b; Kauffmann, *Romanesque Manuscripts*, no. 46, Plates 127, 128.

[77] Piper, 'Durham'.

[78] Gatherings of 10 first appear in the New Testament section of St Calais's Bible (now DCL A II 4), and are found, together with the more standard 8s, in Cambridge, Jesus College, Q C 29 and Q G 16, and with 12s in DCL B IV 16, B III 14, B IV 5, B IV 14 and B IV 15. Amongst manuscripts which use only 10s are B II 21, B III 9 and B IV 13, all associated with the Martyrology Scribe. Early twelfth-century manuscripts which use gatherings of 10 are Jesus Q A 14, and DCL A I 10, B II 7 and B III 4, as well as B II 8.

the Cîteaux manuscripts associated with Stephen Harding.[79] The human figures in B II 8, however, are rather different from those in B II 26.[80] The latter are rather clumsily drawn, with strong lines and no sign of Anglo-Saxon influence. By contrast, several of the figures of B II 8 seem to have taken the artist of B IV 14 and Univ. 165 as a stylistic model. The figure forming the right-hand upright of the initial N on fol. 128r, for instance, shows the curious drooping curves on the chest, the emphasised teardrop-shaped stomach, and the soft drapery folds emphasised by small circles. The hems of these figures show jewelled bands, flutter, and fall into flattened versions of the distinctive fold discussed in Chapter 3, all characteristics of the earliest twelfth-century Durham manuscripts. Still other historiated or inhabited initials have the letter form constructed of coils of foliage, highlighted by rows of open dots, and sometimes filled with rather compressed acanthus, again as seen in Univ. 165 and in the Symeon. However, a third type have trellised or interlaced uprights, a feature again going back to the late eleventh century, and seen also in B II 26. These, the facial types and the more flowing robes all link this manuscript to a contemporary, or slightly earlier, book from Fécamp. This also is a copy of a commentary by Jerome, this time on Jeremiah, and its opening initial, though it has foliage typical of Fécamp, is very close to the type in B II 8.[81] Perhaps the Durham book, like others in this period, was copied from a Norman exemplar? The Fécamp book is now Rouen, BM, A 321 (444) (see Plate 23).[82]

To return to Durham, it has been suggested that the artist of the major initials of B II 8 had a rather eclectic style, drawing partly on B II 26 and partly on Univ. 165/B IV 14 (it is not known when Univ. 165 left Durham, though it had done so by the thirteenth century). Certainly, a repetition of features seen in earlier Durham manuscripts is demonstrated again by the slightly clumsy use of human heads on terminals. In Cosin V ii 6 these emerged, as was standard, from the jaws of dragons and other beasts; but in B II 8, while this does happen (e.g. fol. 34v), they also simply protrude from the top or bottom of the initial, as on fols. 1v and 87r (see Plate 24).

Finally, the arabesque initials of B II 8 show strong links to those of

[79] The Corbie Psalter is now Amiens, BM, MS 18. The remarkable initials in the copy of Gregory's *Moralia in Job*, now Dijon, Bib. Mun., MS 173, made for Cîteaux in 1111, are frequently composed of figures of Cistercian monks.

[80] For DCL B II 26 see Mynors, *Durham Cathedral Manuscripts*, no. 62, and Plate 39; see also Kauffmann, *Romanesque Manuscripts*, no. 28, Plate 65.

[81] The Fécamp manuscript is now Rouen, BM, MS 444 (A 321). For analysis and reproductions, see Avril, *Manuscrits normands*, 76; and Lawrence, 'Anglo-Norman Book Production'.

[82] Given the stress laid on the presence and leading role of Ralph, abbot of Sées, in the accounts of the translation of St Cuthbert's relics in 1104, it would be valuable to know more of the manuscripts of Séez. However, few survive.

contemporary Durham manuscripts. Some are similar to the work seen in B
IV 16. One, however, is an exuberant confection, which manages to mix
almost all the standard Durham motifs in together. It is a green S on fol. 73v.
(Fig. 63). Its foliage is in red and blue, with a yellow-washed ground. The
artist was apparently pleased with it, since he repeated it in BL Harley 3864,
a copy of Bede's *Commentary on the Catholic Epistles* (Fig. 64).

Harley 3864 has only arabesque initials, but is nevertheless very interesting. It is written in a clear, proto-Gothic hand, of a recognisable Durham
type, and has clearly been well used. Omissions are carefully supplied by the
scribe, with finding marks; and frequent *nota* signs, and notes of subjects
discussed, are entered in the margin in another twelfth-century hand. On fol.
87v it has another initial combining clove curls and split petals, but here the
central split petal has small, irregular projections, like those found in
Yorkshire Cistercian manuscripts, particularly from Fountains.[83] Harley
3864 appears to be a Durham product, so it would seem that there was
reciprocal influence between Durham and the Cistercians.[84] However, the
opening initial of Harley 3864, an unusual open trellis-work I constructed
out of curved leaves, split petals and clove curls, is different from Cistercian
work, and similar to the equally bold arabesque initials of DCL A III 10.

Also parts of this group are Cambridge, Jesus College, Q A 14 (Bede's *On
Genesis and Exodus*) and DCL B II 7 (Jerome's *On the Psalms*).[85] The opening
initial of B II 7 is an I, on fol. 2r. It is largely lost in the binding, but its right-
hand edge shows knobs, outlined with red dots, as in B II 8 and others.
Several initials show bold clove-curl designs, related to those already
discussed. Most impressive are those of Jerome's Preface, and the opening
of the main text, on fols. 11v and 12r. They are constructed of open panels,
dragons, and a lion-mask, and filled with sprawling foliage, all set on strong
blue grounds (see Plate 25). This links them both to other books in this
Durham group, and to a small group from Kirkham (discussed in Chapter
8); and also makes them rather old-fashioned for the date of the manuscript.
Jesus Q A 14 is similar in several respects. It has work by the same scribe, and
its clove-curl initials are very close to those of B II 7. Its main initials are also
open-panelled and set on a blue ground, though there are no dragons, and
the foliage here is more advanced.

The use of old-fashioned elements is found also in two other books which

[83] See Chapter 9.

[84] For the most recent survey of the arguments on this problem, see Meehan, 'Durham
Twelfth-Century Manuscripts'; and C. Norton, 'History, Wisdom and Illumination', in Rollason, *Symeon of Durham*, 61–105.

[85] Mynors, *Durham Cathedral Manuscripts*, nos. 69 and 67. Gullick has found contributions
by Symeon in both; see 'The Hand of Symeon of Durham', 28 and 29.

FIG. 63 Initial S from Durham, DCL, MS B II 8, fol. 73v

FIG. 64 Initial S from London, BL, MS Harley 3864, fol. 84v

appear to be products of the Durham scriptorium of this period: DCL B IV
17 (*Decretum Burchardi vel Ivonis*); and BL Harley 1924 (*Life of St Cuthbert*).
Of these two, the latter is most clearly a Durham product, and the styles of its
display script and main hand appear to show something of a generation gap
in the styles of the Durham scriptorium. The opening words of the text of
Bede's letter, on fol. 1r, are in the round, curving style of early-twelfth-
century Durham script. But the main hand uses a clearly proto-Gothic style,
dating the manuscript towards the middle of the century.[86] The initial for the
prefatory letter, on the same folio, is an eleven-line-high D, open-panelled
and filled with fleshy, Anglo-Norman foliage (for details, see Fig. 65). The
ground is equally old-fashioned. On fol. 4r is the opening initial for the main
text, a P, which has a clambering figure clearly related to the figures in B II 8,
and looking back to those in B IV 14 and Hunter 100. In a similar way, B IV
17 has an initial on fol. 39r, for the opening of book II, which has old-
fashioned features. It is drawn in red outline, on a blue and green ground,
with dragon-head terminals and a form of lion-mask. Equally old-fashioned,
if more unusual, is the foliage of the arabesque initials. On fol. 69v is a nine-
line-high red P, with a tail composed of strikingly Norman foliage (Fig. 66).
It would appear that Durham scribes and artists were still using prestigious
older books as models. One of the most impressive manuscripts of the whole
group is DCL A I 10. This contains three separate texts, copied out by several
scribes, all using the rounded, Durham, style of script of the first half of the
century. The first text is an anonymous commentary on Matthew's Gospel,
identified in other manuscripts as that of Anselm of Laon, and confirming
again the scholarly interests of the monks of Durham.[87] The minor initials
here use the established motifs, but its major initials are in some ways more
advanced. The letters are still partially panelled, but the grounds are plain
blue, and the coils of foliage are much more symmetrically controlled. The
foliage is beginning to take on the form which becomes dominant by the
mid-century, and the humans and beasts are smaller in scale. A curious
feature is the large, bell-shaped terminals, as on the C on fol. 1v. The palette,
and especially the heavy use of white, is reminiscent of the Cosin Symeon,
but is here more sophisticated, and there is also use of gold.[88] The same artist
almost certainly illuminated the second text, Berengaudus' *Commentary on the
Apocalypse*. This opens on fol. 170r with an impressive historiated A,
containing the apocalyptic Christ. The clearest link to the initials of the
Matthew commentary are the terminals of the letter. The third text is
Cassiodorus' *De Anima*, and this opens with a fully painted initial, almost

---

[86] Piper, 'Durham', 30.
[87] Mynors, *Durham Cathedral Manuscripts*, no. 66.
[88] Ibid. Plates 40 and 41.

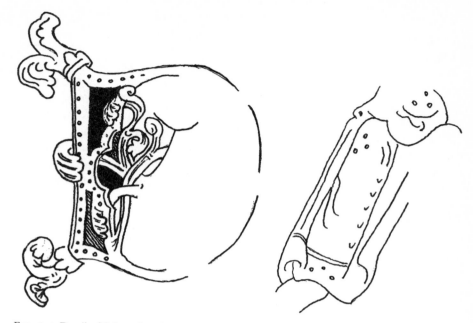

FIG. 65A Detail of foliage from initial D, in London,
BL, MS Harley 1924, fol. 1r

FIG. 65B Detail of human figure,
from the initial on fol. 4r

FIG. 66 Leaf motif from Durham, DCL, MS B IV 17, fol. 69v

certainly by the same artist as the opening initials of the Anselm and
Berengaudus. The simple letter form, the swelling terminals, and the painting
style are all the same. A note in the fourteenth-century catalogue shows that
this manuscript, like B II 8, was used for reading in the refectory.

The final manuscripts in this group are DCL A III 10 and Glasgow,
Hunterian, T 4 2.[89] The former is one of the few volumes dated by Piper to

[89] Ibid. nos. 124 and 71. Gullick has identified contributions by Symeon of Durham in
Glasgow UL Hunterian 85/T 4 2. Op. cit. 29.

the mid-century, and it appears to show a mixture of the elements already discussed, together with large and elaborate flowers. It contains the second part of Gilbert de la Porrée's gloss on the Psalter, another up-to-date theological work from the school of Paris, although this time of a less innovative type. Its script is large, upright and proto-Gothic, and the major initial, on fol. 2r, shows four elaborate, tentacular flowers, similar to those found in other English manuscripts of the period.[90] However, here they are combined with elements traditional in Durham manuscripts. Shaggy beast-heads are still used as terminals, and from their jaws emerge profile human heads. Mynors points out the similarity of design between the initial on fol. 36r of A III 10 and that on fol. 235r of A I 10; the initial on fol. 2r is also related, this time by the large, bell-shaped terminal on the central bar of the E, which is close to several in A I 10. Equally striking are the arabesque initials of A III 10 (see Fig. 67). These use once again the traditional elements of the split petal, as well as the newly popular 'spouted 1'.[91] The split petals also take on a variant wedge-form, again seen in several Yorkshire manuscripts.[92]

This analysis has demonstrated that the scriptorium of Durham remained active up to the arrival of Hugh du Puiset, despite the disruption caused to the life of the priory by the activities of William Cumin in the early 1140s. The work of the scriptorium appears as strikingly conservative, continuing to repeat and to make variations upon forms and motifs which originated around the turn of the century, or even before. Some links with northern Cistercian manuscripts begin to appear from the 1130s, although, as most of the motifs used by the Cistercians were already in use at Durham, this is a matter of nuances and is difficult to prove. It is not the motifs, but rather the way they are used, and the flatter handling of colour, which suggests that the Durham artists were affected by Cistercian work. Other outside influences or links do appear, however, as in the up-to-date flowers in A III 10. All this makes it very difficult to determine whether or not Durham UL Cosin V iii 1, the 'presentation copy' of the works of Laurence of Durham, is a product of the Durham scriptorium.[93] As Michael Kauffmann points out, it is most likely to have been made while Laurence was prior, 1149–54.[94] Thus, it could well be a professional product, made to a special order. Its standard, mid-century script is unhelpful, and the full-page miniature of the author at

[90] For the development of such foliage motifs, see Kauffmann, *Romanesque Manuscripts*, 26.
[91] On the 'spouted I' see Mynors, *Durham Cathedral Manuscripts*, 7.
[92] See for instance Cambridge, Trinity College, R 5 27, the copy of Bede's *Historia Ecclesiastica* most probably from St Mary's, and B II 10, a Pontifical, probably from York Minster.
[93] Mynors, *Durham Cathedral Manuscripts*, no. 110.
[94] Kauffmann, *Romanesque Manuscripts*, no. 76, Plate 215.

FIG. 67 Initial B from Durham, DCL, MS A III 10, fol. 126r

work is different from anything seen in the Durham manuscripts already discussed. Similarly, the tentacular flower in the bowl of the opening initial P is more developed than those in A III 10, and the palette is different. It seems likely, therefore, that this is not the work of the Durham scriptorium, especially as the arabesque initials do not use the so-familiar motifs. Indeed, this luxury book may represent one of the first means by which the artists of Durham learnt of the new type of foliate decoration.[95]

Thus, a pattern of manuscript production and collection at Durham emerges. Neither Ranulf Flambard nor Geoffrey Rufus were themselves scholars or interested in the collecton of books. Their gifts to the Durham library were minimal, and their energies were directed elsewhere. Ranulf Flambard paid for numerous large-scale building projects, and for the defences of Durham and of Norham. Geoffrey Rufus was apparently a less militaristic character, but made use of the financial and diplomatic skills learned in the royal court to keep his see and its lands as peaceful as possible during the outbreak of the civil war and the Scottish invasions. Meanwhile,

---

[95] Given the conservative style of the other Durham manuscripts discussed, it is unlikely that this up-to-date professional was based in Durham itself. However, St Mary's, York, was very wealthy at this time, and the importance of York as an ecclesiastical and economic centre may well have attracted professional artists. Certainly royal nephews such as William fitz Herbert and Hugh du Puiset, accustomed to spending time in the legate's cosmopolitan household at Winchester, can be expected to have been familiar with southern developments. Moreover, Durham had connections further afield than York. Perhaps the most striking example is Magister Laurence, who became a monk at St Albans in 1153, and then abbot of Westminster, and who certainly remained in touch with Aelred of Rievaulx. Thus, it is by no means impossible that Durham priory could have made contact with a professional artist based elsewhere.

the priors, subpriors and schoolmasters of the cathedral priory pursued and encouraged very advanced scholarly activity, obtaining up-to-date texts from the schools of France and of Canterbury (if Anselm's Canterbury can be counted as a school). They built up close contacts with the rising black-monk and Cistercian houses of Northumbria, exchanging texts with these also. In the process, a set of palaeographically unimpressive, but textually interesting, books were collected, which subsequently entered the Durham library.

At the same time, it is clear that an organised set of scribes and artists collaborated to produce a series of high-quality books. The texts were presumably selected by one of the officials of the monastery, and reasons for many of the choices can be suggested. Some, like the collection of canon law, would have had important functions in the life of the community. Others were intended for formal reading aloud in the Refectory; while still others were written by authors held in high regard at Durham, amongst whom Bede is very prominent. Their size, and the conservatism of their illumination (there is virtually no trace of the Byzantinising fashionable elsewhere) suggests that these latter were intended to be added to the equally impressive books of St Calais, as high-quality volumes for the *lectio divina*. There are few imported luxury books, the Laurence of Durham being the sole probable exception, which again fits with the absence of gifts of books from bishops. If the fashionable foliage of the Laurence of Durham was influential, as I have suggested, then the absence of such gifts may also have been partly responsible for the conservatism of the Durham scriptorium.

CHAPTER EIGHT

&⁊

The Augustinians and their libraries

T he settlement of the Augustinians in northern England is striking both for its rapidity and its geographical pattern.[1] During the reign of Henry I, a period when Anglo-Norman control of Northumbria was still being secured, there were six major foundations in Yorkshire, all made by members of the new aristocracy of the region, and during the reign of Stephen a further two. By contrast there were none at all in County Durham, and only two in Northumberland: the archbishop of York's priory at Hexham, founded in 1113, and another at the aristocratic stronghold of Bamburgh, founded in 1121.[2] It would therefore seem both that the bishops and priors of Durham kept Augustinian foundations out of their sphere of direct influence, and that the canons were particularly suitable for conditions in Yorkshire in the generation prior to the arrival of the Cistercians. It is therefore necessary to look both at the foundations themselves and at the state of Yorkshire in the early twelfth century.[3]

Perhaps the most influential foundation was Nostell, originally established as the home of a group of hermits, on a site associated with the cult of St Oswald, perhaps at the end of the eleventh century.[4] In Domesday Book the

[1] An earlier discussion of the surviving Augustinian manuscripts is given in Lawrence, 'A Northern English School?'.

[2] This is the date at which Henry I granted the estate to Nostell; but canons cannot be proved to have been settled there until the thirteenth century. See J. C. Dickinson, *The Origins of the Austin Canons and Their Introduction into England*, London, 1950, 160 and n. 5. Ch. iii of this work gives a full discussion of the foundation of Augustinian houses in England, but concentrates on patrons and filiations. A more succinct account is given by Janet Burton, who also makes a series of valuable points about the practical functions which patrons expected the houses of canons to perform. See her *Monastic and Religious Orders*, 43–62. On the role of Archbishop Thurstan in supporting Augustinian foundations in the north, see Nicholl, *Thurstan*, 127–39.

[3] Valuable information on lands granted to the Augustinians in Yorkshire is given by Robinson, *The Geography of Augustinian Settlement*.

[4] See Jane Herbert, 'The Transformation of Hermitages into Augustinian Priories in Twelfth-Century England', in *Monks, Hermits and the Ascetic Tradition*, Studies in Church History 22, Oxford, 1985, 131–45.

whole manor is recorded as being held by Ilbert de Lacy. Early in the twelfth century it was refounded as an Augustinian priory, and its first prior, Aldulf, Athelulf, or Æthelwulf, seems to have been Henry I's confessor.[5] Athelulf left in 1133, when he was made first bishop of the new diocese of Carlisle by Henry I. But it was whilst Athelulf was prior that Waldef, grandson of Earl Waltheof, stepson of David, king of Scots, and kinsman of William of Aumale, earl of York, entered the house, rising to become sacristan.[6] Ilbert de Lacy himself was one of the group of what were effectively military governors established in Yorkshire by the Conqueror.[7] De Lacy was given charge of a castle at Pontefract, where he founded a Cluniac priory as part of the compact fee he was given.[8] Like most of the new lords of Yorkshire, he was also given supporting estates in wealthier shires further south, and was one of the eight major landholders in Yorkshire itself.[9]

No others of this group founded Augustinian houses on their Yorkshire estates, but Bridlington, founded in 1113, Guisborough c.1119 and Kirkham c.1122 were all founded on parts of the great Yorkshire honour held at the time of Domesday by Robert, count of Mortain and earl of Cornwall, the son of the Conqueror's half-brother, Robert. He had declared his support for Robert Curthose in 1104 and, after the battle of Tinchebrai in 1106, was imprisoned for life. His English lands were retained by Henry I, who used them to reward his supporters.[10] One beneficiary was Walter Espec, one of Henry I's most important supporters in the north, who received Kirkham together with the valuable honour of Helmsley. Walter de Gant received the soke of Bridlington, while Robert de Brus received Guisborough, a large estate on the northern edge of the North Yorkshire moors. William of Aumale, made earl of York in 1140, followed this tradition by founding Thornton in 1139, as a daughter house of Kirkham.[11]

The remaining northern Augustinian houses were founded by men of smaller influence, all of whom were also members of the emerging local aristocracy. Bolton was founded in c.1120 by William Meschin and his wife;

[5] T. N. Burrows, 'The Foundation of Nostell Priory', *Yorkshire Archaeological Journal* 53, 1981, 31–5. The suggestion about Æthelwulf was first made by Dickinson, *Origins*, 120.

[6] On Waldef's career see D. Baker, 'Legend and Reality: The Case of Waldef of Melrose', in *Studies in Church History* 12, 1975, 59–82.

[7] For a discussion of the sweeping tenurial changes by which their consolidated fees were created, and a map, see R. Fleming, *Kings and Lords in Conquest England*, Cambridge, 1991, 149–59.

[8] See B. Golding, 'The Coming of the Cluniacs', in *Proceedings of the Battle Conference on Anglo-Norman Studies* 3, 1980, 65–77.

[9] For the extent of his fee, see Fleming, *Kings and Lords*, 153.

[10] See Kapelle, *The Norman Conquest of the North*, 195–9.

[11] Nicholl brings out the importance of the support given by Archbishop Thurstan to the Augustinian foundations; see note 2 above.

Worksop in the 1120s by William de Lovetot and Drax in the 1130s by William Paynel, with the support of the archbishop of York, who also established an Augustinian priory at Hexham in 1113. The last of the group was Newburgh, founded in 1145 on part of the large and wealthy manor of Coxwold by the Mowbrays, who also founded Byland in the same parish.[12]

This survey suggests that the newly established aristocracy of Yorkshire was following a pattern already well established by the dukes of Normandy and their supporters in Lower Normandy and in Wales. That is, expansion into a new and relatively insecure area was secured and made more stable by the establishment of a network of religious houses.[13] These houses were endowed with lands by collaborating groups of patrons; and in return their stability of tenure helped to support that of the patrons. Indeed, Margaret Gibson goes further, and argues that monasteries could provide their patrons with a range of specialised services: 'a supply of literate men and written documents, a means of control over a complex of estates, a source of ready cash, and a community to pray for the patron'.[14] However, whilst the Augustinian houses of Yorkshire fit this pattern up to a point, patrons in the first half of the twelfth century had an increasing range of religious orders to choose amongst, and several of the founders of Augustinian priories made other foundations also. Thurstan, archbishop of York, for instance, was patron of the Cistercian house of Fountains in the 1130s,[15] while Walter Espec, founder of Kirkham, was also patron of Rievaulx, and the Mowbrays, as has been said, founded both Newburgh and Byland. Furthermore, de Lacy founded a Cluniac priory at Pontefract as well as Augustinian Nostell, while the increasingly wealthy Benedictine house of St Mary's, York, received endowments from a wide range of northern patrons.[16] The question which arises is thus why the Augustinians were so successful in Yorkshire in the early twelfth century.

Part of the answer to this question clearly lies in the patronage given to the Augustinians by Henry I and his queen, Edith-Matilda, which appears to have made the new order fashionable.[17] However, in the case of Yorkshire it is possible to go a little further, by looking at the evidence of Domesday

---

[12] For discussion see Dickinson, *Origins*, 108–25 and 141.
[13] On this practice in Normandy see Gibson, *Lanfranc*, 30–4.
[14] Ibid. 102.
[15] This was under rather exceptional circumstances: see Nicholl, *Thurstan*, 151–91; Bethell, 'The Foundation of Fountains Abbey'; Baker, 'The Foundation of Fountains Abbey'; J. Burton, 'The Foundation of the British Cistercian Houses', in Norton and Park, *Cistercian Art and Architecture*, at 26–7.
[16] See Burton, 'Monastic Revival', 50.
[17] Dickinson, *Origins*, 125–30; Burton, *Monastic and Religious Orders*, 46.

Book.[18] Argument continues about the seriousness of the damage done to the agricultural economy of Yorkshire by the Conqueror's harrying of the north in 1069/70. However, the fall in the value of Yorkshire estates between 1066 and 1086 is very clear.[19] The lands of the archbishop of York, one of the largest landholders in Yorkshire, were almost unaltered in extent but were halved in value. The pattern is even more marked in the king's own estates. These comprised about 20 per cent of Yorkshire, and in 1066 had made up also about 20 per cent of its value, but in 1086 they appear to have made up only about 4 per cent of its value, as well as holding only about 4 per cent of its recorded population.[20] However, as this contrast would suggest, the fall in value is not uniform. Both estates whose value had fallen, and those recorded as wholly waste, were unevenly distributed, not only between the holdings of different lords but also within the holdings of individuals. Moreover, the whole question of waste manors is very difficult, as the Domesday commissioners seem to have been unable to obtain any information for some areas, and in others to have based their figures on geld records or even hypothesis.[21] Nevertheless, there can be little doubt that the destruction had been both severe and extensive, and that the population had been seriously affected. Chroniclers in the West Midlands and elsewhere speak of starving refugees fleeing Yorkshire for the south, some of them dying on the way, while unknown numbers were presumably killed outright or died soon after the winter of 1069.[22] It has been estimated that, of nearly 1900 villages, over 1100 were either depopulated or recorded as containing some waste, while another 400 were significantly under-populated. Even in the Vale of York, the most fertile and potentially valuable area, there was an average population of only two men per square mile.[23] Thus, the conditions in late-eleventh-century Yorkshire do not seem propitious for the establishment of a flourishing monastic culture of the traditional kind.

However, Domesday Book also contains evidence which suggests deliberate moving and resettling of peasants by 'improving' lords. This argument was first put forward by T. A. M. Bishop, who also suggested that the areas in which resettlement and redevelopment were most advanced fall into two

[18] A full account of the Yorkshire Domesday is given by Farrer, 'Introduction to the Yorkshire Domesday'. A map showing the manors described in Domesday as 'waste' is given by H. C. Darby, 'Domesday England', in Darby, ed., *A New Historical Geography of England before 1600*, Cambridge, 1976, 60.
[19] See T. A. M. Bishop, 'The Norman Settlement of Yorkshire', in *Studies in Medieval History presented to F. M. Powicke*, Oxford, 1948, 1–14; le Patourel, 'The Norman Conquest of Yorkshire'; and Kapelle, *The Norman Conquest of the North*, 158–90.
[20] Bishop, 'Norman Settlement', 2–10. See also Jewell, *The North–South Divide*, 86–91.
[21] F. W. Maitland, *Domesday Book and Beyond*, 3rd edn, London, 1960, 423.
[22] Kapelle, *The Norman Conquest of the North*, 161–3.
[23] Ibid. 162.

distinct types: good farming land held by powerful lords or subtenants; and areas of military and strategic importance.[24] Not surprisingly, there is also evidence for the imposition of heavier labour obligations on these manors. Finally, there are in the Domesday record of Yorkshire some fifty villages which were apparently over-populated and over-stocked in relation to their stated capacity. These 'overstocked manors' are difficult to interpret, but they do suggest that some kind of redevelopment was under way by 1086.[25]

The evidence of Domesday Book thus suggests that Yorkshire constituted a sort of frontier society, in which land was plentiful but population was sparse, and in which the numbers of both settlements and functioning churches had been reduced.[26] Moreover, political divisions meant that land tenure was still relatively fluid in the reign of Henry I. Augustinian priories had several characteristics which might have been of value in such circumstances.[27] First, they were smaller and needed fewer resources than Benedictine abbeys. Second, to judge from evidence from southern England, they might be expected to undertake some pastoral duties. Third, they might also accept educational responsibilities.[28] What is particularly interesting is that there is a considerable correspondence between the areas where the Augustinian houses were founded, and the regions in which the majority of the so-called 'overstocked manors' were recorded in Domesday.[29] Kapelle points out that these manors were in relatively secure locations, had apparently not been laid waste in 1069/70, and that most of them had demesne land.[30] This would suggest that these were areas being deliberately developed by their lords; and that the Augustinians were both given potentially valuable land, and perceived as able to contribute to this development.

In very broad terms, then, the foundation of the Augustinian houses represents a particular phase in the settlement of Yorkshire and in the re-establishment of monastic life there. They came later than the great Benedictine houses of Selby, Pontefract and St Mary's, York: but overlap

---

[24] Bishop, 'Norman Settlement', 10.

[25] The fullest discussion of these 'overstocked manors' is that of Kapelle, *The Norman Conquest of the North*, ch. 6, 'The Impact of the Normans on the Northern Village'. Kapelle provides a map on p. 168.

[26] For a map of functioning churches see Kapelle, *The Norman Conquest of the North*, 171.

[27] On this, see Burton, *Monastic and Religious Orders*, 46–50.

[28] The attractiveness to patrons of the Augustinians' capacity to undertake 'involvement with the world around' is stressed also by J. Blair, in 'Secular Minster Churches in Domesday Book', in P. Sawyer, ed., *Domesday Book: A Reassessment*, London, 1985, 104–42, at 138. A number of examples of schools run by Augustinians are cited by Barlow, *The English Church 1066–1154*, 231–3.

[29] See Kapelle, *The Norman Conquest of the North*, 168; and Robinson, *The Geography of Augustinian Settlement*, 28–31.

[30] Kapelle, *The Norman Conquest of the North*, 167–73.

to some extent with the foundation of the Cistercian abbeys. In these circumstances, and especially given their small size and relatively remote locations, the building up of book collections might well have posed special difficulties. Some help may have been given by patrons, and by parent houses where these existed, but unfortunately no documentary evidence survives.

Fortunately, there is clear evidence, both in the Augustinian Rule and in a twelfth-century treatise from Bridlington, about the use and production of manuscripts in these houses.[31] The Rule assumes the presence of books, not only for the liturgy and for reading aloud during meals, but also for devotional reading on a daily basis. Moreover, it is made clear that the books are to be the property of the community rather than of individuals, and that they are to be under the care of an official.[32] The Bridlington treatise goes much further, and gives a valuable picture of how these basic regulations were interpreted in at least one Yorkshire priory. It is an exposition of the Rule, written in the popular form of a dialogue between a master and a pupil, and is almost certainly the work of Robert, known as 'the Scribe'.[33]

Robert became prior of Bridlington c. 1 1 47–50, and was the compiler of glosses on Exodus, on the Minor Prophets and on St Paul, the latter being popular in the twelfth century, and surviving in a number of copies. It seems likely that Robert was in contact with other scholars, as he states that the gloss on the Minor Prophets was compiled at the request of Gervase, abbot of Louth Park.[34] This Gervase was subprior of St Mary's, York, and was one of the founding members of Fountains, whose daughter Louth Park was. To compile his gloss, Robert had access to the older *Commentaries* of Lambert of Utrecht and Anselm of Laon, relatively rare texts and suggestive of access to a well-stocked library.[35] Robert's glosses also demonstrate considerable knowledge of patristic works, and especially those of Augustine. The autobiographical remarks included in the prologue to the treatise do not make it clear that this work of compilation was done at Bridlington, but neither is there mention of any significant study before he came there. Indeed, there is a suggestion that Robert was at Bridlington from the time of Wickmann, the first prior, which would suggest that Robert himself may have been relatively young when he arrived.[36] It is therefore at least a possibility that Bridlington had a good collection of patristic works and biblical commentaries.

---

[31] For the Rule, see G. Lawless, ed., *Augustine of Hippo and His Monastic Rule*, Oxford, 1987; for the Bridlington text, see *The Bridlington Dialogue* (ed. and trans. by a religious of CSMV), London, 1960.

[32] The bans on individual ownership are in ch. iv and xiv. The official in charge of the books is mentioned in ch. xv.

[33] For a brief outline of Robert's career as a compiler of glosses, see Smalley, *The Study of the Bible in the Middle Ages*, 5 1 and 60–1.

[34] Ibid.   [35] Ibid.   [36] *Bridlington Dialogue*, VII–VIII.

The treatise itself suggests that the Augustinian canons were expected not only to study, but also to produce books. At one point the master discusses suitable work for the canons, and at the top of the list come 'Reading, expounding and preaching the Word of God before the brethren, and practising for divine worship by reading'. This is closely followed by 'Preparing parchments for the scribes, writing, illuminating, ruling lines, scoring music, correcting and binding books.'[37] The list is slightly ambiguous, in that there is some suggestion that 'the scribes' may be a separate group, but overall it would appear that Robert expects all stages in the production of books to take place within the priory itself. Later, Robert confirms the importance he attaches to books and to reading, when his master argues strongly against those who suggest that Augustine intended reading to take place during only one hour a day, and even asserts that the superior might modify the Rule's stipulation that 'Anyone who asks for a book at the wrong time is not to have it'.[38] There is a tone of defending a practice against criticism here, and a suggestion of some debate amongst the canons about the correct amount of reading and studying. It is perhaps as part of this debate that Robert emphasises that the central functions of reading and study were not the increase of personal scholarship, but the preparation for divine service, and the exposition of the Scriptures to the brethren. The evidence of the treatise therefore is that the canons of Bridlington were expected, in the mid-twelfth century, both to study and to produce books. What is especially interesting is the suggestion that reading scripture or patristic works was seen as a form of preparation for divine service; there are perhaps similarities between this and the Cistercian idea of a continuity between meditating on a text and praying in the church.[39] What the Bridlington treatise does not contain, however, is any mention of a school. There is also no information on how texts were obtained for copying, or on how scribes and illuminators were trained. The implication would seem to be that, by the middle of the twelfth century, a supply of both texts and scribes could be taken for granted.

Some answers to these questions, however, may be found in surviving Bridlington books. Six twelfth-century manuscripts have been identified, all from the second half of the century, out of a total of nine surviving Bridlington books.[40] As this relatively high survival rate suggests, the

---

[37] Ibid. 154.   [38] Ibid. 163–4.

[39] See 'Codex Manuscriptus 31 Bibliothecae Universitatis Labacensis', ed. C. Noschitzka, *Analecta Sacri Ordinis Cisterciensis* 6, 1950; at cap. L80, p. 37. For discussion, see A. Lawrence, 'English Cistercian Manuscripts of the Twelfth Century', in Norton and Park, *Cistercian Art and Architecture*, at 288.

[40] See Ker, *Medieval Libraries*, 12–13. Lists for the other Augustinian houses discussed here are given in the same work.

twelfth-century books are of good quality and, if they may be taken as at all representative, demonstrate interest in good, glossed copies of biblical texts, and in historical works. Three of the books also carry shelf-marks, with glossed copies of the Apocalypse and of Luke carrying the letter D, and the copy of William of Malmesbury having the letter J.[41] This would suggest that, at least by the fourteenth century (the latest date of a manuscript carrying such a letter) there was a fairly extensive, and organised, library at Bridlington. Moreover, its twelfth-century books fit the attitude towards books set out by the treatise, although there are no surviving copies of the works of Robert the Scribe himself.

The appearance and style of the Bridlington books are also interesting. The three glossed texts are in clear, skilled bookhands of the mid to later twelfth century, with considerable care taken in both ruling and copying to produce a clear arrangement of the glosses around the main text, although no academic apparatus or special signs are given. The layout of the Gospel of Mark (BL Harley 50) is the most complex, and its script is latest in appearance. The hands of all the manuscripts are both skilled and clear but, whilst there is generally uniformity in script and layout within each volume, there is no apparent attempt to produce a set of manuscripts of uniform style. Thus, they represent the work of a number of skilled scribes, but with no clear attempt at a 'house style'. There is then no clear evidence on whether these books were produced at Bridlington itself; but there are suggestions that several, at least, were Northumbrian products.

The evidence for this consists in what appears to be influence from the Yorkshire Cistercian houses in these Bridlington books. Like contemporary manuscripts from these houses, the Bridlington books generally lack rubrication and display script at the beginning of the text. Initial decoration is also very restricted, and is often slightly clumsy in appearance, in contrast to the high quality of the script. When decorated initials do occur, they use several colours (unlike the Yorkshire Cistercian houses other than Fountains); but their stylised foliage motifs are smaller and less complex than those found in contemporary Yorkshire Cistercian initials. Taken together, this would suggest that the Bridlington manuscripts were not Cistercian products, but that there was a clear concept of how books should be set out and decorated, and that this was strongly influenced by the books of the Yorkshire Cistercians.[42] Further evidence that the Bridlington books were probably of Northumbrian origin is found in BL Cotton Claudius A v, fols. 46–135, another copy of William of Malmesbury. Like most of the other Bridlington

---

[41] These are respectively: Ripon Cathedral, MS 3; Bodleian Fairfax 15; and Bodleian Bodley 357.

[42] On these Cistercian books, see Chapter 9.

books, this has initials in the common colours of red, blue and green, but on fol. 84v it has a four-line initial C, in red and blue, decorated with the distinctive split-petal motif. This motif originated at Durham, but became a dominant element in the initials of Yorkshire Cistercian books; it is not found in southern England. Its use in the Bridlington manuscript is very simple, in contrast to the complex patterns found in Cistercian books, so that the suggestion here also is of Cistercian influence, rather than Cistercian origins. It should, however, be noted that the attribution of this manuscript to Bridlington is not supported by an inscription or other definite evidence. The link with Bridlington is suggested by Ker, and fits the overall style and presentation of the book, but Gullick has attributed it to Belvoir, although without citing his evidence.[43]

So far, the evidence is suggestive, but not conclusive. It would appear that Bridlington, by the mid-twelfth century, had developed a clear attitude towards the production, decoration and use of books; and that this book culture was to some extent influenced by the Yorkshire Cistercian houses, with one of which, at least, Robert the Scribe was in contact. It also seems that the books so far discussed, as well as fitting in with this book culture, were produced in Northumbria, but were probably not Cistercian products. All this makes Bridlington itself the most likely centre of production, with the lack of scribal uniformity fitting in with the absence of a school. One surviving manuscript, Bodleian, Digby 53, does seem to confirm literary work on the part of the canons. This is a small volume containing a miscellany of items. Each item is in a different hand, and has a different ruling pattern, while the initials have simple decoration, with no distinctive motifs. This manuscript seems most likely to represent a gathering together of short pieces copied out by members of the community; and the inclusion of a treatise on rhetoric again suggests some literary interests. It therefore seems likely, though it cannot be proved, that the canons of Bridlington did engage in the production of books, as the treatise suggests.

Finally, it has been argued that the library of Bridlington was extensive and well organised by the fourteenth century; but it may be possible to go further than this. BL Harley 50, the glossed copy of Mark's Gospel, also contains, on fol. 48v, a book-list believed to be that of Bridlington in the late twelfth century.[44] The list contains some seventy-seven major titles, as well as some forty works listed as 'Parvi libelli'. They are set out in groups, the first starting

---

[43] See Gullick, 'The Origin and Importance of Cambridge, Trinity College R. 5. 27', 257, n. 43.

[44] This is published by H. Omont, in *Centralblatt für Bibliothekswesen* 9, 1892, 203. For a recent edition see T. Webber and A. Watson, eds., *The Libraries of the Augustinian Canons*, Corpus of British Medieval Library Catalogues 6, London, 1997.

with the works of Gregory the Great, then going on to the *Commentaries* of one Robert, presumably Robert the Scribe himself. In addition to those still extant, there are several other titles, including one on the Apocalypse, which may be related to the extensive glosses and commentary surviving in a Bridlington copy of the Apocalypse, now in Ripon/Leeds.[45] The next group contains principally the works of Ambrose and Isidore, whilst another group is headed 'Libri Glosali' and includes what may be the surviving Mark and Luke. So far, all the books are entered under the general heading of 'libri magni armarii' but the next, and largest, group has the heading 'Libri Hugonis'. There is no evidence on the identity of this Hugh, but the books themselves suggest wide interests. The list opens with the works of Hugh of St Victor, but includes also works by Rabanus, Smaragdus, Cassian and Gregory Nazianzen. There are other works on the monastic life, a number of saints' *Lives* and a Bestiary, as well as other more obscure works. The inclusion of a Priscian suggests the study of Latin grammar, but this is the collection of a monk rather than a schoolman. He had presumably joined the priory of Bridlington at some stage, and given the community his books.[46]

It is thus possible to build up a picture of the book culture of Bridlington, and of its manuscripts. One of the most striking features of the latter is the degree of Cistercian influence they suggest. What is more, it is possible to demonstrate that contacts between the Cistercians and the Augustinians were close in Yorkshire in the twelfth century. The contact between Robert of Bridlington and Gervase of Louth Park has already been mentioned; but contact between Kirkham and Rievaulx was closer still. Both had been founded by Walter Espec, and Waldef, prior of Kirkham from 1139, was a close friend of Aelred of Rievaulx, and indeed left Kirkham, with Everard his lifelong supporter, to become a Cistercian himself in 1147.[47] A surviving document outlines a plan, never carried out, to convert Kirkham itself to a Cistercian house.[48] Moreover, under Waldef, Kirkham became very much involved in ecclesiastical politics. When Thurstan of York resigned in 1140, and retired to Pontefract, William of Aumale offered to have Waldef made

[45] Ripon Cathedral, MSS 3 and 4. These are now lodged at the Brotherton Library, Leeds.

[46] It is tempting to speculate that this individual may have undertaken some teaching, especially as Bridlington was a prosperous town in the late twelfth century, but of this there can be no proof. William of Newburgh, the historian, was born in Bridlington c.1135 (see Barlow, *The English Church 1066–1154*, 22); he gives no details about his own education, but it seems to have taken place entirely at Newburgh.

[47] See Baker, 'Legend and Reality'.

[48] This is a draft agreement preserved in the Rievaulx cartulary. See J. C. Atkinson, ed., *Cartularium Abbathiae de Rievalle*, Surtees Society 83, London, 1887, 108–9. For recent discussion see J. Burton, *Kirkham Priory, from Foundation to Dissolution*, Borthwick Papers 84, York, 1995.

archbishop. Waldef refused but, in 1142, supported Cuthbert, prior of Augustinian Guisborough, William of Rievaulx and Richard of Fountains in accusing William, the archbishop-elect of York and nephew of King Stephen, of simony. By contrast, William's supporters, according to Richard of Hexham, were primarily Benedictines (though they did not include Durham, at this point engrossed in the struggle against William Cumin).[49] Finally, a little later, William of Newburgh was given information and encouraged to write his *History* by Abbot Ernald of Rievaulx, while his *Commentary on the Song of Songs* was requested by Abbot Roger of Byland.[50]

In order to take further this question of a network of contacts between the newer Yorkshire houses, and between them and Durham, it is necessary to examine the surviving manuscripts. The Cistercian books will be discussed in the next chapter, but here the manuscripts from the other Augustinian houses will be compared against the evidence from Bridlington. Unfortunately, these manuscripts are few in number, with Drax and Nostell having no surviving books, and Thornton none from the twelfth century. The most interesting cases are Newburgh, with three twelfth-century manuscripts, Guisborough also with three, Kirkham with five and Hexham with one eleventh-century manuscript and four twelfth-century.[51]

At Newburgh, William was encouraged in his historical writing by Ernald of Rievaulx, and appears to have been given information by Byland as well as Rievaulx. He also made use of chronicle material deriving from Durham, and compiled there *c.*1148–61, though whether this came direct or via the Cistercians is not known.[52] At all events, the impression of a network of literary and intellectual exchanges, perhaps involving the lending and copying of books, is reinforced. Of the surviving Newburgh manuscripts, perhaps the most striking is BL Stowe 62, a copy of William's own work. This work was completed in 1198 and the Stowe copy dates from perhaps 1200 and has a Newburgh *ex libris*. Like the Bridlington manuscripts it is of high quality, and its initials, in three colours, are similar to those in Cistercian manuscripts (see Fig. 68). It uses cable patterns in the stems of letters, complex versions of the split-petal motif and a three-lobed-bud motif, all characteristics of Yorkshire Cistercian initial decoration. Again, BL Arundel 252, the Newburgh copy of Ivo Carnotensis, dates from the turn of the century, and shows some Cistercian influence. It is plain in appearance, with most of its initials having only minimal decoration, but uses a range of colours very close to those found in Cistercian manuscripts: red, acid green, a distinctive pale blue

[49] See 'The Chronicle of John, Prior of Hexham', *sub anno* 1143, in Raine, *Hexham*, 142–3.
[50] See William of Newburgh, *History of English Affairs*, 3.
[51] For all of these, see Ker, *Medieval Libraries*, under their respective entries.
[52] See Taylor, *Medieval Historical Writing in Yorkshire*, 10–12.

FIG. 68 Initial R from London, BL,   FIG. 69 Initial C from London, BL,
MS Stowe 62, fol. 59r   MS Arundel 252, fol. 6v

and dull yellow. However, the only initial with relatively complex decoration, a six-line-high C on fol. 6v, does not use the distinctive cable and split-petal motifs (Fig. 69). Instead, the hollow of the letter is filled with regular, repeating, symmetrically arranged elements, closest in design to some initials in twelfth-century manuscripts from St Mary's, York (see Fig. 54).[53] However, the evidence is too sparse to be able to put forward any argument about the origins of the Newburgh books. All that can be said is that they appear to fit in with the pattern already established, and to be Northumbrian products.

As has already been said, Kirkham was perhaps most closely tied to the Cistercians of all the Augustinian priories, through its prior, Waldef. More-over, the draft agreement to make Kirkham Cistercian, preserved in the Rievaulx cartulary, is an interesting document, especially for the light its sheds on the attitudes of its apparently Cistercian authors. There is special mention of what is to be done about the stained-glass windows, since these were in contradiction to Cisterican regulations; but there is no mention of

[53] See Chapter 5.

any problem about the books or their bindings. No book-list survives from Kirkham, and, like Guisborough, it did not produce any historical work until the sixteenth century. However, a small set of its books are especially interesting, and may represent the collection and special interest of one of the canons. They are now: BL Arundel 36, containing Possidius' *Life of St Augustine* and other shorter texts; BL Add. 38817, containing works by Bede; and BL Cotton Vespasian B xi, fols. 84–125, containing short works by Aelred of Rievaulx. The Arundel and Add. manuscripts were originally part of the same volume, and they are unusual amongst these Yorkshire manuscripts (see Plate 26). They appear to be of the mid-twelfth century, and are written on high-quality vellum, in a large, clear proto-Gothic script. Their main initials are fully painted, in a style reminiscent of Durham and Canterbury in the first part of the twelfth century. The letters are formed from the sinuous bodies of dragons, and contain roundels with heads, including one of a tonsured religious. Even more unusually, Arundel 36 contains a series of outline drawings of heads on the margin of fol. 13r. These are executed in clear, confident ink drawing, and are rather elongated and heavy-jawed, with a preference for the three-quarter view. Perhaps the nearest northern parallels are in books from Durham such as DCL B II 8, or Cosin V ii 6. A link with Durham many also be suggested by the repeated occurrence of the split-petal motif, in complex patterns, in the minor initials (Fig. 70). How these books were obtained and where they were made cannot be proven. Work by the same scribe has been found in BL MS 216, which has therefore been tentatively identified as a Kirkham manuscript, especially because its textual contents link it to a surviving manuscript from Rievaulx. These are Orosius' *Historia adversus Paganos* and Dares Phrygius' *De Excidio Troiae Historia* and they connect both to the other Kirkham books and to Northumbrian historical interests more generally.[54] Where the artist was trained is unknown, but the decorated initials are certainly old-fashioned in comparison to the script of these volumes. However, it appears almost certain that they are Northumbrian work, and possible that they were copied from an older exemplar, perhaps borrowed from Durham. In themselves, these manuscripts are perhaps too few to prove the existence of a scriptorium at Kirkham; but they certainly testify both to an interest in building a collection of high-quality books, and to Kirkham's intellectual and artistic links with other Northumbrian houses. The implications of the works by Bede found in BL Add. 38817 and Arundel 36 will be taken up in Chapter 10, but some further observations can be made here. Firstly, the Kirkham books contain evidence for the existence of a communal book collection by the second half

[54] On BL Burney 216 see Webber and Watson, *The Libraries of the Augustinian Canons*, 32.

FIG. 70 Initial P from London, BL, MS Arundel 36, fol. 14r

of the twelfth century; they contain a large and impressive twelfth-century *ex libris* inscription. Secondly, the interests represented by the surviving books are slightly different from those at Bridlington. The strongest interests appear to be in the history and the authors of Northumbria. Kirkham's intellectual interests are further represented by what is known of one canon resident there in this period, namely Maurice, the prior. He was connected to both Gerard and Roger, archbishops of York, and spent some time studying in York as a young man. He was apparently able to learn Hebrew from the Jewish community of York, as well as having access to the books of Archbishop Gerard. Further evidence of his scholarship, and his slightly unusual interests, is his treatise *Contra Salomitas*, dedicated to Gilbert of Sempringham, with whom he was probably also in touch. It is tempting to link the high-quality Kirkham manuscripts, with the rather scholarly marginal notes which survive in Arundel 36 and were apparently made by its then owner, with this well-connected individual; but there is no evidence.[55]

From Guisborough, the evidence is even more sparse, consisting of only three books. However, it would appear that Guisborough also had a communal library, since BL Arundel 218, a late-twelfth-century book, has a shelf-mark of uncertain date, suggesting the presence of a shelved library. Of the three surviving books, one is by Bede, one by Cassiodorus, and one contains a collection of extracts from Alcuin, Bede, Gregory and

[55] On Maurice of Kirkham, see R. B. Dobson, *The Jews of Medieval York and the Massacre of March 1190*, Borthwick papers 45, York, 1974.

Augustine.[56] Thus here also there seems to have been study of patristic works and an interest in the great figures of the Northumbrian past. Moreover, the collection of extracts, Arundel 218, contains evidence that Guisborough also was influenced by Durham. This manuscript is written in one hand throughout, although it is not completely regular, and its initials use a motif very common in Durham books but not found in other Augustinian or Cistercian manuscripts, the clove curl. This motif is found in Arundel 218 in an elaborated version, again frequent in Durham books, where small strokes of contrast colour are added to the basic form. However, the initials of the Guisborough manuscript are rather sketchily executed, and, as has been said, the script is somewhat irregular. It is therefore possible that this book is not a Durham product, although it seems to copy motifs from Durham manuscripts. Whether the copyist was a Guisborough scribe it is impossible to say; but this manuscript again confirms the existence of the network of contacts already posited.

In the case of Hexham, in Northumberland and more closely linked to Durham, there is again evidence of influence from both Durham itself and from Rievaulx. Hexham had been granted to Alfred Westoue, the early-eleventh-century sacrist of Durham, and his descendant, Eilaf, the father of Aelred of Rievaulx, was the last hereditary priest of Hexham. The advowson had passed to the archbishops of York after the harrying of the north and in 1112 Archbishop Thomas divided the property, and introduced Augustinians to tend the church and provide services.[57] In 1114 Archbishop Thurstan strengthened the new priory's link with York, and introduced Prior Aschatil, from the influential house of Huntingdon. He is also recorded as having given relics, candlesticks and books, presumably obtained from York.[58] Eilaf retired into Durham cathedral priory and presumably took his own books with him or gave them to his children. Nevertheless, whilst the close tie with Durham would thus appear to have been broken, Eilaf's son, Aelred, retained a strong interest in the history and saints of both Durham and Hexham, and was to write a treatise on the latter, as well as being a major supporter of the cult of St Cuthbert.[59]

Five twelfth-century Hexham books survive, and they suggest the study of scripture and of patristic commentaries. They include three volumes of the

[56] These books, and especially those containing works by Bede, show considerable scholarly interest in selecting and editing their contacts; an activity presumably engaged in by a member of the community. See Chapter 10 below.

[57] For a fuller discussion of this, see Chapter 11 below.

[58] See Prior Richard's *History of the Church of Hexham*, cap. xi, in Raine, *Hexham*, 57–8.

[59] See Chapter 11 below. For recent work on Hexham see E. Cambridge, A. Williams, *et al.*, 'Hexham Abbey: a Review of Recent Work and Its Implications', *Archaeologia Aeliana*, 5th series 23, 1995, 51–138.

works of Augustine, and the sermons of Gregory Nazianzen (a text available at Durham and Bridlington, and listed in the Whitby library catalogue). Care for the book collection is also suggested by the presence of early *ex libris* inscriptions in all these books. The Hexham copy of Augustine's *Contra Faustum*, now Bodleian, Bodley 236, has a split petal initial on fol. 1v (Fig. 71). It is in an unusual colour scheme, including grey, a colour not found in Durham books, and does not appear to be a Durham product. Moreover, the book cannot have been part of Archbishop Thurstan's gift of 1114, since it dates from the mid-twelfth century. This book therefore suggests the presence at Hexham of a scriptorium, perhaps borrowing exemplars from Durham, and influenced by Durham initials, although using a distinctive range of colours.

Therefore, despite the scarcity of manuscripts, certain patterns of both production and collection in the Augustinian priories do begin to appear. Moreover, they build up a picture of developing scholarly and artistic activity in twelfth-century Yorkshire, paralleling the county's economic revival, and linked to its place in the reform movements of the period. The majority of the Augustinian houses appear to have had book collections capable of support- ing both the *lectio divina* and scholarly activity. In some houses at least a considerable importance appears to have been attached to such activity, and there seems to have been an expectation that both copying and decorating would go on inside the priories themselves. This work was, however, supplemented by gifts, and possibly by the commissioning of work from professionals. There are considerable signs of influence from Cistercian views about the appearance and decoration of books, but this is not uniformly applied. There is also one interesting difference, in that the Augustinians, unlike the Cistercians, do not appear to have produced their own parchment.

FIG. 71 Diagram of initial F from Oxford, Bodleian, MS Bodley 236, fol. 1v

Characteristically, the parchment in the Augustinian books is smooth and white, with few holes and regular edges, but very varied in thickness and tone. In all these ways it is different from Cistercian parchment. All this suggests purchase, which gives further evidence of the increasing wealth of the Augustinians, and of their readiness to purchase both books and materials. Suppliers were to be found no further away than York. Ink also is generally of good quality, often with different shades used for main text and gloss, but pigments are few, and paints are usually restricted to red, green and blue, frequently rather uneven in texture. This may therefore suggest the lack of skilled painters or deliberate restriction; and, again like the Cistercians, no Augustinian book contains gold or silver decoration. The execution of the initials in the majority of books also suggests the work of rather inexperienced hands.

Finally, there is considerable evidence of the emergence of a regional style of book production. All this produces a picture of a self-contained Northumbrian monastic community, of which the Augustinians formed a part, and in which the houses of all orders were linked to one another intellectually and artistically, despite some divisions in matters of ecclesiastical politics.

CHAPTER NINE

&❧

The Cistercians and their libraries

If the reign of Henry I saw the establishment of an impressive number of well-endowed Augustinian priories in Northumbria, the succeeding period, the troubled reign of King Stephen, saw the triumph of the Cistercians.[1] Two factors in this creation of another group of major monasteries are particularly striking: first, that many of the same patrons who had founded or contributed to Augustinian priories also supported the Cistercians; and second, the speed with which the Cistercians achieved a leading position in the ecclesiastical culture of Northumbria. While the Augustinian priories seem to have applied themselves steadily, as has been seen, to the improvement of their estates, the establishment of libraries and scriptoria and the encouragement of intellectual activities on the part of the canons, they seem never to have grown beyond moderate size. Such shreds of evidence as remain suggest that they tended to reach a level of twenty to thirty canons, but not to grow further.[2] Moreover, although their original endowments were often generous, and capable of considerable development, as at Kirkham and Bridlington, subsequent gifts tended to be on a smaller scale.[3] Finally, with the partial exception of St Waltheof, or Waldef, whose saintly qualities, however, seem mainly to have been recognised after he had become a Cistercian, the Augustinians did not produce any great and dominant figures.[4] In almost every respect the

---

[1] On the arrival of the Cistercians, see Knowles, *Monastic Order*, 227–45; and Burton, 'The Foundation of the British Cistercian Houses'.

[2] Figures are given in Robinson, *The Geography of Augustinian Settlement*, Appendix 20, 399–403. Bridlington had 6 canons in 1148, and 25 by 1380; Guisborough 26 by 1380; Kirkham 17 in 1380; Newburgh may have had 26 at its foundation, but only 16 by 1380; Nostell had 26 in 1312. The few figures available for the twelfth century suggest that, in the better-recorded southern houses, 8–16 was most common, though Merton and Llanthony I were considerably larger.

[3] For general comments see Dickinson, *Origins*. On the endowment of Kirkham, see Burton, *Kirkham Priory*, 4–15.

[4] For Waldef's career, see Baker, 'Legend and Reality'. Outstanding at the organisational level was Athelulf of Nostell, made bishop of Carlisle by Henry I (1133–56). It was he who, besides

Cistercians present a contrast, and this raises the important question of the nature of the impact of the Cistercians upon the developing monastic culture of Northumbria.

The traditional image of the Cistercians, nurtured by their own early writings and foundation narratives, is that they were given large tracts of empty wasteland, and settled there in rural isolation, far from the world.[5] The actual history is more complex, although just as impressive. First, both Rievaulx and Fountains, the two first and greatest of the northern Cistercian houses, were founded on relatively small estates, and were close to established settlements. Second, the evidence from foundation charters and registers of land gifts suggests that the initial grants, at least, were of established agricultural land, and that little actual clearing of waste ground had to be done in the early stages of each house.[6]

Indeed, Kirkstall, an early member of the 'second generation', being founded from Fountains in 1147, accepted as integral parts of its endowment a vill and two parish churches.[7] And finally, the Cistercians played an active part in the ecclesiastical affairs of the archdiocese of York, culminating in the appointment of Henry Murdac, abbot of Fountains, as archbishop of York, against the wishes of King Stephen, and leading the northern Cistercians into opposition to the king.[8] Thus, whilst this is not the place for a detailed review of English Cistercian history, it is important to look briefly at the establishment of the Cistercian monasteries, as necessary background for the examination of their contribution to the book culture of twelfth-century Northumbria.

There were several circumstances which may have led to or encouraged contact between Cistercian and Augustinian houses, and one of these was the role of the founders and patrons. The first patron of the Cistercians in the

obtaining significant privileges from Henry I for Nostell, was involved in the foundation of Nostell's daughter house, at Scone, c. 1120. This in turn provided its prior, Robert, to be bishop of St Andrews, 1127. In intellectual activity, the two outstanding figures were: Robert the Scribe, prior of Bridlington (see Chapter 8); and Maurice, prior of Kirkham, and author of a treatise *Contra Salomitas*. On this, see Burton, *Kirkham Priory*.

[5] For the account of the foundation of Fountains, see *Memorials of the Abbey of St Mary of Fountains*, ed. J. R. Walbran and J. Fowler, vol. i, Surtees Society 42, 1863.

[6] See Burton, 'The Foundation of the British Cistercian Houses', 26–7; and Burton, *Kirkham Priory*, 4–7.

[7] Burton, 'The Foundation of the British Cistercian Houses', 32–3.

[8] The story of the alliance of the Yorkshire Cistercians and Augustinians against William fitz Herbert, archbishop-elect of York, is briefly told in John the Prior's *History of the Church of Hexham*, under 1143; see Raine, *Hexham*, 142–6. The resulting conflict is outlined by Barlow, *The English Church 1066–1154*, 98–102; Cistercian opposition to Stephen is discussed by C. J. Holdsworth in *The Piper and the Tune: Medieval Patrons and Monks*, University of Reading, Stenton Lecture, 1991 for 1990.

north was Walter Espec. He had already founded Kirkham on one of his estates in 1123, and later established Waldef, stepson of David, king of Scots, as its prior.[9] But during the 1120s, St Bernard of Clairvaux was already in contact with a small number of Yorkshiremen, including: Henry Murdac, a scholar from York who went to Clairvaux and became abbot of Vauclair; one William, also a monk of Clairvaux; and Thomas, provost of Beverley.[10] By 1131 an agreement seems to have been reached to found a daughter house of Clairvaux on a site provided by Espec near his Yorkshire caput of Helmsley, with advice and patronage from Thurstan, archbishop of York, and Henry I. And by late 1132 William, the first abbot, and his twelve companions from Clairvaux, after a brief stay at St Mary's, York, were establishing themselves on their nine carucates of land at Rievaulx.[11] Moreover, their arrival attracted a great deal of interest. Symptomatic of this was the visit of Aelred, steward of King David, in 1134. He had been sent on a visit to the archbishop of York, but turned aside on his journey back to visit Walter Espec, and to see Rievaulx, which he then immediately entered as a novice.[12]

An impressive number of patrons added to Rievaulx's endowment, and by 1146 it had already established several granges and five daughter houses, each of the latter requiring an abbot, twelve monks and a group of lay brothers from the founding house, as well as a core set of books.[13] Walter Espec's own enthusiasm for the Cistercians is demonstrated by his founding of another house, Warden, in 1136, near his southern caput in Bedfordshire. Moreover, King David, an early patron of both Espec's northern foundations, went on to found Melrose in 1136 and Dundrennan in 1142, both as daughters of Rievaulx. He further founded or encouraged Newbattle in 1140 and Kinloss and Holm Cultram in 1150, all as daughters of Melrose.[14] When Waldef left Kirkham to become a Cistercian it was at Warden that he served his novitiate, and at Melrose that he very soon became abbot, while his friend, Everard, who had been a canon of Kirkham, became abbot of Holm Cultram.[15] Meanwhile, an agreement for Kirkham itself to become a Cistercian monastery was entered into the Rievaulx cartulary and, although it was never

[9]   See Baker, 'Legend and Reality', 61–2.

[10]   Knowles, *Monastic Order*, 228–9.

[11]   For St Bernard's letter to Henry I on the foundation of Rievaulx, see St Bernard, *Opera Omnia*, ed. J. Leclercq and H. Rochais, vol. vii, Ep. 92, p. 241. Rievaulx's late-twelfth-century cartulary is published by J. C. Atkinson, *Chartularium Rievallense*, Surtees Society 83, 1889.

[12]   Walter Daniel, *Life of Ailred of Rievaulx*, 10–16.

[13]   These books are specified as: 'Missale, textus, epistolare, collectaneum, gradale, antiphonarium, hymnarium, psalterium, lectionarium, regula, Kalendarium, . . .', in the chapter headed 'Quos libros non licet habere diversos' of the Capitula of 1098–*c*.1100. See Norton and Park, *Cistercian Art and Architecture*, 319.

[14]   On David's monastic patronage, see Chapters 9 and 11.

[15]   Baker, 'Legend and Reality', 66–8.

carried out, it does suggest a strong link between the two.[16] Much more could be said about Rievaulx, but the career, writings and influence of its most famous abbot, Aelred, will be discussed in a later chapter. Here, one further example of its influence, this time on a member of the Durham community, will be given. The man concerned was Maurice who, by 1138, was subprior of Durham and already famous for his learning. In about 1140 he also decided to become a Cistercian, and entered Rievaulx where, in 1145, he succeeded William as abbot.[17] Indeed, the very fact that two of Rievaulx's first three abbots were recognised as saints while the other was a well-known scholar perhaps best sums up its fame.

Equally fascinating is the case of the other great Cistercian monastery founded in 1132, Fountains. In this case, however, there was no process of negotiation, and no prepared site; Fountains was the result of a series of spontaneous events. It appears that the process began with the visit of the Clairvaux monks to St Mary's, York, on their way to establish themselves at Rievaulx. They inspired a group of reformers to approach Geoffrey, the abbot of St Mary's, seeking a more stringent application of the Rule. The resulting controversy culminated in a formal visit by the archbishop of York, when the archbishop and the would-be reformers had to take refuge from threatened violence by the monks of St Mary's. Having been rescued by the archbishop's entourage, the reformers were forced to leave St Mary's forthwith, and spent the Christmas of 1132 with Archbishop Thurstan at Ripon.[18] He thus became their patron, and gave them land at his manor of Studley, some three miles from the manor of Ripon, and in the kind of river-valley site favoured by the Cistercians. Here the community struggled to survive, sending an appeal to St Bernard, who responded by sending them one Geoffrey, a monk of Clairvaux experienced in inducting converts. Janet Burton argues that it was this acceptance into the Cistercian movement, apparently complete by 1134, which led to Fountains' rapid acquisition of patrons.[19] Already, in 1134, Dean Hugh of York and Serlo, a canon, arrived to join the community, bringing wealth and, in the case of Hugh, a collection of books.[20] By 1150 Fountains had established six granges and no less than eight daughter houses, and two examples will show the extent of its impact on secular patrons. In 1137, Ralph de Merlay visited Fountains and, according to Serlo's *Narratio*, was so impressed that he gave a valuable

---

[16] The most recent analysis is Burton, *Kirkham Priory*, 6–9.

[17] For Maurice's career, see Powicke, 'Maurice of Rievaulx'.

[18] The story is told by Serlo, see *Memorials*, vol. i, 31–4. The 'letter of Thurstan' describing the events is given on 11–29. For comment, see D. Bethell, 'The Foundation of Fountains Abbey'; and Knowles, *Monastic Order*, 231–5.

[19] Burton, 'The Foundation of the British Cistercian Houses', 27.

[20] See Lawrence, 'English Cistercian Manuscripts', 290.

estate in Northumberland as the site for Newminster.[21] Even more interesting is the case of William of Aumale, earl of York, described by both William of Newburgh and the Meaux chronicler as a virtual king in the north during Stephen's reign. Despite the tension between Fountains and the king over the election of the archbishop of York, the earl visited Fountains during the 1140s. He became a patron, and founded Vaudey in 1147, and then went on to found Meaux in 1151, at the height of the conflict between Henry Murdac and Stephen.[22]

This political conflict is in itself significant for its demonstration of Cistercian influence on the affairs of the northern province. It began when Willliam fitz Herbert, treasurer of York and Stephen's nephew, was elected as Thurstan's successor under considerable pressure from William of Aumale. A reform party was quickly assembled in opposition, led by the archdeacons of York and by Richard of Fountains, William of Rievaulx, Waldef of Kirkham and Cuthbert of Guisborough.[23] The reformers were not immediately successful, but when Richard II of Fountains died, St Bernard (in 1143) sent Henry Murdac as the new abbot of Fountains, and seems to have made him senior abbot of all the northern houses in Clairvaux's affiliation, deputing to him the duties of visitation.[24] Murdac revived the struggle and, in 1147, the Cistercian pope, Eugenius III, deposed William fitz Herbert. By this stage William of Ste Barbe, bishop of Durham and ex-dean of York, and Aldulf, bishop of Carlisle and ex-prior of Nostell, had been drawn into the affair, giving their support to Murdac.[25] In a council at Trier, still in 1147, the Pope made Murdac himself the new archbishop, and he then found himself in open conflict with Stephen and Henry of Winchester. To William of Aumale, with the support of Hugh du Puiset, treasurer of York and another royal nephew, fell the task of keeping Murdac out of York, and Murdac excommunicated them both. Murdac was only able to enter his cathedral in 1151, whilst William fitz Herbert remained in the household of his uncle, Henry of Blois.[26] It was as a result of this affair that a mob of fitz Herbert's supporters attacked Fountains, in 1147, causing serious damage and setting it on fire, but failing to murder the abbot, as was apparently their declared intention.[27]

---

[21] Burton, 'The Foundation of the British Cistercian Houses', 32.

[22] Ibid. For discussion, see Holdsworth, *The Piper and the Tune*, 10–12.

[23] See note 8 above. The involvement of both Waltheof and Aelred of Rievaulx in this affair has led to considerable interest. For the role of William of Aumale see John of Hexham, *Historia*, under 1141, in Raine, *Hexham*, 133–4. The accusation of simony is on page 139.

[24] C. Brooke, 'St Bernard, the Patrons and Monastic Planning', in Norton and Park, *Cistercian Art and Architecture*, at 18.

[25] See John of Hexham, *Historia*, 1147, Raine, *Hexham*, 154–6.

[26] Barlow, *The English Church 1066–1154*, 99.

[27] This assertion is from Serlo's *Narratio*; see *Memorials*, vol. i, 101.

All this raises the question of how the Cistercians in Northumbria were seen by their contemporaries and here, like the affair just outlined, the evidence is complex. On the one hand it seems that, presumably because of the fitz Herbert affair, the Cistercians became associated with the opposition to Stephen. In 1142/3 William de Roumare, earl of Lincoln, with the collaboration of his step-brother, Ranulf, earl of Chester, founded Revesby Abbey, a daughter of Rievaulx. These two men had been amongst the leaders of the force which defeated and imprisoned Stephen at the battle of Lincoln in 1141. Also in about 1142 Earl Ranulf collaborated in the foundation of Pipewell, another Midlands house.[28] Interestingly, the foundation charter of Revesby leaves a blank where the name of the king should be, and Christopher Holdsworth has pointed out that neither Revesby nor Fountains ever got a confirmatory charter from Stephen.[29] Indeed, Holdsworth has also suggested the solution to the problem of William of Aumale's foundation of two daughter houses of Fountains; namely, that it was part of a reconciliation with the Cistercians, at a time when Aumale himself was ageing and Stephen's control in the north was very fragile.[30]

However, if some saw Rievaulx, Fountains and their supporters at least partly in political terms, others were more straightforwardly impressed by their form of the monastic life. Perhaps the most striking patron was King David of Scotland. However, there are also the examples of Gilbert de Gant, de Roumare's successor, and Henry de Lacy, lord of Pontefract. De Gant was already patron of his father's Augustinian foundation of Bridlington, but in 1146 he became a patron of Rievaulx also, giving it his estate at Rufford in Nottinghamshire, which subsequently became the site of a daughter house.[31] De Lacy also was already patron of the family monasteries of Cluniac Pontefract and Augustinian Nostell, but in 1147 he gave the churches and vill at Barnoldswick, not far from Pontefract, to Fountains. When Barnolds-wick itself proved unsuitable as the site for a daughter house, the new abbot approached a group of hermits established at a site in the Aire valley. Impressively, the hermits agreed to make over their site to the Cistercians, many of them joining the new abbey. De Lacy acted as negotiator with the original donor of the site, and so Kirkstall was founded.[32]

1147 perhaps marked the high point of Cistercian influence. It was in that year that Savigny decided to affiliate with all its subordinate houses, and so, with some reluctance, Stephen's foundation of Furness (established in 1124)

---

[28] See Holdsworth, *The Piper and the Tune*, 11.
[29] Ibid.
[30] Ibid. 12 and n. 32.
[31] Burton, 'The Foundation of the British Cistercian Houses', 31–2.
[32] Ibid. 32–3.

and Byland, founded by Roger de Mowbray in 1138 (on the same estate where he also founded Augustinian Newburgh in 1145) became Cistercian. This process was complete by 1150 and involved also Jervaulx, founded in 1145 as a daughter of Byland.[33] However, 1147–50 perhaps also marked the turning of the tide. The later foundations, such as Sawley and Roche, remained small throughout their existence, and in 1152 the General Chapter prohibited further new foundations. For the rest of the twelfth century the great Cistercian abbeys continued to prosper, with Fountains receiving impressive donations until c.1189, and became famous for their wealth. But the era of explosive growth ended, in England, with the death of King Stephen in 1154. Perhaps even more significant was 1153, when Pope Eugenius III, St Bernard, Henry Murdac and William of Ste Barbe all died. In the resulting negotiations, William fitz Herbert was restored to York, to be succeeded on his sudden death by another royal nephew, Roger of Pont l'Eveque; while their cousin, Hugh de Puiset, just succeeded in becoming bishop of Durham.

Nevertheless, recruitment remained good, at least at the larger houses, until the end of the twelfth century. Largest of all was Rievaulx, which must have sent out some sixty-five choir-monks by 1147, and yet was said by Walter Daniel to have reached a level of one hundred and forty monks and five to six hundred lay-brothers and servants under Aelred.[34] Fountains is less well recorded, but would have sent out ninety-one monks by 1150, and is argued to have had at least fifty monks and two hundred lay-brothers by the end of the century.[35] King David's Melrose was nearly as large, with no figures for monks but reputedly with two hundred lay-brothers by the turn of the century; while Kirkstall's buildings made provision for some thirty-six monks and far more lay-brothers.[36] At the bottom of the scale, houses such as Roche and Sawley probably never exceeded twenty monks and perhaps sixty lay-brothers. A very poorly recorded group are the servants; these were certainly employed by the Cistercians, at least in the second half of the century (as craftsmen were employed from an early stage, to assist with building work) but there is no evidence on their numbers.[37]

From all this it is clear that the contribution made by the Cistercians to the development of twelfth-century Northumbria was very considerable. What is also fascinating is that the Cistercians had developed very distinctive

---

[33] For the complexities surrounding the merging of the Savigniac abbeys of Furness, Byland and Jervaulx into the Cistercian hierarchy, see Knowles, *Monastic Order*, 249–51.

[34] See Walter Daniel, *Life of Ailred of Rievaulx*, 38.

[35] L. Butler and C. Given-Wilson, *Medieval Monasteries of Great Britain*, London, 1979, 238.

[36] Ibid. 293 and 274.

[37] See Brooke, 'St Bernard, the Patrons and Monastic Planning', 17–19.

regulations about the production and decoration of books by the 1140s. It is therefore necessary to give some account of these before turning to the surviving manuscripts, in order to see how far the northern English houses followed the regulations. Also interesting is the question of whether St Bernard directly influenced those houses in the affiliation of Clairvaux. Both questions are important for this enquiry, since the leading position of figures such as Henry Murdac and Aelred may well have helped to spread Cistercian ideas to other Northumbrian centres.

In the matter of books, the first concern of the Cistercian statutes was for uniformity in basic texts. Of the capitula datable to 1098–*c.*1100, the chapter 'De Construendis Abbatiis' deals with what is required for unity amongst future Cistercian houses and notes: 'Dehinc ut idem libri quantum dumtaxat ad divinum pertinet officium, idem vestitus, idem victus, idem denique per omnia mores atque consuetudines inveniantur.'[38] The 'Carta Caritatis Prior' expands on this: 'Et hoc etiam volumus, ut mores et cantum, et omnes libros ad horas diurnas et nocturnas et ad missas necessarios secundum formam morum et librorum novi monasterii possideant.'[39] Also amongst the very early capitula is one 'Quos Libros non Licet Habere Diversos', which lists as fundamental texts a Missal, Evangeliary, Epistolary, Collectar, Gradual, Antiphoner, Hymnal, Psalter, Lectionary, Rule, and liturgical Calendar; while an extended version of 'De Construendis', datable before 1113, repeats much of this list, omitting the Epistolary, Evangeliary and liturgical Calendar.[40] Beyond the general concern that these books should be consonant with the customs and ideals of Cîteaux, there is no specific interest in their appearance.

The first interest in this aspect of books comes in *c.*1109–19, at the same time as detailed instructions 'Quid liceat vel non liceat nobis habere de auro, argento, gemmis et serico'. This statute is very much in accordance with the instructions set out in the 'Exordium Parvum', and severely restricts the use of gold and silver for the celebration of divine service or the furnishings of the altar.[41] Similarly, the statute 'De Firmaculis Librorum', as its name suggests, is concerned to forbid the use of gold or silver for the making of book clasps.[42] Again, just as the use of silk or rich fabrics is forbidden for vestments and altar cloths, so the same statute notes that no book is to be draped ('tegatur') with rich fabric.[43] However, the first statute to be concerned with the internal decoration of books is datable to no earlier than *c.*1145–51.[44] This has led to speculation that it represents the final triumph of the views of .

[38] Norton and Park, *Cistercian Art and Architecture*, Table of legislation, 318–19.
[39] Ibid.   [40] Ibid.   [41] Ibid. 323.   [42] Ibid.
[43] The phrase is: 'pallio tegatur'. See ibid. 323.   [44] Ibid. 325.

St Bernard over those of Stephen Harding, who had died in 1134.[45] There are several difficulties with this view. The first is that nowhere, either in the famous 'Apologia' to William of St Thierry or in the treatise on 'The Twelve Steps of Humility and Pride' which sets out his central points of advice to monks, or indeed in his correspondence (including in those letters which take both individuals and institutions to task for various infringements), does St Bernard show any interest in the decoration of books.[46] The second is that the enigmatic wording of the statute suggests that it is intended simply as a reminder of what is, in fact, already well established in practice. What the statute says is: 'Littere unius coloris fiant, et non depicte.' Miniatures appear to be unthinkable, and it is not clear whether initials only, or rubrics also, are intended to be included.[47] More detail is provided in the codification of 1202, which sought to unify and order all the regulatory material accepted up to that time. This gives a compound statute, 'De Firmaculis Librorum et Litteris', which begins by repeating the early prohibition of rich clasps and covers. It then continues: 'Littere autem de cetero absque omni fiant imagine, et sine auro, et sine argento.'[48] This seems to set out what were considered the fundamentals; there are to be no images, no gold and no silver, but the ban on the use of more than one colour is removed, suggesting that it had not found general approval.

Despite the uncertainties, however, it is clear that the attitude of the legislation towards manuscript decoration was both distinctive and restrictive. There is no simple ban on all decoration; it appears to be completely accepted that initials will have some sort of decorative aspect, but this decoration is to be kept within quite narrow bounds, including most distinctively the prohibition of all images. However, it is possible to go further than this, and to find in the legislative material a set of attitudes and assumptions about how and by whom books are to be written, copied, read and stored, and it will be of value to look briefly at this. Since the material has already been discussed in a published article, it will be unnecessary to repeat this discussion at length.[49]

Briefly, it is clear that copying of books is expected to take place, and that monks will have primary responsibility for such work. Moreover, there is an implication, in a statute dating probably from the mid-twelfth century, that

[45] See particularly C. Rudolph, *The 'Things of Greater Importance': Bernard of Clairvaux's 'Apologia' and the Medieval Attitude toward Art*, Philadelphia, 1990, 198.

[46] For a fuller exposition, see A. Lawrence, 'Cistercian Decoration: Twelfth-Century Legislation on Illumination, and Its Interpretation in England', *Reading Medieval Studies* 21, 1995, 31–52.

[47] Norton and Park, 'Table of Legislation', 325.

[48] Ibid. 345.

[49] Lawrence, 'English Cistercian Manuscripts'.

rooms may actually be designated as scriptoria: 'In omnibus scriptoriis, ubicumque ex consuetudine monachi scribunt, silentium teneatur sicut in claustro.'⁵⁰ There is no mention of the preparation of parchment; presumably this was not a matter which needed legislation. In accordance with general practice, it was the cantor who had responsibility for the provision and supervision of books.⁵¹ What was unusual, however, was the suggestion in the *Ecclesiastica Officia* that the abbot should appoint another individual, apparently a lay-brother, to be a sort of caretaker of the books. He was apparently to carry books to and from the scriptorium, the novices' quarters and the infirmary, and to be responsible for closing up the 'armarium' after collation, and watching it during times of work, sleep and eating and whilst vespers was being sung.⁵²

This raises the question of reading, and of the particular nature of the *lectio divina*. Here, what was emphasised was the meditative and prayerful nature of the reading, indicated by the regulation that monks might move from the cloister directly into the church, during reading time, leaving their books in the care of their neighbours.⁵³ Although it is not explicitly stated, this implies that the Rule's stipulation that each monk should be allocated a book on an annual basis was carried out, so that each monastery would require at least as many 'library' books as there were choir monks. In the case of Rievaulx, in particular, this would imply a need for a fair-sized library, and one which would have to be built up rapidly, to supply the growing numbers of recruits. When the requirement to supply each daughter house with a basic set of some ten or eleven liturgical books is also taken into account, then the need for a productive scriptorium is apparent.

It is unfortunate that the survival rate of English Cistercian manuscripts has been rather low, and that the only relevant catalogue is that of Rievaulx, from the thirteenth century.⁵⁴ However, both the books and the catalogue do, in general, accord with Professor Cheney's conclusions on the size and contents of English Cistercian libraries. The Rievaulx catalogue gives a total of some 212 manuscripts, rather low in comparison with Durham's 500+ by the same time, Glastonbury's 400+, Christ Church Canterbury's 600+ or

⁵⁰ Ibid. 'Table of Legislation', 325.
⁵¹ Lawrence, 'English Cistercian Manuscripts', 288.
⁵² *Ecclesiastica Officia*, CXV. See Guignard, *Les Monuments primitifs de la Règle cistercienne*, Dijon, 1878, 237.
⁵³ Cap. L80, in 'Codex Manuscriptus 31', at 37.
⁵⁴ A thirteenth-century library catalogue is preserved in Cambridge, Jesus College, MS 34. This was printed by A. Hoste, *Bibliotheca Aelrediana*, Instrumenta Patristica 2, 1962, 150–76; and by James, *Catalogue of the Manuscripts of Jesus College*, 44–52. For comment, see C. R. Cheney, 'English Cistercian Libraries: The First Century', in his *Medieval Texts and Studies*, Oxford, 1973, 328–45. See also D. Bell, ed., *The Libraries of the Cistercians, Gilbertines and Premonstratensians*, Corpus of British Medieval Library Catalogues 3, London, 1992.

even Rochester's *c.*300. The choice of texts is also interesting, and is in general agreement with the attitude to reading outlined above. Of the 212, 36 were Bibles or parts of Bibles; while another 38 were patristic works. Clearly popular were works by Cistercian writers (Bernard and Aelred were represented by 8 volumes each), as were florilegia (12 volumes) and saints' *Lives* (8 volumes). There were only 4 histories, and a noticeable absence of newer writers, apart from Cistercians and Hugh and Richard of St Victor. However, there was clear interest in the works of Bede, who is also represented by 8 volumes.

Before turning to the surviving manuscripts, however, there is one further aspect of the Cistercian attitude to books which requires discussion. This is the question of the attitude taken towards intellectual activities, which was unusual in several respects. First, in the absence of oblates, the running of a school was specifically ruled out.[55] Second, there was a clear disapproval of study for its own sake, implicit both in the attitude to reading and in the choice of texts for libraries.[56] Third, there was an increasing prohibition of the composition of new works by Cistercians without the explicit permission of General Chapter. The last point can be illustrated by a statute datable to 1119–51 which states: 'Nulli liceat abbati nec monacho nec novicio libros facere, nisi forte cuiquam id in generali capitulo abbatum concessum fuerit.'[57] By 1175 this had been expanded to include treatises and collections of sermons, although abbots still had to deliver, and therefore presumably to compose, sermons.[58] The second point is less clear-cut, but there was certainly a restrictive attitude towards the study of canon law. In 1188 the General Chapter ruled that 'Liber qui dicitur Corpus Canonum, et Decreta Gratiani, apud eos qui habuerint secretius custodiantur, . . . in communi armario non resideant, propter varios qui inde possunt provenire errores.'[59] Similarly, while they were not explicitly restricted, Cheney has shown that the new theological and grammatical studies tended to be absent from English Cistercian libraries, as they were from Rievaulx's.[60]

Comments by both St Bernard and Aelred of Rievaulx help to shed further light on this attitude, and to demonstrate that it was put into practice in Northumbria. In several of his letters, St Bernard refers to studying in the schools as 'pursuing a career in the world' and contrasts such a life with his as

[55] See note 53 above.

[56] This is the subject of some debate, but there is no intention here to suggest that the Cistercians were anti-intellectual. St Bernard himself clearly read Ovid with his monks, and encouraged the composition of new works by those considered suitable, such as Aelred of Rievaulx.

[57] Norton and Park, 'Table of Legislation', 325.

[58] Ibid. 329.

[59] Ibid. 333.

[60] Cheney, 'English Cistercian Libraries', *passim.*

'a rustic and a monk' whose business is 'not teaching but lamenting'.[61] In letters to fellow Cistercians this attitude is uncompromisingly expressed. Having heard that Henry Murdac was intending to compose a commentary on the Prophets, St Bernard wrote: 'I hear, brother, that you are reading the Prophets. Do you think that you understand what you read? Why seek the Word amongst written words, when He stands before your eyes in the flesh? . . . You will find much more labouring amongst the woods than you ever will amongst books.'[62] Murdac had been a scholar before becoming a monk, and there is a clear implication that the two are separate. However, to the self-confessedly unlearned Aelred, St Bernard writes with approval, encouraging him to set down his meditations on charity: 'Knowledge that comes from the school of the Holy Spirit rather than the schools of rhetoric will savour all the sweeter to me. I think that you will be able to strike something out of your rocks that you have not got from the bookshelves of the schoolmen.'[63]

That Aelred was strongly influenced by St Bernard is suggested, not only by his *Speculum Caritatis* itself, but also in the language of the Prologue to his *De Spirituali Amicitia*.[64] Here he briefly describes his call to the monastic life, and says that the 'little learning' he had acquired 'in the world' was entirely secular, with Cicero's *De Amicitia* as his favourite work. But once he became a monk 'nothing which had not been sweetened by the honey of the most sweet name of Jesus, nothing which had not been seasoned with the salt of sacred Scripture' could attract him. What is interesting is not only the suggested change of attitude, but the fact that it is expressed through a paraphrase of an expression of St Bernard's. His fifteenth sermon on the Song of Songs, chapter 6, states 'the name of Jesus is more than light, it is also food. . . . Every food of the mind . . . is tasteless if not seasoned by that salt. . . . Jesus to me is honey in the mouth . . .'.[65] Finally, Aelred's own follower and biographer, Walter Daniel, expressed a related attitude when he wrote 'Our master Christ did not teach grammar, rhetoric, dialectic in his school; he taught humility, charity and righteousness.' That such ideas were not restricted only to Rievaulx, however, but continued into the thirteenth century in several English houses, is demonstrated by comments from both Gilbert of Hoyland and Ralph of Coggeshall.[66]

---

[61] See St Bernard's letters to Fulk, later Archdeacon of Langres, and to Oger, Canon of Mont-St-Eloi: *Sancti Bernardi Opera*, VII, 12–22 and 235–6.

[62] *Sancti Bernardi Opera*, VIII, 486–9.   [63] Ibid. VII, 266.

[64] For the latin text, see J. P. Migne, ed., *Beati Aelredi Abbatis Rievallensis Opera Omnia*, PL 195: 659–702. Quotations here are from: Aelred of Rievaulx, *Spiritual Friendship*, trans. M. E. Laker SSND, Cistercian Fathers Number Five, Kalamazoo, 1977, 45–7.

[65] Quoted by Laker, op. cit., 47.

[66] See Gilbert of Hoyland, *Sermo VII in Cantica Canticorum*, PL 184, 43.

Thus far it has been argued that the Cistercians had very clearly defined, and distinctive, ideas about reading, study and books and their decoration. The remainder of this chapter will examine the surviving books from their Northumbrian houses in the twelfth century. Two central questions will be addressed. First, do the manuscripts accord with the ideals and regulations outlined? Second, do they suggest a self-sufficient development of scriptoria and libraries, or is there evidence of contact with black-monk and Augustinian houses, as the events outlined at the beginning of the chapter would suggest?

According to Ker's fundamental *Medieval Libraries*, twelfth-century manuscripts survive from eleven Cistercian and Savigniac/Cistercian monasteries in the area from the Scottish borders to south Yorkshire. (Melrose is included in this group, because of its strong links with both Rievaulx and Holm Cultram.) The survival rate has been low, although from all these monasteries twelfth-century manuscripts survive in considerably larger numbers than those from later periods. From Byland there are eleven such manuscripts and six fragments of manuscripts; from Fountains thirteen manuscripts and one fragment; from Rievaulx eleven manuscripts and two fragments; from Holm Cultram six manuscripts; from Roche five manuscripts; from Kirkstall and Sawley three each; from Jervaulx and Newminster two each; and from Meaux and Melrose one each.

Early care for the book collection is demonstrated by the fact that all these manuscripts, with the exception only of those from Kirkstall, Meaux and Melrose, show early ex-libris inscriptions. Only from Byland, Fountains and Rievaulx are there sufficient numbers for questions of organisation and uniformity of practice, demonstrating the existence of a scriptorium, to be raised with any point. Briefly, the evidence suggests strongly that each of these had an organised scriptorium, producing books of relatively uniform size and construction.

In the case of the surviving Rievaulx manuscripts, codicological evidence suggests strongly that they were the products of one scriptorium. Firstly, they fall into two coherent groups in terms of their size, with the smaller books being about 150×230mm and the larger about 200×280mm. A second shared feature is that they all contain unusually few folios, with all but one having only sixty to seventy; even the exception has only 133 folios. Most distinctive of all is their vellum, which has a strikingly 'home-made' appearance. It is stiff and rather thick, greyish in colour, and rather rough in texture on the hair side with some patches of hair follicles still visible. In several cases, the margins of folios are unusually discoloured and uneven, suggesting that the very edges of the available sheets of vellum were used. Additionally, holes are rather more frequent than in contemporary manuscripts from non-Cistercian scriptoria. The dark colour of the vellum was apparently recognised, since there is often heavy application of a white substance, to improve the contrast with the ink. Finally, there is some uniformity in the ruling patterns used. Ruling itself is carried out in a mixture of dry-point, lead and crayon; nevertheless, the majority of the surviving books have thirty-five to thirty-seven lines per page, and almost all the larger books use a two-column format. Pricking, gathering, quire signatures and ink are also fairly uniform. Single pin-pricks at the outer ends of each line are the standard, and all but one of the manuscripts used simply gatherings of eight. Quire signatures are prominent, and are placed at the bottom centre of each last verso; they are executed in the good-quality, dark ink which is also found throughout the texts of those datable to the third quarter of the century. In other words, it seems extremely likely that they are all local products and were most probably made in the scriptorium of Rievaulx itself.

Matching the lack of a school, and the apparent requirement that novices were already able to read and write when they were recruited as adults, as well as the ban on teaching literacy to the lay-brothers, there is no evidence of an attempt to teach a uniform style of writing to those who acted as scribes. The best hands are simply clear, well-spaced versions of the standard English proto-Gothic style, while the less good can appear somewhat hesitant. A particularly interesting feature is that, where a manuscript shows several hands, details of the ruling often change with the script, suggesting that scribes ruled up the vellum for their own stints. This is in contrast with Robert of Bridlington's assumption that ruling parchment for the scribes constituted a separate task and, together with the rather short stints found in some books, may suggest that the Rievaulx scriptorium depended on monk-scribes whose copying of books was treated as a part of the tasks carried out within the Rule's stipulations about the organisation of work.

The Byland books, interestingly, seem all to date from the time of the merger with the Cistercians, or later. The majority show vellum very similar in character to that of Rievaulx, and again they are all gathered in quires of eight. There are, however, some differences. They fall into three rough categories of size, with the majority of the books being about 150×230mm., a smaller group $c.180 \times 250$mm., and two reaching the large size of $c.230 \times 330$mm. They are also a little longer than the Rievaulx books, the majority containing about a hundred folios, while ruling patterns tend to be very simple, and in hard point or lead. There are also fewer quire signatures. However, pricking and lines per page are as in the Rievaulx books. Again, there is no clearly recognisable house style of script, but those of about the third quarter of the century are mostly proficient versions of the standard proto-Gothic style. What is interesting here is that, whilst the character of the earliest Byland books cannot be known, those which survive suggest the existence of an organised scriptorium which showed considerable conformity with the practices of Rievaulx. Clearly, considerable effort was made to make Byland books adapt to Cistercian regulations; and it would appear likely that instruction on what was now required came from Rievaulx. It must be very likely that this instruction was given also to Byland's daughter house, Jervaulx, but the survival of only two relevant Jervaulx manuscripts means that there is insufficient evidence to prove this.

At Fountains there is again a similar pattern, despite Fountains' unortho-dox beginnings and the presence of a group of monks originally from St Mary's, York, in leading positions. The vellum here has a rather smoother surface, but is otherwise of the same character as that from Rievaulx and Byland. Again, the majority of the books are about 1 50 × 2 30mm or a little larger, suggesting perhaps, if the vellum is accepted to have been made in-house, that this size made efficient use of the skins available from Cistercian animals. The majority are again gathered in the usual fashion, although here there are a few quires of twelve. Quire signatures are rare. Here, single-column ruling patterns dominate, but pricking is as at Rievaulx and Byland. Again, there is no house-style of script, but the majority of the hands are proficient versions of the standard English style, although without the marked regularity found in books from, for instance, Winchester or St Albans. In other words, there appears to have been an organised scriptorium here also, and again producing books of recognisable type. The lack of regularity in ruling and script at all three suggests that monks, with varied training as scribes, worked in the scriptoria. Those few manuscripts which show the complete regularity of script which might suggest a professional scribe, also show very different vellum, rubrication and initials, and are almost certainly not Cistercian products.[67]

This raises the question of decoration, and here also the manuscripts from these three monasteries show considerable agreement in both style and motifs, but with enough areas of difference to confirm the impression of three separate but interrelated scriptoria. This may be demonstrated by looking at the rubrication of the manuscripts. In those from Rievaulx, rubrics are usually reduced to two or three lines, in ordinary minuscule, done in plain red and without decoration or display script. The capitula also lack the usual coloured letters, spacing and decorative touches. Contents lists are extremely rare. Of the Byland books, the majority have brief headings in red, in the text

---

[67] The books in question are: the Ennodius and Job from Rievaulx, BL Royal 8 E IV and Harley 5273; and, perhaps, the History of Durham from Fountains, now BL Cotton Faustina A v (which may be a Durham product).

script, though sometimes actually smaller than the main text script, and without decoration. There are some variations, however, which may perhaps be continuations of earlier practice. BL Royal 5 E XXII, a copy of the sermons of Gregory Nazianzen, of the mid-twelfth century, has a list of the sermons set out on fol. 4r, done in red minuscule, and opening with a two-line pale green initial. And Cambridge, Trinity College, O 3 42, a copy of Palladius' *Opus Agriculture*, of the later twelfth century, has a full title in red at the top of the first folio, followed by the capitula, each on its own line, with a red or green one-line-high initial. In the Fountains books, rubrication is again generally reduced to a minimum, with the exception of one mid-twelfth-century book, now BL Arundel 217, a copy of the letters of St Cyprian, which has one line written in one-line-high red display script. Thus it seems that, at all three of these houses, there was a deliberate attempt to apply the statute on letters to rubrication, and that, in fact, more stringent limitations were imposed than were actually required by the General Chapter.

Broadly, the same is true of the illumination of these manuscripts. At the risk of stating the obvious, there are no miniatures, and there are no human figures incorporated into initials. Even more unusually, there are virtually none of the creatures elsewhere so dominant in twelfth-century decoration, the dragons, grotesque birds and lions. The ban on 'images' could hardly be taken further. Indeed, the majority of the books contain only plain initials, usually in only one colour, and sometimes, even in the case of the first initial of the main text, not exceeding three lines high. The decorative touches on these letters are restricted to elongated serifs, or sometimes a strip of plain vellum left in the centre of the thicker portions of letters. Colours are few, generally being restricted to red, dark green and pale blue, with occasional use of yellow, and, rarely, orange-red. However, some manuscripts do have initials with simple stylised foliage terminals or pen-scrolling, and it is a little surprising that these details are frequently done in contrast colours. The size of the letters remains generally small, with few exceeding about three lines in height. Colours are still those already given. However, such minor decoration is rare in the Fountains books.

In discussing books with more elaborate initials, some seem almost certainly to occur in books which were not products of these scriptoria, and so are scarcely relevant to this enquiry, except as demonstrating that the Northumbrian Cistercians were prepared to accept gifts of manuscripts which did not adhere to their regulations. Perhaps most striking is the Rievaulx copy of Ennodius, now BL Royal 8 E IV, which has soft vellum, a unique ruling pattern, a professional-looking script, and a gold initial U, set in a ten-line-high blue box, and containing a fully painted image of an ass playing the harp, which breaks almost every part of the regulations on letters. Also from Rievaulx is a glossed copy of the book of Job, probably from the mid-twelfth century, whose main initial is a six-line-high V, painted in red, blue, yellow and green, and decorated with stylised foliage of the type characteristic of St Swithun's, Winchester. This initial also is unique among the Rievaulx manuscripts, and suggests that the book may have been acquired from elsewhere (Fig. 72).

The remaining manuscripts, however, which constitute perhaps one third of the total now surviving, contain examples of a very distinctive type of initial, found at all three houses. These occur as both major and minor initials, and are painted in the colours already described. What is distinctive is their complex and technically skilled use of a very restricted set of decorative motifs (see Fig. 73). These are: scallop and cable patterns left in relief in the thick portions of letters; a simple three-lobed floret motif; and the motif dubbed by Mynors the split petal.[68] It is the latter which is the dominant characteristic of these initials, occurring with a variety of elaborations, such as flanking leaves, stalks and hair-like projections. They are most common in Fountains books, occurring in six manuscripts from that house, as well as in four from Byland and five from Rievaulx.[69] Moreover, while different hands are clearly at work, there are examples in each group of initials which use more than one colour; this is frequently restricted to the use of a yellow wash around portions of the letter, particularly in the Rievaulx books, but can include the execution of portions of the decoration in a contrast colour. Finally, all three groups of manuscripts use the split-petal motif in an elaborated, as well as plain, form.

It is clear, then, that letters in this very distinctive style occur in manuscripts from all three of these great Northumbrian Cistercian monasteries; what is not so clear is where they originated. The simplest hypothesis would be that Rievaulx and Fountains copied them from Clairvaux books, and that Byland thus copied in turn when it too became Cistercian and needed to obtain copies of the basic Cistercian texts. However, examination of initials from surviving Clairvaux manuscripts demonstrates that this was not the case.[70] Moreover, these initials are not found in books from southern English Cistercian monasteries. Their closest parallels, and they are sometimes very close, are in

[68] Mynors, *Durham Cathedral Manuscripts*, 7.

[69] The Rievaulx books are: BL Royal 8 D XXII; BL Royal 6 C VIII; BL Arundel 346; BL Add. 46203; and BL Harley 5273. The Byland books are: BL Harley 3641; BL Royal 5 E XXII; BL Add. 35180; and Trinity, Cambridge, O152. The Fountains books include: Oxford, Corpus Christi College, D 209; BL Cotton Faustina B 1; Bodleian, Laud. Misc. 310; Camb. Gonville and Caius MS 126; BL Arundel 217.

[70] For published examples, see F. Bibolet, 'Les Manuscrits de Clairvaux au XIIe siècle', in *Congrès archéologique de France, Troyes*, Paris, 1955, 174–9.

FIG. 72 Initial V from London, BL, MS Harley 5273, fol. 2r

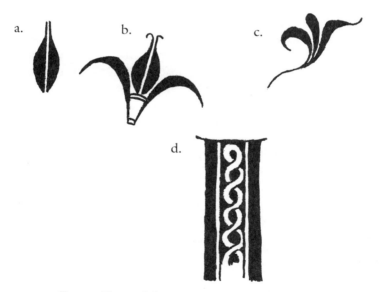

FIG. 73 Characteristic motifs from Cistercian manuscripts:
a. Split-petal motif, b. Complex split-petal motif, c. Tri-lobed floret, d. Cable

books from Durham and other Northumbrian houses.[71] This in turn raises the question of whether they were a Cistercian development, subsequently imitated elsewhere in Northumbria, or whether the Cistercians copied them from elsewhere.

Both the cable pattern and the three-lobed floret are variants on widely distributed motifs, and are of little use in seeking an answer to this question. But the split petal is more interesting. Mynors identified this motif in a group of Durham manuscripts of the third quarter of the twelfth century, in which it already occurs in complex and developed forms, clearly related to those in contemporary Cistercian books. For this reason, and because a motif related to the split petal occurs in three of the four surviving twelfth-century manuscripts from York, I originally believed that the motif had originated at St Mary's, York, and had been taken on to Fountains by its founding group, also spreading to other Northumbrian houses, including Durham.[72] However, further examination of Durham manuscripts has changed the position, as simple forms of the split petal do occur in two books of almost certain Durham origin, dated by Ker to the early twelfth century. These are BL Harley 4688, and DCL B IV 15, a copy of Isidore's *Etymologies* (Fig. 48). It therefore seems most likely that the motif originated at Durham, and was subsequently taken up at St Mary's.[73]

For geographical reasons, it would seem logical for the new Cistercian monasteries, as they built up their libraries, to borrow books from York. Indeed, as the founders of Fountains came from St Mary's, and one of them was known as Geoffrey 'pictor', it is possible that some of them had already been trained as scribes and artists there, and had learnt this motif, amongst others. Serlo records that, when Henry Murdac became abbot, he was shocked to find 'images' at Fountains, and had them burnt to drive home the importance of the regulations.[74] Moreover, it seems probable that Fountains' earliest books were supplied by Archbishop Thurstan, and supplemented by those of Dean Hugh of York, both of whom probably drew on the work of clerks and professionals based in York. However, this hypothesis of a 'York' connection, although attractive, appears to be wrong. First, the St Mary's manuscripts with the split petal, or closely related motifs, which are discussed in more detail in the chapter on the Benedictine Revival, are almost certainly later than the two Durham manuscripts cited. Second, there is evidence which suggests that St Mary's maintained a hostile attitude towards the rebel monks of Fountains and their Cistercian colleagues. This is contained in BL Add. 38816, which contains a list

---

[71] See Chapter 7.
[72] See Lawrence, 'English Cistercian Manuscripts', 296–7.
[73] See Chapter 3.
[74] See *Memorials*, vol. i, 84–6.

of confraternity agreements entered into by St Mary's.[75] They are wide-ranging, including continental, southern English and Northumbrian houses, but the Cistercians are conspicuous by their absence. This absence is made all the more pointed by a late entry, added in a hand of the 1150s or 1160s, and stating that for Richard of Fountains, when he died, St Mary's would do as it would for one of its own monks.[76] This was possibly Richard III, a native of York, who was in Burgundy during Fountains' early years, and came to take up the post of abbot in 1149.[77] For all these reasons, then, it is unlikely that Fountains, seeking to build up its library, could turn to St Mary's. And St Peter's Cathedral, despite apparently friendly relations with the Cistercians, was served by secular canons, with no obligation to engage in the *lectio divina*, and no communal library.

This leaves Durham as a likely source for books and exemplars, and there is evidence for both. Reginald of Durham describes how the monks of Fountains borrowed a *Life of St Godric of Finchale* to copy it, and goes on to relate how, in gratitude, the prior of Fountains asked the cantor to decorate the book (apparently the Durham examplar) with bright colours.[78] It is a pity that the book does not seem to survive, as Fountains decoration in a Durham book would be an interesting combination. What is certain is that Fountains at some point came into possession of an early-twelfth-century Durham manuscript. This is the copy of Symeon's *Libellus*, now BL Cotton Faustina A v, fols. 25r–98r, already discussed in Chapter 3, and whose decorated initials use characteristic Durham motifs (though not the split petal). Unfortunately, it is unknown when and how Fountains acquired this manuscript, whose main initials clearly break the Cistercian 'legislation'.[79]

There is also evidence for similar contacts on the part of both Rievaulx and Byland with Durham. In the case of Byland, Durham may well have provided exemplars for Palladius' *Opus Agriculture* and the writings of Remigius of Auxerre. These were not common texts, but both are listed in the Durham catalogue.[80] Between Rievaulx and Durham, contact was particularly close. Both Maurice's move from Durham to Rievaulx, and Aelred's dedication to St Cuthbert and numerous visits to Durham, would help to maintain links. Mynors noted that the Rievaulx copies of works by Jerome, Rabanus Maurus and Ennodius, as well as of a short collection of miracles of the Virgin, seem

[75] On this list, see also Burton, 'Confraternity List'.
[76] See BL Add. 38816, fol. 38v.
[77] See D. Knowles, C. N. L. Brooke and V. London, eds., *The Heads of Religious Houses: England and Wales, 940–1216*, Cambridge, 1972, and *Memorials*, 'Chronicle of the Abbots', at i, 131.
[78] See Reginald of Durham, *Libellus de Vita et Miraculis S. Godrici*, 466–8.
[79] For similar letters in Durham manuscripts, see Chapter 7 and references there.
[80] See *Catalogi Veteres*, 3 and 4.

to be based on Durham exemplars.[81] Especially interesting is BL Royal 8 D XXII, the Rievaulx copy of the sermons of Petrus Chrysologus. This is datable by its script to the later twelfth century, but its main initial is very close in design to those produced by the Martyrology Scribe at Durham at the end of the eleventh century (see Plate 27). No Durham copy of the text exists, but it seems possible that the Rievaulx book was copied from a Durham book, including the design of its main initial. There is also at least one manuscript at Durham with split-petal initials which are closely connected to those in manuscripts from both Rievaulx and Byland. The Durham manuscript is DCL A III 4, a glossed copy of I–IV Kings, the Rievaulx manuscript is BL Royal 6 C VIII, an Orosius, and the Byland manuscript is BL Add. 35180, a Peter Cantor (see Plates 28, 29 and 30). Exchange of books is suggested also by Durham UL Cosin V ii 2, a Durham copy of a short work by Aelred of Rievaulx in a hand which is, as Mynors noted, similar to that of the portion of the Durham historical manuscript, B II 35, which is datable to 1166.[82] This latter also contains genealogical texts which appear to be related to the sources used by Aelred in compiling his treatise for Henry II on the Anglo-Saxon kings. Durham also had early copies of several of the works of St Bernard.[83]

Clearly, no simple pattern emerges from all this. However, the evidence above does suggest that, of the range of motifs developed at Durham in the late eleventh and early twelfth centuries, several became known to the members of the new Cistercian monasteries of Yorkshire, certainly through the borrowing of exemplars, and almost certainly through the acquisition of books produced at Durham. Of all these motifs, one, which was also known at St Mary's, York, by the 1130s, was adopted by these early Cistercians, and incorporated into the repertoire of motifs used in a distinctive type of initial which, by the mid-twelfth century, was popular at all three of the houses discussed. By the 1160s, these initials were also to be found at Durham, where they may well have been influenced by Cistercian designs. However, at Durham other early motifs, such as the clove curl, also continued in use. Finally, the evidence of the interpretation of, and obedience to, the Cistercian regulations is extremely interesting. Since Fountains contained at least one 'pictor' from St Mary's, who may or may not have been the cantor capable of illuminating 'with bright colours' who appears in Reginald of Durham's

---

[81] See Mynors, *Durham Cathedral Manuscripts*, 26, 38, 40.

[82] Ibid. no. 120, 72.

[83] For these, see *Catalogi Veteres*, 5, where they are given as: 'Liber Bernardi Abbatis de Epistolis'; 'Bernardus super Cantica Canticorum'. Prior Laurence (8) owned 'Libri duo Sermonum Abbatis de Claravalle' (Laurence died in the same year as St Bernard, so these, like those which precede them in the Catalogue, were presumably acquired during Bernard's lifetime).

story, it seems almost certain that the avoidance of images and elaborate rubrication in the Fountains manuscripts was the result of deliberate application of the regulations. However, neither at Fountains nor at Rievaulx, where the first monks came from Clairvaux, does there seem to have been any attempt to copy initials from Clairvaux books. Instead, a local style was developed, which seems to have been taken up very rapidly at Byland, after its conversion to the Cistercian movement.

The last question for this chapter is whether this distinctive style of book also appeared at other Cistercian houses of subsequent 'generations'. Here, it is unfortunate that no twelfth or early-thirteenth-century manuscripts survive from Stephen's wealthy Savigniac foundation of Furness. This absence of evidence means that there is nothing with which directly to compare what is known from Byland. Furness's remoteness might make it seem likely that it would develop independently, but there is evidence that, by the reign of Henry II, it was in touch with Durham. Reginald tells of how the abbot of Furness set up an altar to St Cuthbert, and then rode to Durham to tell of the miraculous protection given by the saint.[84] It is not recorded whether he took books back with him; but *Lives* of Northumbrian saints and bishops, including St Cuthbert, were available to the hagiographer Jocelin of Furness in the late twelfth century.[85]

Manuscripts from the daughter houses of Rievaulx and Fountains are few. Of the affiliation of Rievaulx, there is only one relevant book from Melrose, its Chronicle, and this has completely plain initials and rubrication. However, from Melrose's daughter house, Holm Cultram, there are six twelfth-century books, which fit well into the pattern outlined. They are: a Bestiary (with spaces for pictures, which were never filled in); two volumes of saints' *Lives*; a copy of the letters of Jerome; and two volumes of sermons.[86] Of these, the volume of *Lives* of English saints (including St Bee and St John of York, but not St Cuthbert) has initials in the split-petal style. The rest have simple scrolling and very simple stylised foliage, and are plain in appearance.

Of the family of Fountains, there are two manuscripts from Newminster, three from Kirkstall, and one from Meaux, as well as those from Newminster's daughters, Roche and Sawley. Their texts are all in accordance with Cistercian tastes. Moreover, two of the Kirkstall books, one from Newminster and three from Roche all have versions of the split-petal initials.

[84] See Reginald, *De Admirandis*, cap. lv, pp. 112–14.

[85] On Jocelin of Furness see G. McFadden, 'The *Life of Waldef* and Its Author Jocelin of Furness', *Innes Review*, Glasgow, 1955, 5–13. He certainly wrote a *Life of St Kentigern*, and was in touch with both Melrose and the bishop of Glasgow.

[86] These are: BL Cotton Nero A v. fols. 1–82; Cotton Claudius A v. fols. 135–99; Cotton Faustina B iv, fols. 3–179; Oxford, Bodleian, Lyell 2; Bodleian, Hatton 101 and Oxford, University College, MS 15.

These presumably were derived from those of the earlier Cistercian houses; but there is also possible evidence for direct contact with Durham on the part of Roche and Newminster. This is because manuscripts from both contain versions of the curious 'spouted I' which seems to have originated at Durham, although it was also copied at Augustinian priories in both Northumberland and Yorkshire. The books in question are a copy of Bede's *Historia Ecclesiastica* from Newminster, and the last volume of Lethbertus' *Flores Psalterii* from Roche.[87] It is the books from Sawley whose appearance comes as a surprise. They form a collection of historical texts, including a copy of Symeon's *Libellus*, and two of them may originally have been bound together. There is no other evidence that the monks of Sawley had either the inclination or the capacity to produce books with figurative illustrations so different from the decoration of all the Cistercian books so far discussed. Given the textual links with Durham it is most likely that these books were produced at Durham, and that they reached Sawley as gifts. These manuscripts raise complex problems which will be discussed in a subsequent chapter, when looking at the circulation of historical texts in twelfth-century Northumbria.

The coming of the Cistercians, then, affected the developing monastic culture of Northumbria significantly. First, together with the Augustinians, they introduced, and put into practice, reforming ideas about limiting the interference of the king in the affairs of the Church. Secondly, this champion-ship of reform was accompanied by the establishment of a group of very successful and influential monasteries, led by men whose spirituality and convictions provoked both reverence and controversy. Thirdly, whilst they played no part in the development of schools, their success in the recruitment of educated adolescents and adults is in itself testimony to the degree to which formal education had already spread among the free groups in society. Fourthly, a part of their very influential spirituality was a clearly defined attitude towards both reading and books. As a result of their participation in the network of contacts outlined in this chapter, this attitude influenced both the Augustinians and the monks of Durham, although St Mary's, York, may have been more resistant. Finally, they made a major contribution to the design of a simple but technically sophisticated type of initial, which, by its ubiquity in Northumbria and absence in the south, helps to demonstrate the strong sense of cultural unity in the northern province.

---

[87] These are, respectively, BL Add. 25014 and Oxford, Bodleian, Laud Misc. 145.

CHAPTER TEN

&⚜

Readers of Bede

The importance of Bede in the revival of Northumbrian monasticism

The previous chapter argued for the existence of a surprisingly uniform and widespread type of manuscript illumination in twelfth-century Northumbria. This chapter will examine one possible source for this sense of Northumbrian cultural unity: the works and reputation of the Venerable Bede. It will begin with the house which held Bede's relics, namely Durham, and attempt to put the surviving evidence into the context of Bede's widespread popularity at this time.

It has already been pointed out by other writers, most recently David Rollason, that the monks of Durham at the end of the eleventh century were engaged in a rather delicate political and historical enterprise.[1] On the one hand, they were clearly interlopers, newcomers who were mostly from outside the region, who had displaced the long-established Community of St Cuthbert. They had demolished the Anglo-Saxon cathedral and, under the leadership of their alien, and frequently absent, bishops, had begun the construction of a new and very different cathedral.[2] They had ejected the families of the 'clerks' of St Cuthbert from the cathedral area, and had gone so far as to ban women, and even little girls, not only from the cloister area but also from the cathedral itself and the graveyard beside it.[3] This must presumably have made visits to family graves very difficult for women of the clerks' families, and seems strikingly harsh. They were also projecting, and enforcing, a reorganisation of the lands controlled by the bishop and the cathedral chapter, and were imposing harsher conditions of tenancy on the

---

[1] See Rollason, 'Symeon of Durham and the Community of Durham'; and Piper, 'The First Generations of Durham Monks'.

[2] The new cathedral was strikingly different from the existing stone churches of the region and, presumably, from the Anglo-Saxon cathedral. See Cambridge, 'Early Romanesque Architecture'.

[3] See Symeon, *Libellus*, lib. II, cap. viii–ix, and lib. III, cap. xi; Arnold, i, 60–1 and 94–5. See also V. Tudor, 'The Misogyny of St Cuthbert', *Archaeologia Aeliana*, 5th series 12, 1984, 151–62; and Reginald, *De Admirandis*, cap. lxii, lxxiv, c, cxix.

'haliwerfolc' or tenants of the territories of St Cuthbert.[4] Indeed, the assassination of Bishop Walcher, who had attempted to cooperate with the Community of St Cuthbert, and had been drawn into local politics and feuds, must have emphasised the gulf between themselves and the populace of Northumbria.[5] However, on the other hand, they also saw, or represented, themselves as the true spiritual heirs to the monks of Lindisfarne, Wearmouth and Jarrow. Symeon's *Libellus* puts forward this idea of the revival of true monasticism very clearly, and smoothes over the rupture by emphasising that, whilst the Community had slowly declined from monastic observance over the years, the bishops of the see of Lindisfarne/Durham had maintained their monastic status.[6]

Central to this presentation of the change as a necessary revival were two figures from the Northumbrian ecclesiastical past: St Cuthbert and Bede. St Cuthbert's triple status as bishop, monk and hermit, as forcefully depicted by Bede, was emphasised in the cult as it was developed at Durham throughout the century after the Conquest.[7] The importance of the cult of St Cuthbert, and the ways in which it affected the political, spiritual, intellectual and artistic history of Durham in this period are examined in other chapters. This chapter is concerned with the quieter, but nevertheless significant, influence of the Venerable Bede, whose relics were also possessed by the monks of Durham, and who was himself the biographer of St Cuthbert.

What is immediately striking is the difference between the representations of St Cuthbert and of Bede created in post-Conquest Durham. St Cuthbert was the figure of power, a defender of his Church capable of striking terror into the hearts of pagan Vikings and of William the Conqueror alike.[8] He could release prisoners, save sailors from shipwreck, and appeared always in full, awe-inspiring regalia as bishop.[9] In his most benign aspects, he healed the sick of both sexes, and promoted the education of boys and monks; but women and girls who dared to enter Durham cathedral, even unknowingly, were punished by illness, madness and death.[10] The image of Bede was very different. Alcuin attributed miracles to his relics, then at Jarrow, and Alfred Westoue, the early-eleventh-century sacristan of Durham, removed them from there, bringing them to Durham.[11] However, neither then nor after the

---

[4] See particularly Kapelle, *The Norman Conquest of the North*, especially ch. 4 and 5.
[5] See *Libellus*, lib. III, cap. xxiv; Arnold, i, 116–18.   [6] Ibid. 85–7.
[7] See V. Tudor, 'The Cult of St Cuthbert in the Twelfth Century: The Evidence of Reginald of Durham', in Bonner *et al.*, *St Cuthbert*, 447–57.
[8] See *Libellus*, lib. III, cap. xv and lib. III, cap. xix and xx; Arnold, i, 71–2, 106–8.
[9] Ibid. lib. III, cap. xvi and xx. Reginald's descriptions are still more elaborate.
[10] For Cuthbert's interest in education, see Reginald, *De Admirandis*, cap. lxxiii and lxxv.
[11] See Whitelock, *After Bede*. On Alfred Westoue's treatment of the relics, see *Libellus*, lib. III, cap. vii; Arnold, i, 88–9.

Conquest, when they were installed in the new cathedral beside those of St Cuthbert, were miracles attributed to them.[12] When Bede is represented in early-twelfth-century Durham illumination it is always as an author and scholar (see the chapter on the *Life of St Cuthbert*). This is also how he is presented by Symeon of Durham, who clearly knew Bede's writings. Symeon took Bede's historical method as a model for his own, as well as making direct use of Bede's historical and hagiographical writings.[13] He also seems to have visited Jarrow, and to have paid special attention to the building he believed to be Bede's 'study', describing rather wistfully how Bede could sit there and 'meditate, read, dictate and write, without disturbance'.[14] When Symeon mentioned Bede, it was as a scholar whose 'books were famed throughout the world', and who possessed the rare distinction of knowing Greek.[15] He had read at least some of Bede's biblical commentaries, and quotes from Bede's *Commentary on the Song of Songs*.[16] From Bede's own writings, Symeon was aware of the strength of the library available to him, and of the impressive level of learning in the Northumbria which produced Bede and Alcuin.[17] Thus Bede represented a scholarly ideal, to which monks like Symeon could aspire, rather than an image of power. Nevertheless, he was also a Father of the Church, whose testimony had considerable weight; and whose association with Durham helped to make it a centre of historical knowledge and scholarship.

The power of Bede's historical writing was most strikingly represented by a phenomenon which has been thoroughly investigated by several writers, and needs only brief treatment here; this is Bede's influence on the three monks from Winchcombe and Evesham who came to Northumbria to live an eremitical life amongst the places 'once crowded with communities of monks and packed with multitudes of saints' as Symeon put it.[18] The three

---

[12] The view of Bede as a scholar, rather than a miracle-worker, was shared at Worcester. Wulfstan dedicated a church to Bede, and Wulfstan's biographer, Coleman, justified this by calling Bede the 'first in fame as a man of letters among the English people'. See *The Vita Wulfstani of William of Malmesbury*, ed. R. R. Darlington, Camden Society, 3rd series 40, 1928, 20.

[13] Lib. I, cap. i declares Symeon's intention to excerpt from the *Historia Ecclesiastica* all the 'various incidents' which 'illustrate the origin and the progress of this holy church of Durham'. This is to be supplemented with 'other treatises' by 'historians', with 'documents' and with 'the information of our trustworthy elders, who had either been eye-witnesses of these incidents, or had frequently heard them recounted by religious and credible personages, who themselves had personal knowledge of the same'. The translation is by Stevenson, *Church Historians*, iii, 2, 627.

[14] *Libellus*, lib. I, cap. xiv.

[15] See the letter to dean Hugh of York, in Arnold, i, 227–8.

[16] Arnold, i, 228. This work was amongst the books given to Durham by St Calais.

[17] See note 15 above.

[18] *Libellus*, lib. III, cap. xxi; Arnold, i, 108. For recent analyses, see particularly: A. Gransden, 'Bede's Reputation as an Historian in Medieval England', in A. Gransden, *Legends, Traditions and History in Medieval England*, London and Rio Grande, 1992, 1–30; and Davis, 'Bede after Bede'.

individuals had different backgrounds, and doubtless different motivations. Reinfrid, not an Anglo-Saxon, was apparently a knight who took part in the Conqueror's harrying of the north. He seems to have visited the ruins at Streoneshalch/Whitby, and been deeply affected; he subsequently became a monk at Evesham, but clearly retained an interest in Whitby and North-umbria.[19] It was to Evesham that some refugees from Yorkshire made their way, and were given food and shelter by Abbot Æthelwig.[20] At this time Æthelwig was also in charge of Winchcombe, whose abbot had been deposed by the Conqueror. The prior of Winchcombe was Aldwin, and it was he who was apparently familiar with Bede's *Historia Ecclesiastica*.[21] From this reading Aldwin had clearly derived a list of major monastic sites; and he, Reinfrid, and a third monk, Ælfwy, received the permission of Æthelwig to set off on foot, with a donkey carrying books and other necessities, on a sort of pilgrimage to Bede's Northumbria.[22] What their precise intentions were cannot be known, as they left no written testimony of their own. Symeon's *Libellus*, and the *Historia Regum* attributed to him, give detailed accounts of their activities in Northumbria, but written with hindsight. By the early twelfth century, when these accounts were composed, the activities of the three monks had produced striking results. The *Historia Regum*, cutting a long story very short, describes them as the founders of Durham, Whitby, and St Mary's, York.[23] For Symeon, they were the supporters of Bishop Walcher's desire to bring monks back to the shrine of St Cuthbert, and the *Libellus* lists the places subject to the bishop of Durham at which they established groups of monks: Wearmouth, Jarrow, Tynemouth and, finally, Durham itself. He is understandably less interested in Whitby, Lastingham, Hackness and York.[24] One final point is of interest, and that is the move of Aldwin, with his new follower, Turgot, introduced to him by Bishop Walcher, to Melrose.[25] It was presumably at this time that Turgot came into contact with St Margaret, queen of Scotland, whose chaplain he probably became. What is even more interesting is that this move to Melrose was cut short. Melrose was still claimed by Durham but, although it was part of the kingdom of Northumbria when Bede wrote, by the late eleventh century it was part of Scotland.[26] This political boundary seems not to have

---

[19] For Reinfrid, see Burton, 'Monastic Revival', 41–52.
[20] For discussion of this, see Davis, 'Bede after Bede', 108.
[21] See *Libellus*, lib. III, cap. xxi; Arnold, i, 108.   [22] Ibid.
[23] *Historia Regum*, in Arnold, ii, *sub anno* 1074.
[24] *Libellus*, lib. III, cap. xxi–xxii; Arnold, i, 108–13.   [25] Ibid.
[26] It seems probable that the bishops of Durham continued to claim episcopal jurisdiction beyond the Tweed, in Lothian, perhaps until 1150; and that King Edgar (1097–1107) recognised their claim. See D. Matthew, 'Durham and the Anglo-Norman World', in Rollason *et al.*, *Anglo-Norman Durham*, 1–22, at 4, n. 12.

troubled Aldwin and Turgot, and the Scottish royal house were apparently happy to become their patrons; but nevertheless Aldwin and Turgot soon returned to Bishop Walcher, to be given Wearmouth by him.[27] For this reason the move to Melrose is usually said to have failed; but Davis has made the interesting suggestion that Walcher, not wishing to lose control of Aldwin and Turgot, deliberately recalled them.[28] Since both Aldwin and Turgot were Anglo-Saxons, as was Queen Margaret, Walcher may well have wished to prevent the monastic revival from becoming associated with Anglo-Saxon political loyalties.[29]

Whether or not this argument is correct, it raises the problem of the political significance of Bede's work, and thus the further question of how that political significance was perceived at Durham. Aldwin and Ælfwy were both Anglo-Saxons, as was Turgot. They came from two of the last monasteries in the country to have an Anglo-Saxon abbot, and from the diocese of Worcester, which had one of the last Anglo-Saxon bishops, Wulfstan II (1062–95). They were inspired by Bede's account of the past glories of the Anglo-Saxon Church, and they did their best to revive that Church in the places about which Bede had written. Does this mean that Bede should be seen as the inspiration for an Anglo-Saxon movement to resist Norman domination of the English Church? This is an interesting idea, but one which is impossible to prove. Reinfrid was a Norman knight or mercenary, who wished to live an eremitical life, and was particularly affected by Whitby; he may well have reacted against the harrying of the north, but that does not make him a proponent of the Anglo-Saxon Church. Similarly, Walcher was a Lotharingian, appointed to an isolated and dangerous post by the Conqueror. He was attempting to secure his hold on Durham, but for him to arouse Anglo-Saxon feeling would be very dangerous. His patronage of the three monks, and his recall of Aldwin and Turgot from Melrose, make most sense as part of an attempt to build up groups of monks who would be loyal to him, and would help to counterbalance the dominance of the Community of St Cuthbert. Whether it was Walcher's intention to turn Durham into a Benedictine monastery, as Symeon stated some twenty years after Walcher's death, cannot be certain.[30]

What all this does emphasise is that Bede's legacy to Anglo-Norman Durham was not entirely straightforward. On the one hand there was Bede

[27] *Libellus*, lib. III, cap. xxii; Arnold, i, 110–13.

[28] See Davis, 'Bede after Bede', 108–9.

[29] The *Libellus* confirms that Walcher recalled the party from Melrose; but stresses Malcolm's hostility, caused by the monks' refusal to swear fidelity to him (lib. III, cap. xxii; Arnold, i, 111–12).

[30] For this assertion, see *Libellus* 'Epitome', Arnold, i, 9–10.

the scholar-saint and father of the Church, whose relics and writings added to the glory of the cathedral and priory of Durham. But there was also Bede the Anglo-Saxon, one of whose best-known works was the *Ecclesiastical History of the English People*, and whose account of the glorious Anglo-Saxon past was translated into Old English, and was used by compilers of various versions of the *Anglo-Saxon Chronicle*.[31] In order to try to understand how Bede was perceived in Anglo-Norman Durham, it is necessary to look at the evidence from surviving manuscripts, catalogues and texts. One of the most difficult problems, unfortunately, is to get any idea of which of Bede's works was available at Durham before the Conquest. First, the copy of Bede's *Life of St Cuthbert*, given to the shrine by King Athelstan in the early tenth century, was part of the treasures of the shrine at Durham.[32] Second, Alfred Westoue's relic-hunting activities make it virtually certain that he was using a copy of the *Historia Ecclesiastica* as his guide.[33] Third, the mid-twelfth-century Durham book-list includes a 'Historia Anglorum Anglice' and something listed as 'Scutum Bedae'. There is no trace amongst the surviving Durham books of these last three items. On the whole, it seems unlikely that the 'Historia Anglorum Anglice' would be Alfred Westoue's copy of the *Historia Ecclesiastica*. It is possible that it may have been Aldwin's copy of this work, since the Old English translation was available at Worcester in the eleventh century,[34] and the surviving Winchcombe manuscript of the *Historia Ecclesiastica* (the Latin version) is apparently twelfth-century (it is now Bodleian, Douce 368).

The volume referred to as 'Scutum Bedae' appears in the book-list isolated from both Bede's theological works and the main listing of historical works. It comes between a group of classical works and Christian Latin poetry, which precede it, and a rather miscellaneous set of epistles, sermons, hagiography and recent theological works (Anselm and St Bernard) which follow it.[35] If this placing is significant, then the book may have been a collection of prayers, religious poems, or something of the kind. At any rate, its chief interest seems to have been its attribution to Bede, which, since no such work appears to be known from any other centre, may have been a piece

---

[31] On this, see especially Whitelock, *After Bede*.

[32] See *Historia de Sancto Cuthberto* in Arnold, i, 196–214, at 211. The manuscript concerned is now Cambridge, Corpus Christi College, MS 183. However, David Rollason has questioned this identification, see 'St Cuthbert and Wessex', in Bonner *et al.*, *St Cuthbert*, 413–24.

[33] Davis comes to the same conclusion. See 'Bede after Bede', 113, n. 35. That Alfred Westoue's grandson, Eilaf, Aelred of Rievaulx's father, owned some books is confirmed by Laurence of Durham's letter to Aelred, and, perhaps, by Aelred's account of his grandfather at Hexham, given in Aelred's treatise on the saints of Hexham (see Chapter 11).

[34] This is now Cambridge UL Kk 3 18, datable by its script to the late eleventh century.

[35] *Catalogi Veteres*, 1–10.

of Durham tradition. It is unfortunate that it does not appear to survive. A copy of the *Commentary on the Apocalypse* does, but is almost equally frustrating. DCL A IV 28 is clumsily written by several scribes, apparently working in haste, in a not very good version of English Caroline miniscule. Its low quality and lack of decoration make it difficult to date, but the consensus is for the early eleventh century. It has no early provenance, and it is tempting to see it as a local product, which passed to the monks after 1083. However, there is no evidence that it was at Durham before the middle of the twelfth century. The mid-twelfth-century book-list gives the works of Bede by name, but the list does not include this text. DCL B IV 16, of the second half of the twelfth century, appears to be copied from A IV 28, so that two possibilities arise.[36] First, A IV 28 was at Durham in the early twelfth century, but was not listed in B IV 24; B IV 16 would then be produced from it as a better copy. Second, A IV 28 was acquired in the second half of the century, used as an exemplar, and itself added to the library.

By contrast to this unimpressive total, the book-list in B IV 24 gives eight theological commentaries, as well as the *De Temporibus*, *Historia Ecclesiastica* and *Liber de Vitis Abbatum de Weremuth*.[37] This would appear to suggest considerable activity in building up a collection of Bede's works, which accords with Symeon of Durham's clear admiration for Bede, although also with the general popularity of Bede's theological works in the twelfth century. In order to understand how Bede and his works were perceived at Durham it is therefore worth looking at the surviving evidence for the creation of this collection in some detail.

Not very much activity in book-collecting is attributed to Walcher, as might be expected. He is represented by Symeon as interested in reading about the history of his see, which may well have included consulting the *Historia Ecclesiastica*, and certainly looked at King Athelstan's copy of the *Life of St Cuthbert*, but he is not recorded as leaving any books to the shrine.[38] Much more active was St Calais. His list of books given to Durham includes Bede's *Commentaries* on Mark and Luke, and on the Song of Songs, as well as the *Historia Ecclesiastica*, here interestingly listed as 'Historia Anglorum'.[39] Of these, the only one which survives is the 'Historia Anglorum', to which various other historical texts were added during the twelfth century, which is now DCL B II 35. It was probably St Calais's copies of the *Historia* and the

---

[36] See Mynors, *Durham Cathedral Manuscripts*, 55.

[37] See note 35. Of course, where the books do not survive, and thus cannot be dated, it is possible that they were of Anglo-Saxon origin; although St Calais's gift of several volumes of Bede makes it unlikely that there was a large collection.

[38] For Walcher's use of Cambridge, Corpus Christi College, MS 138, see Hohler and Hughes, 'The Durham Services'.

[39] See Chapter 2.

Commentary on the Song of Songs which recur in the B IV 24 book-list. The book-list's 'Super Marcum et Lucam' (apparently one volume) also presumably refers to St Calais's gift. This would seem to suggest that the other Bedan items on the list were produced or acquired by the priory; these were *De Temporibus* (lost); *Super Genesim ad Litteram* (almost certainly Cambridge, Jesus College, Q A 14); *De Tabernaculo* (lost, but a Kirkham manuscript has extracts from this text); *Super Samuhel* (lost); *Super Canonicas Epistolas* (almost certainly BL Harley 3864); *Super Actus Apostolorum* (lost); and *Super Parabolas Salomonis* (presumably the work usually known as *De Proverbis*, and almost certainly BL Harley 4688; copies of the work survive from Jervaulx and Kirkstall). The *Liber de Vitis Abbatum de Weremuth* appears separately in the B IV 24 list, and is now lost. However, it was presumably the exemplar for the twelfth-century copy of this work which was added to St Calais's 'Historia Anglorum' in a Durham hand.[40]

All this raises the question of where St Calais found exemplars for his copies of Bede's works. As has already been seen, he showed a clear preference for Norman styles of scholarship and book production. His copy of the *Historia Ecclesiastica* was produced by a Norman scribe who seems to have been brought to Durham by St Calais, and is wholly Norman in style.[41] Davis suggests that a 'local copy' was probably used as an exemplar, but this is not as simple a hypothesis as might appear.[42] For a start, St Calais's text was apparently not the same as that used by Symeon; and secondly, this copy might have been made during St Calais's exile. It is certainly possible that it came from a Norman or northern French exemplar. St Wandrille, near Rouen, had a copy by the end of the eighth century. This may have been destroyed, like St Wandrille itself, by Vikings. The eleventh-century catalogue of Fécamp has only Bede's theological works and the *De Temporibus*. However, the work rose in popularity in Normandy from the Conquest on, and Orderic Vitalis himself made a copy for St Evroult, now Rouen, BM, 1343. Interestingly, this belongs to the same general family of texts as St Calais's, a family which Colgrave and Mynors show to have been dominant in both England and Normandy, although in various sub-versions.[43] It is clear, however, that B II 35 is at least ten years older than Rouen 1343, and is the oldest post-Conquest representative of this textual family – an unhelpful fact. What is striking is that B II 35 belongs to the so-called 'c' family of manuscripts, which appear to descend from an early version of the work by Bede. One of the main characteristics of this version is that it lacks a

[40] Now DCL B II 35. See Mynors, *Durham Cathedral Manuscripts*, no. 47.
[41] See Chapter 2.
[42] Davis, 'Bede after Bede', 113.
[43] *Bede's Ecclesiastical History*, lxi and xlvii–lii.

miracle of St Oswald, which is added as book IV, chapter xiv, in the revised or 'm' version. Interestingly, the absence of this miracle seems not to have been noticed at Durham, which had relics of St Oswald, even though it was noticed at Peterborough by 1100 (St Oswald was important at Peterborough also, as an early-eleventh-century bishop of Durham, an ex-monk of Peterborough, had apparently stolen the arm of St Oswald, and given it to Peterborough).[44] In defence of Durham scholarship it may be pointed out that reference to the Old English translation would not have shown up the omission, since it too came from the 'c' family.[45]

Where does all this leave the enquiry? A Norman exemplar is possible, but not demonstrable. Invoking a 'local copy' is problematic, since there is no other clear trace of it at Durham. A York exemplar is possible, assuming that it had survived the destruction at York, but there is a problem; Dorothy Whitelock says that the version of the *Historia Ecclesiastica* used in the tenth century by the compilers of the northern (York) version of the *Anglo-Saxon Chronicle* was of the other, 'm', family.[46] There remain two other alternatives: an exemplar from the Winchcombe area; or Canterbury. The idea of an exemplar brought north by Aldwin and copied for St Calais is attractive, but must again be ruled out. Both BL Royal 13 C V, the eleventh-century copy from Gloucester, and Bodleian Douce 368, the early twelfth-century copy from Winchcombe, are related to something like BL Cotton Tiberius A xiv, and are therefore of a different branch of the 'c' family. So Canterbury raises possibilities, and the results are a little more encouraging than those encountered so far. The 'c' family itself appears to be linked to St Augustine's, and Whitelock argues that it may be derived from the version sent by Bede to Albinus at Canterbury.[47] The oldest surviving representative of the 'c' family, C itself, is BL Cotton Tiberius C ii, written in southern England in the eighth century, and glossed, using Kentish forms, in the ninth century. Most strikingly, this has a curious mistake at the beginning of the Preface, which is repeated by Symeon of Durham.[48] So it would appear that either C itself, or a close copy from it, was known at Durham c. 1100. But, to add further complexity to the problem, this mistake is *not* found in B II 35. Moreover, the twelfth-century copies from Battle, Waltham, Rochester and Bury, which seem to represent the twelfth-century Canterbury versions, although of the 'c' type, are not closely related to B II 35.[49] So all

[44] For this accusation see Symeon, *Libellus*, lib. III, cap. vii. On the Peterborough copy of the *Historia Ecclesiastica*, see *Bede's Ecclesiastical History*, li.

[45] See D. Whitelock, 'The Old English Bede', *Proceedings of the British Academy* 48, 1962, 57–90.

[46] Whitelock, *After Bede*. [47] Ibid.

[48] See *Bede's Ecclesiastical History*, xlii. [49] Ibid. lvi–lix.

that can be said is that an early copy of the Canterbury 'C' manuscript seems to have been available to Symeon of Durham. The source of St Calais's exemplar remains obscure, but perhaps the Norman connections are the most promising.

Thus, it does seem that St Calais gave to Durham a copy of the *Historia Ecclesiastica* taken from an examplar not otherwise known there, and in a wholly Norman style. His view of the work is perhaps represented by the title it is given in both St Calais's book-list and the B IV 24 list, 'Historia Anglorum'. The title 'Historia Ecclesiastica' seems to have been reserved for Eusebius, as translated by Rufinus, a work on which Bede himself drew. This is perhaps the fundamental importance of the work: Bede gave the 'English', and especially those of Northumbria, a history. How influential his history could be is suggested both by the story of Aldwin and his companions, and by Symeon of Durham's picture of St Calais himself studying the history of his see before deciding to 'restore' monks to the church and shrine of St Cuthbert.[50]

Sadly, St Calais's other Bede manuscripts have been lost. Nevertheless, surviving Durham books show the interest in Bede and his work understandably felt by the monks. The copies of Bede *On Genesis*, *On the Catholic Epistles*, *On the Apocalypse* and *On Proverbs* all appear to be Durham products. Jesus Q A 14 (*On Genesis*) and DCL B IV 16, fols. 1–45 (*On the Apocalypse*) both have distinctive 'clove-curl' initials, while Mynors has identified the hand of BL Harley 4688 (*On Proverbs*) in an added 'Life of St Jerome' in DCL B II 10.[51] The sources drawn on for exemplars cannot be identified, but these were not rare works. By the twelfth century, the Norman houses were building up their collections also. St Wandrille's ninth-century copy of *On Genesis* may have been lost, but the work was in the libraries of Le Bec and Lyre, while St Thierry, in close touch with St Bernard's Clairvaux, preserved its own ninth-century copy. Indeed, it is interesting that the St Thierry version was the longer text, and that this is the version which survives from Durham and from Clairvaux, as well as from Augustinian Llanthony.[52] *On the Catholic Epistles* was more popular, and Le Bec had a copy, as well as St Wandrille. Interestingly, both St Thierry and St Bénigne had tenth-century copies, while Cîteaux, Fleury and Peterborough all had eleventh-century versions. The copies from Christ Church, Canterbury, Rochester and Clairvaux, like Durham's, are all twelfth century.[53] For the commentary on the Apocalypse, an English copy of unknown provenance (DCL A IV 28)

[50] Symeon, *Libellus*, lib. IV, cap. ii; Arnold, i, 120–1.
[51] See Mynors, *Durham Cathedral Manuscripts*, no. 38, 37.
[52] See M. L. W. Laistner and H. H. King, *A Hand-List of Bede Manuscripts*, New York, 1943, 41–3.   [53] Ibid. 30–7.

was found; whether there is any direct connection between it and the twelfth-century copies from St Evroult, Le Bec, Jumièges and Christ Church, Canterbury, is unknown.[54] Finally, of the surviving works, *On Proverbs* was also popular. Twelfth-century copies survive from Canterbury, Fécamp, Clairvaux, St Thierry and Peterborough, of which the Durham copy (BL Harley 4688) is perhaps the oldest.[55]

However, if little can be said of the sources drawn upon by the monks of Durham in building up their collection of Bede's works, there is a little more evidence on the influence exerted by the Durham copies on other Northumbrian libraries. The twelfth-century library list from Whitby shows six works by Bede, namely the *Life of St Cuthbert*, and the *Commentaries* on Acts, the Catholic Epistles, Luke, Mark and Proverbs.[56] None of these survive, but as they were all to be found at Durham, some borrowing seems likely. The Rievaulx catalogue, of twelfth/thirteenth-century date, shows a larger collection of Bede than mid-twelfth-century Durham, but the two lists have the *Commentaries* on Luke, Mark, the Catholic Epistles, Samuel and *De Tabernaculo* in common.[57] I have argued elsewhere that Rievaulx borrowed and copied Durham books, so that Rievaulx may well have drawn on Durham for some of its list of Bede's works. A twelfth-century manuscript of the *Historia Ecclesiastica*, from Kirkham, also contains extracts from the *De Tabernaculo*, which may be derived from Durham's lost copy;[58] while Guisborough's twelfth-century copy of book VII of Bede's *On the Song of Songs* may have been derived from St Calais's lost gift to Durham.[59] Similarly, Fountains' copy of the *Commentary on St Mark* and Louth Park's *On St Luke* may go back to St Calais's lost books.[60] More substantial are the surviving copies of *On Proverbs* from Kirkstall and Jervaulx.[61] The Kirkstall copy gives the work a different title from the Durham version, and has initials which are as close to those of St Mary's, York, as to Durham styles; while the Jervaulx copy is thirteenth century. Nevertheless, the Jervaulx copy at least may be

---

[54] Ibid. 25–30.   [55] Ibid. 56–62.

[56] See Atkinson, J. G., ed., *Cartularium Abbathiae de Whitby*, Surtees Society 69, Durham, 1878, i, 341.

[57] For the full Rievaulx catalogue, see now D. N. Bell, ed., *The Libraries of the Cistercians, Gilbertines and Premonstratensians*, Corpus of British Medieval Library Catalogues 3, London, 1992. For the copies of Bede's works held by Rievaulx and Durham, the most convenient means of comparison is to use the listings in Laistner and King, *Hand-List*.

[58] This is now BL Add. 38817.

[59] This is one section in the collection of excerpts which is now BL Arundel 218. Durham influence is demonstrated by the use of the clove-curl motif in this manuscript.

[60] These are, respectively, Cambridge, Trinity College, MS 54 (B 2 11) and Cambridge UL Dd i 29.

[61] These are: Oxford, Bodleian, Laud misc. 216 (not listed by Laistner and King, but with an *ex libris*): and Bodleian, Lat. Th. f 3.

related to the Durham text. A final comparison which might be of interest would be of fols. 128–36 of BL Arundel 218 (the Guisborough copy of part of Bede's *On the Song of Songs*) with Le Mans, BM, MS 20. The latter is an eleventh-century copy of the text from St Vincent, Le Mans, the house of which St Calais had been abbot, and thus may have provided the exemplar for his own copy of this work.[62]

In all this, one thing stands out clearly, and that is the influence exerted by St Calais's copy of the *Historia Ecclesiastica/Anglorum*. Colgrave and Mynors have demonstrated that it was the ancestor of copies from Worksop (BL Harley 4124), Tynemouth (Cambridge, Pembroke College, MS 82), Newminster (BL Add. 25014) and, in the thirteenth century, Coupar Angus (Rome, Vat., Reg. Lat. 694).[63] What is interesting here is that, while these houses are Augustinian and Cistercian, thus confirming the intellectual similarities between Durham and the new orders, they are all, with the exception of Worksop, situated to the north of Durham, and none of them is in Yorkshire. Copies of the *Historia Ecclesiastica* survive from Selby (Bodleian, Fairfax 12), Jervaulx (Oxford, St John's College, MS 99) and Kirkham (BL Add. 38817). All these come from a common exemplar, which was faulty at the end, as did Cambridge, Trinity College, R 5 27, which I have argued to be a St Mary's manuscript, and which is the oldest of the group.[64] BL Cotton Vitellius E i is a twelfth-century copy from Guisborough. It was badly burnt in the Cotton fire, and is now seriously charred. Much of the text is lost, but enough survives to show it does not belong to the Durham group. It is written in a confident hand, perhaps of the mid-twelfth century, and its initials, which appear to have been in red and blue, show some similarities to those in York manuscripts, though there are no distinctive motifs. Both Rievaulx and Augustinian Bridlington had copies, now lost; it would have been interesting to know which version Rievaulx, with its close contacts with Durham, followed. In the absence of other evidence, it seems likely that St Mary's, the offspring of Reinfrid's Whitby, obtained a copy of this work independent of that of St Calais, and had it copied in the first quarter of the twelfth century. This may also have been used by Selby, Jervaulx and Kirkham, each of which add selected further historical and hagiographical material, drawn from texts circulating in Cistercian circles and at Durham in the early to mid-twelfth century. It is also interesting that the Selby and

---

[62] For St Calais's possession of this text, see the list of his books, on fol. 1 of DCL A II 4.

[63] See *Bede's Ecclesiastical History*, xlix–l.

[64] On this 'Yorkshire' group, see *Bede's Ecclesiastical History*, liii–lv. It may be of significance that Selby was placed under the supervision of the archbishop of York by William Rufus, when he became a patron of St Mary's, thus creating a link between this group and York which avoids the problem of the hostility between St Mary's and the Cistercian houses.

Kirkham copies have similar script and 'Anglo-Norman' initials, although the Selby manuscript is slightly earlier. Thus, even though the Yorkshire copies of the *Historia Ecclesiastica* did not apparently derive from Durham, their scribes and readers drew upon a pool of material which linked Yorkshire, and especially the Cistercian houses, to Durham.[65]

This then raises perhaps the most interesting, and the most difficult, question of all; whether the works of Bede contributed to the development of a distinctive monastic and intellectual culture in post-Conquest Northumbria, and whether this can be distinguished from Bede's general popularity at this time (already demonstrated by the number of French houses cited as having copies of his works).

Perhaps the first point is that Bede's appeal seems to have been twofold. First there was Bede the scholar, whose works were equally popular in the more scholarly houses of Normandy and in those Anglo-Norman houses, like Durham and Christ Church, Canterbury, most directly affected by continental scholarship.[66] However, there was also Bede, the Father of the Church, who made a very strong appeal to the Cistercians, despite their disapproval of scholarship for its own sake, or of scholarship as the path to a career 'in the world'.[67] A glance at the surviving books of Cîteaux and Clairvaux demonstrates the strength of this appeal. From Cîteaux, twelfth-century copies of the *Commentaries* on Acts, the Catholic Epistles and Tobit survive together with the *De Templo*, the *Historia Ecclesiastica* and the *Life of St Cuthbert*. Clairvaux appears to have had an extremely impressive collection, with surviving twelfth-century copies of the *Commentaries* on Acts, the Apocalypse, the Catholic Epistles, Ezra and Nehemiah, Tobit, Genesis, Luke, Mark, Proverbs and the Song of Songs as well as the *De Temporum Ratione*, *De Tabernaculo*, *De Templo*, the *Life of St Cuthbert* and the rare *Life of St Felix*.[68] St Bernard himself makes use of several of Bede's *Commentaries*, and his own well-known *Sermons on the Song of Songs* take fundamental points from Bede's work on the same text.

The popularity of Bede's works with St Bernard thus suggests a rather different Bede. For the Cistercians, what was presumably important was that

---

[65] For details see Conclusion.

[66] William of St Calais's interest in Bede has already been noted, as has the activity of Orderic Vitalis at St-Evroult, in copying out the *Historia Ecclesiastica*. In the case of Canterbury, Anselm wrote from Le Bec to Maurice, a Norman monk at Christ Church, asking for a good text of the *De Temporibus* (see F. S. Schmitt, ed., *S. Anselmi Opera Omnia*, vol. iii, Rome/Edinburgh, 1946). By the late twelfth century, Laistner demonstrates that Christ Church had no less than twelve of Bede's theological works (see Laistner and King, *Hand-List*, 11).

[67] For this view see e.g. St Bernard, Epistle to Fulk, Archdeacon of Langres, in *S. Bernardi Opera*, vol. vii, Rome, 1974, 12–22.

[68] For these, see Laistner and King, *Hand-List, passim*.

Bede was a monk, who spent his entire life in one monastery, which was, as he himself wrote, remote from almost all the world, and who dedicated his life, not to an ambitious career, but to the teaching of his fellow monks.[69] Many of his commentaries were dedicated to fellow monks, or to monk-bishops; and the majority were sent to bishops, either for approval or because they had requested them. This is strikingly in accordance with the way in which St Bernard conducted his own theological work, presenting his sermons and commentaries as dedicated to others, or written at the request of others. Indeed, Bede's humility is in accordance with the growing Cistercian practice of requiring that would-be authors received the approval of General Chapter before they wrote.[70] Moreover, Bede is humble in his treatment of his authorities. He presents his material straightforwardly, and supplies marginal source-marks in some commentaries, indicating which passages came from which Father, which he asked future scribes to copy. Bede's historical and hagiographical writing might also be of especial interest to Cistercians. For he is not only telling an important part of the early history of the Western Church; his heroes, and St Cuthbert particularly, are both monks and men of humility. St Cuthbert's preference for living as a hermit, and for praying for extended periods alone in the open air, his love of animals and sympathy with natural phenomena, are reminiscent of St Bernard's dictum that trees can teach the faithful more than books can.[71]

If all this is accurate, then certain questions or suggestions follow. The first point, which was already implicit in the analysis of textual filiations above, is that, despite Durham's possession of Bede's relics, and of the site of Bede's study, Cistercian houses in northern England need not necessarily have looked to Durham for exemplars of Bede's works. All these Cistercian houses belonged to the family of Clairvaux, and their abbots may have been aware that their mother-house's collection of Bede's works was more extensive than Durham's own. Thus, whilst an interest in Bede and his works was clearly widespread in Northumbria, this did not necessarily imply any simple pre-eminence for Durham, but rather a network of links and related interests. This is rather in contradiction to Bernard Meehan's recent arguments on the Yorkshire Cistercians' dependence on Durham, and I certainly do not wish to imply that the Cistercians did not have a high regard for Durham as a source

[69] Bede himself wrote that he was 'born and nurtured far away' and this view was echoed in the twelfth century by Symeon of Durham and by William of Malmesbury. See Gransden, 'Bede's Reputation as an Historian', at 13.

[70] For this prohibition, datable to c.1119–51, see 'Table of Cistercian legislation', in Norton and Park, *Cistercian Art and Architecture*, 325.

[71] See St Bernard, epistles to Aelred of Rievaulx and Henry Murdac, in *Opera Omnia*, vii, 266, and viii, 486–9.

of books; but, at least in this area, dependence cannot be assumed.[72] Second, and rather more interesting, is the question of whether Bede's works were used, or read, differently in different houses. Any answer to this question given here can only be a preliminary sketch, but some evidence can be found.

The survey can start with the work of which the largest number of copies survive, that is the *Historia Ecclesiastica*. It has already been observed that, to St Calais and to the monastic officials of Anglo-Norman Durham, this was the 'Historia Anglorum'. This implies that it was seen as 'history', rather than 'Church history', and this impression is confirmed by the fact that it occurs in the B IV 24 book-list separated from Bede's other works, and grouped together with the 'De Gestis Francorum' and the 'De Gestis Normannorum'. The additions to B II 35, St Calais's copy, give the same impression. The chief additions are: Bede's *Historia Abbatum*; a *Life of Bede*; Nennius' *Historia Brittonum*; Pope Sergius' letter to Ceolfrid; a *Life of Gildas*; lists of kings of England and Scotland; and lists of bishops of the provinces of Canterbury and York. Interestingly, the surviving copy which shows the closest interests to these is that from another 'traditional' house, Cambridge, Pembroke College, MS 82, from Tynemouth.[73] This is a twelfth-century derivative from B II 35, but its additions are slightly different, if equally historical. They include the *Historia Abbatum* and the *Life of Bede*, but then diverge to a list of the bishops of Lindisfarne and a genealogy of the kings of Northumbria. Thus, at Tynemouth the emphasis was more simply on 'northern history'. However, at Cistercian Newminster, things were slightly different. The Newminster copy, now BL Add. 25014, is the only Cistercian derivative of B II 35.[74] However, here the additional material focuses more strongly on the ecclesiastical politics of Northumbria and Scotland, consisting as it does of: the letter on the death of Bede, written by Cuthbert, one of his disciples; a piece on Whithorn and the see of York; and a piece on the Scottish veneration of St Andrew. The other surviving Cistercian copy, Oxford, St John's College, MS 99, comes from Jervaulx, and is textually of the 'Yorkshire' group. This adds Cuthbert's letter, Nennius' *Historia Brittonum* (both this and the Fountains/Sawley version are related to that in B II 35) and St Bernard's *Life of St Malachy* (d. 1148). It is difficult to make much of this, although the fact that the Nennius text was known at other Yorkshire Cistercian houses suggests that this should be seen as a Cistercian collection, rather than one which looks to Durham.

[72] Meehan, 'Durham Twelfth-Century Manuscripts'.

[73] Tynemouth was a priory of St Albans, although Durham maintained an unsuccessful claim to it well into the twelfth century. The exchange of books, and of initial-forms, between the two houses however demonstrates that friendly contacts took place.

[74] Newminster's location is, of course, far closer to Durham and especially to Tynemouth than to its own 'Fountains' family, or even to the 'Rievaulx' family in the border regions.

What of the members of the 'Yorkshire' group from Selby (Bodleian, Fairfax 12) and St Mary's (Cambridge, Trinity College, R 5 27)? Interestingly, both incorporate marginal notes suggesting that the *Historia Ecclesiastica* was here read as a sort of official history of the diocese of York. Those in Fairfax 12 are very interesting. The text is here titled 'Historia de Gestis Anglorum', suggesting an attitude similar to that at Durham. However, fol. 77 has a contemporary note, in red, emphasised by a red box: 'Nota quod Lindisfarnensis insula perpetuo habuerit episcopum'. On fol. 78 is another, again emphasised by a red box: 'Nota quod Hripensis ecclesia perpetuo habuerit episcopum'. By the early twelfth century Selby had been placed under the supervision of the archbishop of York, and these notes seem to demonstrate a strong interest in the possible diocesans of the archdiocese. It is tempting to imagine an advisor of Archbishop Thurstan consulting the *Historia Ecclesiastica* for information on the rights of the archdiocese, but sadly there is no clear proof of this.

Finally, the two surviving copies from Augustinian houses suggest still other approaches to the text. The Guisborough copy is too badly damaged for marginal annotations to survive, but the supplementary texts are again interesting, as they turn it into a sort of compendium on Bede. They include Cuthbert's letter, the *Historia Abbatum*, the *Life of Bede*, Bede's prose *Life of St Cuthbert*, a list of the bishops of Lindisfarne and Durham, and a Durham relic-list including the relics of Bede and St Cuthbert. BL Add. 38817, the Kirkham manuscript, again had what looks like a carefully selected set of additions. It opens with a short extract from Bede's *De Tabernaculo*, accompanied by a detailed diagram, painted in red, blue and yellow. This is followed by an account of the discovery of the body of St Ragner, which is set in Northampton, in the time of Edward the Confessor. Then comes the *Historia Ecclesiastica*, with the same additions as in the Jervaulx copy, suggesting that the Kirkham scribe may have used that as his exemplar. Finally, and uniquely, came a collection of visions of the other world. These are now lost, but the contemporary contents list on fol. 4v gives them as the visions of Wettin, the twelve dancers, Barontus, and the boy Orm (d. 1126). Whoever compiled this set of visions was clearly familiar with the *Historia Ecclesiastica* since, in book V, which they follow, Bede devotes three chapters to visions, including a long account of the otherworld vision of a dying man, which was popular enough to have a circulation alone as an extract. Copies of it survive from St Thierry and Clairvaux, which does not seem to have had a complete text of the major work.[75] Some link with Durham is also clear, as

---

[75] See Laistner and King, *Hand-List*, 108.

the story of Orm derives from a letter written by his parish priest to Symeon of Durham.[76]

Here also there are some marginal notes in the *Historia Ecclesiastica* itself, again suggesting a rather hagiographical approach to the text, almost that of someone selecting martyrological material. Fol. 24r has 'de obitu s. augustini', fol. 38v 'Oswaldo', fol. 41 'de moribus sci Oswini', and fol. 48 the simple notes 'Coleman' and 'Wilfrid'. In all, this volume may have been intended for reading aloud, rather than for historical study. That readers at Guisborough were very interested in, and discerning about, the contents of their books is suggested by other notes and annotations. BL Arundel 218, a Guisborough book, contains three texts, and a contemporary inscription on the flyleaf explains that the first is a set of excerpts from Gregory's *Moralia*, first put together by Alcuin, who was called by Charlemagne; that the second is a collection of excerpts on the Song of Songs, taken by Bede from the works of Gregory; and that the third is Augustine's *De Disciplina Christiana*. There is no evidence on where this information came from, but its presence again demonstrates an informed interest in Bede.

This analysis has so far dealt with Bede the historian, and with how his chief historical work was read in the monastic houses of twelfth-century Northumbria. The question of his use by twelfth-century chroniclers is examined in some detail by Davis and, particularly, Gransden, and there is no need to repeat that work here. Instead, Bede the schoolmaster and Bede the theoretical writer on time, neither of which have attracted so much attention, will be briefly discussed. Indeed, Bede the schoolmaster *can* only be briefly discussed, since Bede's 'school text-books' are notable in twelfth-century Northumbria by their absence. In the case of Cistercian houses their absence is hardly surprising, since the Cistercians did not run schools. Very few Augustinian books survive; but the detailed twelfth-century book-list from Bridlington, which has the *Historia Ecclesiastica*, does not have the text-books.[77] Most surprising is their absence from Durham. Symeon of Durham was clearly aware of Bede's pedagogical activities, and outlines Bede's teaching on 'rules of metre, astronomy and ecclesiastical calculation' as well as giving in its entirety Bede's list of his own works.[78] This account was based on the *Historia Ecclesiastica*, since there is nothing in the B IV 24 book-list, with its long lists of school books, identifiable as Bede's *De Arte Metrica* or *De Schematibus et Tropis*. This absence is all the more striking as Canterbury had a tenth-century copy of both works, and both Fécamp and Rochester had

[76] See D. H. Farmer, 'The vision of Orm', Analecta Bollandiana 75, 1957, 72–82; also Gransden, *Historical Writing in England*, 116.
[77] For this list, see Chapter 8 above.
[78] Symeon, *Libellus*, lib. I, cap. xiv; Arnold i, 41–3.

copies by the early twelfth century.[79] The conclusion would seem to be that the school at Durham preferred to use Priscian, Boethius and other late-classical authors. However, there is one small way in which Bede the pedagogue may have influenced Anglo-Norman Durham. It has already been observed that Durham was precocious in producing a full set of illustrations for copies of the *Life of St Cuthbert*; perhaps it is only a coincidence, but Bede comments favourably on the educational and spiritual value of pictures at several points in his writings, and he particularly emphasises an illustrated manuscript of the *Life of St Paul* which had been brought to England from Rome.[80] It cannot be proved that the relevant treatise was known at Durham *c.*1100; but the fuller description of the volume containing Bede's *Commentary on Acts*, given in the fourteenth-century catalogue, states that it also contained many other short pieces, so that it is at least a possibility.[81]

Finally, there is the question of the influence of Bede's works on time, and on the computus. This was an aspect of his work which was valued in the late eleventh century. St Augustine's, Canterbury, had a copy of Bede's *De Temporibus*, probably copied under Scolland's abbacy (1070–87),[82] while Anselm wrote from Le Bec, asking Maurice, a monk who had gone with Lanfranc to Christ Church, to find and copy a good text of the same work.[83] Robert de Lotharingia, the bishop of Hereford who died in 1095 and who was interested in science, knew Bede's writings on time thoroughly. He himself wrote a work on computus, based on Bede's treatises, which was mostly known in the region around Hereford (copies survive from Winchcombe, Malmesbury and Abbey Dore). However, the only other copy is in Glasgow UL, Hunterian T 4 2, a twelfth-century book from Durham.[84] This manuscript is later than DCL Hunter 100, which it partly copies, but is earlier than 1140, as the death of Geoffrey Rufus is added in the margin of fol. 26r. It thus represents a fairly early copy of Robert's text, confirming again the scholarly interests and contacts of the priory of Durham. The influence at Durham of Bede's chronological and computistical works is demonstrated by the presence in the B IV 24 list of *De Temporibus* 'in duobus voluminibus', presumably both the short 'de temporibus' and the 'de temporibus liber maior' or *De Temporum Ratione*. This does not survive, but probably corresponds to the volume listed as E under 'Libri Bedae' in the

---

[79] See Laistner and King, *Hand-List*, 131–7.
[80] See G. Henderson, *Bede and the Visual Arts*, Jarrow Lecture, 1980, 7.
[81] See *Catalogi Veteres*, 20.
[82] This is Cambridge, Corpus Christi College, MS 291. It was written by an Englishman.
[83] See *S. Anselmi Opera Omnia*, ed. F. S. Schmitt, Edinburgh, 1946, vol. iii, letter 60.
[84] Mynors, *Durham Cathedral Manuscripts*, no. 71, 55–6.

fourteenth-century catalogue.[85] Besides the two versions of *De Temporibus* this also had a work 'de Creatione Mundi' attributed to Bede, Johannes Scotus' *De Natura* and Bede's *Martyrology*. That the compilation of works on the computus was already advanced at Durham *c.* 1100 is demonstrated by Hunter 100. Besides its better-known medical texts, this compendious volume assembles tracts by Dionysius Exiguus (a rare work, used by Bede); Abbo of Fleury (who himself used Bede's *De Temporibus*); Isidore; Helperic of Grandval; Bede himself (extracts from the *De Temporibus*); and the same Robert de Lotharingia or Losinga (suggesting that contact with him was esablished very early).[86] In this field, then, Durham clearly excelled, just as it did in the compilation and composition of historical works; and in both these areas the influence of Bede was fundamental.

Thus, while it is clear that no single 'Northumbrian' view of Bede can be constructed, the very breadth of Bede's work was part of his importance. He offered models for many of the projects undertaken by both 'traditional' and 'reforming' houses, and the popularity and status of his works contributed largely to the development of the network of intellectual contacts which is one of the features of Anglo-Norman Northumbria. His relics at Durham may not have attracted as much attention as those of St Cuthbert, but Symeon's description suggests a sense of closeness; and there can be no doubt of the contribution made by Bede to the concept of Northumbria as a region with a distinctive monastic history. Only a Northumbrian writer could refer to Bede, as did William of Newburgh, as 'our Bede'.[87]

---

[85] *Catalogi Veteres*, 64.

[86] The presence of the rare work of Dionysius Exiguus raises the possibility that it was derived from an early manuscript which had remained at Durham; but this cannot be proven.

[87] William of Newburgh, *History of English Affairs*, 76.

CHAPTER ELEVEN

❧

Aelred of Rievaulx

Aelred of Rievaulx was described by Jocelyn of Furness, biographer of Aelred's friend, St Waltheof, as being born of an illustrious Old English line ('ex veterum Anglorum illustri stirpe procreatus').[1] This identity was important throughout his life, and is also stressed by Aelred's own biographer, Walter Daniel, who describes how Aelred called out repeatedly in (Middle) English on his death-bed.[2] Such a background and identity made Aelred distinctive as a link between two very different aspects of twelfth-century Northumbria. On the one hand, he represents one of the last known descendants of the porters of St Cuthbert; thus, he was a member of that old aristocracy which, like Aelred's own family, was increasingly displaced during the century after the Conquest.[3] On the other hand, he was also a leader of the newest and most influential monastic reform movement to arrive in twelfth-century Britain. In this guise, he took a major part in the reform of both religious houses and local clergy in a region which extended from Lincolnshire to Lothian and Galloway and which was, for him, still a unity. This unique duality was, moreover, recognised by Aelred's contemporaries. When an authoritative *Life* of a pre-Conquest saint was needed, whether it were Ninian of Galloway, the Anglo-Saxon bishops of Hexham, or King Edward the Confessor, Aelred was called upon. Equally, he corresponded with both Gilbert Foliot, bishop of London, and Robert, earl of Leicester, as well as offering political advice to Fergus of Galloway and information to Henry II of England, to whom he gave details about his Anglo-Saxon ancestors. Thus, Aelred's career and writings constitute another important element in the cultural unity of twelfth-century Northumbria.

[1] Quoted by Powicke in Walter Daniel, *The Life of Ailred of Rievaulx*, xxxiii.

[2] Ibid. 60.

[3] On the porters of St Cuthbert, and the regional aristocracy's links with them, see Symeon, *Libellus*, lib. II, cap. xiii in Arnold, i, 65–8; and Reginald, *De Admirandis*, cap. xv. On Aelred's ancestry see Raine, *Hexham*, l–lxvii; and Powicke in Walter Daniel, *The Life of Ailred of Rievaulx*, xxxiv. See also M. L. Dutton, 'The Conversion and Vocation of Aelred of Rievaulx: A Historical Hypothesis', in Williams, *England in the Twelfth Century*, 31–49, at 34–5.

Family and history

This recognition of Aelred as a link between the Northumbrian past and the twelfth-century present makes Aelred's background an important problem. It is not entirely straightforward, even though it has been written about several times. The argument that Aelred was descended from one of the porters of St Cuthbert's coffin is Powicke's, and cannot be certainly proved. Nevertheless, it is quite certain that Aelred's great-grandfather was Alfred Westoue, the early-eleventh-century sacrist of Durham.[4] Alfred held a prominent position in the Community of St Cuthbert, since he was the keeper of St Cuthbert's relics, a scholar and teacher, and responsible for adding considerably to the Community's collection of relics.[5] The family's connection with the church of Hexham also begins with him. The churches and monastery of Hexham were founded by Wilfrid, who was given the region known as Hexhamshire by Etheldreda, wife of King Ecgfrith of Northumbria.[6] From the late seventh century to the ninth century Hexham was the seat of bishops, and the lands given to Wilfrid were presumably shared between the monks and the bishops; what rights the archbishops of York retained is unclear. Raine, however, argued that the discovery at Hexham of ninth-century coins minted by archbishops of York demonstrated that the archbishops retained some supervision of Hexhamshire.[7] When the see and monastery of Hexham were brought to an end by Viking invasions in the later ninth century, control of Hexham passed to the bishops of Lindisfarne/Durham. However, the archbishops of York retained some interest in Hexham and, in the early eleventh century, Archbishop Alfric questioned the control of Hexham by Bishop Edmund of Durham.[8] At some point a division was made between the lands directly controlled by the bishops of Durham, which were supervised by a provost or thane, and those allocated to the old monastery church, which formed the living for a priest. Alfred Westoue was given possession of the church and its lands, but appears to have remained at Durham, appointing a priest to serve the church.[9] Possession of Hexham church thus passed down in Alfred Westoue's family, although its value must have been considerably reduced

[4] For Alfred son of Westou, and Aelred's explanation that 'larwa' means 'doctor', see Raine, *Hexham*, 190.

[5] Symeon also gives Alfred the title 'larwa', and describes his teaching of boys at the cathedral. *Libellus*, lib. III, cap. vii; Arnold, i, 87–9.

[6] See Raine, *Hexham*, xxix.

[7] Ibid. xliv.

[8] Ibid. 1.

[9] See Aelred, *On the Saints of the Church of Hexham*, in Raine, *Hexham*, 173–203, and appendix, viii.

when Hexham and its surrounding area were devastated by William the Conqueror's army in 1069/70.[10]

It seems to have been this devastation, together with the plight of Bishop Egelwin and the Community of St Cuthbert, which led the then provost, Uctred, to place the temporalities of Hexham in the hands of Archbishop Thomas I of York.[11] Rather surprisingly, this loss of Hexhamshire was accepted by both Walcher and St Calais, for no attempt to reclaim Hexham is recorded, although the church remained in the possession of Eilaf I, son of Alfred Westoue. In 1083, Eilaf chose to leave Durham, and to keep his family together by retiring to Hexham.[12] In turn his son, Eilaf II, Aelred's father, inherited the church; but he was to be the last of the family to do so. Meanwhile, the position at Hexham became increasingly complex. At first, Archbishop Thomas I simply made the Hexham lands in his control a part of the prebend of Holme, and installed a canon of Beverley as prebendary, with a stall in York Minster.[13] Thus, when Thomas II of York decided to install canons at Hexham, and to create the basis for an Augustinian priory, completed by Archbishop Thurstan, it was necessary to remove the lands from the canon of Beverley, and the church from Eilaf II and his family. The compromise reached was that Eilaf remained parish priest of Hexham, and retained a life interest in the church lands; but his sons were barred from succession, and the church was taken over by the Augustinians.[14] The latter also took possession of the relics carefully identified and enshrined at Hexham by Aelred's family; and of an ancient book, apparently a book of Gospels, known as the Red Book, on which oaths were sworn.[15] Aelred's uncle, Aldred, who had acted as relic-keeper for Eilaf II, chose to join the priory and become an Augustinian, but Eilaf II, to judge from a recorded jest against the archbishop of York, strongly resented this further dispossession.[16]

Nevertheless, Eilaf and his family were still treated with considerable respect. Richard of Hexham, prior and historian of the house, was later to argue that the prior and archbishop would have been entitled to remove both

[10]   The region is not included in the Domesday survey, but the sack of Hexham is discussed by Orderic Vitalis; see Raine, *Hexham*, lvi. See also the 'Account of the Early Provosts', ibid. Appendix IV, viii.

[11]   Ibid.

[12]   Aelred, in *On the Saints of Hexham*, 191, describes Eilaf as requesting permission to rebuild the church. See also Symeon, in Arnold, i, 122–3. The 'Account of the Early Provosts' stresses that 'Eilaf Larwa' received the church of Hexham from the archbishop.

[13]   See Nicholl, *Thurstan*, 129.

[14]   Ibid.; and Dutton, 'Conversion', 37.

[15]   Raine, *Hexham*, lxvii–lxviii.

[16]   Walter Daniel, *Life of Ailred of Rievaulx*, 72; for Powicke's comments, see xxxv–xxxvi. Raine states that Aldred became a canon at Hexham, but Dutton believes he was a monk of Durham ('Conversion', 37).

church and lands from Eilaf (whose position as a married, hereditary parish priest was clearly open to attack), but they did not.[17] Instead, Aelred and his brothers seem to have received some formal education; and Aelred's relations with the canons appear to have been friendly.[18] It is also possible that Aelred received some education at Durham. Certainly, Eilaf II gave a copy of a *Life of St Bridget* to Laurence, the future prior of Durham; and Laurence later dedicated his version of the story to Aelred, and seems to have sent him a copy. In his surviving letter, Laurence addresses Aelred in a very friendly style, and describes him as 'accustomed to have a care for letters'.[19]

Eilaf's continuing status is demonstrated in two further ways. First, he was able to arrange for Aelred to be taken into the court of David, king of Scots, very soon after David had become king. How this was arranged is unclear, but Jocelyn of Furness suggests that Aelred broke off his formal education to take up his place at court, and the event is usually dated to *c*.1124/5.[20] Laurence of Durham was clearly aware of it, and of the prominent position which Aelred achieved, since he wrote to Aelred at the Scottish court. The second suggestion that Eilaf II retained some wealth and status comes from the events leading up to his death. In 1138, only months before his death, Eilaf returned to Durham. In a formal ceremony, witnessed by his sons, the prior of Hexham, and probably the abbot of Rievaulx, as well as by members of the cathedral priory of Durham, he gave over to the Augustinians of Hexham the church lands he had retained.[21] It appears that he also had other lands, since he gave to Durham and to St Cuthbert the vill of Cocken, close to the future site of Godric of Finchale's hermitage. He also possessed an impressive cross, made of gold and silver, and containing relics (apparently of Hexham origin). Finally, whilst two of his sons became Cistercian monks, and his daughter almost certainly became a recluse, one of his sons appears to have been able to marry well.[22] Reginald of Durham tells of how, on a later

[17] Prior Richard, *History of the Church of Hexham*, cap. ix; Raine, *Hexham*, 55–6.

[18] Aelred's work *On the Saints of Hexham*, written for the translation of the relics in 1154/5, and apparently read on the occasion by Aelred himself, stresses this friendship, represented particularly by Aelred's uncle, who had become a canon of Hexham. See Raine, *Hexham*, 173–203, particularly 173–6.

[19] Laurence's letter occurs as a preface to his *Life of St Bridget*, in Oxford, Bodleian, Laud misc. 668, fol. 106v. See Walter Daniel, *Life of Ailred of Rievaulx*, xl.

[20] Aelred himself mentions a time when he was at school, with a group of friends and companions, in the Prologue to his *De Spiritualis Amicitia*; See *PL* 195: 659. For Jocelyn of Furness's comment, see A. Squire, *Aelred of Rievaulx: A Study*, London, 1969, 12 and n. 32.

[21] Prior Richard, *History*, cap. x, Raine, *Hexham*, 56. See also n. 15 above.

[22] The evidence for the daughter rests on Aelred's authorship of the *De Institutione Inclusarum*. This is printed as a work of St Bernard in *PL* 32: 1451–65, but its authorship, and the real existence of the 'sister' addressed, are not in doubt. Aelred's brother, the subcellarer of Revesby, is mentioned by Walter Daniel, *Life of Ailred of Rievaulx*, 31. Raine names Eilaf's sons as Samuel, Ethelwold and Aelred (*Hexham*, lxviii).

visit to Lothian, Aelred visited a knight of that region who was married to his (Aelred's) niece.[23] This would suggest that some further lands may also have been available, to enable one family member to marry and raise at least one daughter who could marry into the lower aristocracy of the region. It may also suggest David I's continuing interest in a family who could give support to his claims to Cumbria, which played an important part in the twelfth-century history of the region.

The heritage of this family history is very clear in Aelred's own life. First, there is his strong devotion to St Cuthbert, the saint on whom his father continued to call.[24] Reginald of Durham tells stories of how Aelred composed a sort of prose-poem to St Cuthbert while on his way to a general chapter at Cîteaux; and of how he spread St Cuthbert's reputation amongst other Cistercian abbots by calling on the saint during difficulties at sea.[25] Aelred also took pains to celebrate St Cuthbert's feast in a church dedicated to him, whilst on a visit to Galloway.[26] Perhaps most strikingly of all, when Aelred was novice master at Rievaulx he had some sort of bath or chamber constructed beneath the floor of the novice-chamber, so that he could immerse himself in cold water, as Bede had described St Cuthbert doing on the inner Farne.[27] Thus, Aelred acted as a very influential link with the old Northumbria, in the new world of the twelfth century.

Secondly, there is Aelred's expert knowledge of the saints and history of Hexham. When the Augustinians of Hexham carried out a major translation of their relics in 1154, it seems to have been Aelred, now abbot of Rievaulx, whom they asked to preach on the occasion, and to compose an account of the Hexham saints and their miracles.[28] This became the tract 'On the Miracles of the Holy Fathers who Rest in Hexham Church', and it demonstrates how well Aelred, like his father and ancestors before him, knew Bede's *Historia Ecclesiastica*.[29] To this is added information from the *Life of Wilfrid*, together with more recent stories derived, amongst others, from Aelred's uncle and from his own experience. Aelred demonstrates familiarity with Hexham's ancient rights of sanctuary, and, as Squire suggests, seems to have been aware of the 'modern' need to provide attested miracle stories for traditional saints.[30] He also identifies himself clearly as a native of Hexham

---

[23] Reginald, *De Admirandis*, cap. lxxxviii, pp. 185–8. Aelred's niece had married one Robert, son of Philip, a knight of Lothian, presumably of Norman ancestry.

[24] See Walter Daniel, *Life of Ailred of Rievaulx*, xxxvii–xxxviii.

[25] Reginald, *De Admirandis*, cap. lxxxiii, pp. 175–7.

[26] Ibid. cap. lxxxiv, pp. 177–8.

[27] Walter Daniel, *Life of Ailred of Rievaulx*, 25.

[28] See note 18 above.

[29] For a more general discussion of the influence of Bede on Northumbrian monastic culture, see Chapter 10.   [30] See Squire, *Aelred of Rievaulx*, 115.

when he writes of York as 'foreigners' country', and describes feelingly how the Hexham saints resist all attempts, including those by Thomas II of York, to move their relics.[31] Moreover, another story places Hexham clearly within a broadly defined Northumbria. This is the story of how, when Hexham was faced by a particularly dangerous army of marauding Scots, St Cuthbert and St Wilfrid came literally riding to the rescue.[32] Neither had relics at Hexham, but Wilfrid is clearly thought of as retaining a special affection for Hexham, and he is made to explain that he stopped at Durham on his way, to call upon the help of St Cuthbert. Thus, the two 'senior' saints of Northumbria spring to the defence of Hexham; it is interesting that St John of Beverley, who had been bishop of Hexham, is not included.

Finally, Aelred was able to inspire other writers with similar concerns, most strikingly Reginald, not a member of Aelred's own Rievaulx, but a monk of Durham. Reginald's collection of the recent miracles of St Cuthbert, written at a time when the cult was in need of some revitalisation, was inspired by Aelred. It was Aelred who personally collected and passed on stories, especially from his visitations to houses in Lothian and Galloway, and whose telling of them at Durham started the process of collection.[33] And it was also Aelred to whom the final work was dedicated, even though he died before it was finished. Reginald's *Life of St Godric of Finchale*, one of the new group of hermits associated with Durham, also seems to have been inspired, or at least encouraged, by Aelred. The two future saints, abbot and hermit, met on at least one occasion, when Aelred visited Godric at Finchale, on a site near an estate which once belonged to his family.[34] Thus, in a variety of ways, Aelred, like Bede and like St Cuthbert himself, helped to infuse into the ecclesiastical and intellectual culture of post-Conquest Northumbria a real interest in, and identification with, its pre-Conquest past. This could even be of immediate, practical use, as when Aelred was called upon to help resolve a dispute over the exact status of the prior at Durham.[35] It also gave a particular identity to Aelred's position as abbot of Rievaulx.

Aelred and the Cistercians

The most problematic aspect of Aelred's career as a Cistercian monk and abbot is how it came to start. Recent interpretations have seen Aelred's entry into Rievaulx, in 1134, as carefully planned by King David and by Walter

[31] See text in Raine, *Hexham*, 173–203, at 202–3.
[32] Aelred, in Raine, *Hexham*, 178–80.
[33] Reginald, *De Admirandis*, 4 and 32.
[34] Reginald of Durham, *De Vita et Miraculis S. Godrici Heremitae de Finchale*, Surtees Society, 1847, 176–7.
[35] See *Durham Episcopal Charters 1071–1152*, no. 36, 142–51.

Espec, one of David's supporters and the founder of Rievaulx.[36] Walter Daniel's account of how Aelred was welcomed into Rievaulx by the prior, guest-master and gate-keeper has been seen as evidence that Aelred's visit was expected and was carefully stage-managed. The fact that another member of David's court, Waltheof, son of David's queen by her first marriage, had recently become an Augustinian, and became prior of Kirkham, another of Walter Espec's foundations, in 1134, the same year in which Aelred entered Rievaulx, gives circumstantial support to this argument. Aelred's choice of Rievaulx, unexpected as it was a new house, of a new 'order', and had no connection with the past of his family or of Northumbria, could thus be explained as the outcome of the pressures or influences of patronage.

However, this argument is not entirely straightforward, as there is evidence that David's decision to send Aelred to Rievaulx must have been, if it happened, a rather sudden change of mind. Walter Daniel stresses that Aelred achieved an important and influential position in David's court and household, with responsibility for allocating some of the king's resources, and for presiding over, and serving at, formal meals.[37] This is supported by Laurence of Durham's letter to Aelred, where he is addressed as the king's steward; and by Aelred's later protestations that he came to Rievaulx from the kitchens, not from the schools.[38] Walter Daniel states quite clearly that Aelred experienced an increasingly strong monastic vocation, but felt constrained to hide this from David; while Aelred himself was to write of a period of confusion and despair before he left the Scottish court, from which he was rescued by divine providence.[39] None of this suggests a long-established plan for Aelred to become a monk. What is even more striking is that there is no sign of any intention for Aelred to enter the Church. This is in contrast to Waltheof, whose biographer, Jocelyn of Furness, suggests that he was prepared to enter the Church from childhood on.[40] Walter Daniel states that Aelred hid his desire to become a monk because David intended to make him a bishop; but this only makes the situation still more confusing.[41] David's chancellor, William Cumin, had himself been trained in Henry I's writing-office, under Henry I's chancellor, and David supported Cumin's

---

[36] See especially Dutton, 'Conversion'.

[37] Walter Daniel, *Life of Ailred of Rievaulx*, 3–4.

[38] On Laurence of Durham's letter, see Powicke in Walter Daniel, *Life of Ailred of Rievaulx*, xl. Aelred's modest comment is referred to by St Bernard, in his letter calling Aelred to write the *Speculum Caritatis*, which was used as a preface to that work. See *Sancti Bernardi Opera*, vii, Rome, 1974, 266.

[39] For Walter Daniel see his *Life of Ailred of Rievaulx*, 9–10. For Aelred's own comment, see Squire, *Aelred of Rievaulx*, 15 and n. 43.

[40] See Squire, *Aelred of Rievaulx*, 13.

[41] See Walter Daniel, *Life of Ailred of Rievaulx*, 3 and 10.

attempt to become bishop of Durham. By contrast, Aelred's formal education was cut short; almost all contemporaries comment on his lack of the increasingly important training in the schools, and there seems to have been no question of his being any sort of clerk at David's court. Thus, while Aelred's statement that he was regarded as extremely fortunate in the patronage he received at David's court rings true, Walter Daniel's argument that David intended to make Aelred a bishop is extremely surprising. As for the entry into Rievaulx, both Walter Daniel and Aelred himself, though in different ways, represent it as an almost fortuitous decision. Walter Daniel's story has been shaped to emphasise how God reached out to call Aelred to Rievaulx. Nevertheless, Walter Daniel also states that Aelred was fond of recalling how his final decision to enter Rievaulx, and not to return to David's court, rested on the wish of one of his companions.[42] What this story emphasises is that Aelred did have a choice; he was not simply sent into Rievaulx by patron or family, even if their contacts must have been important.

Once at Rievaulx, Aelred rose to prominence as he had at the Scottish court. Some five years after completing his novitiate he was sent to the papal court as Abbot William's representative in the dispute over the election of Archbishop Thurstan's successor. On his return, he was made novice-master, and was effectively summoned by St Bernard to write what became his *Speculum Caritatis*.[43] The very next year, he was made abbot of Rievaulx's daughter house of Revesby, in Lincolnshire. Here, as well as continuing with the *Speculum Caritatis* he began to give sermons; and he was asked by the bishop of Lincoln to preach at local synods, to help reform the clergy.[44] It was also during this time that he successfully defended his friend Waltheof's decision to leave Kirkham, of which he was now prior, and to become a Cistercian. In 1147 he was elected as abbot of Rievaulx, when Maurice, ex subprior of Durham, resigned. Aelred held this post until his death in 1167. As abbot of Rievaulx, Aelred's influence was even greater, and there is further evidence of the effectiveness of his preaching. He was now asked by the bishop of Troyes to preach at a synod in his own diocese.[45] His reputation as a preacher is confirmed by John of Hexham, who presumably heard his sermon in 1154, on the ceremonial translation of the Hexham relics. John of Hexham supplies interesting characterisations of the prominent men he discusses. An archdeacon of York, Geoffrey Turcople, is described as 'scholarly'; Maurice of Rievaulx is noteworthy for his decision to leave 'the cloister

[42] Ibid. 15.
[43] See note 38 above; also Squire, *Aelred of Rievaulx*, 25.
[44] Ibid. 53.
[45] Ibid. 65.

of Durham' for 'the rigour of the Cistercian discipline', 'from a desire for perfection'; while Henry Murdac, abbot of Fountains and archbishop of York, is described in terms of his powerful friends and contacts.[46] In contrast to all these, Aelred is 'one who had obtained from the Lord an excellent grace in the preaching of wisdom'.[47] His sermons were noted down by listeners, as were St Bernard's.[48]

This preaching of wisdom was called upon in a range of ways. First, when Savigny and its daughter houses joined the Cistercians in 1147, Aelred was asked to send a group of monks from Rievaulx to advise Swineshead (Hoyland), in Lincolnshire, on Cistercian life.[49] Moreover, no request or agreement is recorded, but Aelred's Rievaulx seems also to have played a similar role for another, nearer, daughter of Furness, namely Byland. Certainly, literary and artistic links between the two were strong, and Walter Daniel suggests a close relationship between Aelred and Abbot Roger of Byland (1146–96) who was abbot throughout the transitional period. Roger was present, with Richard, abbot of Fountains (1147–70), at Aelred's death; and it was Roger who anointed Aelred on his deathbed, despite the fact that the abbot of Fountains was senior to the abbot of Byland in the Cistercian hierarchy.[50] Indeed, under Abbot Roger, and perhaps with Aelred's advice, Byland had grown and prospered, so that William of Newburgh, another Augustinian writer, calls the three Cistercian houses 'the three lights of our province, shining out as prime examples of holy religious life'.[51] In 1151, Aelred settled the dispute between Savigny and Furness over Byland.

It thus seems that Aelred helped to establish the fame of both Rievaulx and other northern Cistercian houses, and may well have done much to help build up their network of friendly contacts with houses of other orders. His own interest in Durham and Hexham has already been demonstrated; and he was also influential in the relationship between the northern Cistercians and the Gilbertines. In 1164 he went to Kirkstead, Lincolnshire, to agree a formal decision between the Cistercians and the Gilbertines over relations between their houses, granges, and other activities; and it was to Aelred that the Gilbertine nuns of Watton looked for advice and judgement, when a

---

[46] John, Prior of Hexham, *Historia*, in Raine, *Hexham*, at 31, 149–50, 150.

[47] Ibid. 150.

[48] Walter Daniel states that Aelred preached about two hundred sermons, while a slightly later writer states that he wrote one hundred sermons, as well as thirty-three homilies on the burdens of Isaiah. See Walter Daniel, *Life of Ailred of Rievaulx*, 42 and n. 1.

[49] Ibid. 35.

[50] Ibid. 60 and 63.

[51] See William of Newburgh, *History of English Affairs*, 79.

scandal broke out over the conduct of one of their members, who had been placed in the house as a child by Henry Murdac.[52]

Moreover, although Aelred made no claim to formal scholarship himself, he seems to have respected it in others, and to have encouraged and supported it at Rievaulx, perhaps following the tradition of his mentor, Abbot William, who had been *magister scholarum* in York before becoming a Cistercian. Maurice of Rievaulx apparently continued his studies and writing at Rievaulx, and Powicke's study of Walter Daniel shows something similar.[53] Walter, on his own evidence, acted as scribe and secretary for Aelred, but was also evidently himself free to write. Unlike Aelred, Walter is described as 'Magister', and his recorded works, like those of Maurice, suggest an interest in some of the theological issues of the day. Only the *Life of Aelred* and the *Centum Sententiae* survive; but Leland lists a collection of homilies, another of letters and a treatise 'on the burdens of the beasts of the south', as well as works on the topical issues of true friendship; the virginity of Mary; the sending of the angel Gabriel to Mary; and the immaculate conception. The latter was written specifically against the treatise of Nicholas, monk of St Albans, suggesting that Walter Daniel was informed on contemporary debates, and able to obtain copies of new works. Nevertheless, Walter Daniel, whilst clearly familiar with contemporary study of logic, and with scholastic exegetical procedure, strongly distinguishes both from true spirituality, and writes specifically to defend the views of St Bernard, thus harnessing his scholarship to contemporary Cistercian views.[54]

Aelred's own learning was more individual, as would be expected from his history. His views on elaboration in musical services, sculpture and wall paintings are close to those expressed by St Bernard in the *Apologia to William of St Thierry*: and, again like St Bernard, his own writings are full of scriptural references and phrases.[55] His knowledge of the writings of Augustine, Jerome and Ambrose was extensive, while his own exegetical methods are described as 'old-fashioned' by Squire.[56] Rather more surprising is his

---

[52] The text of Aelred's letter recounting the events survives in Cambridge, Corpus Christi College, MS 139, which belonged to the small Cistercian house of Sawley, of the family of Fountains, by the early thirteenth century. See G. Constable, 'Aelred of Rievaulx and the Nun of Watton: An Episode in the Early History of the Gilbertine Order', in D. Baker, ed., *Medieval Women*, Studies in Church History, Subsidia 1, Oxford, 1978, 205–26.

[53] See F. M. Powicke, *Aelred of Rievaulx and His Biographer Walter Daniel*, Manchester, 1922, especially 3–23; and Powicke, 'Maurice of Rievaulx'.

[54] Walter Daniel, *Life of Ailred of Rievaulx*, 3–23.

[55] For Aelred's views on sculpture and wall paintings see particularly the *Speculum Caritatis*, II, xxiv, in *Aelredi Rievallensis*, *Opera Omnia 1*, ed. A. Hoste and C. H. Talbot, Corpus Christianorum, Continuatio Mediaevalis 1, Turnhout, 1971, 99–100. There are further comments in the *De Institutione Inclusarum*, para.24; ibid. 656.

[56] See Squire, *Aelred of Rievaulx*, 149–50.

apparent familiarity with Pseudo-Dionysius the Areopagite, whom he quotes briefly in his *De Anima*.[57] Equally distinctive is his awareness of Greek theology, demonstrated, as Squire points out, by the First Homily of *De Oneribus Isaiae*, where God is called 'the primordial and efficient cause'. Squire speculates that this may be derived from Hugh of St Victor, whose works, as has been seen, were being collected at Durham.[58] However, more direct knowledge, again drawing upon the Durham library, is also possible. Mynors has suggested that the Rievaulx copies of works by Jerome, Rabanus Maurus, and Ennodius may be based on Durham exemplars.[59] It also seems that the Rievaulx copy of the sermons of Petrus Chrysologus, now BL Royal 8 D XXII, was copied from a Durham book, with an initial in the style of the Martyrology Scribe. The Durham book-list, as has already been demonstrated, contains the works of several Greek Fathers, including Gregory Nazianzen, whose sermons were copied at Byland, whilst Fountains also is recorded as borrowing exemplars from Durham. Thus Aelred's unexpected knowledge of Greek theology may be the product of the Northumbrian monastic culture of which he was an important part.

Aelred, Northumbria and 'Scocia'

Also of importance for an understanding of Northumbrian regional identity are what might be called Aelred's political ideas. A recent commentator on William of Newburgh has stated that 'he lacked Aelred's appreciation of the religious heritage of Northumbria as being common to the English and the Scots'.[60] This is extremely interesting, but it still simplifies the problem of the definition of 'the English' and 'the Scots'. Certainly, the details of Aelred's life already discussed show that he felt genuine loyalty to both the king of England and to the king of Scots; and he moved freely, both as a courtier and as a monk, between the lands of the one and the lands of the other. In this, he was similar to the secular lords of the region, such as Walter Espec, Bernard de Balliol and Robert de Brus, who held land from both kings, and for whom the 'border' was apparently simply the place where the lands of the two kings met. However, Aelred's writings make it possible to clarify his view of the complex definitions of the north in the twelfth century, and to compare it with the concepts used by other writers.

Perhaps most complex of all was the situation in the west of the region, in

---

[57] Aelred, *De Anima*, ii, and first homily on Isaiah (*PL* 195, col. 363), cited by Squire, *Aelred of Rievaulx*, 137 and 170, n. 25.

[58] Ibid. 136.

[59] Mynors, *Durham Cathedral Manuscripts*, 38 and 40.

[60] Walsh and Kennedy, 'Introduction' to William of Newburgh, *History of English Affairs*, 18.

Cumbria/Strathclyde and Galloway. Aelred had knowledge of this area from several sources: first, there was Bede's *Historia Ecclesiastica*, from which Aelred derived his knowledge of the Anglo-Saxon invasion of the whole area; second, there was his apparent knowledge of a version of the *Anglo-Saxon Chronicle*; and finally, there was information gained on his visits to the district, whilst carrying out visitations at Rievaulx's daughter house of Dundrennan.[61] It is clear that these visits were not confined to Dundrennan alone. Aelred met Fergus, lord of Galloway, cofounder of Dundrennan with King David, on at least one occasion.[62] He also visited St Cuthbert's church at Kirkcudbright, and it was presumably he who told Reginald of Durham of the scholars or clerks who served the church, known as 'Scollofthes' in the regional (Reginald says 'Pictish') dialect.[63] Aelred's view of this region, once the Brittonic kingdom of Strathclyde, is most clearly stated in his *Life of St Ninian*. Ninian's see of Whithorn, destroyed by Norse invasions, was revived by David, and the new bishop, with the Celtic name of Gilla Aldan, was sent to Thurstan of York for consecration in 1126.[64] This is interesting in itself, as it argues that Galloway was recognised as having been part of Northumbria, and as coming under the authority of the archbishops of York. However, if David hoped to extend the see into southern Strathclyde, which had been conquered and settled by William Rufus, and split off to become Cumbria, he was disappointed. In 1133 Henry I responded by making Carlisle the seat of a new bishopric, and brought in a man of unquestioned loyalty, Athelulf of Nostell, once his own chaplain, as the first bishop.

Aelred was asked to write a *Life of St Ninian* by Christian, who was consecrated bishop of Whithorn in 1154, although the work itself is not clearly dated.[65] He based his work both on Bede and on an early Latin *Life of Ninian*, as well as reliable stories. In his Prologue, he makes clear that he has undertaken the work at the request of Christian and his 'clergy and people'.[66] Interestingly, there is also a hint that he sees the Galloway region as

---

[61] Aelred's use of Bede for his definition of Northumbria is discussed on the following pages. It is clear that, like most northern contemporaries, Aelred knew Bede's work very well, and regarded it as fundamental. Indeed, Aelred opens his *Life of St Ninian* by quoting verbatim Bede's brief account of Ninian's work. See *Life of St Ninian*, Preface, in *Lives of S. Ninian and S. Kentigern*, ed. A. P. Forbes, *The Historians of Scotland*, vol. v, Edinburgh, 1874, 6–7. Aelred's knowledge of the Anglo-Saxon Chronicle is perhaps most strongly suggested by his *Genealogy of the Kings*, which uses the genealogy of King Æthelwulf given by the Chronicle (though also used by Asser), as well as details on the kings from Alfred to Ethelred which may be partly drawn from the Chronicle.

[62] See Walter Daniel, *Life of Ailred of Rievaulx*, 45–6.

[63] Reginald, *De Admirandis*, cap. lxxxiii–lxxxiv, pp. 175–8.

[64] See *Life of St Ninian*, 'General Introduction, Part 1', xlvi.

[65] Ibid. xlviii. Powicke suggests 1154–60; see Walter Daniel, *Life of Ailred of Rievaulx*, xcvii.

[66] *Life of St Ninian*, 3–5.

barbarous, at least at the time when the old *Life* was written. In chapter 1, Aelred states clearly that, in his own time, the 'realms of the Scots and the Angles' were separated in the west by a major arm of the sea.[67] This seems to be the Solway Firth, and suggests that Aelred saw Cumbria as 'English' and Galloway as 'Scottish'. However, he goes on to say that until recently 'the whole region' (that is, both Cumbria and Galloway) 'belonged to the Angles'. He also knows from both 'written record and oral testimony' that the region once had kings of its own, and he perhaps saw Fergus of Galloway as their modern successor. Certainly Walter Daniel, who may well have accompanied Aelred, calls Fergus 'the petty king of that land'.[68] The statement that Galloway 'belonged to the Angles' is curious, since it was ceded to Malcolm, king of Scots, in the mid-tenth century, and was part of the lands of the kings of Scots from then on. However, Aelred was presumably taking his information from Bede's repeated statements that Ninian's see of Candida Casa/Whithorn was part of Northumbria and was ruled, in Bede's time, by Ceolwulf.[69] Again, Aelred's story of a miracle performed by Ninian's staff tells how a boy 'ran away from Galloway, and fled to Scocia by sea'. Where exactly he landed is a matter of debate, but if 'Scocia' is taken to be the lands of the Scots, then Aelred did not see Galloway as an integral part of it; and David, in sending its bishops to the archbishops of York, apparently agreed.[70] The region rebelled against the rule of the kings of Scots after David's death, and it was some years before Malcolm IV, David's successor, finally defeated the rebels. As part of the settlement, Fergus retired to become a canon at Holyrood, and it is presumably to this that Walter Daniel is referring, when he says that Aelred helped to settle a rebellion in Galloway, and persuaded its 'petty king' to retire into a monastery.[71]

It is Aelred's historical works which bring out most clearly the complexities of Northumbrian politics, and offer a complement to the anti-Scottish stance of Durham writers, especially in their account of the career of David I, and his invasions of Cumbria, Northumberland, Durham and Yorkshire. Aelred is far from being the only twelfth-century 'English' writer to give an account of the Battle of the Standard, fought near Northallerton in 1138, but his account is unique in several ways. Squire argues convincingly that Aelred based his account on that in the final version of Henry of Huntingdon's *Historia Anglorum*.[72] However, one unusual feature in Aelred's account is the

[67] *Life of St Ninian*, 7.
[68] Walter Daniel, *Life of Ailred of Rievaulx*, 45.
[69] See Aelred's quotations from Bede in his Preface, *Life of St Ninian*, 6–7.
[70] *Life of St Ninian*, cap. x, 19–20.
[71] See note 63 above.
[72] Squire, *Aelred of Rievaulx*, 76.

prominence given to Walter Espec, Rievaulx's founder, who, according to the Rievaulx Cartulary retired to Rievaulx in 1153, and died there in 1155.[73] However this may be, Aelred demonstrates an awareness of the complexities of political allegiance and ethnic identity of the time. The army raised by Archbishop Thurstan and fighting, at least in theory, for King Stephen, is referred to as 'English', but is also called 'southern'. Moreover, the Normans are clearly distinct from the Angles, and a long speech on the nature and victories of the Normans is given to Espec, whose own Norman identity is emphasised.[74] Robert de Brus, another Norman friend of David I, was also fighting on Thurstan's side, and Espec is made to encourage such men by emphasising that they are fighting not only for Stephen but also, and more fundamentally, for their land, families and churches, and are fulfilling their duty to 'repel an imminent peril'.[75] Aelred's portrait of David's army is still more complex, and brings out very clearly the divisions amongst those ruled by the kings of Scots. Men from both Cumbria and Galloway are there, and indeed it is the ferocity and ungovernability of the 'Galwegians' which contributes to David's defeat. Also separately identified are the 'men of the Isles' and the 'Moray men', while David himself is shown as sharing Espec's view of the military capacity of the Normans, and wishing to use his 'Norman bodyguard' as the front line in his army, something which is rejected by the rest.[76]

The theme of the difficulties faced by David in ruling his disunited realm is taken up still more strongly in Aelred's lament, composed after David's death (in May 1153). Here, David is presented, as he also is by John of Hexham, as a model ruler, and a man 'necessary to the world'.[77] Aelred describes David's attempts to unify the different categories of 'Scots', who are 'hostile to each other on account of differences of language and custom'.[78] Aelred's own political and economic perceptiveness come out when he lists David's enlightened modernising efforts. Not only has he begun to unify the 'Scots', but he has founded numerous monasteries, built castles, encouraged the growth of towns and developed overseas trade, as well as modernising agriculture, and promoting horticulture. As in the account of the Battle of the Standard, it is the invasion of Yorkshire in which David is seen as going too far. It is for this that David is shown as repenting, and as having been

---

[73] See J. C. Atkinson, ed., *Chartularium Rievallense*, Surtees Society 83, 1889, 264–5.

[74] For the text see *Chronicles of the Reigns of Stephen, Henry II and Richard I*, ed. R. Howlett, vol. iii, Rolls Series, 1886, 181–99. Espec's speech on the Normans is at 185–6.

[75] Ibid. 186–7.

[76] Ibid. 188.

[77] An abbreviated text is given in *PL* 195: 711–38. Translated extracts are given by Squire, *Aelred of Rievaulx*, 85–7. For this phrase see Squire, *Aelred of Rievaulx*, 82.

[78] Squire, *Aelred of Rievaulx*, 84.

purged by various sufferings.[79] Thus, whilst Cumbria, and perhaps even Hexhamshire, represented 'marchlands', Yorkshire was clearly seen as outside the sphere of the Scots.

In much of this, Aelred's account is corroborated by other evidence and other writers. Indeed, the list of David's monastic foundations shows him as something of an expert on the range of orders available. He founded, or helped to found the Tironensian house of Kelso; the Augustinian houses of Jedburgh, Holyrood, and Cambuskenneth; Cistercian Melrose, Newbattle, Dundrennan and Kinloss; Premonstratensian Dryburgh; Benedictine Dunfermline (and perhaps Coldingham); and Cluniac St Andrew's, Northampton.[80] Moreover, he was generous to Hexham, Nostell, Rievaulx and Kirkham. When Rievaulx faced financial problems it was to David that Aelred turned for help.[81] John of Hexham, writing very soon after Aelred, expresses many of the same views. David's capture of Cumbria and Northumberland is treated sympathetically, as the result of his devotion to his niece, the empress Matilda. But in the account of the Battle of the Standard, Robert de Brus and Bernard de Balliol are said to have held a formal meeting with David. For them, as for Aelred, David's control of Northumberland seems to be acceptable; but the invasion of Yorkshire is seen as wholly unjustified.[82] Finally, Richard of Hexham's account makes explicit something which Aelred leaves implicit; namely, that the lands of Hexham and of St Cuthbert constitute a sort of border region between the 'debatable lands' and the territory which is clearly 'English'. Unsurprisingly, it is Hexham's role which is covered in detail, and Hexham emerges as a sort of neutral base, from which individuals such as the papal legate could be conducted to meetings with David in Carlisle.[83] This role is also suggested by the pattern of the lands given to Hexham in the twelfth century. These are described by Raine as 'very large indeed', and it seems that 'from the borders of Cumberland to Newcastle-on-Tyne, there was no parish in which the prior and canons did not have a large interest. They could not have had less than 20,000 acres of land in Northumberland.'[84] Whether Aelred influenced John of Hexham is uncertain, but the two writers do seem to have a related sense of their region.

Nevertheless, what is striking about Aelred is the sense that, for him,

---

[79] Squire, *Aelred of Rievaulx*, 83.

[80] See Brooke, 'St Bernard, the Patrons and Monastic Planning', at 13–14. See also G. W. S. Barrow, 'Scottish Rulers and the Religious Orders, 1070–1153', *Transactions of the Royal Historical Society*, 5th series 3, 1953, 77–100.

[81] The phrase is 'pro quadam necessitate domus nostrae'; see Squire, *Aelred of Rievaulx*, 164, at n. 38.

[82] Richard of Hexham, *De Gestis Regis Stephani, et de Bello Standardii*, in Raine, *Hexham*, 88.

[83] Ibid. 96–104.

[84] Raine, *Hexham*, vol. ii, xv.

Bede's Northumbria was still somehow a reality. It was the old Northumbria which covered all the regions in which Aelred was active, linking Rievaulx's Yorkshire lands to those of its daughter houses of Melrose and Dundrennan, as well as to Melrose's own daughter of Holm Cultram. For Aelred, it was the first English Cistercian house, Waverley in Surrey, which was 'tucked away in a corner', and it was perhaps a sign of the power of Aelred's views that Rievaulx took its next two abbots from Dundrennan and Melrose successively.[85] Finally, however, Aelred consoled himself for the deaths of Prince Henry and of David by the reflection that the old Anglo-Saxon royal line, of which David was such a prominent member, also lived on in David's great-nephew, Henry II of England. It was to Henry II that Aelred looked to join the English and the Normans together in a prosperous future.[86] In 1157, Henry II had taken Northumberland and Cumberland into his control without oppositon from Malcolm IV of Scotland; and by the end of the twelfth century Aelred's and John of Hexham's strong sense of the different territories which made up 'the north' had given way to William of Newburgh's much vaguer terminology, already discussed in the Introduction.

[85] The remark is in Aelred's work on the Battle of the Standard, in *Chronicles of the Reigns of Stephen, Henry II and Richard I*, 184. For the abbots of Rievaulx, see Knowles *et al.*, *The Heads of Religious Houses*.

[86] This view is explicitly expressed in the *Genealogy of the Kings*. Another work directly addressed to Henry II, the Prologue to Aelred's *Life of Edward*, portrays the new king as the fruit of the restored tree seen in a vision by Edward the Confessor, and as the 'cornerstone' joining the English and the Normans. See *The Life of King Edward Who Rests at Westminster*, ed. and trans. F. Barlow, London, 1962, appendix A. See also *PL* 195: 740.

CONCLUSION

❧

History and regional identity

A recurring theme of this study has been the extent of the exchange and circulation of texts, ideas and artistic influences between the religious houses of Northumbria. Moreover, one of the most important of these is the idea of Northumbria itself, still meaningful to William of Newburgh at the end of the twelfth century.[1] It was also William who gave the idea of regional history and regional identity wider importance by writing, at the request of the abbot of Rievaulx, to expose the 'fables and lies' of Geoffrey of Monmouth through contrasting them with the authoritative witness of 'our Bede'.[2] Thus, the exchange and the composition of histories brought Benedictines, Augustinians and Cistercians together in the twelfth century, in what was almost a collaborative enterprise, as well as one which further strengthened the sense of a shared regional identity. This historical enterprise therefore forms a suitable centre for this conclusion, in bringing together many of the themes and arguments of preceding chapters.

The story necessarily begins at Durham, where the library taken over by the new Benedictine priory, although small, constituted one of the major surviving remnants of the great days of Northumbrian monasticism and scholarship. The members of the Community of St Cuthbert at the time of the Conquest have a rather poor reputation, but this is largely the result of the Anglo-Norman historical works themselves.[3] One family at least, that of Alfred Westoue and his descendants, seems to have maintained some tradition of scholarship, and there is considerable evidence of historical records of various sorts produced by the Community which were taken over by the Benedictine monks. The tenth-century compilation known as the *Historia de Sancto Cuthberto* was still being updated in the first half of the eleventh century, and was passed on to the monks.[4] Moreover, a narrative

---

[1] William of Newburgh, *History of English Affairs*, 76.   [2] Ibid.
[3] See, for instance, *Libellus*, lib. III, cap. ix–xi; Arnold, i, 90–5.
[4] On the composition of the *Historia de Sancto Cuthberto* see Gransden, *Historical Writing in England*, 76–7; and Simpson, 'The King Alfred/St Cuthbert Episode'.

account covering the Conquest period, and going up to 1072, seems also to have been composed, and also passed on to the monks.[5] The text known as the *De Obsessione Dunelmi* deals with events in the time of Bishop Aldhun (995–1018) and, although its actual date of composition is unknown, it was presumably the work of a member of the Community, or of someone connected with it, and it too survives in a later copy.[6] All this is clearly in accordance with the depictions of Walcher and William of St Calais as reading about the history of their remote and complex see, in order to inform their decisions about it.[7]

Moreover, the unusual circumstances created at Durham by the displacement of the established community of St Cuthbert, and the installation of Benedictine monks, led to the creation of a rather unusual type of history, the *Libellus de Exordio atque Procursu Istius, Hoc est Dunelmensis, Ecclesiae* (also known as the *Historia Dunelmensis Ecclesiae*).[8] This is specifically an institutional history, rather than a hagiographical text, a collection of the *Lives* of bishops, or a broader chronicle, and thus something distinctive for the early twelfth century. Its author is traditionally identified as 'Symeon of Durham', although there is no evidence for the name in the *Libellus* itself. Indeed, the surviving Durham copy of the work, now Durham UL Cosin V ii 6, which is believed to be partly autograph, gives the author no name. Interestingly, the name is supplied in a late-twelfth-century copy of the work, in a compound manuscript which belonged to the Cistercian house of Sawley, in Yorkshire; the authority for the name is not given, though Dean Hugh of York had been in correspondence with a Durham historian called Symeon, and it was perhaps knowledge of this, or a strong local tradition, which led to the attribution.[9] The sources used, as would be expected in such an institutional history, are almost exclusively local, but nevertheless reflect the strengths of the historical materials available to the monks of Durham. Considerable use is made of Bede's *Historia Ecclesiastica*, in a version which, as has been seen, went back to an early exemplar, and was not that given to the priory by

---

[5] On this see Craster, 'The Red Book of Durham', 523–9.

[6] This work is printed by Arnold, i, 215–20. It survives in Cambridge, Corpus Christi College, MS 139.

[7] *Libellus*, 'Preface', in Arnold, i, 9–11.

[8] On this work, and its author, see Gransden, *Historical Writing in England*, 114–21.

[9] The manuscript now forms part of Cambridge UL Ff 1 27. For discussion of the complex problems raised by this and its companion volume from Sawley, see Meehan, 'Durham Twelfth-Century Manuscripts'; D. M. Dumville, 'The Sixteenth-Century History of Two Cambridge Books from Sawley', *Transactions of the Cambridge Bibliographical Society* 7, 1980, 440–9; D. Baker, 'Scissors and Paste: Corpus Christi, Cambridge, MS 139 Again', *Studies in Church History* 11, 1975, 84–139; and Norton, 'History, Wisdom and Illumination'. On Symeon's authorship of the work, see contributions by Rollason, Gullick, Aird and Howlett to the same volume.

William of St Calais.[10] Other works of Bede, including the *Life of St Cuthbert*, are also used, together with the *Historia de Sancto Cuthberto*, the *Cronica Monasterii Dunelmensis* and the *De Miraculis et Translationibus Sancti Cuthberti*.[11]

However, there is also evidence that wider-ranging historical works were available at Durham, this time introduced by the newcomers, and representing their broader political interests. The work known as the *Historia Regum* has also been attributed to Symeon of Durham, though analysis of the two texts shows that they cannot in fact be simply by the same author. The two works frequently contradict one another on key points of detail, such as the cause and timing of the death of Bishop Aldhun of Durham, as well as expressing different points of view on problematic issues, whilst the *Historia Regum* is a compilation rather than a new composition like the *Libellus*[12] Nevertheless, Durham is still generally accepted as having played an important part in the making of the *Historia Regum*; and indeed analysis of the text shows that its author/compiler made use of a range of materials which were available at Durham, as the Durham book-list and surviving manuscripts both show. The work is conceived and represented as a continuation of Bede, with additional information from a complex range of sources, still not fully analysed.[13] The author/compiler demonstrates a strong interest in the history of the Anglo-Saxons, as well as in the work of Bede. Nevertheless, there is also much use of Anglo-Norman and Continental sources for the period from the later ninth to the early twelfth century. Indeed, it is possible, as Blair argues, that the early texts, including Asser, may already have been edited together at Durham in the tenth century, although more recent work does not entirely support this.[14] He made heavy use of the Worcester chronicle known as 'Florence of Worcester', which itself used sources only recently brought into England; it may perhaps have been obtained through Durham's links with the West Midlands, and its intellectual contact with Robert, bishop of Hereford.[15] To this was added material from Eadmer of Canterbury and William of Malmesbury; here, links with Canterbury are known to have been

---

[10] See Chapter 7 above.

[11] See *Symeon of Durham: Libellus de Exordio atque Procurso Istius, Hoc est Dunhelmensis, Ecclesie. Tract on the Origins and Progress of This the Church of Durham*, ed. and trans. D. Rollason, Oxford Medieval Texts, Oxford, 2000.

[12] Gransden, *Historical Writing in England*, 148–51.

[13] Ibid. and Whitelock, *After Bede*, 14.

[14] See Hunter-Blair, 'Some Observations on the *Historia Regum*'. See also Lapidge, 'Byrhtferth of Ramsey'.

[15] 'Florence of Worcester' was familiar with Bede's *De Temporibus*, and used the Chronicle of Marianus Scotus, of Fulda, which was brought into England by Robert de Losinga, Bishop of Hereford 1079–95. This places Durham in touch with both historical and scientific work in this region. See also Chapter 7 above.

strong, at least in the late eleventh century, while William of Malmesbury's work occurs in the book-list.[16] Finally, use is made of Dudo of St Quentin and William of Jumièges, and a Durham copy of the latter still survives.[17]

These two 'Durham' works seem to have been influential in twelfth-century Northumbria, and were known and used by members of the new Augustinian and Cistercian houses. The link with Augustinian Hexham is perhaps clearest and may be examined first. Offler has demonstrated that the surviving text of the *Historia Regum* has been re-edited by someone with an interest in Hexham, who interpolated additional Hexham material; this would suggest that the Augustinians of Hexham obtained a copy of this Durham work.[18] Moreover, Prior Richard of Hexham, perhaps modelling himself on the *Libellus*, wrote a history of Hexham to *c.* 1138, while the house also produced a 'continuation' of the *Historia Regum*, dealing with the reign of Stephen, which was taken further by Prior John.[19] Some information about the past also came to Hexham through Aelred of Rievaulx, who drew at least in part on his family's past as members of the Community of St Cuthbert and 'hereditary rectors' of Hexham. This information came in the form of Aelred's treatise *On the Saints of Hexham*.[20] In this, he not only briefly surveys the saints whose relics were preserved at Hexham, but also depicts Hexham as being under the protection of two of the region's greatest saints, Wilfrid and Cuthbert.[21]

However, the Durham historical texts circulated more widely than simply to Hexham. The surviving copy of the *Historia Regum*, in the 'Hexham edition', was certainly known also to at least one Cistercian house, since it belonged by the late twelfth century to Sawley, a small house of the family of Fountains. The manuscript in which the text occurs is now Cambridge, Corpus Christi College, MS 139, which is a historical compendium of some importance.[22] Its other major contents are: Nennius' *Historia Brittonum*; the *Life of Gildas*; and the 'letter of Archbishop Thurstan' on the founding of Fountains. Of these, the last is clearly linked to Fountains, and occurs in Corpus 139 in the same version found in another twelfth-century Fountains

[16] See *Catalogi Veteres*, 3.
[17] This is now London BL Harley 491.
[18] Offler, 'Hexham and the *Historia Regum*'.
[19] The Chronicle of John of Hexham is printed in Raine, *Hexham*, 107–72. Prior Richard's *History of the Church of Hexham* is given on pages 1–62 of the same volume, and his *Account of King Stephen and the Battle of the Standard* is on 63–106. Hexham authors knew not only the Durham works, but also the sources used by Durham authors, though how the latter were obtained is unclear.
[20] For Aelred's treatise on the saints of the church of Hexham, see Raine, *Hexham*, 173–203.
[21] Ibid. 179.
[22] For brief discussions of its importance see Gransden, *Historical Writing in England*, 214 and n. 260, and Raine, *Hexham*, Preface, Part Two, cli–clii.

book, now Oxford, Corpus Christi College, D 209.[23] More puzzling are the 'Nennius' and 'Gildas' texts. Versions of both were known at Durham earlier in the twelfth century, when they were added into St Calais's copy of Bede's *Historia Ecclesiastica* (now DCL B II 35), a fitting place since they all deal with early history. However, the Corpus 139 texts do not derive from the Durham versions, but from new versions, which seem therefore to have come into Northumbria in the middle of the twelfth century. These new versions were known at Durham, where they were used to correct the existing texts in B II 35, demonstrating Durham's continuing concern to build up a reliable collection of historical works.[24] How Corpus 139 came to Sawley is unknown, but the 'Nennius' text was known also at Kirkstall, another daughter house of Fountains. The Kirkstall copy of the work is now Liège, Bibliothèque de l'Université, 369 C, and its place of origin, like that of the Sawley book, is in dispute.[25] Nevertheless, it seems clear that an interest in both Bede, and in Gildas and Nennius as sources related to Bede, was shared by both Durham and the Cistercians of Yorkshire. Finally, it is of some importance that, when a new and highly regarded exemplar of these historical works became available, it circulated rapidly amongst the Northumbrian houses, together with other related material. The importance of Durham as a source of unusual historical texts is again confirmed by Corpus 139 in one other way; fols. 19r–37v contain the chronicle of Regino of Prüm, copied from the early twelfth-century Durham manuscript, which survives as DCL C IV 15.

The strength of the interest in historical material which linked Durham to the Yorkshire Cistercians is also demonstrated by another Sawley book, now apparently divided between Cambridge, Corpus Christi College, MS 66 and Cambridge UL Ff 1 27.[26] These two sections appear once to have made up another mostly historical compilation, the work of numerous hands, which again belonged to Sawley by the end of the twelfth century.[27] Numerous complications, dealt with by Meehan, Baker, Dumville and Norton, amongst others, arise from this compound manuscript; but they are not the concern of this Conclusion. It is clearly unlikely that either this compound manuscript,

[23] For Aelred's work, see Chapter 11.

[24] On DCL B II 35 and its contents see M. Gullick, D. Marner and A. Piper, *Anglo-Norman Durham 1093–1193: A Catalogue for an Exhibition of Manuscripts in the Treasury, Durham Cathedral*, Durham, 1993, 16–17.

[25] On this, see Meehan, 'Geoffrey of Monmouth, *Prophecies of Merlin*'.

[26] On the complexities of this see Meehan, 'Durham Twelfth-Century Manuscripts'. Similar conclusions on Parker's handling of his manuscripts were already reached by Raine, *Hexham*, cli–clii. See also M. R. James, *A Descriptive Catalogue of the Manuscripts of Corpus Christi College, Cambridge*, Cambridge, 1912, at 1, 138 and 145.

[27] The *ex libris* of Sawley is on page 2 of the twelfth-century portion of Cambridge, Corpus Christi College, MS 66.

or Corpus 139, were produced at the small house of Sawley; either Durham or Fountains, both of which have been suggested, would be more likely as a place of origin. What is of importance here, however, is the very strength of the link between Durham and Fountains, which makes the argument possible, as well as the speed with which these texts were circulating. One of the main works found in the relevant section of Ff 1 27, indeed, is the *Libellus*, with the Durham continuations on William Cumin, William of Ste Barbe and Hugh of le Puiset, which are also added to Durham UL Cosin V ii 6, the Durham copy of the same work. The last of these must have been very new when the 'Sawley' copy was made, and Meehan even argues that the hand of Ff 1 27 is earlier than that of the addition in Cosin V ii 6.[28] If this is correct, then the Durham text must have become known to the Yorkshire Cistercians effectively as soon as it was written. Close links with Durham are also demonstrated by other material in the same section of the manuscript, which includes the *Historia de Sancto Cuthberto*, a Durham relic-list, and a charter relating to Lindisfarne. Why the Cistercians of Sawley would be interested in the last item is not very clear, but it does seem that Ff 1 27/ Corpus 66 was used as a companion volume to Corpus 139, with its copy of the *Historia Regum* (although in a Hexham recension). The evidence for this is that Corpus 139's text of the *Historia Regum* has been annotated in several places, to bring it into line with Ff 1 27/Corpus 66's text of the *Libellus*.[29] Ff 1 27 also contains book I of Gildas' *De Excidio*, which would make it a valuable complement to the *Life of Gildas* found in Corpus 139. More confusingly, however, Ff 1 27/Corpus 66 also contains a second copy of 'Nennius', based on the same exemplar as those in Corpus 139 and Liège, Bibliotèque de l'Université, 369 C (and the corrections in DCL B II 35). However, this extra version has further amplifications, unknown elsewhere in Northumbria (so far as is known), and of unknown origin.[30] Interest in the early history of Northumbria is again demonstrated by the presence of a copy of Æthelwulf's *De Abbatibus*, here 'edited' so that it refers to Lindisfarne, rather than to an anonymous house. Finally, Ff 1 27/Corpus 66 also shows interest in Hexham, since it concludes with the work of Richard of Hexham.

Altogether, it is difficult to come to any clear conclusion on the origins of Corpus 139 and Ff 1 27/Corpus 66. Clearly much of the historical material is of Durham origin, as with the *Libellus* and its continuation, and yet there are links also with Hexham. Finally, much of the rest was known at both Durham and other Northumbrian houses, without having originated at

---

[28] Meehan 'Durham Twelfth-Century Manuscripts', 444.

[29] Ibid. 441–2.

[30] See D. M. Dumville, 'Celtic-Latin Texts in Northern England c.1150–c.1250', *Celtica* 12, 1977, 19–49.

either, so that its point of entry into Northumbria is impossible to determine. In this category, as well as the 'Gildas' and 'Nennius' texts already discussed, is Gilbert of Limerick's *De Statu Ecclesiae*, which is also added into DCL B II 35, as well as occurring in Ff 1 27/Corpus 66. Only one text is primarily Cistercian in content and that is the 'letter of Thurstan'. However, for the purposes of this Conclusion, as has already been argued, what is of importance is the very closeness, and speed, of intellectual contact between at least Durham, Hexham, and the family of Fountains.

A similar conclusion also emerges from a comparison of some of the further material added into DCL B II 35 with the historical works of Aelred of Rievaulx. Aelred, writing in the 1150s, made use of genealogies of the Anglo-Saxon kings, and had precise information on the kings of England and of Scots.[31] Relevant additions to B II 35 are: 'Nomina Regum Britanniae'; 'Genealogia'; 'De Regibus Regnorum Anglorum' (down to Henry II); and 'Nomina Regum Scottorum' (to William the Lion). Thus again, much of the information on which Aelred drew, and which he wished to impart to Henry II himself, was shared with Durham, just as were Aelred's interests in St Cuthbert, and in the Northumbria of Bede.

However, this Northumbrian concern for an accurate version of early English history seems to have been increasingly remote from the interests of court circles. For in the mid-twelfth century a new version of history was rapidly growing in popularity elsewhere, and that was the exciting work of Geoffrey of Monmouth, in his *Historia Regum Britanniae*. An early copy was brought into Yorkshire by Walter Espec, patron of Rievaulx and Kirkham, who is said to have kept it for some time at Helmsley.[32] It may have been to this work that Aelred referred when he wrote of the popularity of someone called Arthur, disclaiming personal knowledge, and calling the stories about him 'fables and lies'.[33] More sympathetic was Alfred, treasurer and sacrist of Beverley, who was sufficiently interested in the current disputes about history to compose a 'History of England', from the British period to 1129, working probably in the 1140s.[34] Like the monks of Durham, Rievaulx and Kirkstall, he had an early copy of Henry of Huntingdon's chronicle, and he also made use of Bede, and of Symeon of Durham. Alfred of Beverley states that Geoffrey's work was being widely read and talked about, but he was clearly uneasy about it. He quotes extensively from it, but says he only uses the passages which he found credible; and he does his best to combine it with material from Bede and Symeon.

[31] For discussion, see Chapter 10.
[32] See Gransden, *Historical Writing in England*, 209.
[33] Aelred of Rievaulx, *Speculum Caritatis*, PL 195, 565.
[34] Gransden, *Historical Writing in England*, 212.

Much more forceful, and more scholarly, is the Augustinian William of Newburgh, who was asked to write, and was supplied with information, by Abbot Ernald of Rievaulx, and who called his work the *Historia Rerum Anglicarum*, in contradiction to Geoffrey's focus on the Britons.[35] William clearly knew and admired the Cistercians of Rievaulx, Fountains and Byland, and quotes briefly from their own foundation histories in his account of the founding of the Yorkshire houses.[36] Interestingly, he does not attribute Ernald's inability to compose a history himself to the Cistercian legislation which required members to gain permission from General Chapter before writing books. In his Preface, William says rather that he, as an Augustinian, had more time than had the Cistercians, because of the high level of work they undertook.[37] Moreover, as Abbot Ernald supplied William with sources and information, it may be presumed that William's approach to his task was approved by the abbot of Rievaulx, as well as the prior of Newburgh. This approach, as defined by William's Prologue, consists largely of a strong attack on the authenticity and credibility of the *Historia Regum Britanniae*, in which Geoffrey of Monmouth's 'fables and lies' are exposed by contrasting his narrative with the evidence of Gildas and of 'our Bede'.[38] The possessive attitude towards Bede is especially interesting; not only was Bede an authority beyond question but, in the eyes of this late-twelfth-century Augustinian, he was a fellow Northumbrian.

This opposition to the 'lies' of Geoffrey of Monmouth can, as has been seen, demonstrate the existence of a shared sense of identity and of history, on the part of twelfth-century Northumbrian writers in a wide range of religious houses. Something similar may perhaps also be seen in works with a more strictly local focus, in the form of the popularity of the writing of foundation histories. Symeon of Durham's impressive work has already been discussed, but almost contemporary with it, if more modest in scale, is the account of the foundation of St Mary's, York, probably composed by Abbot Stephen. This is a difficult work, which has been carefully analysed by Janet Burton; but in one aspect it is a further testament to the importance and influence of Bede.[39] Again, later in the century, the composition of a narrative account for Selby seems to testify to the same influences, as well as to the importance now attached to the possession of an authenticated historical account.[40] The same forces, together with a desire to emphasise

---

[35] For the whole work, see *Chronicles of the Reigns of Stephen, Henry II and Richard I*, vol. i, 3–408, vol. ii, 411–583. A recent edition and translation by Walsh and Kennedy of book I is William of Newburgh, *History of English Affairs*. [36] Ibid. 74–8.
[37] Ibid. 26. [38] Ibid. 28–37. [39] Burton, 'Monastic Revival', 41–52.
[40] For the *Historia Selebiensis Monasterii* see J. T. Fowler, *The Coucher Book of Selby*, Yorkshire Archaeological and Topographical Association, Record Series 10, xiii, 1891, 1893, 2 vols., vol. i, 1–54.

independence from Durham, may have been working in the case of Hexham, although here Cistercian influence may also have been felt. Indeed, the arrival of the Cistercians had meant, as has been seen, that they played a major part in the development of a distinctive monastic culture in Northumbria, influencing both the writings and the illumination of the Augustinians as well as of Durham. Here it is interesting that the northern Cistercians were particularly active in the composition of foundation histories, despite the difficulties experienced by Cistercians in writing. None seems to have been composed for Rievaulx, but Fountains, with its more troubled early history, did produce a long and carefully documented example, drawing on the models provided by Cîteaux and by Clairvaux, and setting out also the story of the foundations of each of Fountains' daughter houses.[41] Kirkstall also had a difficult start, though for different reasons, and it also produced a foundation history.[42] Finally, the abbot of Byland, once a Savigniac house, wrote a careful account both of Byland itself, and of its daughter house, Jervaulx. Like the Fountains narrative, this also made use of documents from what must already have been an archive kept in the monastery.[43]

From all this, it may be argued that, by the middle of the twelfth century, a genuine, and shared, sense of regional identity existed in the religous houses of Northumbria. This identity was complex, and necessarily partly deter-mined by the new political and spiritual forces of the twelfth century. Nevertheless, a shared interest in the saints of the region, and a sense of pride in its past, seem to have overcome differences between orders, as well as differences of political affiliation. Indeed, it is fitting for this chapter to close with a demonstration of the important role of saints' cults in the creation and realisation of this shared culture. It has already been demonstrated that Rievaulx received both scholars and books from Durham, and that some Rievaulx initials, as well as borrowing decorative motifs from Durham books, are effectively copies of distinctive initials found in manuscripts written and decorated at Durham.[44] However, a miracle story concerning St Godric of Finchale demonstrates that it was also perfectly possible for initials by a Fountains artist to be executed in a Durham book.[45] This is the story of the sacrist of Fountains, who was asked by his superiors to illuminate a copy, borrowed from Durham, of Reginald of Durham's *Life of St Godric of*

[41] The *Narratio de Fundatione Fontanis Monasterii* is edited in *Memorials*, vol. i, 1–129.
[42] On Kirkstall, see E. K. Clark, 'The Foundation of Kirkstall Abbey', in *Miscellanea*, Thoresby Society 4, 1895, 169–208.
[43] The Byland Chronicle is discussed by C. T. Clay, 'The Early Abbots of the Yorkshire Cistercian Houses', *Yorkshire Archaeological Journal* 38, 1952–5, 8–43.
[44] See Chapter 8.
[45] See Reginald of Durham, *Vita S. Godrici*, 466–8.

Finchale. The book had been borrowed from Durham in order that Fountains might produce a copy of the text; but the work of the sacrist of Fountains, intended as a gift both to Durham and to St Godric, was to travel in the opposite direction, back to Durham. The reaction of the monks of Durham is not recorded, but they were presumably impressed by the evident approval of St Godric himself, who intervened to restore the work when it was accidentally damaged by the weather. Indeed, by passing the story of the miracle back to Durham, the monks of Fountains made their own contribution to the creation of a Durham text, just as Aelred of Rievaulx had in the case of the miracles of St Cuthbert. Certainly, the study of both the historical works and the surviving manuscripts produced in Northumbria in this period testifies to the importance of the sharing of both books and ideas across the whole region, within what emerges as a very distinctive spiritual and intellectual culture.

APPENDIX

&❧

List of manuscripts

Manuscripts marked * in this list are those argued in the text to be the products of the houses under which they are listed.

1. Manuscripts from Northumbrian houses

Bridlington

* London, BL, Cotton Claudius A v. fols. 46–135; William of Malmesbury, *de gestis Pontificum Anglorum*; mid-twelfth century.
  London, BL, Harley 50; Mark's Gospel (glossed); later twelfth century.
  Oxford, Bodleian, Bodley 357; William of Malmesbury, *de gestis Pontificum Anglorum*; mid-twelfth century.
* Oxford, Bodleian, Digby 53; Poetic works of Serlo, florilegia; mid-twelfth century.
  Oxford, Bodleian, Fairfax 15/Auct. D infr. 2–7; Luke's Gospel (glossed); mid-twelfth century.
  Ripon Cathedral, MSS 3 and 4; Apocalypse (glossed) and commentary (originally one volume); mid-twelfth century.

Byland

* Cambridge, Trinity College, O 1 52; Remigius, *Super Missa* etc.; mid-twelfth century.
* Cambridge, Trinity College, O 3 42; Palladius, *Opus Agriculture*; later twelfth century.
* London, BL, Add. 35180; Peter Cantor etc.; *c.*1200.
  London, BL, Arundel 368; Peter Comestor, *Historia Scholastica*; *c.*1200.
  London, BL, Cotton Julius A xi, fol. 114; Verses 'De Contemptu Mundi'; later twelfth century.

London, BL, Cotton Tiberius D. vi, fols. 149v–150; 'De Dedicatione Altarum'; later twelfth century.

London, BL, Cotton Vespasian E iv, fols. 100–3, 211; *Vita S. Eufrosine*; later twelfth century.

* London, BL, Cotton Cleopatra B iv, fols. 2–30; Henry of Huntingdon; later twelfth century.

London, BL, Cotton Faustina B i, fols. 2–11; Epistles of Pope Alexander III etc.; later twelfth century.

London, BL, Cotton Faustina B iv, fols. 180–2; *Vita S. Alexis*; mid-twelfth century.

* London, BL, Harley 3641; William of Malmesbury, *de gestis Pontificum Anglorum*; later twelfth century.

* London, BL, Royal 5 E XXII; Gregory Nazianzen, *Orationes*; mid-twelfth century.

* London, BL, Royal 15 A XX; Cicero, Anselm, Ivo; *c.* 1200.

* London, BL, Royal 8 F XV; St Bernard, *Letters* and *Opuscula*; *c.* 1200.

Oxford, St John's College, MS 46; Robert of Bridlington; mid-twelfth century.

York, Minster Library, XVI I 7; Psalter (glossed); mid-twelfth century.

Carlisle

Oxford, Bodleian, Bodley 728; Pseudo-Clemens, *Historia Clementis*; mid-twelfth century.

Durham

Cambridge, Corpus Christi College, MS 183; Bede, *Life of St Cuthbert*; early tenth century.

* Cambridge, Jesus College, Q A 14 (14); Bede, *On Genesis and Exodus*; mid-twelfth century.

Cambridge, Jesus College, Q B 6 (23); Psalter, Canticles, Calendar; twelfth century.

* Cambridge, Jesus College, Q B 8 (25); Astronomica, Augustine; twelfth century.

* Cambridge, Jesus College, Q B 11 (28); Priscian; early twelfth century.

Cambridge, Jesus College, Q D 2 (44); Medica; twelfth century.

Cambridge, Jesus College, Q G 2 (50); Isaiah, Tobit, Ruth (all glossed); twelfth century.

* Cambridge, Jesus College, Q G 4 (52); Sermons; early twelfth century.

Cambridge, Jesus College, Q G 5 (53); Ivo of Chartres, *Epistolae*; early twelfth century.

Cambridge, Jesus College, Q G 16 (64); Boethius; twelfth century.

Cambridge, Jesus College, Q G 29 (76); Jerome etc.; twelfth century.

Cambridge, King's College, MS 22; Hugh of St Victor, *De Sacramentis* (part ii); twelfth century.

Cambridge, Peterhouse, MS 74; Pseudo-Isidore; later eleventh century.

Cambridge, Sidney Sussex College, MS 51; Hildebert; twelfth century.

Cambridge, Sidney Sussex College, MS 100, ii; Pontifical; eleventh century.

Cambridge, Sidney Sussex College, MS 101; Decretals; twelfth century.

Cambridge, Trinity College, O 3 55; Bede, *Life of St Cuthbert*, etc.; twelfth century.

Cambridge UL Gg 4 33; Pauline Epistles; mid-twelfth century.

Cambridge UL Add. 3303(6); Calendar; mid-twelfth century.

* Durham, DCL, A I 10; Anselm, Berengandus, Cassiodorus; mid-twelfth century.

Durham, DCL, A II 4; Bible (part II); St Calais.

Durham, DCL, A III 1; Genesis (glossed); twelfth century.

Durham, DCL, A III 2; Leviticus (glossed); twelfth century.

* Durham, DCL, A III 10; Gilbert de la Porrée; mid-twelfth century.

Durham, DCL, A III 29; Sermons; eleventh century.

Durham, DCL, A IV 15; John's Gospel (glossed) etc.; mid-twelfth century.

* Durham, DCL, A IV 16; John's Gospel (glossed) etc.; twelfth century.

Durham, DCL, A IV 28; Bede; twelfth century.

Durham, DCL, A IV 34; Notes on the Song of Songs; early twelfth century.

Durham, DCL, A IV 35; Bede etc.; later twelfth century.

Durham, DCL, B II 1; Josephus; twelfth century (first half).

Durham, DCL, B II 2; Sermons; St Calais.

* Durham, DCL, B II 6; Ambrose (+ sermon, Augustine); St Calais.

* Durham, DCL, B II 7; Jerome, *On the Psalms*; mid-twelfth century.

* Durham, DCL, B II 8; Jerome, *On Isaiah*; early twelfth century.

Durham, DCL, B II 9; Jerome, *On the Twelve Minor Prophets*; St Calais.

Durham, DCL, B II 10; Jerome, *Epistles*, + Origen; St Calais?

* Durham, DCL, B II 11; Jerome, minor works; St Calais.

* Durham, DCL, B II 13; Augustine, *On the Psalms*, vol. ii; St Calais.

Durham, DCL, B II 14; Augustine, *On the Psalms*, vol. iii; St Calais.

Durham, DCL, B II 16; Augustine, *On St John*; St Calais?

Durham, DCL, B II 17; Augustine, *On St John*; St Calais?

* Durham, DCL, B II 18; Augustine, *Sermons*; early twelfth century.

* Durham, DCL, B II 21; Augustine, *Epistles*; late eleventh century.

Durham, DCL, B II 22; Augustine, *The City of God*; St Calais?

* Durham, DCL, B II 26; Augustine, *On the Trinity*; early twelfth century.

Durham, DCL, B II 35; Bede, *Historia Ecclesiastica*, + additions; St Calais.

Durham, DCL, B III 1; Origen, *Homilies*; St Calais.

* Durham, DCL, B III 3; Augustine, *De Octoginta Tribus Quaestionibus*; early twelfth century.

Durham, DCL, B III 5; Augustine, opuscula; twelfth century.

* Durham, DCL, B III 9; Gregory, *Registrum*; St Calais.

Durham, DCL, B III 10; Gregory, *Moralia in Job*; St Calais.

Durham, DCL, B III 11; Gregory, *Homilies on the Gospels*; St Calais?

Durham, DCL, B III 14; Isidore, Peter Damian, John Chrysostom; early twelfth century.

* Durham, DCL, B III 16 (+ B III 10, flyleaves); Rabanus Maurus, *On St Matthew*; late eleventh century.

Durham, DCL, B III 32; Hymnal, Grammar; eleventh century.

Durham, DCL, B IV 1; Gregory Nazianzen, *Orationes*; early twelfth century.

* Durham, DCL, B IV 4; Ambrose, *Hexaemeron*; early twelfth century.

* Durham, DCL, B IV 5; Ambrose, opuscula; early twelfth century.

* Durham, DCL, B IV 6; Augustine, *Confessions*, *On Diverse Heresies*, *Retractations*, *Dialectica*; early twelfth century.

* Durham, DCL, B IV 7; Augustine, *De Caritate*; early twelfth century.

Durham, DCL, B IV 8; Augustine, *De Caritate*; epitome of Josephus; Hugh of St Victor; early twelfth century.

Durham, DCL, B IV 12; Augustine, opuscula; early twelfth century.

* Durham, DCL, B IV 13; Gregory, *On Ezekiel*; St Calais.

* Durham, DCL, B IV 14; Saints' *Lives*; early twelfth century.

* Durham, DCL, B IV 15; Isidore; early twelfth century.

* Durham, DCL, B IV 16; Bede, *On the Apocalypse*, Odo of Cluny, John Chrysostom etc.; early twelfth century.

* Durham, DCL, B IV 17; Decretum Burchardi; twelfth century.

Durham, DCL, B IV 18; *Collectanea Iuris Canonici*; *c.*1123.

Durham, DCL, B IV 24; Martyrology, Calendar, Rule, Constitutions; St Calais.

Durham, DCL, B IV 37; Florilegia; early twelfth century.

Durham, DCL, C III 18; Suetonius; late eleventh century.

Durham, DCL, C IV 5; Cicero; twelfth century.

Durham, DCL, C IV 7; Glosses on Cicero; early twelfth century.

Durham, DCL, C IV 10; Glosses on Boethius; early twelfth century.

Durham, DCL, C IV 12; Constantinus Africanus; twelfth century.

* Durham, DCL, C IV 15; Chronicles; early twelfth century.

Durham, DCL, C IV 29; Notes on Priscian and Cicero; early twelfth century.

* Durham, DCL, Hunter 100; Medical works; *c.*1100.

* Durham UL Cosin V ii 6; Symeon of Durham; early twelfth century.

Durham UL Cosin V iii 1; Laurence of Durham; mid-twelfth century.

Durham UL Cosin V v 6; Gradual; *c.*1100.

Edinburgh, National Library, Adv. 18 4 3; 'Paradysus'; twelfth century.

Edinburgh, National Library, Adv. 18 6 11; Medical works; twelfth century.

* Glasgow UL Hunterian 85(T 4 2); Calendar etc.; twelfth century.

London, BL, Cotton Julius A vi; Hymnal; eleventh century.

* London, BL, Cotton Vitellius D xx; Miscellany on St Cuthbert; mid-twelfth century.

London, BL, Cotton Otho B ix; Gospels; ninth and tenth century (given by Athelstan).

London, BL, Cotton Domitian vii; *Liber Vitae*; ninth century to dissolution.

London, BL, Harley 491; William of Jumièges; twelfth century.

* London, BL, Harley 1924, *Life of St Cuthbert*, etc.; Bede; mid-twelfth century.

* London, BL, Harley 3864; Bede, *On Epistles*; mid-twelfth century.

* London, BL, Harley 4688; Bede, *In Parabolas Salomonis*; early twelfth century.

London, BL, Royal 6 A v; Fulgentius, *Works*; mid-eleventh century.

* London, Society of Antiquaries, 7; Anselm; early twelfth century.

Oxford, Bodleian, Bodley 596, fols. 175–214; Bede, *Life of St Cuthbert*; St Calais?

* Oxford, Bodleian, Digby 20, fols. 194–227; Bede, *Life of St Cuthbert*; *c.*1100.

Oxford, Bodleian, Digby 41, fols. 91, 91*, 92, 101; List of Relics; twelfth century.

Oxford, Bodleian, Lat. liturg. f. 5; Evangeliary; eleventh century.

Oxford, Bodleian, Laud Misc. 52; Ivo of Chartres etc.; mid-twelfth century.

Oxford, Bodleian, Laud Misc. 277; Hugh of St Victor, St Bernard, etc.; mid-twelfth century.

Oxford, Bodleian, Laud Misc. 359; Jerome etc.; twelfth century.

* Oxford, Bodleian, Laud Misc. 392; Hugh of St Victor, *Summa Santentiarum*; mid-twelfth century.

Oxford, Bodleian, Laud Misc. 491; Julian of Toledo; late eleventh century.

Oxford, Bodleian, Rawl. D. 338; Jerome etc. twelfth century.

Oxford, Bodleian, Wood empt. 24; Augustine etc.; twelfth century.

* Oxford, University College, 165; Bede, *Life of St Cuthbert*; *c.*1100.

* Shrewsbury, Shrewsbury School, XX 1; Gregory, *Pastoral Care*; late eleventh century.

Fountains

Cambridge, Gonville and Caius College, 126; Augustine etc.; later twelfth century.

* Cambridge, Trinity College, B 2 11; Bede, *On St Mark*; later twelfth century.

* London, BL, Add. 46203; Missal; later twelfth century.

London, BL, Add. 62129; Basil etc.; later twelfth century.

* London, BL, Arundel 217; Cyprian, Letters; later twelfth century.

London, BL, Cotton Faustina A v; *Libellus* (Symeon); later twelfth century.

* London, BL, Cotton Faustina B i, fols. 192–205; *Itinerarium Trium Monachorum*; late twelfth century.

London, BL, Harley 3173; *Expositio Missae*; mid-twelfth century.

London, BL, Henry Davis Gift M.49; Ezekiel (glossed); twelfth century.

* Oxford, Bodleian, Laud Misc. 310, Hugh of St Victor, *De Sacramentis*; mid-twelfth century.

* Oxford, Corpus Christi College, D 209; *Life of St Olaf*, 'Letter of Thurstan' etc.; late twelfth century.

Oxford, University College, MS 124; *Liber Florum*; late twelfth century.

Guisborough

Cambridge, Gonville and Caius College, MS 109, vol. ii; Bestiary, Cassiodorus; *c.*1200.

London, BL, Arundel 218; Alcuin, Epistles. etc.; late twelfth century.

London, BL, Cotton Vitellius E i (+ fragments in Vitellius E vii); Bede etc.; mid-twelfth century.

Hexham

Cambridge, Corpus Christi College MS 149; Hegesippus; eleventh century.

Cambridge, Jesus College, Q B 21 (38); Gregory Nazianzen, *Works*; mid-twelfth century.

Cambridge, St John's college, MS 46; Augustine, *On John*; later twelfth century.

Durham, DCL, Hunter 57; Augustine; later twelfth century.

* Oxford, Bodleian, Bodley 236; Augustine, *Contra Faustum*; later twelfth century.

Holm Cultram

London, BL, Cotton Nero A v, fols. 1–82; Calendar, Zodiac, Bestiary; early twelfth century.

* London, BL, Cotton Claudius A v, fols. 135–99; *Lives* of Anglo-Saxon saints; late twelfth century.
* London, BL, Cotton Faustina B iv, fols. 3–179; Saints' *Lives*; *c.* 1200.
  Oxford, Bodleian, Lyell 2; Jerome, *Letters*; later twelfth century.
  Oxford, University College, MS 15; Sermons; later twelfth century.

Jervaulx

Oxford, Bodleian, Lat. th. f. 3; Bede, *In Parabolas Salomonis*; later twelfth century.
Oxford, St John's College, MS 99; Bede etc.; later twelfth century.

Kirkham

Cambridge UL Dd. 9 6; Augustine; late twelfth century.
London, BL, Add. 38817; Bede, *Historia Ecclesiastica*; mid-twelfth century.
London, BL, Arundel 36; Possidius etc., Saints' *Lives*; later twelfth century.
London, BL, Cotton Vespasian B xi, fols. 84–125; Aelred, *Life of St Edward*; later twelfth century.
London, BL, Royal 13 A xxi, fols. 151–92; Jerome, Cassiodorus; later twelfth century.

Kirkstall

Liège, Bibliothèque de l'Université, 369C; Eutropius etc.; mid-twelfth century.
* Oxford, Bodleian, E Mus. 195; Smaragdus; later twelfth century.
* Oxford, Bodleian, Laud Misc. 216; Bede, *On Proverbs* etc.; mid-twelfth century.

Lindisfarne

Durham, DCL, A II 17; Gospels (Durham Gospels); seventh/eighth century.
London, BL, Cotton Nero D iv; Gospels (Lindisfarne Gospels); seventh/eighth century.

Meaux

Oxford, Bodleian, Rawl. C. 415; Augustine; later twelfth century.

Melrose

London, BL, Cotton Faustina B ix, fols. 2–75; Chronicle of Melrose; twelfth/thirteenth century.

Newburgh

London, BL, Arundel 252; Ivo of Chartres; *c.*1200.
London, BL, Stowe 62; William of Newburgh; *c.*1200.
Winchester, Winchester College, MS 20; Augustine, *De Doctrina Christiana*, etc.; twelfth century.

Newcastle

London, BL, Add. 35110; Saints' *Lives*, Aelred; late twelfth century.

Newminster

*London, BL, Add. 25014; Bede, *Historia Ecclesiastica*; later twelfth century.
London, BL, Harley 3013; *Hymn to the Virgin*, Aldhelm; later twelfth century.

Rievaulx

Cambridge, Corpus Christi College, MS 86; Rabanus Maurus; later twelfth century.
Cambridge, Jesus College, Q B 17 (34); Willelmus de Monte; *c.*1200.
Dublin, Trinity College, MS 279, fols. 33–111; Hugh of St Victor; late twelfth century.
London, BL, Add. 31826; Hymns (2 fols. only); later twelfth century.
London, BL, Add. 63077; Genesis (glossed); late twelfth century.
London, BL, Arundel 346; *De Officiis Ecclesiasticis* etc.; *c.*1200.
*London, BL, Cotton Vitellius C viii, fols. 4–22; Peter Abelard etc.; late twelfth century.
*London, BL, Cotton Vitellius F iii; Aelred etc.; late twelfth century.
London, BL, Harley 5273; Job (glossed); mid-twelfth century.
*London, BL, Royal 6 C viii; Orosius and Dares Phrygius; late twelfth century.
*London, BL, Royal 8 D xxii; P. Chrysologus, *Sermons*; *c.*1200.

London, BL, Royal 8 E iv; Ennodius, *Letters* and *Opuscula*; late twelfth century.

* Manchester, John Rylands Library, Lat. 196; Walter Daniel; *c.*1200.
  York, Minster Library, XVI I 8; Jerome, etc.; mid-twelfth century.

Roche

Oxford, Bodleian, Laud Misc. 145; Lethbertus, *Flores Psalterii*; *c.*1200.
* Oxford, Bodleian, Laud Misc. 241; Gregory, *Homilies*; later twelfth century.
* Oxford, Bodleian, Laud Misc. 308; Augustine, *On the Psalms*, vol. iii; late twelfth century.
  Oxford, Bodleian, Laud Misc. 309, *On the Psalms*, vol. i; Augustine; late twelfth century.
* Oxford, Bodleian, Rawl. C 329; Ambrose, opuscula; late twelfth century.
  Yale UL Beinecke 590; Geoffrey of Monmouth; *c.*1200.

Sawley

Cambridge, Corpus Christi College, MS 66, pp. 1–114; Historical works; late twelfth century.
Cambridge, Corpus Christi College, MS 139; Symeon of Durham etc.; late twelfth century.
Cambridge UL Ff 1 27, pp. 1–40, 73–252; Historical works; late twelfth century.

Selby

London, BL, Add. 36652,C; Easter tables and annals; late twelfth century.
Oxford, Bodleian, Fairfax 12; Bede, *Historia Ecclesiastica*; mid-twelfth century.

Sweetheart

Oxford, Bodleian, Fairfax 5; Jerome, opuscula; twelfth century.

Tynemouth

Cambridge, Pembroke College, MS 82; Bede, *Historia Ecclesiastica*; mid-twelfth century.
London, BL, Cotton Julius A x, fols. 2–43; Saints' *Lives*; late twelfth century.

London, BL, Harley 3847; Hugh of St Victor, *De Sacramentis*; mid-twelfth century.

Oxford, Bodleian, Laud Misc. 4; Processional; mid-twelfth century.

Oxford, Corpus Christi College, MS 134; Saints' *Lives*; later twelfth century.

Oxford, Magdalen College, Lat. 171; Geoffrey of Monmouth; later twelfth century.

York, St Mary's

* Cambridge, Trinity College, R 5 27; Bede, *Historia Ecclesiastica*; early twelfth century.

Cambridge UL Ee 6 40; Plato, *Timaeus*; mid-twelfth century.

* London, BL, Add. 38816, fols. 21–39; Chronicle etc.; later twelfth century.

London, BL, Add. 4007; Ranulph de Diceto; *c.*1200.

* London, BL, Burney 220; Ovid, *Epistolae ex Ponto*; mid-twelfth century.

* London, BL, Harley 56; *Life of St Dunstan*; mid-twelfth century.

Oxford, Corpus Christi College, MS 224; Boethius etc.; late twelfth century.

York, Minster

Lincoln Cathedral, MS 101; Eutropius etc.; late twelfth century.

Lincoln Cathedral, MS 102; Orosius; late twelfth century.

London, BL, Harley 46; Gospels of Matthew and Mark (glossed); late twelfth century.

Oxford, Bodleian, Laud Misc. 140; Augustine, *De Trinitate*; early twelfth century.

York, Minster Library, XVI A 8; Boethius, *De Trinitate* etc.; mid-twelfth century.

York, Minster Library, XVI Q 3 + 4; Bible (vols. ii and iii); *c.*1100.

2. Manuscripts from other regions, discussed for purposes of comparison

a. England

Canterbury, Christ Church

Cambridge, Trinity College, R 15 22; Boethius, Guido; early twelfth century.

Cambridge, Trinity College, B 3 4; Jerome, *On Psalms*; early twelfth century.

Cambridge, Trinity College, B 4 2; Augustine, *On John*; late eleventh century.

Cambridge UL Ii III 12; Boethius; early twelfth century.

Canterbury, St Augustine's

Cambridge, Trinity College, O 2 51; Priscian; late eleventh century.

Cambridge UL Kk 1 17; Jerome and Origen; early twelfth century.

Exeter

Oxford, Bodleian, Bodley 301; Augustine, *On John*; late eleventh century.

Oxford, Bodleian, Bodley 717; Jerome, *On Isaiah*, etc.; late eleventh century.

Oxford, Bodleian, Bodley 810; Pseudo-Isidore; late eleventh century.

Rochester

Cambridge, Trinity College, R 3 30; Lucan, *Pharsalia*; c. 1100.

Winchester, Old Minster

?Cambridge, Corpus Christi College, MS 183; Bede, *Life of St Cuthbert*; early tenth century.

Winchester Cathedral, MS 2; Augustine, *On St John*; late eleventh century.

b. Normandy

Fécamp

Rouen, BM, U 3; Saints' *Lives*; late eleventh century.

Rouen, A 321; Jerome, *On Jeremiah*; c. 1100.

Jumièges

Paris, Bibliothèque Nationale, Lat. 13765; Liturgical fragment; late eleventh century.

Rouen, BM, A 286; Augustine, Opuscula; late eleventh century.

Rouen, BM, A 88; Jerome, *On Minor Prophets*; late eleventh century.

Rouen, BM, A 102; Augustine, *On Psalms* (3 vols.); late eleventh century.

Rouen, BM, A 195; Ambrosiaster; late eleventh century.

Rouen, BM, A 278; Gregory, Homilies; late eleventh century.

Rouen, BM, A 298; John Chrysostom, *Homilies* and Opuscula; late eleventh century.

Rouen, BM, A 366; Anselm, Opuscula; late eleventh century.

Rouen, BM, I 69; Boethius, Alcuin, etc.; late eleventh century.

Rouen, BM, U 61; Josephus, *Jewish Antiquities*; late eleventh century.

Rouen, BM, Y 109; Saints' *Lives*; late eleventh century.

Lyre

Rouen, BM, A 296; Smaragdus, Cassian; later eleventh century.

Rouen, BM, A 85; Augustine, *On John*; late eleventh century.

Rouen, BM, Y 21; Orationes et capitula; late eleventh century.

Rouen, BM, Y 41; Saints' *Lives*; mid-eleventh century.

St Evroult

Rouen, BM, A 259; Augustine, *De Verbis Domini*, Anselm; late eleventh century.

Bibliography

❧

PRINTED PRIMARY SOURCES

Aelred of Rievaulx, *Genealogia Regum Anglorum, PL* 195: 736.
—— *Life of St Ninian*, ed. A. P. Forbes, *The Historians of Scotland*, vol. v, Edinburgh, 1874.
—— *On the Saints of the Church of Hexham*, in J. Raine, ed., *The Priory of Hexham*, vol. i, Surtees Society 44, 1864, 173–206.
—— *De Speculo Caritatis*, ed. A. Hoste, Corpus Christianorum, Continuatio Mediaevalis 1, Turnhout, Belgium, 1971.
—— *Spiritual Friendship*, trans. M. E. Laker SSND, Kalamazoo, 1977.
—— *De Spirituali Amicitia*, in *PL* 195: 659–702.
—— *Treatises: The Pastoral Prayer*, trans T. Berkeley, M. P. Macpherson and R. P. Lawson, in *The Works of Aelred of Rievaulx*, vol. i, Spence, Massachusetts, 1971.
The Anglo-Saxon Chronicle, ed. and trans. D. Whitelock, in *English Historical Documents, Volume 1, c.500–1042*, London, 1979.
Bede, *Bede's Ecclesiastical History of the English People*, ed. B. Colgrave and R. A. B. Mynors, Oxford, 1969.
—— *Opera Historica Minora*, ed. J. Stevenson, London, 1841.
St Bernard of Clairvaux, *An Apology to Abbot William*, trans M. Casey, intro. by J. Leclercq, in *The Works of St Bernard of Clairvaux, 1, Treatises*, Cistercian Fathers Series 1, Shannon, 1970, 3–69.
—— *Epistolae*, in *Opera Omnia*, ed. J. Leclercq and H. Rochais, vols. vii and viii, Rome, 1974.
Cartularium Abbathiae de Rievalle, ed. J. C. Atkinson, Surtees Society 83, 1887.
Cartularium Abbathiae de Whitby, ed. J. C. Atkinson, Surtees Society 69, 1878.
Catalogi Veteres Librorum Ecclesie Cathedralis Dunelm, ed. B. B. (Beriah Botfield), Surtees Society 7, 1838.
Chartularium Abbathiae de Novo Monasterio, vol. i, ed. J. T. Fowler, Surtees Society 66, 1878.

Chartulary of the Cistercian Abbey of Salley in Craven, ed. J. McNulty, Yorkshire Archaeological and Topographical Association, Record Series 87 and 90, Leeds, 1933–4.

Chronicles of the Reigns of Stephen, Henry II and Richard I, ed. R. Howlett, Rolls Series, 1884–9.

'Codex Manuscriptus 31 Bibliothecae Universitatis Labacensis', ed. C. Noschitzka, *Analecta Sacri Ordinis Cisterciensis* 6, 1950, 1–124.

Coucher Book of Selby Abbey, ed. J. T. Fowler, Yorkshire Archaeological and Topographical Association, Record Series 10, 1891 for 1890, and 1893.

The Durham Collectar, ed. A. Correa, Henry Bradshaw Society 107, 1992.

Durham Episcopal Charters, 1071–1152, ed. W. H. Offler, Surtees Society 179, 1968.

Early Yorkshire Charters, 3 vols., ed. W. Farrer, Edinburgh, 1914–16.

Ecclesiastica Officia, ed. P. Guignard, *Les Monuments Primitifs de la Règle Cistercienne*, Dijon, 1878.

Historia Dunelmensis Ecclesiae Continuatio usque ad Electionem Willelmi de Sancta Barbara, in T. Arnold, ed., *Symeonis Monachi Opera Omnia*, vol. i, Rolls Series 75, London, 1882, 135–60.

Historia de Sancto Cuthberto, in T. Arnold, ed., *Symeonis Monachi Opera Omnia*, vol. i, Rolls Series 75, London, 1882, 169–214.

Historia Selebiensis Monasterii, in J. T. Fowler, ed., *The Coucher Book of Selby Abbey*, Yorkshire Archaeological and Topographical Association, Record Series 10, 1891, 1893, vol. i, 1–54.

Historians of the Church of York and Its Archbishops, 2 vols, ed. J. Raine, Rolls Series, London, 1879–94.

Hugh the Chanter, *The History of the Church of York, 1066–1127*, ed. and trans. C. Johnson, M. Brett, C. N. L. Brooke and M. Winterbottom, Oxford, 1990.

De Iniusta Vexatione Willelmi Episcopi Primi, in T. Arnold, ed., *Symeonis Monachi Opera Omnia*, vol. i, Rolls Series 75, London, 1882, 171–94.

John of Hexham, *Historia*, in J. Raine, ed., *The Priory of Hexham*, vol. i, Surtees Society 44, 1864, 107–72.

Lanfranc, *The Monastic Constitutions*, ed. and trans. M. D. Knowles, Nelson's Medieval Classics, London, 1951.

Laurence of Durham, *Dialogi Laurentii Dunelmensis Monachi ac Prioris*, ed. J. Raine, Surtees Society 70, 1880.

Liber de Miraculis et Translationibus Sancti Cuthberti, in T. Arnold, ed., *Symeonis Monachi Opera Omnia*, vol. i, Rolls Series 75, London, 1882, 229–61 and ii, 333–62.

Liber Vitae Ecclesiae Dunelmensis, ed. J. Stevenson, Surtees Society 13, 1841.

The Life of King Edward Who Lies at Westminster, ed. and trans. F. Barlow, Nelson's Medieval Texts, London, 1962.

The Life of St Oswald, in J. Raine, ed., *The Historians of the Church of York and Its Archbishops*, vol. i, Rolls Series, London, 399–475.

Memorials of the Abbey of St Mary of Fountains, 2 vols., ed. J. R. Walbran and J. Fowler, Surtees Society 42, 1863.

De Obsessione Dunelmi, in J. Hodgson Hinde, ed., *Symeonis Dunelmensis Opera et Collectanea*, Surtees Society 51, 1868, 154–8.

Orderic Vitalis, *The Ecclesiastical History of Orderic Vitalis*, 6 vols., ed. M. Chibnall, Oxford, 1969–80.

Reginald of Durham, *Reginaldi Monachi Dunelmensis Libellus de Admirandis Beati Cuthberti Virtutibus Quae Novellis Patratae sunt Temporibus*, ed. J. Raine, Surtees Society 1, 1835.

Libellus de Vita et Miraculis S. Godrici, Heremitae de Finchale, ed. J. Stevenson, Surtees Society 20, 1847.

Richard of Hexham, *Account of King Stephen and the Battle of the Standard*, in J. Raine, ed., *The Priory of Hexham*, vol. i, Surtees Society 44, 1864, 63–106.

—— *History of the Church of Hexham*, in J. Raine, ed., *The Priory of Hexham*, vol. i, Surtees Society 44, 1864, 1–62.

Robert 'the Scribe', *The Bridlington Dialogue*, ed. and trans. by a religious of CSM, London, 1960.

Statuta Capitulorum Generalium Ordinis Cisterciensis ab Anno 1116 ad Annum 1786, 8 vols., ed. J.-M. Canivez, Louvain, 1933–41.

Symeon of Durham, *Historia Dunelmensis Ecclesiae* (also known as *Libellus de Exordio atque Procursu Istius, Hoc est Dunelmensis, Ecclesie*), in T. Arnold, ed., *Symeonis Monachi Opera Omnia*, vol. i, Rolls Series 75, 1882–5, 3–169.

—— (?) *Historia regum*, in T. Arnold, ed., *Symeonis Monachi Opera Omnia*, vol. ii, Rolls Series 75, 1882–5, 3–283.

—— ed. and trans. D. Rollason, *Libellus de Exordio atque Procurso Istius, Hoc est Dunelmensis, ecclesiae*, Oxford Medieval Texts, Oxford, 2000.

Thomas Walsingham, *Gesta Abbatum Monasterii Sancti Albani a Thoma Walsingham*, 3 vols., ed. H. T. Riley, Rolls Series 25, London, 1867–9.

Turgot of Durham (?), *Life of St Margaret*, Appendix III in J. Hodgson Hinde, ed., *Symeonis Dunelmensis Opera et Collectanea*, vol. i, Surtees Society 51, 1868.

Two 'Lives' of St Cuthbert, ed. B. Colgrave, Cambridge, 1940.

Walter Daniel, *The Life of Ailred of Rievaulx*, ed. and trans, F. M. Powicke, London, 1950.

William of Malmesbury, *Vita Wulfstani*, ed. R. R. Darlington, Camden Society, 3rd series 40, 1928.

William of Newburgh, *The History of English Affairs, Book One*, ed. and trans. P. G. Walsh and M. J. Kennedy, Warminster, 1988.

William of St Thierry, *Exposition on the Song of Songs*, trans. M. C. Hart, in *The Works of William of St Thierry*, vol. ii, Shannon, 1970.

SECONDARY SOURCES

Abou-El-Haj, B., 'Bury St Edmunds Abbey between 1070 and 1124: A History of Property, Privilege and Monastic Art Production', in *Art History* 6, 1983, 1–29.

—— *The Medieval Cult of Saints: Formations and Transformations*, Cambridge, 1994.

Aird, W. M., 'The Origins and Development of the Church of St Cuthbert, 635–1153, with Special Reference to Durham in the Period 1071–1153', unpublished Ph.D. thesis, University of Edinburgh, 1991

—— 'An Absent Friend: The Career of Bishop William of St Calais', in D. Rollason *et al.*, eds., *Anglo-Norman Durham 1093–1193*, Woodbridge, 1994, 283–98.

—— 'St Cuthbert, the Scots and the Normans', in M. Chibnall, ed., *Anglo-Norman Studies XVI: Proceedings of the Battle Conference, 1993*, Woodbridge, 1994, 1–20.

—— *St Cuthbert and the Normans. The Church of Durham 1071–1153*, Woodbridge, 1998.

Alexander, J. J. G., *Norman Illumination at Mont St Michel 966–1100*, Oxford, 1970.

—— 'Some Aesthetic Principles in the Use of Colour in Anglo-Saxon Art', *Anglo-Saxon England* 4, 1975, 137–54.

—— *Insular Manuscripts 6th to 9th Centuries* (A Survey of Manuscripts Illuminated in the British Isles, general editor J. J. G. Alexander, vol. i), London, 1978.

—— 'Scribes as Artists: The Arabesque Initial in Twelfth-Century English Manuscripts', in M. B. Parkes and A. G. Watson, eds., *Medieval Scribes, Manuscripts and Libraries. Essays Presented to N. R. Ker*, London, 1978, 87–116.

—— *Medieval Illuminators and Their Methods of Work*, New Haven and London, 1992.

—— and Temple, E., *Illuminated Manuscripts in Oxford College Libraries, the University Archives and the Taylor Institution*, Oxford, 1985.

Arngart, O., *The Leningrad Bede*, Early English Manuscripts in Facsimile II, Copenhagen, 1952.

Avril, F., *Manuscrits Normands XI–XIIème siècles*, Rouen, 1975.

Aylmer, G. E., and Cant, R., eds., *A History of York Minster*, Oxford, 1977.

Baker, D., 'The Foundation of Fountains Abbey', *Northern History* 4, 1969, 29–43.

—— 'The Desert in the North', *Northern History* 5, 1970, 1–11.

—— '"Viri Religiosi" and the York Election Dispute', in *Studies in Church History* 7, 1971, 87–100.

—— 'The Genesis of English Cistercian Chronicles: The Foundation History of Fountains Abbey', i and ii, *Analecta Sacri Ordinis Cisterciensis* 25, 1969, 14–41, and 31, 1975, 179–212.

—— 'Legend and Reality: The Case of Waldef of Melrose', *Studies in Church History* 12, 1975, 59–82.

—— 'Scissors and Paste: Corpus Christi, Cambridge, MS 139 Again', *Studies in Church History* 11, 1975, 84–139.

—— '"A nursery of saints": St Margaret of Scotland Reconsidered', in D. Baker, ed., *Medieval Women*, Studies in Church History Subsidia 1, Oxford, 1978, 119–41.

Baker, M., 'Medieval Illustrations of Bede's *Life of St Cuthbert*', *Journal of the Warburg and Courtauld Institutes* 41, 1978, 16–49.

Barlow, F., *The English Church 1000–1066*, 2nd edn, London, 1979.

—— *The English Church 1066–1154*, London and New York, 1979.

—— *The Norman Conquest and Beyond*, London, 1983.

—— *William Rufus*, London, 1983.

—— *The Feudal Kingdom of England, 1042–1216*, 4th edn, London and New York, 1988.

Barr, C. B. L., 'The Minster Library', in G. Aylmer and R. Cant, eds., *A History of York Minster*, Oxford, 1977, 487–539.

Barrow, G. W. S., 'Scottish Rulers and the Religious Orders, 1070–1153', *Transactions of the Royal Historical Society*, 5th series 3, 1953, 77–100.

—— 'The Anglo-Scottish Border', in *The Kingdom of the Scots*, London, 1973, 139–61.

—— *David I of Scotland (1124–1153): The Balance of New and Old*, Stenton Lecture, 1984, University of Reading, 1985.

—— 'The Kings of Scotland and Durham', in D. Rollason *et al.*, eds., *Anglo-Norman Durham 1093–1193*, Woodbridge, 1994, 311–24.

—— 'The Scots and the North of England', in E. King, ed., *The Anarchy of King Stephen's Reign*, Oxford, 1994, 231–54.

Barrow, J., 'English Cathedral Communities and Reform in the Late Tenth and the Eleventh Centuries', in D. Rollason *et al.*, eds., *Anglo-Norman Durham 1093–1193*, Woodbridge, 1994, 25–39.

Bates, D., 'Normandy and England after 1066', *English Historical Review* 104, 413, 1989, 851–80.

Battiscombe, C. F., ed., *The Relics of St Cuthbert*, Oxford, 1956.

Bethell, D., 'The Foundation of Fountains Abbey and the State of St Mary's, York, in 1132', *Journal of Ecclesiastical History* 17, 1966, 11–27.

Bibolet, F., 'Les Manuscrits de Clairvaux au XIIe siècle', in *Congrès archéologique de France, Troyes*, Paris, 1955, 174–9.

Bishop, T. A. M., 'The Norman Settlement of Yorkshire', in *Studies in Medieval History presented to F. M. Powicke*, Oxford, 1948, 1–14.

—— 'A Canterbury Scribe's Work', *Durham Philobiblon* 2, 1, 1955, 435–7.

—— *Scriptores Regis*, Oxford, 1961.

—— and Chaplais, P., *Facsimiles of English Royal Writs to AD 1100*, Oxford, 1957.

Blair, John, 'Secular Minster Churches in Domesday Book', in P. Sawyer, ed., *Domesday Book: A Reassessment*, London, 1985, 104–42.

Blumenfeld-Kosinski, R., and Szell, T., eds., *Images of Sainthood in Medieval Europe*, Ithaca, 1991.

Boase, T. S. R., *English Art 1100–1216*, 2nd edn, Oxford, 1968.

Bonner, G., 'St Cuthbert at Chester-le-Street', in G. Bonner *et al.*, eds., *St Cuthbert, His Cult and His Community to AD 1200*, Woodbridge, 1989, 387–96.

——, Rollason, D., and Stancliffe, C., eds., *St Cuthbert, His Cult and His Community to AD 1200*, Woodbridge, 1989.

Brett, M., *The English Church under Henry I*, Oxford, 1970.

Brooke, C., 'Gregorian Reform in Action: Clerical Marriage in England 1050–1200', in *Medieval Church and Society*, New York, 1972, 69–99.

—— 'St Bernard, the Patrons and Monastic Planning', in C. Norton and D. Park, eds., *Cistercian Art and Architecture in the British Isles*, Cambridge, 1986, 11–23.

—— 'King David I of Scotland as a Connoisseur of the Religious Orders', in C. G. Viola, ed., *Mediaevalia Christiana XIe–XIIIe siècles. Hommage à Raymonde Foreville*, Paris, 1989, 320–34.

—— and Hill, R. M. T., 'From 627 until the Early Thirteenth Century', in G. E. Aylmer and R. Cant, eds., *A History of York Minster*, Oxford, 1977, 1–43.

Browne, A. C., 'Bishop William of St Carilef's Book Donations to Durham Cathedral Priory', *Scriptorium* 42, vol. ii, 1988, 140–55.

Burrows, T. N., 'The Foundation of Nostell Priory', *Yorkshire Archaeological Journal* 53, 1981, 31–5.

Burton, J., 'A Confraternity List from St Mary's Abbey, York', *Revue bénédictine* 89, 1979, 325–33.

Burton, J., 'The Foundation of the British Cistercian Houses', in C. Norton and D. Park, eds., *Cistercian Art and Architecture in the British Isles*, Cambridge, 1986, 24–39.

—— 'The Abbeys of Byland and Jervaulx, and the Problems of the English Savigniacs, 1134–1156', in J. Loades, ed., *Monastic Studies*, vol. ii, Bangor, 1991, 119–31.

—— 'The Eremitical Tradition and the Development of Post-Conquest Religious Life in Northern England', in N. Crossley-Holland, ed., *Eternal Values in Medieval life*, Lampeter, 1991, 18–39.

—— 'The Monastic Revival in Yorkshire: Whitby and St Mary's, York', in D. Rollason *et al.*, eds., *Anglo-Norman Durham 1093–1193*, Woodbridge, 1994, 41–65.

—— *Monastic and Religious Orders in Britain, 1000–1300*, Cambridge, 1994.

—— *Kirkham Priory, from Foundation to Dissolution*, Borthwick Papers no. 84, York, 1995.

Butler, L., and Given-Wilson, C., *Medieval Monasteries of Great Britain*, London, 1979.

Buytaert, P. E. M., 'An Earlier Redaction of the *Theologia Christiana* of Abelard', *Antonianum* 37, 1962, fasc. 4, 481–95.

Cahn, W., *Romanesque Bible Illumination*, Ithaca, 1982.

Cambridge, E., 'Early Romanesque Architecture in North-East England: A Style and Its Patrons', in D. Rollason *et al.*, eds., *Anglo-Norman Durham 1093–1193*, Woodbridge, 1994, 141–60.

——, Williams, A., *et al.*, eds., 'Hexham Abbey: A Review of Recent Work and Its Implications', *Archaeologia Aeliana*, 5th series 23, 1995, 51–138.

Carrasco, M., 'Notes on the Iconography of the Romanesque Illustrated Manuscript of the Life of St Albinus of Angers', *Zeitschrift für Kunstgeschichte* 47, 1984, 333–48.

—— 'Spirituality and Historicity in Pictorial Hagiography: Two Miracles by Saint Albinus of Angers', *Art History* 12, 1989, 1–21.

—— 'Spirituality in Context: The Romanesque Illustrated Life of St Radegund of Poitiers (Poitiers, Bibl. Mun., MS 250)', *Art Bulletin* 72, 1990, 414–35.

Chaplais, P., 'William of St Calais and the Domesday Survey', in J. C. Holt, ed., *Domesday Studies*, Woodbridge, 1987, 65–77.

Cheney, C. R., 'English Cistercian Libraries: The First Century', in C. R. Cheney, *Medieval Texts and Studies*, Oxford, 1973, 328–45.

Chibnall, M., 'Monks and Pastoral Work: A Problem in Anglo-Norman History', *Journal of Ecclesiastical History* 18, 1967, 165–72.

—— *Anglo-Norman England 1066–1166*, Oxford, 1986.

Clark, E. K., 'The Foundation of Kirkstall Abbey', in *Miscellanea*, Thoresby Society 4, 1895, 169–208.

Clay, C. T., 'The Early Abbots of the Yorkshire Cistercian Houses', *Yorkshire Archaeological Journal* 38, 1952–5, 8–43.

Coates, A., *English Medieval Books*, Oxford, 1999.

Colgrave, B., 'The Post-Bedan Miracles and Translations of St Cuthbert', in C. Fox and B. Dickins, eds., *The Early Cultures of North-West Europe*, Cambridge, 1950, 305–32.

Colvin, H. M., *The White Canons in England*, Oxford, 1951.

Constable, G., 'Aelred of Rievaulx and the Nun of Watton: An Episode in the Early History of the Gilbertine Order', in D. Baker, ed., *Medieval Women*, Studies in Church History, Subsidia 1, Oxford, 1978, 205–26.

Cooper, J. M., *The Last Four Anglo-Saxon Archbishops of York*, Borthwick Papers 38, York, 1970.

Cramp, R., 'Excavations at the Saxon Monastic Sites of Monkwearmouth and Jarrow, Co. Durham: An Interim Report', *Medieval Archaeology* 13, 1969, 21–65.

—— 'The Window Glass from the Monastic Site of Jarrow', *Journal of Glass Studies* 17, 1975, 88–95.

—— *The Background to St Cuthbert's Life*, Durham Cathedral Lecture, 1980.

—— and Mills, S., *Bede's Writings: Early Manuscripts and Finds*, catalogue of an exhibition at Bede's World, Jarrow, 1995.

Craster, H. H. E., 'The Red Book of Durham', *English Historical Review* 40, 1925, 504–32.

Croydon, G. E., 'Abbot Laurence of Westminster and Hugh of St Victor', *Medieval and Renaissance Studies* 2, 1950, 169–171.

Curtius, E. R., *European Literature and the Latin Middle Ages*, trans. W. R. Trask, London and Henley, 1979.

Dalton, P., *Conquest, Anarchy and Lordship: Yorkshire 1066–1154*, Cambridge, 1994.

Davies, R. R., *Domination and Conquest: The Experience of Ireland, Scotland and Wales, 1100–1300*, Cambridge, 1990.

Davis, R. H. C., 'Bede after Bede', in C. Harper-Bill, C. J. Holdsworth and J. L. Nelson, eds., *Studies in Medieval History Presented to R. Allen Brown*, Woodbridge, 1989, 103–16.

Dawtry, A., 'The Benedictine Revival in the North: The Last Bulwark of Anglo-Saxon Monasticism', *Studies in Church History* 18, 1982, 87–98.

Delalonde, M., *Manuscrits du Mont-Saint-Michel*, Rennes, 1981.

De la Mare, A. C., 'A Probable Addition to the Bodleian's Holdings of Exeter Cathedral Manuscripts', *Bodleian Library Record* 11, 1983, 79–83.

Deshman, R., 'Anglo-Saxon Art after Alfred', *Art Bulletin* 56, 1974, 176–200.

Dickinson, J. C., 'The Origins of the Cathedral of Carlisle', *Transactions of the Cumberland and Westmorland Antiquarian and Archaeological Society*, n.s. 45, 1946, 134–43.

—— *The Origins of the Austin Canons and Their Introduction into England*, London, 1950.

Dobson, R. B., 'The First Norman Abbey in Northern England', *Ampleforth Journal* 74, 1969, 161–76.

—— *The Jews of Medieval York and the Massacre of March 1190*, Borthwick Papers 45, York, 1974.

Dodwell, C. R., *The Canterbury School of Illumination, 1066–1200*, Cambridge, 1954.

Donkin, R. A., 'The English Cistercians and Assarting *c.*1128–1350', *Analecta Sacri Ordinis Cisterciensis* 20, 1964, 49–75.

—— *A Check-List of Printed Works Relating to the Cistercian Order as a Whole and to the Houses of the British Isles in Particular*, Rochefort, 1969.

—— *The Cistercians: Studies in the Geography of Medieval England and Wales*, Pontifical Institute of Medieval Studies, Studies and Texts 38, Toronto, 1978.

Doutreleau, L., 'Étude d'une tradition manuscrite: le *De Spiritu Sancto* de Didyme', in P. Granfield and J. A. Jungmann, eds., *Kyriakon: Festschrift Johannes Quasten*, Münster, 1970, 352–89.

Dumville, D. M., 'Celtic-Latin Texts in Northern England *c.*1150–*c.*1250', *Celtica* 12, 1977, 19–49.

—— 'The Sixteenth-Century History of Two Cambridge Books from Sawley', *Transactions of the Cambridge Bibliographical Society* 7, 1980, 440–9.

Dutton, M. L., 'The Conversion and Vocation of Aelred of Rievaulx: A Historical Hypothesis', in D. Williams, ed., *England in the Twelfth Century. Proceedings of the 1988 Harlaxton Symposium*, Woodbridge, 1990, 31–49.

Dutton, P. E., '"Illustre civitatis et populi exemplum": Plato's *Timaeus* and the Transmission from Calcidius to the End of the Twelfth Century of a Tripartite Scheme of Society', *Medieval Studies* 45, 1983, 79–119.

—— *The Glossae super Platonem*, Toronto, 1991.

Farrer, W., 'Introduction to the Yorkshire Domesday', in W. Page, ed., *Victoria History of the County of York*, London, 1912, vol. ii, 133–90.

Faull, M., and Stinson, M., eds., *Domesday Book, 30, Yorkshire*, 2 vols., Chichester, 1986.

Fergusson, P. J., 'The Builders of Cistercian Monasteries in Twelfth Century England', in M. P. Lillich, ed., *Studies in Cistercian Art and Architecture*, vol. ii, Kalamazoo, 1984, 14–29.

Fernie, E., 'The Romanesque Church of Selby Abbey', in L. R. Hoey, ed., *Yorkshire Monasticism*, British Archaeological Association Conference Transactions 16, 1995, 40–9.

—— 'The Architectural Influence of Durham Cathedral', in D. Rollason *et al.*, eds., *Anglo-Norman Durham 1093–1193*, Woodbridge, 1995, 269–82.

Fleming, R., *Kings and Lords in Conquest England*, Cambridge, 1991.

Foster, M., 'Custodians of St Cuthbert: The Durham Monks' Views of Their Predecessors, 1083–c.1200', in D. Rollason, *et al.*, eds., *Anglo-Norman Durham 1093–1193*, Woodbridge, 1994, 53–67.

Gameson, R. G., 'English Manuscript Art in the Mid-Eleventh Century: The Decorative Tradition', *Antiquaries Journal* 71, 1991, 64–122.

—— 'The Cost of the Codex Amiatinus', *Notes and Queries* 237/1, 1992, 2–9.

—— 'The Royal I. B. vii Gospels and English Book Production in the Seventh and Eighth Centuries', in R. Gameson, ed., *The Early Medieval Bible*, Cambridge, 1994, 24–52.

—— 'English Manuscript Art in the Late Eleventh Century: Canterbury and Its Context', in R. Eales and R. Sharpe, eds., *Canterbury and the Norman Conquest: Churches, Saints and Scholars 1066–1109*, London and Rio Grande, 1995, 95–144.

—— 'Hugo Pictor, enlumineur normand', *Cahiers de civilisation medievale* 44, 2001, 122–38.

Gibson, M., *Lanfranc of Bec*, Oxford, 1978.

Ginzburg, C., *The Cheese and the Worms*, London, 1980.

—— *The Enigma of Piero*, London, 1985.

Gneuss, H., 'A Preliminary List of Manuscripts Written or Owned in England up to 1100', *Anglo-Saxon England* 9, 1981, 1–60.

Golding, B., 'The Coming of the Cluniacs', in *Proceedings of the Battle Conference on Anglo-Norman Studies* 3, 1980, 65–77.

Gransden, A., *Historical Writing in England c.550 to c.1307*, vol. i, London, 1974.

—— 'Bede's Reputation as an Historian in Medieval England', in A. Gransden, *Legends, Traditions and History in Medieval England*, London and Rio Grande, 1992, 1–30.

Green, J., 'William Rufus, Henry I and the Royal Demesne', *History* 64, 1979, 337–52.

—— *The Government of England under Henry I*, Cambridge, 1986.

—— 'Aristocratic Loyalties on the Northern Frontier of England, c.1100–1174', in D. Williams, ed., *England in the Twelfth Century. Proceedings of the 1988 Harlaxton Symposium*, Woodbridge, 1990, 83–100.

Guignard, P., *Les Monuments primitifs de la Règle cistercienne*, Dijon, 1878.

Gullick, M., 'The Scribe of the Carilef Bible: A New Look at Some Late

Eleventh Century Durham Cathedral Manuscripts', in L. Brownrigg, ed., *Medieval Book Production: Assessing the Evidence*, Los Altos Hills, 1990, 61–83.

—— 'The Scribes of the Durham Cantor's Book (Durham, Dean and Chapter Library, MS B. IV.24) and the Durham Martyrology Scribe', in D. Rollason *et al.*, eds., *Anglo-Norman Durham 1093–1193*, Woodbridge, 1994, 93–110.

—— 'The Hand of Symeon of Durham: Further Observations on the Durham Martyrology Scribe', in D. Rollason, ed., *Symeon of Durham: Historian of Durham and the North*, Stamford, 1998, 14–31.

—— 'The Two Earliest Manuscripts of the *Libellus de Exordio*', in D. Rollason, ed., *Symeon of Durham: Historian of Durham and the North*, Stamford, 1998, 106–19.

—— 'The Origin and Importance of Cambridge, Trinity College R. 5. 27', *Transactions of the Cambridge Bibliographical Society* 11, Part 3, 1998, 239–62.

—— Marner, D., and Piper, A., *Anglo-Norman Durham 1093–1193: A Catalogue for an Exhibition of Manuscripts in the Treasury, Durham Cathedral*, Durham, 1993.

Hahn, C., 'Picturing the Text: Narrative in the Life of the Saints', *Art History* 13, 1990, 1–33.

Hallam, E. M., 'Monasteries as 'War Memorials': Battle Abbey and La Victoire', *Studies in Church History* 20, Oxford, 1983, 47–57.

Hallam, H. E., *Rural England 1066–1348*, Glasgow, 1981.

Hamilton Thompson, A., ed., *Bede: His Life, Times, and Writings*, Oxford, 1935.

Harrison, S., 'Observations on the Architecture of the Galilee Chapel', in D. Rollason *et al.*, eds., *Anglo-Norman Durham 1093–1193*, Woodbridge, 1994, 212–21.

Hartzell, K. D., 'An Unknown English Benedictine Gradual of the Eleventh Century', *Anglo-Saxon England* 4, 1975, 131–44.

Henderson, G., *Bede and the Visual Arts*, Jarrow Lecture, Jarrow, 1980.

Herbert, J., 'The Transformation of Hermitages into Augustinian Priories in Twelfth-Century England', in *Monks, Hermits and the Ascetic Tradition*, Studies in Church History 22, Oxford, 1985, 131–45.

Heslop, T. A., '"Dunstanus Archiepiscopus" and Painting in Kent around 1120', *The Burlington Magazine*, 126, 973, 1984, 195–204.

Higham, N. J., *The Kingdom of Northumbria AD 350–1100*, Stroud, 1993.

Hill, B. D., *English Cistercian Monasteries and Their Patrons in the Twelfth Century*, Urbana, 1968.

Hohler, C., and Hughes, A., 'The Durham Services in Honour of St

Cuthbert', in C. F. Battiscombe, ed., *The Relics of St Cuthbert*, Oxford, 1956, 155–91.

Holdsworth, C. J., The Chronology and Character of Early Cistercian Legislation on Art and Architecture', in C. Norton and D. Park, eds., *Cistercian Art and Architecture in the British Isles*, Cambridge, 1986, 40–55.

—— *The Piper and the Tune: Medieval Patrons and Monks*, University of Reading, Stenton Lecture, 1991 for 1990.

—— 'The Church', in E. King, ed., *The Anarchy of King Stephen's Reign*, Oxford, 1994, 207–30.

—— 'The Early Writings of Bernard of Clairvaux', *Cîteaux*, fasc. 1–2, vol. xlv, 1994, 21–61.

Hoste, A., 'A Survey of the Unedited Work of Laurence of Durham with an Edition of His Letter to Aelred of Rievaulx', *Sacris Erudiri* 2, 1960, 249–65.

—— *Bibliotheca Aelrediana*, Instrumenta Patristica 2, 1962.

Hunter-Blair, P., 'Some Observations on the *Historia Regum* Attributed to Symeon of Durham', in K. Jackson *et al.*, eds., *Celt and Saxon: Studies in the Early British Border*, Cambridge, 1963, 63–118.

—— *The World of Bede*, London, 1970.

James, M. R., *A Descriptive Catalogue of the Manuscripts in the Library of Jesus College, Cambridge*, Cambridge, 1895.

—— *A Descriptive Catalogue of the Manuscripts of Corpus Christi College, Cambridge*, Cambridge, 1912.

Jewell, H., *The North–South Divide*, Manchester, 1994.

Kapelle, W., *The Norman Conquest of the North: The Region and Its Transformation 1000–1135*, Chapel Hill and London, 1979.

Kauffmann, C. M., *Romanesque Manuscripts, 1066–1190*, A Survey of Manuscrpts Illuminated in the British Isles (general editor J. J. G. Alexander) 3, London, 1975.

Ker, N. R., 'Medieval Manuscripts from Norwich Cathedral Priory', *Transactions of the Cambridge Bibliographical Society* 1, 1949–53, 1–28.

—— *English Manuscripts in the Century After the Norman Conquest*, Oxford, 1960.

—— *Medieval Libraries of Great Britain: A List of Surviving Books*, Royal Historical Society Guides and Handbooks 3, 2nd edn, London, 1964.

—— and Watson, Andrew G., *Medieval Libraries of Great Britain: Supplement to the Second Edition*, Royal Historical Society Guides and Handbooks 15, London, 1987.

Keynes, S., 'King Athelstan's Books', in M. Lapidge and H. Gneuss, eds., *Learning and Literature in Anglo-Saxon England*, Cambridge, 1985, 170–201.

King, E., ed., *The Anarchy of King Stephen's Reign*, Oxford, 1994.

Kitzinger, E., and McIntyre, D., *The Coffin of St Cuthbert*, Oxford, 1950.

Knowles, D., 'The Case of St William of York', *Cambridge Historical Journal* 5, 2, 1936, 162–77.

—— *The Monastic Order in England, 940–1216*, 2nd edn, Cambridge, 1963.

——, Brooke, C. N. L., and London, V., eds., *The Heads of Religious Houses: England and Wales 940–1216*, Cambridge, 1972.

——, and Hadcock, R. N., eds., *Medieval Religous Houses: England and Wales*, 2nd edn, London, 1971.

Laistner, M. L. W., with King, H. H., *A Hand-List of Bede Manuscripts*, New York, 1943.

Lapidge, M., 'Byrhtferth of Ramsey and the Early Sections of the *Historia Regum* Attributed to Symeon of Durham', *Anglo-Saxon England* 10, 1981, 97–122.

—— 'The Study of Latin Texts in Late Anglo-Saxon England: The Evidence of Latin Glosses', in N. Brooks, ed., *Latin and the Vernacular Languages in Early Medieval Britain*, Leicester, 1982, 99–140.

—— *Bede the Poet*, Jarrow Lecture, Jarrow, 1993.

Lawless, G., ed., *Augustine of Hippo and His Monastic Rule*, Oxford, 1987.

Lawrence, A., 'The Influence of Canterbury on the Collection and Production of Manuscripts at Durham in the Anglo-Norman Period', in A. Borg and A. Martindale, eds., *The Vanishing Past: Studies of Medieval Art, Liturgy and Metrology Presented to Christopher Hohler*, British Archaeolical Reports, International Series 3, Oxford, 1981, 95–104.

—— 'Manuscripts of Early Anglo-Norman Canterbury', in *British Archaeological Association Conference Proceedings, 5, 1979*, 1982, 101–11.

—— 'English Cistercian Manuscripts of the Twelfth Century', in C. Norton and D. Park, eds., *Cistercian Art and Architecture in the British Isles*, Cambridge, 1986, 284–98.

—— 'Alfred, His Heirs and the Traditions of Manuscript Production in Tenth Century England', *Reading Medieval Studies* 13, 1987, 35–56.

—— 'Anglo-Norman Book Production', in D. Bates and A. Curry, eds., *England and Normandy in the Middle Ages*, London and Rio Grande, 1994, 79–94.

—— 'The Artistic Influence of Durham Manuscripts', in D. Rollason *et al.*, eds., *Anglo-Norman Durham 1093–1193*, Woodbridge, 1994, 451–70.

—— 'Cistercian Decoration: Twelfth-Century Legislation on Illumination, and Its Interpretation in England', *Reading Medieval Studies* 21, 1995, 31–52.

—— 'A Northern English School? Patterns of Production and Collection of Manuscripts in the Augustinian Houses of Yorkshire in the Twelfth and

Thirteenth Centuries', in L. R. Hoey, ed., *Yorkshire Monasticism*, British Archaeological Association Conference Transactions 16, Leeds, 1995, 145–53.

Le Patourel, J., 'The Norman Conquest of Yorkshire', *Northern History* 6, 1971, 1–21.

Le Roy Ladurie, E., *Les Paysans de Languedoc*, Paris, 1966.

—— *L'Argent, l'amour et la mort en pays d'oc*, Paris, 1980.

—— *Carnival: A People's Uprising at Romans*, London, 1980.

—— *Montaillou: Cathars and Catholics in a French Village, 1294–1324*, Harmondsworth, 1980.

Leyser, H., *Hermits and the New Monasticism*, London, 1984.

Lillich, M. P., ed., *Studies in Cistercian Art and Architecture*, vol. ii, Kalamazoo, 1984.

—— ed., *Studies in Cistercian Art and Architecture*, vol. iii, Kalamazoo, 1987.

Lomas, R., *North-East England in the Middle Ages*, Edinburgh, 1992.

Maitland, F. W., *Domesday Book and Beyond*, 3rd edn, London, 1960.

Markus, R. A., *Bede and the Tradition of Ecclesiastical Historiography*, Jarrow Lecture, Jarrow, 1975.

Matthew, D., 'Durham and the Anglo-Norman World', in Rollason *et al.*, eds., *Anglo-Norman Durham 1093–1193*, Woodbridge, 1994, 1–22.

McFadden, G., 'The *Life of Waldef* and Its Author, Jocelin of Furness', *Innes Review*, Glasgow, 1955, 5–13.

Meehan, B., 'Insiders, Outsiders and Property at Durham around 1100', *Studies in Church History* 12, 1975, 45–58.

—— 'Geoffrey of Monmouth, *Prophecies of Merlin*: New Manuscript Evidence', *Bulletin of the Board of Celtic Studies* 28, 1978, 37–44.

—— 'Durham Twelfth-Century Manuscripts in Cistercian Houses', in D. Rollason *et al.*, eds., *Anglo-Norman Durham 1093–1193*, Woodbridge, 1994, 439–49.

Meyvaert, P., 'Bede and the Church Paintings at Wearmouth–Jarrow', *Anglo-Saxon England* 8, 1979, 63–77.

Muratova, X., 'Bestiaries: An Aspect of Medieval Patronage', in S. Macready and F. H. Thompson, eds., *Art and Patronage in the English Romanesque*, Society of Antiquaries, Occasional Papers, n.s. 8, London, 1986, 118–44.

Mynors, R. A. B., *Durham Cathedral Manuscripts to the End of the Twelfth Century*, Durham, 1939.

Nicholl, D., *Thurstan, Archbishop of York 1114–1140*, York, 1964.

Norton, C., 'The Buildings of St Mary's Abbey, York, and Their Destruction', *The Antiquaries Journal* 74, 1994, 256–88.

—— 'History, Wisdom and Illumination', in D. Rollason, *Symeon of Durham: Historian of Durham and the North*, Stamford, 1998, 61–105.

Norton, C. and Park, D., eds., *Cistercian Art and Architecture in the British Isles*, Cambridge, 1986.

Offler, H. S., *Medieval Historians of Durham*, Durham, 1958.

—— 'Hexham and the *Historia Regum*', *Transactions of the Architectural and Archaeological Society of Durham and Northumberland* 2, 1971, 51–62.

Offler, W. H., 'William of Saint-Calais, First Norman Bishop of Durham', *Transactions of the Archaeological and Architectural Society of Durham and Northumberland* 10, 1950, 258–79.

Pächt, O., 'Hugo Pictor', *Bodleian Library Record* 3, 1950, 96–103.

—— *The Rise of Pictorial Narrative in Twelfth-Century England*, Oxford, 1962.

—— *Book Illumination in the Middle Ages: An Introduction*, London, 1986.

—— and Alexander, J. J. G., *Illuminated Manuscripts in the Bodleian Library Oxford*, vol. ii, *The Italian School*, Oxford, 1970.

—— , Dodwell, C. R., and Wormald, F., *The St Albans Psalter/Albani Psalter*, London, 1960.

Parkes, M. B., *The Scriptorium of Wearmouth–Jarrow*, Jarrow Lecture, Jarrow, 1982.

Peers, Sir Charles, and Ralegh Radford, C. A., 'The Saxon Monastery of Whitby', *Archaeologia* 89, 1943, 27–88.

Piper, A. J., 'The Libraries of the Monks of Durham', in M. B. Parkes and A. G. Watson, eds., *Medieval Scribes, Manuscripts and Libraries. Essays Presented to N. R. Ker*, London, 1978, 213–250.

—— 'Durham', in N. R. Ker and A. G. Watson, *Medieval Libraries of Great Britain: Supplement to the Second Edition*, Royal Historical Society Guides and Handbooks 15, London, 1987, 16–34.

—— 'The First Generations of Durham Monks', in G. Bonner *et al.*, eds., *St Cuthbert, His Cult and His Community to AD1200*, Woodbridge, 1989, 437–446.

—— 'The Durham Cantor's Book (Durham, Dean and Chapter Library, MS B. IV. 24)', in D. Rollason *et al.*, eds., *Anglo-Norman Durham 1093–1193*, Woodbridge, 1994, 79–92.

—— 'The Early Lists and Obits of the Durham Monks', in D. Rollason, *Symeon of Durham: Historian of Durham and the North*, Stamford, 1998, 161–201.

—— 'The Historical Interests of the Monks of Durham', in D. Rollason, *Symeon of Durham: Historian of Durham and the North*, Stamford, 1998, 301–32

Powicke, F. M., 'Maurice of Rievaulx', *English Historical Review* 36, 1921, 17–25.

—— *Ailred of Rievaulx and His Biographer Walter Daniel*, Manchester, 1922.

Quirk, R. N., 'Winchester Cathedral in the Tenth Century', *Archaeological Journal*, 114, 1957, 28–71.

Raine, J., ed., *The Priory of Hexham*, vol. i, Surtees Society 44, 1864; and vol. ii, Surtees Society 46, 1865.

Ridyard, S., 'Condigna Veneratio: Post-Conquest Attitudes to the Saints of the Anglo-Saxons', in *Anglo-Norman Studies IX. Proceedings of the Bible Conference 1986*, Woodbridge, 1987, 179–206.

—— *Royal Saints of Anglo-Saxon England*, Cambridge, 1988.

Ritchie, R. L. Graeme, *The Normans in Scotland*, Edinburgh, 1954.

Robinson, David M., *The Geography of Augustinian Settlement in Medieval England and Wales*, British Archaeological Reports, British series 80, 2 vols., Oxford, 1980.

Rollason, D., 'St Cuthbert and Wessex: The Evidence of Cambridge, Corpus Christi College MS 183', in G. Bonner *et al.*, eds., *St Cuthbert, His Cult and His Community to AD 1200*, Woodbridge, 1989, 413–24.

—— 'Symeon of Durham and the Community of Durham in the Eleventh Century', in C. Hicks, ed., *England in the Eleventh Century*, Harlaxton Medieval Studies 2, Stamford, 1992, 183–98.

—— , ed., *Symeon of Durham: Historian of Durham and the North*, Stamford, 1998.

—— *et al.*, eds., *Anglo-Norman Durham 1093–1193*, Woodbridge, 1994

Rudolph, C., *The 'Things of Greater Importance'. Bernard of Clairvaux's 'Apologia' and the Medieval Attitude toward Art*, Philadelphia, 1990.

Rumble, A. R., 'The Palaeography of the Domesday Manuscripts', in P. Sawyer, ed., *Domesday Book: A Reassessment*, London, 1985, 28–49.

Sawyer, P., ed., *Domesday Book: A Reassessment*, London, 1985.

Scott, J. G., 'The Origins of Dundrennan and Soulseat Abbeys', *Transactions of the Dumfriesshire and Galloway Natural History and Antiquarian Society* 63, 1988, 35–44.

Sharpe, R., *et al.*, *English Benedictine Libraries*, Corpus of British Medieval Library Catalogues 4, London, 1994.

Sheppard, J. M., 'The Twelfth-Century Library and Scriptorium at Buildwas: Assessing the Evidence', in D. Williams, ed., *England in the Twelfth Century. Proceedings of the 1988 Harlaxton Symposium*, Woodbridge, 1990, 193–204.

—— *The Buildwas Books: Book Production, Acquisition and Use at an English Cistercian Monastery, 1165–c.1400*, OBS, 3rd series 3, Oxford, 1997.

Simpson, L., 'The King Alfred/St Cuthbert Episode in the *Historia de Sancto Cuthberto*: Its Significance for Mid-Tenth-Century English History', in G. Bonner *et al.*, eds., *St Cuthbert, His Cult and His Community to AD 1200*, Woodbridge, 1989, 397–412.

Smalley, B., *The Study of the Bible in the Middle Ages*, Oxford, 1952.

—— *The Gospels in the Schools c.1100–c.1280*, London and Ronceverte, 1985.

Somerville, R., 'Lanfranc's Canonical Collection and Exeter', *Bulletin of the Institute of Historical Research* 45, 1972, 303–6.

Southern, R. W., 'Ranulf Flambard', in R. W. Southern, *Medieval Humanism and Other Studies*, Oxford, 1970, 183–205.

Squire, Aelred, 'The Literary Evidence for the Preaching of Aelred of Rievaulx', *Cîteaux* 11, 1960, 165–77.

—— *Aelred of Rievaulx: A Study*, London, 1969.

Stevenson, J., trans., *The Church Historians of England*, vol. iii, part 2, *The Historical Works of Symeon of Durham*, London, 1855.

Talbot, C. H., 'New Documents in the Case of St William of York', *Cambridge Historical Journal* 10, 1, 1950, 1–15.

Taylor, J., *Medieval Historical Writing in Yorkshire*, St Anthony's Hall Publications 19, York, 1961.

Temple, E., 'The Twelfth-Century Psalter in the Bodleian Library, MS Douce 293', unpublished thesis, University of London, 1971.

—— *Anglo-Saxon Manuscripts 900–1066*, A Survey of Manuscripts Illuminated in the British Isles (general editor J. J. G. Alexander) 2, London, 1976.

—— 'A Note on the University College *Life of St Cuthbert*', *Bodleian Library Record* 9, 6, 1978, 320–2.

Thomson, R. M., *Manuscripts from St Albans Abbey 1066–1235*, Woodbridge, 1982.

—— 'The Norman Conquest and English Libraries', in P. Ganz, ed., *The Role of the Book in Medieval Culture*, Bibliologia 4, Brepols-Turnhout, 1986, 27–40.

—— *Catalogue of the Manuscripts of Lincoln Cathedral Chapter Library*, Cambridge, 1989.

Tudor, V., 'Reginald of Durham and St Godric of Finchale: A Study of a Twelfth-Century Hagiographer and His Major Subject', unpublished thesis, University of Reading, 1979.

—— 'The Misogyny of St Cuthbert', *Archaeologia Aeliana*, 5th series 12, 1984, 151–62.

—— 'The Cult of St Cuthbert in the Twelfth Century: the Evidence of Reginald of Durham', in Bonner *et al.*, eds., *St Cuthbert, His Cult and His Community to AD 1200*, Woodbridge, 1989, 447–57.

—— 'Durham Priory and Its Hermits in the Twelfth Century', in D. Rollason *et al.*, eds., *Anglo-Norman Durham 1093–1193*, Woodbridge, 1994, 67–78.

Turner, D. H., *et al.*, *The Golden Age of Anglo-Saxon Art*, catalogue of an exhibition at the British Museum, London, 1984.

Wall, V., 'Malcolm III and the Foundation of Durham Cathedral', in

D. Rollason *et al.*, eds., *Anglo-Norman Durham 1093–1193*, Woodbridge, 1994, 325–38.

Wardrop, J., *Fountains Abbey and Its Benefactors 1132–1300*, Cistercian Studies 91, Kalamazoo, 1987.

Webber, T., *Scribes and Scholars at Salisbury Cathedral c.1075–c.1125*, Oxford, Clarendon Press, 1992.

—— 'Script and Manuscript Production at Christ Church, Canterbury, after the Norman Conquest', in R. Eales and R. Sharpe, eds., *Canterbury and the Norman Conquest; Churches, Saints and Scholars 1066–1109*, London and Rio Grande, 1995.

—— and Watson, A., eds., *The Libraries of the Augustinian Canons*, Corpus of British Medieval Library Catalogues 6, London, 1997.

Whitelock, D., 'The Dealings of the Kings of England with Northumbria in the Tenth and Eleventh Centuries', in P. Clemoes *et al.*, eds., *The Anglo-Saxons: Studies Presented to Bruce Dickins*, Cambridge, 1959, 70–88.

—— *After Bede*, Jarrow Lecture, Jarrow, 1960.

—— 'The Old English Bede', *Proceedings of the British Academy* 48, 1962, 57–90.

Wightman, W. E., 'Henry I and the Founding of Nostell Priory', *Yorkshire Archaeological Journal* 41, 1966, 57–60.

Williams, D., ed., *England in the Twelfth Century. Proceedings of the 1988 Harlaxton Symposium*, Woodbridge, 1990.

Williams, R., *Keywords*, London, 1976.

Wilson, J., 'The Foundation of the Austin Priories of Nostell and Scone', *Scottish Historical Review* 7, 1910, 141–59.

Wormald, F., *English Benedictine Kalendars after 1100*, Henry Bradshaw Society 77 and 81, 1939–42.

—— 'The Survival of Anglo-Saxon Illumination after the Norman Conquest', *Proceedings of the British Academy* 30, 1944, 127–45.

—— 'Some Illustrated Manuscripts of the Lives of the Saints', *Bulletin of the John Rylands Library* 35, 1952, 248–66.

Young, A., *William Cumin: Border Politics and the Bishopric of Durham 1141–1144*, Borthwick Papers 54, York, 1995.

Zarnecki, G., *et al.*, *English Romanesque Art 1066–1200*, London, 1984.

Index

&❧

References to manuscripts have been grouped under the heading 'manuscripts'. A similar procedure has been followed with 'illuminators' and 'scribes'.

Manuscripts, Oxford, Bodleian Library (*cont.*)
MS Laud Misc. 140 131–2; Fig. 55
MS Laud Misc. 145 216
MS Laud Misc. 216 215
MS Laud Misc. 241 215
MS Laud Misc. 308 215
MS Laud Misc. 309 215
MS Laud Misc. 310 210n
MS Laud Misc. 392 165–6
MS Lyell 2 215n
MS Rawl. C 415 215
Corpus Christi College, MS D 209 210n, 256
St John's College, MS 99 228, 231
St John's College, MS 154 23
University College, MS 15 215n
University College, MS 165 26, 55, 56, 68–9, 70, 73, 80, 84–8, 96, 165; Plates 13, 15, 16, 18, 19, 20, 21
historiated initial 90
dedication miniature 90
narrative miniatures 97–107, 140
Paris
Bibliothèque Mazarine, MS 404/729 49
Bibliothèque Nationale
MS lat. 7963 50
MS lat. 10575 15
MS lat. 13765 54
Ripon Cathedral, MSS 3 and 4 186
Rome, Vatican Library MS Reg. Lat. 694 228
Rouen
Bibliothèque Municipale
MS A 28; Fig. 23
MS A 47 54
MS A 85 50
MS A 88 53
MS A 102 53; Figs. 22 & 26
MS A 195 53
MS A 259; Fig. 21
MS A 278; Fig. 25
MS A 296; Fig. 20
MS A 298 53
MS A 321 169; Plate 23
MS A 343 161
MS A 366 54; Fig. 24

MS I 69 Fig. 18
MS U 3 Fig. 17
MS U 43 / 1343 224
MS U 61 53; Fig. 19
MS Y 21 50
MS Y 41 46, 54
MS Y 109 54
Stonyhurst College, Stonyhurst Gospel 20, 25
Winchester, Cathedral Library, MS 2 Fig. 4
York
Minster Library
MS XVI A 7 77
MS XVI I 8 210
MS XVI P 12 123
MS XVI Q 3 130–1; Plate 22
MS Add. 1 15
Matilda (Empress) 135, 140
Maurice of Durham/Rievaulx 145, 151–2, 156, 161, 197, 245
Maurice of Kirkham 119, 129, 190
Maximianus 118, 153
Meaux 206, 215
Meehan, B. 123, 230
Melrose 18, 138, 196, 200, 206, 215, 220, 250
Miracles and Translations of St Cuthbert 24, 156
Monk Bretton 113
Morcar (earl) 4, 5
Motifs (used in illumination)
acanthus foliage 50–1, 53, 54, 86, 87, 112, 131, 169
berries 122
clove-curl 43, 63, 71, 73–5, 124, 167, 170, 191, 214, 226
curved cross 56, 58, 61–3
dragons 52–4, 56, 63, 69, 112, 132, 169, 170, 172
flame motif 36, 56, 58, 61–3, 71, 73, 87
frilled curl 71, 167
human heads 81, 86, 174
scallops 45, 50, 54, 210
split petal 71, 74, 75–6, 112, 122, 123–4, 138, 166, 170, 174, 185, 187–9, 192, 210–11, 214, 215